ENGLISH G

access

1

Lehrerfassung

Dieses Buch gibt es auch auf
www.scook.de

Es kann dort nach Bestätigung der
Allgemeinen Geschäftsbedingungen
genutzt werden.

Buchcode: **voz46-43fcf**

English G Access · Band 1
Lehrerfassung

Im Auftrag des Verlages herausgegeben von
Jörg Rademacher, Mannheim

Erarbeitet von
Laurence Harger, Wellington, Neuseeland
Cecile Niemitz-Rossant, Berlin

unter Mitarbeit von
Dr. Annette Leithner-Brauns, Dresden
Birgit Ohmsieder, Berlin
Mervyn Whittaker, Bad Dürkheim

in Zusammenarbeit mit der Englischredaktion
Dr. Christiane Kallenbach (Projektleitung),
Dr. Philip Devlin (koordinierender Redakteur), Susanne
Bennetreu (Bildredaktion), Filiz Bahsi, Ulrike Berendt,
Gwendolyn Düwel, Gareth Evans, Bonnie Glänzer, Solveig
Heinrich, Stefan Höhne, Uwe Tröger

Beratende Mitwirkung
Peter Brünker, Bad Kreuznach; Anette Fritsch, Dillenburg;
Uli Imig, Wildeshausen; Thomas Neidhardt, Bielefeld;
Wolfgang Neudecker, Mannheim; Angela Ringel-Eichinger,
Bietigheim-Bissingen; Dr. Andreas Sedlatschek, Esslingen;
Sieglinde Spranger, Chemnitz; Marcel Sprunkel, Köln;
Sabine Tudan, Sankt Georgen-Peterzell; Friederike von
Bremen, Hannover; Harald Weißling, Mannheim *sowie für
die Gestaltung* Aksinia Raphael und Korinna Wilkes

Illustrationen
Tobias Dahmen, Utrecht/NL; Elke Hanisch, Köln; Burkhard
Schulz, Düsseldorf *sowie* Roland Beier, Berlin; Judy Brown,
Hove *und* Jane Smith, London

Fotos
Trevor Burrows Photography, Plymouth

Umschlaggestaltung und Layoutkonzept
kleiner & bold, Berlin

Layout
Eric Gira, Rosendahl Berlin

Technische Umsetzung
zweiband.media, Berlin

Für die freundliche Unterstützung danken wir der
Plymstock School in Plymouth.

Legende zur Lehrerfassung

1 ▶ **12**	CD- und Tracknummern
school	Lernwortschatz (produktiv)
°spy	Situativer Wortschatz (nicht produktiv)
Box "when", Voc, S. 197	Verweis auf Wortschatzbox im *Vocabulary*
were	Grammatische Strukturen
KV 1 · FöFo 1.1 · LAS 1.1	Verweise auf Begleitmedien
Grund-schule	Verweis auf Grundschulmethoden
[ˈpriːjaː, ˈpriːjə]	Aussprachehinweis
Lernfeld: Die S können …	Hinweis auf Lernfelder, die abgedeckt werden
Alternative: …	Didaktische Hinweise, Alternativen oder Zusätze
learned · sat	Lösungen (geschlossene Aufgaben)

www.cornelsen.de

Die Internetadressen und -dateien, die in diesem Lehrwerk
angegeben sind, wurden vor Drucklegung geprüft. Der
Verlag übernimmt keine Gewähr für die Aktualität und den
Inhalt dieser Adressen und Dateien oder solcher, die mit
ihnen verlinkt sind.

Dieses Werk berücksichtigt die Regeln der reformierten
Rechtschreibung und Zeichensetzung.

1. Auflage, 2. Druck 2015
Alle Drucke dieser Auflage sind inhaltlich unverändert und
können im Unterricht nebeneinander verwendet werden.

© 2014 Cornelsen Schulverlage GmbH, Berlin

Druck: Mohn Media Mohndruck, Gütersloh

ISBN 978-3-06-033070-6

PEFC zertifiziert
Dieses Produkt stammt aus nachhaltig
bewirtschafteten Wäldern und kontrollierten
Quellen.

PEFC
www.pefc.de
PEFC/04-31-1033

English G Access 1 enthält folgende Teile:

Here we go	Los geht's: der Einstieg ins Buch
Units	die fünf Kapitel des Buches
Access story	*Reading for fun* – eine Geschichte in zwei Teilen
Book rally	eine „Rundfahrt" durch dein Englischbuch
Wordbank	Mini-Bildwörterbuch zu verschiedenen Themen
Skills File	eine Beschreibung wichtiger Lern- und Arbeitstechniken
Grammar File	eine Zusammenfassung der Grammatik jeder Unit
Vocabulary	das Wörterverzeichnis zum Lernen der neuen Wörter jeder Unit
Dictionary	alphabetisches Wörterverzeichnis zum Nachschlagen (Englisch-Deutsch und Deutsch-Englisch)

In den Units findest du diese Überschriften:

Background file	Informationen über Land und Leute
Everyday English	Englisch in Alltagssituationen
Looking at language	Beispiele sammeln und sprachliche Regeln entdecken
Language help	Hilfe in Form von sprachlichen Regeln
Practice	Aufgaben und Übungen
Spelling course	englische Rechtschreibung trainieren
The world behind the picture	vom Bild in den Film – Videoclips mit Aufgaben
Text	eine spannende oder lustige Geschichte

Du findest auch diese Symbole:

〰	Texte, die du dir anhören kannst: *www.englishg.de/access*
■■■■■	Übungssequenz: neue Grammatik intensiv üben und dann anwenden
Early finisher	zusätzliche Aktivitäten und Übungen für Schüler/innen, die früher fertig sind
More help	zusätzliche Hilfen für eine Aufgabe
You choose	eine Aufgabe auswählen
EXTRA	zusätzliche Aktivitäten und Übungen für alle
My Book	schöne und wichtige Arbeiten sammeln
Study skills ▶	Einführung in Lern- und Arbeitstechniken
Your task ▶	Was du gelernt hast, kannst du in der Lernaufgabe am Ende jeder Unit noch mal zeigen und dich auch selbst einschätzen.
🎧 💬 📖 ✏	Hören Sprechen Lesen Schreiben
🏴	Mediation (zwischen zwei Sprachen vermitteln)
👥 👥 👥 🧩	Partnerarbeit Partnercheck Gruppenarbeit Kooperative Lernform

Justin Skinner

Maya Sen

Die hier und auf den Folgeseiten aufgeführten Angebote sind nicht obligatorisch abzuarbeiten. Die Auswahl der Übungen und Übungsteile richtet sich nach den Schwerpunkten des schulinternen Curriculums.

	Lerninhalte	Your task (Lernaufgabe)	Texte
Unit 3 Clubs and hobbies 	• über AGs (*school clubs*) reden • über Hobbys, Sportarten und Freizeitaktivitäten sprechen • um Erlaubnis fragen • sagen, wie oft man etwas tut	**What can we do this week?** Pläne für drei Tage mit einem englischen Jugendlichen in Deutschland machen (S. 74)	**Background file** *Old Plymouth – the Barbican* (S. 69) **Text** *The captain's ghost* (S. 72)

Access story · Part I

	Lerninhalte	Your task (Lernaufgabe)	Texte
Unit 4 Weekends 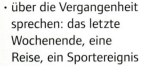	• über die Vergangenheit sprechen: das letzte Wochenende, eine Reise, ein Sportereignis • andere fragen, wie ihr Wochenende war • sagen, dass etwas Spaß gemacht hat • zwei unterschiedliche Versionen einer Geschichte vergleichen	**A memory game** Ein Spiel erstellen und in einer Gruppe spielen (S.100)	**Background file** *Devon – an English county* (S. 90) *Grey seals* (S. 92) **Text** *A baby seal* (S. 98)

Sam Bennet

	Lerninhalte	Your task (Lernaufgabe)	Texte
Unit 5 By the sea 	• sagen, was man gerne tun würde und das auch begründen • sagen, was man sehen, hören, fühlen kann • Bilder beschreiben • Personen beschreiben	**Let's go to Plymouth** Argumente für einen Urlaub in Plymouth sammeln und die Eltern davon überzeugen (S.120)	**Song** *Octopus's garden* (S.103) **Background file** *The aquarium in Plymouth* (S.109) **Text** Theaterstück *The pepper smugglers* (S.118)

Access story · Part II

Abby Blackwell

Kompetenzen	Sprache	
✏️ **Schwerpunkt Writing** **MyBook** Steckbriefe fortführen (S. 58) **Hör-/Sehverstehen** Plymstock school clubs (S. 63) **Methoden** Collecting information (S. 62) Giving a one-minute talk (S. 62)	**Wortschatz** *sports and hobbies, go/play/do* **Strukturen** *simple present*: Fragen und Kurzantworten; Wortstellung der Häufigkeitsadverbien *Everyday English* *How can we join the club?* (S. 63) *Spelling course* [ɔː] gesprochen und geschrieben, Groß- und Kleinschreibung (S. 71)	**56**
		76
📖 **Schwerpunkt Reading** **MyBook** *Plymstock School News* (S. 96) **Hör-/Sehverstehen** *Plymouth, my hometown* (S. 97) **Methoden** *Putting a page together* (S. 96)	**Wortschatz** *weekend activities and places* **Strukturen** *simple past: be*, regelmäßige und unregelmäßige Verben, bejahte und verneinte Aussagesätze, Fragen *Everyday English* *A present for Ruby* (S. 97) *Spelling course* [iː] gesprochen und geschrieben, Plural (S. 91)	**80**
🏴󠁧󠁢󠁥󠁮󠁧󠁿 **Schwerpunkt Mediation** **MyBook** *Summer holidays in Plymouth* (S.120) **Hör-/Sehverstehen** *A ferry trip to Cawsand* (S.116) **Methoden** *Preparing and giving a mini-talk* (S.115)	**Wortschatz** *the seaside, marine life, adjectives* **Strukturen** *present progressive*: bejahte und verneinte Aussagesätze, Fragen; Wortstellung (S-V-O) *Everyday English* *Making plans* (S.116) *Spelling course* [ðeə] *their/there/they're*, Buchstabieren, ein Buchstabe – verschiedene Laute (S.117)	**102**
		122

Lernfeld S. 8–9: Die S können andere **begrüßen**, ihnen **Fragen über die eigene Person** stellen und **sich selber vorstellen**. Sie können dies auch aufschreiben.

Here we go!

My name is Silky.
I'm two years old.

Box "Numbers",
Voc, S. 173

Hello!
I'm a seal.

Silky

Es bietet sich an, auf dieser Seite die Handpuppe *Silky* vorzustellen und sie bei der Bearbeitung einzusetzen.

I'm from Plymouth in England. What about you?

1 Silky's **questions**

a) 👥 Partner A: You're Silky.
Ask the questions.
Partner B: Answer the questions.

A: What's your name?
B: My name is …
A: Are you …?

b) 👥 Partner B:
Now you're Silky.

What's your name?
Are you a boy or a girl?
How old are you?
Where are you from?

2 **Meet your classmates**

👥 Talk to different partners.

A: Hi, my name is …
I'm … years old.
What's your name?
B: Hello, I'm …
I'm from …
What about you?
C: Hi, I'm …
I'm from …

Bei **2** geht es vor allem um den Wohnort der S. Wenn die S auch über ihre Herkunftsländer sprechen wollen, kann L als Hilfe für Europa **Folie 2** zeigen und für außereuropäische Länder die Namen an die Tafel schreiben und die Aussprache üben.

3 A **card to** Silky

Write a card to Silky.

Hello Silky,

My name is Lara. I'm ten years old and I'm from Frankfurt in Germany.
I like the colour red.
What about you?
Lara xxx

xxx steht für "kisses". *xoxo* wäre "hugs and kisses". Beides sind gängige informelle Schlussformeln z.B. bei SMS oder Mails.

➡ **Workbook** *1–2 (p. 2)*

> **TIP**
> Im **Vocabulary** findest du die neuen Wörter.
> Es beginnt auf S. 172.

Lernfeld: Die S können mit dem Vocabulary im SB umgehen.

Let's go to England. Come and see Plymouth – my hometown.

Lernfeld S. 10–11: Die S können verstehen, wenn bestimmte **Gegenstände und Orte** aus dem SB erwähnt werden. Sie können sie auch **auf einer Karte oder einem Bild zeigen**.

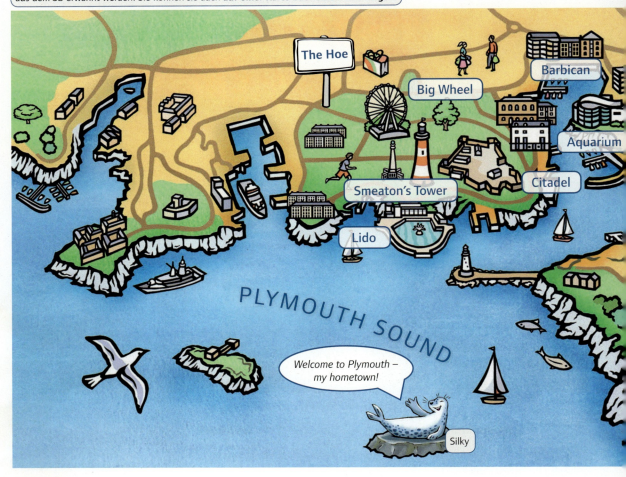

Welcome to Plymouth

Alternativer Einstieg möglich über **KV 1: The British Isles**

1 Silky's tour of Plymouth

Grund-schule

a) 👥 Match the words to the pictures.

> girl · river · castle · pool · tower · hill ·
> boy · boat · sea · big wheel

1 – castle, 2 – …

b) 👥 Talk about the map.

A: I can see a boat / a boy / …
on the map. And you?

B: I can see …

1 ▷ 2 c) Listen to Silky and look at the places on the
Grund-schule   map. Listen again and point to the places.

➔ **Workbook** 3 (p. 3)

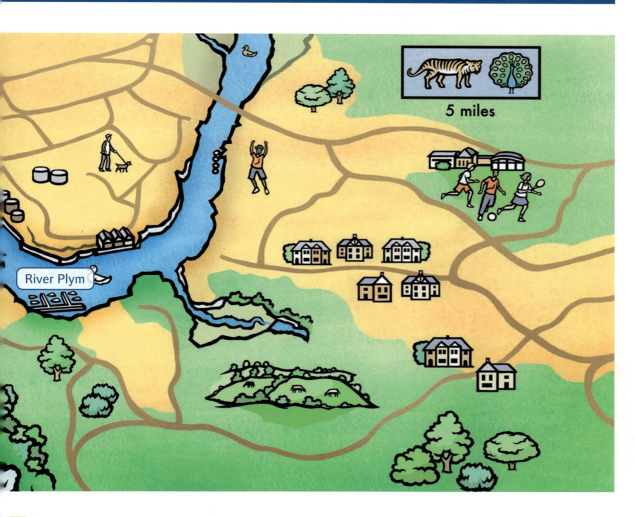

River Plym

Grund-schule **2 Silky's song** 1 3–4

🖐 Listen to Silky's song and sing along.

Chorus: °*Let me show you* Plymouth °*Sound,*
°*It's* my hometown! It's my hometown!
Let me show you Plymouth Sound,
Plymouth, Plymouth Sound.

°*By the sea,* °*there's* the Hoe –
Hey, hey Hoe, here we go!
°*Blue,* blue, blue, the Lido Pool.
The °*water's* °*warm,* the °*kids* are °*cool!*

Chorus

Red and °*white,* °*lots of* °*stripes.*
Red and white, °*tall* and °*bright:*
It's the tower, on the Hoe!
Hey, hey Hoe, here we go!

Chorus

EXTRA Answer the questions.

1 What's blue?
2 What's warm?
3 °Who's cool?
4 What's red and white?
5 What's Silky's hometown?
6 What's your hometown?

1 the Lido Pool ·
2 the water ·
3 the kids ·
4 the tower on the Hoe ·
5 Plymouth

Die im Song vorkommenden Farben *blue, red* und *white* werden nicht als Lernwortschatz eingeführt, sollten den S aber aus der GS bekannt sein. Farben werden auf S. 15 wiederholt/ eingeführt.

Is it Monday, Tuesday, …?
Every day is great in Plymouth!

Box "The days of the week", Voc, S. 175

11

Lernfeld S. 12–13: Die S kennen und verstehen die **Wochentage** auf Englisch und können über sie sprechen und schreiben.

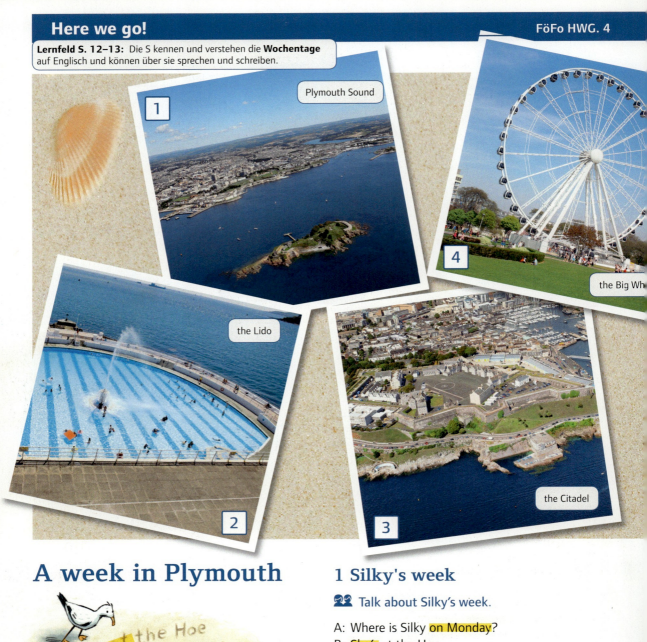

1 Plymouth Sound

4 the Big Wh

2 the Lido

3 the Citadel

A week in Plymouth

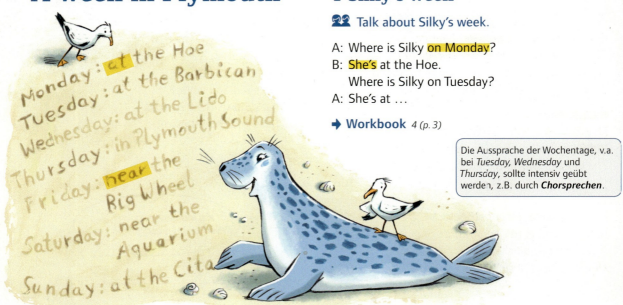

Monday: at the Hoe
Tuesday: at the Barbican
Wednesday: at the Lido
Thursday: in Plymouth Sound
Friday: near the Big Wheel
Saturday: near the Aquarium
Sunday: at the Cita

1 Silky's week

🗣️ Talk about Silky's week.

A: Where is Silky <mark>on Monday</mark>?
B: <mark>She's</mark> at the Hoe.
   Where is Silky on Tuesday?
A: She's at …

➜ **Workbook** *4 (p. 3)*

> Die Aussprache der Wochentage, v.a. bei *Tuesday*, *Wednesday* und *Thursday*, sollte intensiv geübt werden, z.B. durch **Chorsprechen**.

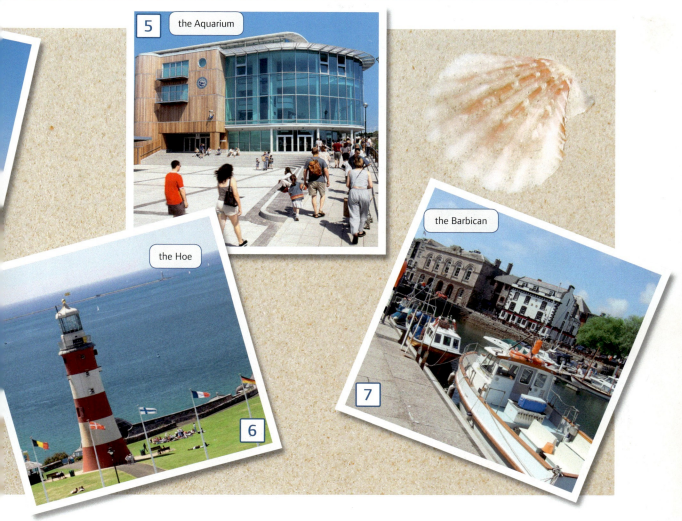

5 the Aquarium

the Hoe

the Barbican

6

7

2 Plymouth photos

Partner A: Look at pages 12–13.
Partner B: Look at pages 10–11.
Now match the Plymouth photos to places on the map.

A: Photo 1 is Plymouth Sound. **Look**, **it's here** on the map.
B: **Yes, that's right.** And photo 2 is …
A: Yes, … / **No, that's wrong.** Photo 2 is …

2 the Lido · 3 the Citadel · 4 the Big Wheel ·
5 the Aquarium · 6 the Hoe · 7 the Barbican

3 Rhyme: The days of the week

 1 ▸ 5

Grund-schule

Copy the **black** lines. Listen and add the green lines. Say the rhyme in class.

Monday, Tuesday, °**school for** you,
Work …   Work with a group and a partner too.

Wednesday, Thursday, can you see
…   Seals in a boat, one, two, three?
Friday, Friday. Hello! Hi!
…   School is over. Say goodbye.
Saturday, Sunday, °**they're so cool** –
…   You and your friends at the swimming pool.

Seals in a boat, one, two, three?
°**Work** °**with** a °**group** and a °**partner** °**too**.
You and your friends at the swimming pool.
°**School is over.** °**Say** °**goodbye**.

There are lots of animals in Plymouth. **Follow me.**

Lernfeld S. 14: Die S können Hörtexte/Gespräche über **Tiere** verstehen sowie über Tiere sprechen und schreiben.

Alternativer Einstieg mit dem Tierquiz auf **KV 2: Animals**.

My **favourite** animal

ant · bear · bird · butterfly · cat · dog · elephant · frog · giraffe

1 Silky's favourite animal

a) 👥 Talk like this:

A: I can see a rabbit / **an** elephant / …
   in the **picture.** What about you?

B: I can see …

 6 b) Listen to Silky and the animals.
   When you hear an animal, point to it in
   the picture.
   What is Silky's favourite animal?

Grund-schule

2 ~~Strange~~ animals?

 Grund-schu e

a) Write the letters in the right order.

~~farfeig~~ · ebar · bratib · pelhaten ·
dirb · tra · ansek · herso · nilo ·
act · ogd · anugie gip

– farfeig   giraffe   giraffe · bear · rabbit · elephant ·
                          bird · rat · snake · horse · lion ·
– ebar   …   cat · dog · guinea pig

b) 👥 Check with a partner.

> **TIP**
> Hinten im Buchdeckel werden die
> **Arbeitsanweisungen** erklärt.

Differenzierung: Schnelle S denken sich eigene "strange
animals" aus und geben sie einem Partner zum Lösen
(*bus stop*-Methode).

FöFo HWG. 6

Here we go!

> **Lernfeld S. 15:** Die S können **Farben** benennen, lesen und schreiben.

guinea pig · horse · lion · monkey · pig · rabbit · rat · snake · whale

> Box "Colours", Voc, S. 176

3 Colours

a) Copy the names of the colours.

> **black**[4] · **blue**[9] · **brown**[7] · **green**[6] · **grey**[1] ·
> **orange**[3] · **pink**[8] · **purple**[11] · **red**[5] · **white**[10] · **yellow**[2]

Then look at the picture.
Write the number for each colour.

b) 👥 Talk like this:

A: Black is number four.
B: Yes, that's right. And blue is …

c) 👥 Make groups of three.
– Say a colour. *Green.*
– Look at the picture.
  Find an animal with the same colour. *The frogs are green.*
– Find a thing in the room
  with the same colour. *My ruler is green.*

➡ **Workbook** 5–6 (pp. 4–5)

4 GAME °I spy with my little eye

👥 Choose an animal from the picture.
Talk to your group.

A: I spy with my little eye a grey / green / …
   animal with two / four / … legs / without legs.
B: Is it a frog / …?
A: Yes, that's right! / No, that's wrong!

5 EXTRA My favourite colour

Draw animals and other things with your
favourite colour. Label your drawing.

Get more words if you need them.
➡ *Wordbank 1 (p.142)*

> *Now it's time for an English lesson.*

Lernfeld S. 16: Die S können richtig reagieren, wenn ihnen jemand sagt, was sie mit **Gegenständen im Klassenzimmer** oder aus ihrer **Schultasche** machen sollen.

Our English class

1 What's in your classroom?

 a) Copy the words from the box.

> board · cupboard · chair · clock ·
> door · desk · poster · window

b) 👥 Talk about the things like this:

A: Board.
B: This is the board. It's black/green/...
B: Chair.
A: This is a chair. It's ...

> **Alternative: KV 3: School things in my room** mit einem Wimmelbild, in dem die S Gegenstände suchen und ausmalen können.

2 What's in your school bag?

1 ▶ 7 a) Listen. Find the things and put them on your desk.

> book · exercise book · ruler · pen · pencil ·
> pencil case · glue stick · rubber · sharpener

Listen again. When you hear a word, put your finger on the thing and say the word.

b) 👥 Talk like this:

A: Let me show you what's on my desk.
   This is my ruler. It's white.
   Now you.
B: This is my pen. It's blue. And here's my ...

3 GAME Simon says

Grund-schule

a) Listen to your teacher. Do only what Simon says.

b) Now you are Simon.

(Simon says) Put your pen on the desk. / Talk to the teacher. / Open the window. / Touch ... / Give me ...

➜ **Workbook** 7–9 (pp. 5–6)

Lernfeld S. 17: Die S können die Zahlen 1–100 verstehen, sagen und schreiben (auch Telefonnummern).

4 The ants go marching 1 8–9

Grundschule

a) Listen and sing along.

The ants go marching one by one,
Hurrah, hurrah!
The ants go marching two by two,
Hurrah, hurrah!
The ants go marching three by three,
The little one stops to climb a tree
And they all go marching
Down … to the ground
To get out … of the rain,
BOOM! BOOM! BOOM!

The ants go marching four by four,
Hurrah, hurrah!
The ants go marching five by five,
Hurrah, hurrah!
The ants go marching six by six,
The little one stops to pick up sticks
And they all go marching
Down … to the ground
To get out … of the rain,
BOOM! BOOM! BOOM!

b) Point to the ants and say
these numbers to your partner:

1–20
21, 22, 30
40, 50 …100

Box "Numbers", Voc, S. 178

6 Telephone numbers

Ask your partner for his/her telephone
number. Write it down. Are you right?

What's your number?

*O three eight two
one o five double
four seven two.*

➔ **Workbook** 10–11 (p. 7)

5 Count them

Count things and people in your classroom.
Tell your group.

– There are … chairs in the classroom.
– There are … girls in the classroom.
– …

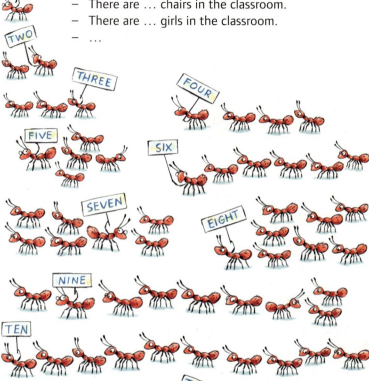

Box "Betonungszeichen und
Bindebogen", Voc, S. 178

See you in Unit 1.

The first day at school

Maya, [ˈmaɪə]
eleven years old

Sam,
eleven years old

Lernfeld S. 18–26: Die S können andere **begrüßen** und sich über **persönliche Dinge** unterhalten. Sie verstehen, wenn andere ihnen etwas über sich erzählen oder sie davon lesen.

Mrs Skinner

Justin

1

Lucy

Maya

2

Mr Bennett

Sam

3

1 Meet the Plymouth kids

1 ▶ 10–12

Box "Personal pronouns + possessive determiners", Voc, S. 179

Grund-schule

 Read texts A, B and C. Then listen and match them to pictures 1, 2 and 3. A2 · B3 · C1

 Check with a partner.

A Sunday

Lucy Pascoe and her best friend Maya Sen are eleven. They're at Maya's flat. Monday is their first day at their new schools.

Lucy: Hey, your Coombe Dean[1] uniform is nice! I like black.

Maya: The Plymstock school uniform is nice too.

Lucy: You know the Plymstock uniform?

Maya: My brother Mukesh[2] is at Plymstock.

Lucy: Oh, yes – in Year 9. My sister Holly is in Year 9 too.

B Monday

Sam Bennett is a student at Plymstock School. But he isn't from Plymouth. He's from London. His mum and dad are in the navy.

Father: Let me look at you. That's a great uniform. Dark blue and grey.

Sam: Your uniform is OK too, Dad.

Father: Thank you, Number One.

C Monday

It's 8:15. Justin Skinner is on Skype with his father in Boston.

Mother: Please, Justin. It's your first day at Plymstock School. And you're late.

Justin: Wait a minute, Mum. I'm on Skype with Dad.

Mother: Hey, what time is it in Boston?

¹[ˌkuːm ˈdiːn] ²[ˈmukeʃ]

Lucy, eleven years old

Justin, twelve years old

Plymstock School
SPECIALIST SPORTS COLLEGE

Lernfeld S. 19: Die S können ein **Kurzprofil** über sich und andere anlegen.

2 Profiles

Start a profile for Lucy, Maya, Justin and Sam.
Get information from page 18. Add more information as you work through the units.

Profile
Name: Lucy Pascoe.
Hometown: Plymouth
School:
Brothers /
Sisters:

Profile
Name: Maya Sen
Hometown:
School:
Brothers /
Sisters:

Die S sollten im *MyBook* für jedes der Lehrwerkskinder eine neue Seite anlegen, damit sie ausreichend Platz haben, alle Informationen im Laufe des Buches zu sammeln.

TIP
Was steckt alles in deinem Englischbuch? Das kannst du mithilfe der **Book rally** herausfinden. (S. 126)

Die S bearbeiten die *Book rally* alleine oder in PA.

3 Meet Morph

Morph is at Plymstock School too. The library is his home.

Box "home", Voc, S. 179

a) Listen to Morph's song and sing along.

1 ▷ 13–14
Grund-schule

Morph's song

I'm Morph, I'm Morph from Plymstock School,
I'm big, I'm small, I'm really cool.
Sometimes I'm blue and sometimes red,
I'm all the colours in your head.
I can change my shape and I can be
An X, Y, I or J, T, D.
Can you find me? Just have a look!
I'm on the shelf, I'm in a book,
I'm always in the library.
That's where I am – come in and see.
I'm Morph, I'm Morph from Plymstock School,
I'm big, I'm small, I'm really cool, I'm Morph.

You choose Act out Morph's song. Or write four more lines.

Neigungsdifferenzierung: Die S haben die Wahl zwischen einer darstellenden Aufgabe und einer kreativen Schreibaufgabe.

b) Listen to Morph again. He talks about the Book rally. What page is it on? Now go to that page.

1 ▷ 15

➜ **Workbook** *1 (p. 8)*

1 Before school 〔1〕▸16

Maya · Lucy

Sam · Lucy

Lucy:	Hey, Maya!
Maya:	Hi, Lucy. My first day at Coombe Dean! It's strange without you.
Lucy:	Oh, Maya, my first day at a new school
5	and you **aren't there**. It's **sad**.
Maya:	Yes, it is. Oh Lucy, look at the time. It's 8:25.
Lucy:	**Don't go**, Maya. We aren't late. °**Give me a hug.**
10 Maya:	**Bye**, Lucy.
Lucy:	Bye, Maya! Bye!
	❖
Lucy:	Hey, **watch out!**
Sam:	Oh, **sorry!** Hey, **you're** at Plymstock School.
15 Lucy:	**So?**
Sam:	I'm at Plymstock school too.
Lucy:	You aren't from Plymouth!
Sam:	No, I'm not. I'm new here. I'm from London.
20 Lucy:	OK.
Sam:	I'm in Year 7 – in class 7EB. What about you?
Lucy:	I'm in 7EB too.
Sam:	Hey, that's cool.
25 Lucy:	Is it?
Sam:	Yes. Er … my name is Sam.
Lucy:	Sam?
Sam:	Sam Bennett. What's your name?
Lucy:	Lucy. Lucy Pascoe.
30 Sam:	Hi, Lucy. **Nice to meet you.**
Lucy:	Hey, **it's** 8:30. **Hurry up** … we're late.

Box "to = zu", Voc, S. 180

Zusatz: Die S können hier dazu angehalten werden, die betreffenden Textstellen betont (un-)freundlich vorzutragen.

2 Who are they?

👥👥 Read the sentences. Say who the people are.

1 She's eleven. She's in Year 7. Maya is her best friend.
    That's …
2 He's in class 7EB. He's new at Plymstock. He's from London.
3 She's eleven. She's at Coombe Dean School. Her best friend is at Plymstock.

1 Lucy · 2 Sam · 3 Maya

Zusatz: Die S formulieren Sätze über andere Lehrwerkskinder oder Mit-S. Die Klasse muss raten, wer gemeint ist.

3 Friendly or not?

Find these phrases in the text and make two lists.

Give me a hug. · Hey, watch out! · So? · Hey, that's cool. · Is it? · Nice to meet you.

 friendly    not friendly

Give me a hug.   …
Hey, that's cool. · Nice to meet you.   Hey, watch out! · So? · Is it?

Listen and check.   〔1〕▸17

Lernfeld S. 21: Die S können sich über **persönliche Dinge** wie Namen und Heimatstadt unterhalten.

4 👆 At school 1 ▶ 18

Justin is late.

> I'm Justin Skinner.

> Skinner?
> Wait a minute…
> Yes, you're in class 7EB.
> That's room HU9.
> Hurry up, you're late.

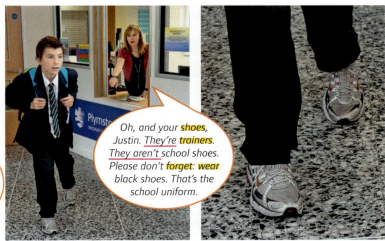

> Oh, and your **shoes**, Justin. They're **trainers**. They aren't school shoes. Please don't **forget**: **wear** black shoes. That's the school uniform.

Background file

There are uniforms at **British** schools. **Different** schools **have** different uniforms.

Lucy

> Dark blue is nice. I like the dark blue uniform.

Maya

> I **don't like** dark green. The uniform **isn't** nice.

> Who is at Plymstock School? Lucy
> Who is at Coombe Dean School? Maya
> Say which uniform you like.

5 Have a go

🧩 Walk around the classroom. Find two partners and talk like this. Change roles.

> Hello, I'm Jan. What's your name?

Jan

> Oh, hello Jan. I'm Ela.

Ela

> And this is Alex. He's from …

> Hello Jan. Nice to meet you.

Alex

Mit **KV 5: My school uniform** erstellen die S ihre eigene Schuluniform, indem sie die Kleidungsstücke bunt ausmalen. Die KV wird auf S. 25 weiter verwendet.

Looking at language

a) Copy and finish the table. You can find the short forms on pages 20–21.

Personal pronouns and the forms of the verb be

Singular		Plural	
long	**short**	long	short
I am	I'm	we are	…
you are	you'…	you are	you're
he is	…	they are	…
she is	…		
it is	…		

b) Make a second table for negative forms: I am not, you are not, he …
Look at pages 20–21 and add the short forms: I'm not, you aren't, he …

➡ GF 1: Personal pronouns (p. 157)
GF 2 a: (to) be: statements (p. 158)

1 *He, she or it?* (Personal pronouns)

■■■■■■

👥 Look at the pictures. Talk like this:
A: I °spy a *she*. ——— B: The bag?
A: No, that's an *it*. —— B: Justin's mum?
A: That's right. ——— B: I spy …

2 Plymouth people and things (Personal pronouns)

■■■■■

Finish the sentences with I, you, he, she, it, we or they.

1 Where's Plymouth? – …'s in England.
2 Lucy and Maya are eleven. …'re friends.
3 Maya: "I like you, Lucy. …'re great!"
4 Sam is eleven too. …'s new in Plymouth.
5 Sam: "…'m in Year 7. What about you?"

6 Maya isn't at Plymstock School. …'s at Coombe Dean.
7 Lucy: "Maya and I are best friends. But …'re at different schools."
8 That's the Plymstock uniform. …'s dark blue.

1 It's · 2 They're · 3 You're · 4 He's ·
5 I'm · 6 She's · 7 we're · 8 It's

➡ **Workbook** 2 (p. 9)

3 I'm Maya *(be: positive)* ▪▪▪□□□

a) Choose the right short forms: 'm, 's or 're.

1 I... from Plymstock in Plymouth.
2 Plymouth? – It... a town in England.
3 I have a big brother. He... OK.
4 My best friend is Lucy. She... great!
5 We... sad – we... at different schools.
6 But I like my new classmates. They... cool.
7 And you? Oh, you... from Germany!

1 I'm · 2 It's · 3 He's · 4 She's ·
5 We're ... we're · 6 They're · 7 you're

Hi, I'm Maya.

b) Make sentences like these about yourself. Use short forms of *be***.**

4 Silly sentences

(be: negative) ▪▪▪▪□□

Correct the sentences. Use short forms.
Then give the right information.

1 Silky is a snake.
　– No, she *isn't* a snake. She's a seal!
2 Sam is at Coombe Dean School.
　– No, he... He's at ...
3 Justin and Sam are in Year 8. – No, ...
4 Plymouth is a town in Germany. – No, ...
5 The sea at Plymouth is red. – No, ...
6 And you? You're in a German lesson now.
　– No, I...

2 isn't ... Plymstock School. · 3 they're not ... Year 7 ·
4 it's not ... England · 5 it isn't ... blue · 6 I'm not ... English

Early finisher Make more silly sentences and
correct them.

5 Who's in the photo?

(be: positive and negative) ▪▪▪▪▪□

👥 **Partner A:**
Go to page 205.

Partner B:
Go to page 140.

6 GAME Team sentences 💬 ▪▪▪▪▪▪

👥 **Work in teams of six.**

Step 1: Think of a sentence with six words. Write each word on a different card.

| LUCY | IS | NEW | AT | PLYMSTOCK | SCHOOL |

Step 2: Swap cards with another team. Don't look at your new cards.
Step 3: Go to the front of the class and stand in a line. Hold up your new cards.

TOWN　　　WE'RE　　　A　　　GERMANY　　　FROM　　　IN

Lisa　　　Sven　　　Cem　　　Iris　　　Marie　　　Jasper

Step 4: The class says: "Sven, you're one. Marie, you're two ...". At the end, the sentence is right.

➡ **Workbook** *3 (p. 9)*

7 Don't wear trainers (Imperatives)

You make positive imperatives like this:

Wait a minute.

Wear black shoes, please.

You make negative imperatives like this:

Don't go, Maya.

Don't wear trainers.

➜ *GF 4: Imperatives (p. 159)*
➜ **Workbook** *4 (p. 10)*

More help: Die Verben sind im Infinitiv in einer Box vorgegeben und müssen Lückensätzen zugeordnet werden.

Make imperatives for the pictures.

touch

give

put

open

forget

talk

More help ➜ *p. 128*

1 Don't touch the picture. • 2 Give me the pen, please. • 3 Don't put the rat in the bag. • 4 Don't open the window. • 5 Don't forget your bag. • 6 Don't talk in the library.

8 Study skills: The Vocabulary

Lernfeld: Die S wissen, was welche Zeichen und Hilfen im *Vocabulary* bedeuten. Sie können diese auch erklären.

Mithilfe des Vocabulary (ab S. 172) lernst du die neuen Wörter einer Unit kennen.

a) Sieh dir die Seiten 172 – 205 an und beantworte diese Fragen:

1 Die Zeichen in [ ] zeigen
a) Geheimschrift.
b) Aussprache.
c) Dialekt.

2 Ein rotes Ausrufezeichen (❗) weist hin auf
a) gefährliche Worte.
b) Vokabeltests.
c) mögliche Fehlerquellen.

3 Die rechte der drei Spalten
a) ist für Notizen.
b) enthält Beispielsätze und Verwendungshinweise.
c) soll auswendig gelernt werden.

4 Das Zeichen ◄ ► steht für
a) Gegenteile.
b) Jahreszahlen.
c) kleiner/größer als.

5 Die blauen Kästen enthalten
a) Hinweise für Lehrer/innen.
b) Bekanntes aus vorigen Units.
c) Übersichten von Wörtern und Wendungen, die du zusammen lernen solltest.

b) Kannst du jetzt diese Fragen beantworten?

1 Was ist das Gegenteil von **new**? (S. 179)
2 Worauf muss man bei der Aussprache von **wrong** achten? (S. 175)
3 Was ist das Besondere am Wort **I** (ich!)? (S. 173)
4 Wie spricht man die englische **Null** in Telefonnummern aus? (S. 178)

1 old • 2 w wird nicht gesprochen • 3 wird immer groß geschrieben • 4 wird wie ein "o" ausgesprochen

Das Vocabulary ist nicht der einzige Weg, wie du Vokabeln lernen kannst.
Weitere Methoden zeigt dir das **Skills File**.
➜ *SF 1: Learning vocabulary (pp. 148 – 149)*

Lernfeld S. 25: Die S können über **sich**, ihre **Familie**, **Freunde** und die Lehrwerksfiguren schreiben.

9 People's profiles

a) There are *four* speakers.
Listen and match each speaker to a picture.
Make a table for your answers.

Speaker	Name	b)
1	...	Maya: Plymouth · 11 · Coombe Dean · Lucy
		Sam: London · 11 · Plymstock School · Tom
2	...	Silky: Plymouth · 2 · Sammy
		Justin: Plymouth · 12 · Plymstock School ·
...	...	his dad

Say who the speakers are.
Speaker number ... is Justin.
1 Maya · 2 Sam · 3 Silky · 4 Justin

b) Choose a picture from a).
Listen again. Find this information about the speaker in your picture:

hometown · ... years old · school · best friend

c) **EXTRA** 👥👥 Find a student with the same picture. Together write a short profile of the speaker.
This is ...'s profile.
... is from ... in England.
He/She ... years old.
... at ... school.
His/Her best friend ...

Give your text to another pair. Read their text.

➡ *SF 7: Listening (pp. 153–154)*
➡ **Workbook** *5 (p. 10)*

10 About me 💬

a) What can you say about yourself?
Find ideas in the profile from 9 c).

My name is ...
I'm from ... in Germany.

More ideas:
My mum and dad are ...
I have ... brothers and sisters.
My favourite animal/colour/day/... is ...
I like ... / I don't like ...

...

b) 🧩 Make appointments with three partners.

Can we meet at 10/11/12 o'clock, please?

Write your appointments
on a card:

My appointments:
10 o'clock – Emil
11 o'clock – Lily
12 o'clock – Leonie

When your teacher says it's 10/11/12 o'clock,
go to your appointments.
Talk to your partners about yourself.

➡ **Workbook** *6 (p. 11)*

11 My profile ✏

a) Write your profile.

b) 👥👥 Read your partner's profile.
Can you give him/her more ideas?

EXTRA Make a mini-poster of your profile.
Hang it up in your classroom.
Then you can put it into your 📓.

MY PROFILE
Name: Boris Köhne
Hometown: Bad Honnef
School:
Brothers:
Sister:

You can put pictures on your mini-poster.

➡ **Workbook** *7 (p. 11)*

Alternative: In a) notieren die S eine Entwurfsfassung, die sie in b) in PA überarbeiten. Erst danach schreiben sie ihren Steckbrief in Reinschrift.

Alternative Erarbeitung bei geschlossenem SB mit **KV 6: A game with Miss Bell**: Die S identifizieren Figuren, die den Ball werfen, und ordnen Personen Zitate zu. Bei Einsatz der KV entfällt Aufgabe 2 im SB.

1 A game with Miss Bell 1 ▷ 20

Good morning.
I'm Miss Bell.

Justin

Miss Bell:	**Good morning**. I'm Miss Bell, your class teacher. It's your first day at Plymstock School, **so** …
Justin:	Sorry I'm late, Miss.
5 Miss Bell:	OK. **Come in**, please.
Justin:	Yes, Miss.
Miss Bell:	Now, let's **start** with a game. Here's a **ball**. **Throw** the ball and **ask** a question. **Catch** it and **answer** the question. OK?
10 Class:	Yes, Miss.
Miss Bell:	Here we go. <u>Are you</u> in a football team?
Sam:	<u>No, I'm not.</u>
Miss Bell:	And now, please, say your name and one or two things about **yourself**.
15 Sam:	I'm Sam Bennett and I'm from London. My **birthday** is in **September**. I **do°kung fu** and I like …
Miss Bell:	Thank you, Sam. Now throw the ball.
20 Sam:	OK. <u>Are you</u> from Plymouth?
Justin:	<u>Yes, I am.</u> My name is Justin Skinner. I **live** with my mum **at 14 Dean Street**. My dad is from the USA. Er … <u>Is your dad</u> from the USA?
25 Lucy:	<u>No, he isn't.</u> My name is … oops!
Sam:	Lucy.
Miss Bell:	<u>Are you</u> Lucy?
Sam:	<u>No, I'm not</u>, Miss.
Miss Bell:	**Then** please don't answer Lucy's question. OK, Lucy, start **again**.
30 Lucy:	My name is Lucy Pascoe. And my favourite animals are rabbits …
❖	
Miss Bell:	Now, here are your **timetables**. And at 11 o'clock it's time for …

Sam

Are you in a
football team?

Justin

Is your dad from the USA?

Lucy

My name is … oops!

2 Who is it?

👥 Read a sentence from the dialogue to your group. Can the others guess who it is?

A: "Sorry I'm late, Miss."
B: That's Justin!
B: "Come in, please."
C: That's …

3 Have a go

👥 Ask and answer questions like this:

A: Are you in class 5b / in a football team / …?
B: Yes, I am. / No, I'm not.
B: Is your mum from England / the USA / …?
A: Yes, she is. / No, she isn't.

EXTRA Play Miss Bell's game in your class.

Das Spiel sollte in Gruppen von 6–8 S gespielt werden. Pro Gruppe wird ein Ball benötigt.

Grund-
schule

Lernfeld S. 27: Die S können **Fragen** über sich und andere **kurz beantworten**.

Looking at language

a) Copy the table and finish the *yes* answers. You can find examples on p. 26.

Are you …?	Yes, I …	No, …
Is he …?	Yes, he is.	
Is she …?	Yes, she …	
Is it …?	Yes, it is.	
Are you …?	Yes, we …	
Are they …?	Yes, … are.	

b) Add negative forms to the table:
No, I'm not. No, he …

TIP
Don't answer *Yes* or *No*.
Say *Yes, I am* or *No, I'm not*.

Lernfeld: Die S verstehen und können sagen, wie spät es ist, und können auch andere nach der **Uhrzeit** fragen.

2 WORDS What time is it?

a) 👥 Point to the clocks and mobile phones and say the time. Talk like this:
A: What time is it, please?   B: It's …
A: Thank you.

ten o'clock	quarter past …	twenty past …
10.00 ten o'clock	10:15 ten fifteen	10:20 ten …
half past …	quarter to …	five to …
10:30 ten …	10:45 ten …	10:55 ten …

b) 👥 Draw five mobile phones with five different times. Talk again.

➡ **Workbook** 9 (p. 12)

1 Yes, I am (*be*: questions and short answers)

a) 👥 Partner A: Ask the questions.
1 Are you in Year 5?
2 Is Sam from London?
3 Are you and your friends in Plymouth now?
4 Are your books in your pencil case?
5 Is your English teacher from England?

1 Yes, I am. • 2 Yes, he is. • 3 No, we aren't. • 4 No, they aren't. • 5 Yes, s/he is. / No, s/he isn't.

Partner B: Ask the questions.
6 Are you nine years old?
7 Are Lucy and Maya friends?
8 Is your English book in your school bag?
9 Is Miss Bell a student?
10 Are your mum and dad from the USA?

6 Yes, I am. / No, I'm not. • 7 Yes, they are. • 8 No, it isn't. • 9 No, she isn't. • 10 Yes, they are. / No, they aren't.

b) 👥 Make more questions for your partner.
A: Is your best friend in our class?
B: – Yes, she is. / No, she isn't.
B: Are your shoes red? …

 More help ➡ *p. 128*

More help: Einige Ideen für Fragen sind vorgegeben.

➡ *GF 2 b–c: (to) be: questions and short answers (p. 158)*
➡ **Workbook** 8 (p. 11)

3 WORDS School subjects

Lernfeld: Die S können über **Schulfächer** sprechen.

a) Look at the school subjects. Can you understand the words?

- English
- German
- French
- Music
- Religion
- PE
- History
- Geography
- Art
- Design and Technology
- Maths
- Science
- ICT

Box "School subjects", Voc, S. 182

b) Listen to Lucy and Maya.
What subjects do they like?
What are their favourite subjects?

 1 ▸ 21

c) What are your favourite subjects?

➡ **Workbook** 10 (p. 12)

Lucy likes Geography and History. Her favourite subject is Design and Technology.
Maya likes Maths, Science, German and Religion. Her favourite subject is ICT.

Lernfeld S. 28: Die S können einen **Stundenplan** lesen und verstehen, um welche Fächer/Pausen es geht und wann sie stattfinden. Sie können darüber auch sprechen.

4 WORDS Lucy's timetable (The school day)

a) Look at Lucy's timetable. Then finish the text below. You need these new words:

> hour · lunch · break

At Plymstock School, there are … lessons every day.

Lessons are one … long.

The first lesson is at …

There's a short … at 11:00.

The … break is at 1:20.

It's … minutes long.

It's time to go home at …

five · hour · 9:00 · break · lunch · 35 · 2:55

Lesson	Monday	Tuesday	Wednesday	Thursday	Friday
9:00 – 10:00	Design and Technology	English	History	Science	Maths
10:00 – 11:00	Music	Geography	French	Maths	Design and Technology
BREAK 11:00 – 11:20					
11:20 – 12:20	PE	ICT	English	German	German
12:20 – 1:20	English	Learning to Learn	Science	History	Science
LUNCH 1:20 – 1:55					
1:55 – 2:55	Maths	Art	PE	Religion	English

b) Talk about Lucy's timetable like this:

A: What is lesson 1 on Monday?
B: Lesson 1 on Monday is Design and Technology.

➜ **Workbook** 11 (p. 13)

5 My timetable

a) Write your timetable in English. Put it into your My Book.

Get more words if you need them.
➜ Wordbank 2 (p. 142)

b) Right or wrong? Correct the sentences about your timetable.

1 There are five school days in the week.
   Right.
2 There are nine lessons on Monday.
   Wrong, there are …
3 The first lesson is at 9:15.
4 Lessons are 35 minutes long.
5 There's a short break at 10:30.
6 There's a lunch break at 12:30.
7 Science is on Thursday and Friday.
8 History lessons are on Monday, Tuesday and Friday.
9 At 12:30, it's time to go home.

c) Write three more wrong sentences. Can your partner correct them?

6 EXTRA A letter to Lucy

Write a letter to Lucy.
Tell her about your school day and your subjects.

More help   ➜ p. 129

More help: Ein Musterbrief mit Lücken bzw. Multiple-Choice-Auswahl.

Put your letter into your My Book.

Lernfeld S. 29: Die S können sagen, wann jemand **Geburtstag** hat. Sie können **Geburtsdaten** und **Geburtstagseinladungen** schreiben.

7 WORDS My birthday is in ... (The months) Box "The months", Voc, S. 182 1 22

a) On a card, write the month of your birthday.

> January · February · March · April ·
> May · June · July · August · September ·
> October · November · December

Alternative: Sollten die Monatsnamen den S bisher unbekannt sein, liest L diese zunächst vor und die S sprechen im Chor nach.

b) Listen. When you hear your month, hold up your card and say "My birthday is in ...".

Grund-schule

My birthday is in May.

→ **Workbook** 12 (p. 13)

Zusatz: Die S basteln aus den Karten einen Geburtstagskalender.

8 WORDS My birthday is on ... (Ordinal numbers) 1 23–24

Grund-schule

a) Listen and say the dates. Put up your hand when you hear the date of your birthday.

1st	**first**	12th	**twelfth**
2nd	**second**	13th	thirteenth
3rd	**third**	14th	fourteenth
4th	fourth	...	
5th	**fifth**	20th	**twentieth**
6th	sixth	21st	twenty-first
7th	seventh	22nd	twenty-second
8th	**eighth**	23rd	twenty-third
9th	**ninth**	...	
10th	tenth	30th	**thirtieth**
11th	eleventh	31st	thirty-first

Box "Numbers", Voc, S. 182

b) Ask other students.

When's your birthday?

My birthday is on the ninth of July.

Box "Birthdays", Voc, S. 182

c) Listen to the children. When are their birthdays? Make a table like this:

Name	Date
Will	13th March
Zoe	
Harry	
Grace	

Zoe: 15th October
Harry: 22nd May
Grace: 13th April

→ **Workbook** 13 (p. 13)

9 *a* [ə] or *an* [ən] ? 1 25

Listen. What presents would the kids like? Write them in the correct column – a or an?

Name	*a*	*an*
Will		
Zoe		
Harry		
Grace		

DVD · elephant · English book · football · giraffe · MP3 player · orange pen · uniform for Teddy

Will: a football · an English book
Zoe: a DVD · an orange pen
Harry: a giraffe · an elephant
Grace: a uniform for Teddy · an MP3 player

→ **Workbook** 14 (p. 14)

10 Come to my party! ✏ (Prepositions)

a) Finish the invitation. Use these words: at (2x) · in · on · to

b) Write an invitation to your party.

Come ... my party!
It's ... Plymouth,
... 19 Hill Street,
... Saturday, 13th March,
... 3 o'clock.

to · in · At · on · at

TIP

You say	You **write**
the second of April	2nd April
the ninth of July	9th July

Early finisher → p. 138

Early finisher: Rätsel

1 Where's Justin? 1 ▷ 26

It's 11 o'clock – time for the Plymstock School °Discovery Quiz. Sam, Lucy and Justin are in Team 3.

Sam:	What's the first question?
5 Lucy:	"Where are your geography lessons? Find the room and count the maps."
Justin:	Here's the geography room – room HU3.
Lucy:	Are there any maps?
Sam:	Yes, there's a map of England, a map
10	of China …
Lucy:	Is there one "n" or two in "China"?
Justin:	I can spell it. It's C - h - …
	❖
Lucy:	OK, second question: "Where can you work with computers?
15	Count the computers there."
Justin:	The computer room. Here it is!
Sam:	Wow! There are lots of computers! Two, four, six, …, 11, 12!
	❖
Lucy:	Good. Third question:
20	"Where can you read a book, watch a DVD and fall asleep?"
Justin:	I can do that at home, in my room.
Sam:	Is your room at Plymstock School, Justin?
25 Justin:	Er … no …
Lucy:	You're silly, Justin.
Justin:	I'm not silly! The answer is the library. I know that.

> Box "look · see · watch", Voc, S. 183

Lucy:	Yes, but the big question is:
30	"When is this place open?"
Sam:	When *is* the library open?
Lucy:	I don't know. Let's go and look.
	❖
Sam:	OK, the library times are here. I can read them for you.
35 Lucy:	OK … Hey, where's Justin?
Sam:	I don't know. Er … What's the fourth question?
Lucy:	"Where can students meet and eat? What colour are the chairs there?"
40 Sam:	That's the canteen – it's near the gym. Hurry up!
	❖
Lucy:	OK, the chairs are red and yellow.
Sam:	We're finished! Now, where is Justin?
45 Lucy:	I don't know. Can we go back now?
Sam:	No, we can't – not without Justin.
Lucy:	Then we can't win. Sam, can we find him?
Sam:	Yes, we can. Let's go!

2 Right or wrong?

Check with a partner.

1 In the geography room, Justin is with Lucy and Sam.
2 He isn't with them in the computer room.
3 He isn't with them at the library door.
4 Sam and Lucy can go back to the classroom without Justin.

1 Right. · 2 Wrong. He is with them. ·
3 Right. · 4 Wrong. They can't go back without him.

3 The winners are … 1 ▷ 27

a) Listen and correct the sentences.

1 Miss Bell is at the canteen.

   No, she isn't. Team 5 are at the canteen.
2 Justin is in the library.
3 There is a map of Plymstock in the geography room.
4 Team 2 are the winners of the quiz.

b) Check your partner's answers.

2 No, he isn't. Justin is in the geography room. · 3 No, there isn't.
There's a map of Germany. · 4 No, they aren't. Team 3 are the winners.

FöFo 1.8　▶　**The world behind the picture**　**1**

Lernfeld S. 31: Die S verstehen und benutzen viele **Sätze, die sie im Klassenraum verwenden**.

1 The Plymstock School Discovery Quiz

a) Look at the photo of the three students. Then watch the film. Say "Stop!" when you know the names of all three students.

b) Watch the film again. You see these places:
   A the canteen　　　D a computer room
   B classroom HU3　　E the library
   C classroom HU6

Put them in the right order.
The first place is C, classroom HU6.
The second place … 2 the canteen · 3 the library · 4 classroom HU 3 · 5 a computer room

c) 👥 Check with a partner.
Then watch the film again. Are you right?

d) 👥 Make two lists about the school like this:

e) Look at a partner's lists.
What's the same? What's different?

☺ I like	☹ I don't like
the uniform	the computer room
…	…

2 EVERYDAY ENGLISH Classroom English　　1 ▶ 28

a) Finish the sentences from an English classroom.

1 Please … your **workbooks** at **page** 15.
2 Can you … with Paul, please?
3 … I'm late.
4 What … are we on?
5 Miss, can I open the …?
6 I can't … number 3.
7 Paul, … you help Lisa, please?
8 Can I … to the **toilet**, please?
9 … for **homework**?
10 Can you … "Scotland", please?

1 open · 2 work ·
3 Sorry · 4 page ·
5 window · 6 do ·
7 can · 8 go ·
9 What's · 10 spell

More help ➡ p. 129　　**More help:** Die passenden Verben sind in einer Box vorgegeben.

b) 👥 Compare your sentences with a partner.

c) Watch the film and check your answers.

d) 👥 Make classroom ladders.

➡ *Classroom English (p. 236)*

Sorry,	Can I	Can you	What's
I don't know.	open the window?	work with …?	for homework?
I'm late. :(	have your sharpener?	spell "Plymouth"?	"Kleber" in English?
	go to the toilet?	help …, please?	

1 At Plymstock School *(there is / there are)*

Box "There are / There aren't any", Voc, S. 183

Make sentences and write them down.

There's a … / There are …	but there isn't a … / there aren't any …
uniforms for the students,	swimming pool.
Discovery Quiz for Year 7,	maps.
red and yellow chairs in the canteen,	Discovery Quiz for Year 8.
map of China in room HU3,	green chairs.
18 computers in the computer room,	map of Mexico.
library at the school,	uniforms for the teachers.

Language help

There's + singular:
- There's a *book* on my desk.

There are + plural:
- There are *two pens* on my desk.

English: There aren't any …
German: Es gibt/sind keine …

English: Are there any …?
German: Gibt es …? / Sind …?

➡ *GF 3: There is … / There are … (p. 159)*

Early finisher Make sentences about your pencil case, desk, …
There are three pencils in my pencil case, but there isn't a rubber.

2 At your school *(there is / there are: questions and short answers)*

👥 Make questions for your partner. Ask and answer your questions in pairs.

A: Is there a swimming pool at our school?   B: Yes, there is. / No, there isn't. Are there any …?

Is there a Are there any	computers · swimming pool · English students · canteen · library · nice teachers	at our school?	Yes, there is. · No, there isn't. Yes, there are. · No, there aren't.

Go on with new ideas.   – Is there a Discovery Quiz/a …?
– Are there any rats/monsters/…?   ➡ **Workbook** 16–17 (p. 15)

3 In the classroom *(can/can't)*

Make correct sentences.

1 you – it – in German? – Can – say
   Can you say it in German?
2 can't – I – in English – say – it.
3 can't – I – spell – "cupboard".
4 I – work – with – Lisa? – Can
5 window, – I – please? – the – Can – open
6 toilet, – go – I – Can – please? – to – the
7 again, – you – say – Can – please? – it
8 I'm finished. do – I – What – can – now?

Early finisher Ask a partner four questions
with *can*. Answer his/her questions.

➡ *GF 5: can (p. 160)*
➡ **Workbook** 18 (p. 15)

2 I can't say it in English. · 3 I can't spell "cupboard". · 4 Can I work with Lisa? ·
5 Can I open the window, please? · 6 Can I go to the toilet, please? ·
7 Can you say it again, please? · 8 I'm finished. What can I do now?

4 EXTRA GAME I can see …

Play the game.

Boris: I can see a yellow pencil.
Anne: Boris can see a yellow pencil and I can write English words.
Liu: Boris can see a yellow pencil, Anne can write English words and I can spell "cupboard".

More help ➡ p. 129

More help: Hier sind einige Ideen vorgegeben.

TIP
English: I can see a pencil.
German: Ich kann einen Bleistift sehen.

L sollte an dieser Stelle darauf hinweisen, dass hinter *can* immer ein Vollverb stehen muss.

Lernfeld S. 33: Die S können das **Alphabet** aufsagen und Wörter **buchstabieren**. Sie können Worte schreiben, die ihnen buchstabiert werden.

1 The alphabet song

1 ▷ 29–31

Grundschule

a) Listen and sing along.

A B C D E F G
H I J K L M N O P
Q R S T U V W X Y Z

*Now you know the ABC
you can spell your name for me.*

> Track 1.30 ist die Instrumentalversion des Songs.

b) Here, the alphabet is in sound groups. Say the letters. Listen and check.

A H J K
B C D E G P T V
F L M N S X Z
I Y Q U W O R

➜ **Workbook** 19 (p. 16)

2 Spell with Morph

1 ▷ 32–33

a) Listen to Morph. Write down the words in the order he spells them.

 ³Coombe Dean · ⁵geography · ¹Justin · ²aren't · ⁴Sam Bennett

You write	You say
oo, nn	double o, double n
n't	n apostrophe t

b) Morph spells more words. Listen and write them down. that's · butterfly · exercise book · o'clock · technology

c) Write down five words and spell them. Your partner says the words.

3 My name and address

1 ▷ 34

a) Listen. What are ä, ö, ü and ß in English?

Ben: Can you spell your name, Jörg?
Jörg: Yes, it's J - o with ... dots - r - g. two
Ben: And your family name?
Jörg: Müller. That's M - u with ... dots, two double l - e - r.
Ben: What's your address?
Jörg: Schäferstraße 24A. I can spell it for you. It's S - c - h - a with ... dots - two f - e - r - s - t - r - a - ... - e. double s

b) Act out a dialogue like in a). Use your name and address. Change roles.

➜ **Workbook** 20 (p. 16)

4 Apostrophes

> **TIP**
> Some English verbs have a short form. In short forms, you use an apostrophe for the missing letter.

a) Make correct sentences from the word snakes. Don't forget the apostrophes.

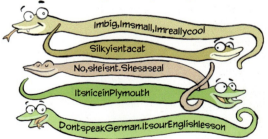

Imbig,Imsmall,Imreallycool
Silkyisntacat
No,sheisnt.Shesaseal
ItsniceinPlymouth
DontspeakGerman.ItsourEnglishlesson

➜ *SF 9: Writing – Check your spelling (p. 155)*

➜ **Workbook** 21 (p. 16)

b) Now write the sentences with long forms.

Zusatz: Die S machen eigene Buchstabenschlangen und tauschen sie untereinander aus.

Lernfeld S. 34–35: Die S können eine Geschichte mündlich oder schriftlich weiterführen.

Chaos at the corner shop   35

Look at the pictures. Say who's in the story and who's new. Then read the story.

1 Right or wrong?

Correct the wrong sentences.

1 Maya is in the Broadway before Lucy.
2 Sam is Lily's big brother.
3 Sam **is good at** kung fu.
4 Maya is Sam's sister.
5 Maya isn't a good swimmer.
6 Sam is in the shop with his sister.

1 Lucy is in the Broadway before Maya. · 4 Lily is Sam's sister. · 5 Maya is the best swimmer in Plymstock. · 6 Sam is with Maya and Lucy.

2 Feelings

Choose a picture in the story. Match the smileys to the people in that picture and talk about them.
Picture 10/smiley 3: Lucy and Maya are angry.

happy   sad   **angry**

surprised   sorry

3 Act it out

Grund-schule

👥 Every student gets a speech bubble from the story. Act out your speech bubbles in the right order.

KV 7: **Chaos at the corner shop** enthält die Sprechblasen für die S zum Ausschneiden und Ordnen.

4 The **next** picture

You choose   Do a) or b).

a) Draw the next picture for the story.

b) What's next? Write speech bubbles for one or more of these people:

Sam – Maya – Lucy – the **man** from the shop

Show your picture or speech bubbles to your classmates. Say which ideas you like.

Neigungsdifferenzierung: Die S haben die Wahl zwischen einer künstlerisch-gestalterischen Aufgabe und einem kreativen Schreibauftrag. Beide befassen sich inhaltlich mit der gleichen Thematik und können gemeinsam oder in PA ausgewertet werden.

→ **Workbook** 22 (p. 17)

Workbook Checkpoint 1 (pp. 18–21)

2 Unit

Homes and families

Box "Straßennamen mit und ohne Hausnummern", Voc, S. 184

I live in Beach Road in Wembury, near Plymouth. This is my house.

Abby

Abby Blackwell is in Year 7 at Plymstock School.

1 What's in the house?

a) Look at the house on page 37. Which rooms are upstairs? Which rooms are downstairs?

b) 👥 You can find these things in a house. Do you know the words?

> armchair · bed · book · chair · clock · cupboard · desk · door · football · lamp · photo · picture · poster · shelf · sofa · table · toilet · toy · TV · window

Alternative Erarbeitung mit **KV 8: Things you can find in a house**.

c) Listen and say the numbers from the picture on page 37.
There's a big table in the dining room.
That's number 12.

Grund-schule

d) 👥 Ask and answer like this:

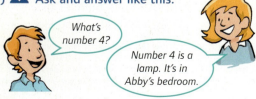

What's number 4?

Number 4 is a lamp. It's in Abby's bedroom.

e) Now listen to Abby and point to the things in the house.

2 My bedroom

a) 👥 Take turns and tell your partner three things about your bedroom.
My bedroom is small. I have an old TV.
From my window, I can see my friend's house.
What about you?

b) Draw a picture or take a photo of your bedroom. Label the things in your picture or photo.

Die S können schon in der Stunde zuvor gebeten werden, Fotos mitzubringen.

Get more words if you need them.
➜ *Wordbank 3 (p. 143)*

👥 Show your picture or photo to your partner. Then you can put it into your 📓 .

Your task

Am Ende dieser Unit wirst du …
… in einem Rollenspiel einem Schüler oder einer Schülerin aus Großbritannien dein Haus oder deine Wohnung vorstellen.

➜ **Workbook** *1–2 (p. 22)*

Lernfeld S. 36–37: Die S können anderen von ihrem **Zimmer**/ihrer **Wohnung**/ihrem **Haus** erzählen und sagen, welche **Gegenstände** sich in welchem Zimmer befinden. Sie können dies auch aufschreiben und auf einem Bild Räume und Gegenstände zeigen, wenn andere über ihr Zimmer/ihre Wohnung/ihr Haus berichten.

Abby's **bedroom**

bathroom

Mr and Mrs Blackwell's bedroom

upstairs

downstairs

dining room

kitchen

living room

garden

1 poster · 2 shelf · 3 book · 4 lamp · 5 desk · 6 toy · 7 toilet · 8 bed · 9 photos · 10 armchair ·
11 window · 12 table · 13 chair · 14 clock · 15 TV · 16 pictures · 17 door · 18 sofa · 19 football

1 My day at home

"This is my home – Plymouth °Sound."

I wake up at 6 o'clock every morning.

My friends wake up too.

Then I have breakfast – a big plate of crabs.

After breakfast, my friends and I swim and swim and swim ...

In the afternoon, we play football in a pool.

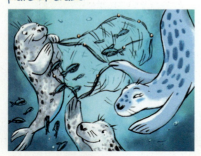

In the evening, we catch fish for dinner.

Box "in the evening", Voc, S. 185
Box "to have breakfast", Voc, S. 185

I sit on my rock and eat lots of fish.

I text my friends or read a book. And then I fall asleep.

Alternative: Die Bilder und Bildunterschriften befinden sich ungeordnet auch auf **KV 9**. Die S schneiden sie aus, ordnen sie einander zu und bringen sie in die richtige Reihenfolge.

2 Now you're Silky

Imagine you're Silky. Talk to your partner about your day. Take turns and don't forget to talk about Silky's friends too.

I meet my friends and we swim and swim and swim.

3 🔊 At the Blackwells' house 2 ▶ 4

Abby has a new friend, Maya. She knows her from Wembury Sailing Club. Maya is at Abby's house.

Abby:	Let's go into the kitchen. I can make a cup of tea for you.
5 Maya:	A cup of tea? Yes, please.
Abby:	Oh no, it's Saturday. Dad is in the kitchen. He always reads the paper there at the weekend. Let's go into the living room.
	❖
Maya:	Who's that?
10 Abby:	Mink, our cat.
Maya:	She likes the sofa!
Abby:	It's her favourite place. She plays at night. And then she sleeps on the sofa in the morning.
15 Maya:	Wow, you have lots of games!
Abby:	Yes, Dad likes games. We play at weekends.
Maya:	That's nice. We watch TV.
Skip:	Woof, woof!
20 Maya:	There's a dog at the door.
Abby:	That's Skip. I feed him in the morning. Then he plays in the garden.
Maya:	Can he come in?
Abby:	No … please! No dogs in the living room, 25 Mum says. Skip! Go to the kitchen door.
Skip:	Woof, woof!
Abby:	OK, we can go upstairs.
Maya:	Can Skip come with us?
Abby:	Of course … he sleeps in my room. His 30 basket is on the floor near my bed.

Maya:	Hey, you have a nice bedroom.
Abby:	Thanks.
Maya:	And you have lots of sailing trophies!
Tim:	Yes, look at Abby's trophies! She's the star of Wembury Sailing Club.
35 Abby:	Tim! This is my room. You can't come in here. Go away. Now!
Tim:	Help! A mad sister …
Skip:	Woof, woof!
40 Tim:	… and a mad dog!
Abby:	Oh, Tim thinks he's so cool. Maya, let's go for a walk with Skip.

4 Right or wrong?

Correct the wrong sentences.

1 Abby and Maya are old friends.
2 Maya is at Abby's house.
3 Mink is on a chair.
4 Skip isn't in the living room.
5 Tim is Abby's father.
6 Abby is friendly to Tim.

➡ **Workbook** 3–5 (pp. 23–24)

1 new friends · 3 on the sofa · 5 Abby's brother · 6 isn't friendly

5 Have a go

Make sentences.

who	what	where
My father	eats	in the bathroom.
My mother	sleeps	in the kitchen.
My brother	plays	…
My sister	reads	
My cat/dog		

Looking at language

a) Copy and finish the table.
The text on p. 39 can help you (lines 10–25).

Singular	Plural
I play football in the afternoon.	We … at weekends.
You play basketball.	You play in the park.
He … in the garden.	They play at home.
She … at night.	
It plays DVDs.	

b) Look at the 3rd person singular (he/she/it). What's different?

➡ *GF 6 a–b: The simple present (pp. 160–161)*

1 I wake up in the morning (Simple present: positive statements)

I wake up in the morning (Abby)
I wake up in the morning (Silky)
I wake up in the morning (Maya)
I wake up in the evening (Morph)

a) Who sings this song?   Silky

I wake up in the morning,
Then I eat my crabs,
Then I eat my crabs,
I wake up in the morning,
Then I eat my crabs.

b) Finish the songs for the other singers.
Use these lines:

Then I text my friends,   Maya
Then I read a book,   Morph
Then I feed the dog,   Abby

c) Listen and sing along.

 EXTRA Write your morning song and sing it.

Als Hintergrund für die Songs der S steht eine
Instrumentalversion zur Verfügung (Track 2.9).

Grund-
schule

2 We play games (Simple present: positive statements)

Abby talks about the weekend. Make sentences for her.

I	fall asleep	in the living room.
Skip and I	play games	in the kitchen.
We	read books	on the Hoe.
My mum and dad	have a big breakfast	in my room.
They	go for a walk	with my friends.
	play football	in the garden.

We play games in the living room.

 Early finisher ➡ *p. 138*   **Early finisher:** Bilderrätsel

Lernfeld S. 41: Die S können Wörter, die auf **-s** enden, richtig **aussprechen** und wissen, welches Lautschriftsymbol sie dafür verwenden.

3 Pronunciation (The "s" sound: [s], [z] or [ɪz])

2 ▶ 10–11 ■■■■□

a) Read and listen to the poem.

A seal comes home at half past eight,
And watches a crab on a rock.
The crab wakes up and thinks, "I'm late!
Oh, no! It's nine o'clock!"

The crab has breakfast and finds his pen,
And swims away to school,
The seal waits a minute, she counts to ten,
Then catches the crab in a pool.

The seal puts the crab on her breakfast plate.
Then she makes a cup of tea.
The crab says, "Thanks, but I can't wait",
And runs into the sea.

b) Copy the table. Then listen to Morph. Put all the verbs in the right place.

c) Practise the sound groups. Then read the poem out loud.

wakes	comes	watches
...	...	...
thinks, waits, counts, puts, makes	has, finds, swims, says, runs	catches

4 Before school, after school (Simple present: positive statements)

■■■■□

a) Say what the kids do before school.

feed · have · read · talk · text

1 Abby feeds her dog Skip before school.
2 Maya ... Lucy before school.
3 Sam ... a big breakfast before school.
4 Justin ... to his dad on Skype before school.
5 Lucy ... emails before school.

2 texts · 3 has · 4 talks · 5 reads

b) Say what the kids do after school.

1 Abby goes for a walk with Skip after school.
2 Maya ... Lucy at the Broadway after school.
3 Sam ... TV after school.
4 Justin ... computer games after school.
5 Lucy ... her mum in the kitchen after school.

More help ➡ p. 130   2 meets · 3 watches · 4 plays · 5 helps

c) 👥 Say what you do before and after school.

More help: Die gesuchten Verben sind im Infinitv vorgegeben.

5 A tour of Sam's house 💬

■■■■□

Sam shows Lucy his house. Finish his sentences and practise them with a partner.

1 Come into the kitchen. We have breakfast here.
2 This is the living room. Dad ... TV here.
3 That's Mum's armchair. She ... there in the evenings.
4 Look at the garden. My sister Lily ... with her rabbit there.
5 Upstairs, now. That's Lily's room. Look, she ... lots of games.
6 And she always ... them on the floor.
7 And this is my room. I ... my homework here.

More help ➡ p. 130   2 watches · 3 sits · 4 plays · 5 has · 6 throws · 7 read/do

Sam
Lucy

➡ Workbook 6–9 (pp. 24–25)

More help: Die gesuchten Verben sind in einer Box vorgegeben.

Lernfeld S. 42: Die S können Wörter mit einer **Mindmap** ordnen und Überschriften für die einzelnen Wortfelder finden. Diese Methode können sie auch **beim Vokabellernen** anwenden.

6 Study skills: Learning words with mind maps

a) How can you learn new words? One way is to make groups and find the umbrella word.
Find the umbrella word in these lists:

brother	elephant	maths
(family)	frog	PE
mother	(animals)	English
father	horse	(subjects)
sister	rat	German

b) Find umbrella words for these word groups:

1 boy · girl · man · woman
2 blue · orange · purple · red
3 April · June · August · October
4 kitchen · bedroom · dining room · bathroom

1 people
2 colours
3 months
4 house

More help ➡ p. 130

More help: Die *umbrella words* sind in einer Box vorgegeben.

👥 Check with a partner.

c) A mind map can help you to make groups of words.
What umbrella words can you see in this mind map? What are the missing umbrella words?

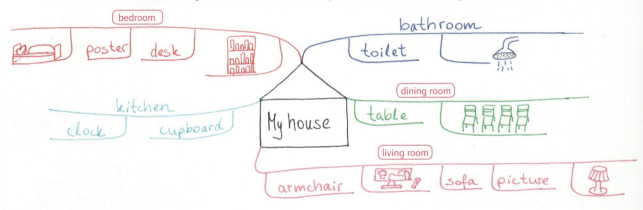

Study skills ▶

Mind maps

1 Du kannst Wortschatz oder Ideen in einer Mindmap ordnen.
Schreibe das Thema (**topic**) in die Mitte.
2 Schreibe deine Oberbegriffe (**umbrella words**) auf die Hauptäste deiner Mindmap.
Verwende verschiedene Farben, Symbole und Zeichnungen. So kannst du dir die Wörter bessser merken.
3 Ergänze weitere Begriffe, Symbole und Zeichnungen auf Nebenästen.

➡ SF 2: Collecting information (pp. 149–150)

d) Make a mind map for your house or flat. The study skills box can help you. Use words from pages 36–37.

➡ *Wordbank 3 (p. 143)*
➡ *SF 1: Learning vocabulary (pp. 148–149)*

➡ **Workbook** *10–11 (p. 26)*

Lernfeld: Die S können den **Laut** [uː] in Wörtern **heraushören**. Sie wissen, dass der Laut [uː] unterschiedlich geschrieben werden kann. Sie können einem Partner Wörter buchstabieren.

1 You say, you write ... [uː]

2 12–13

a) You hear the [uː]-sound in the word "sch**oo**l". Look at the six pictures. Find five words with an [uː]-sound. Then listen and check.

b) How many words with an [uː]-sound can you find: 6, 7 or 8?

> go · glue · double · group · out ·
> Lucy · rubber · school · touch · do ·
> cool · two · who · look

Listen and check.

c) Make a table. Write down the [uː]-words.

You say	You write
uː	glue ... group, Lucy, school, do, cool, two, who

d) Ask your partner to spell the [uː]-words from b).

Can you spell "glue"?

Yes, I can. It's G – L – U – E.

➡ **Workbook** 12 (p. 27)

2 Apostrophes again: *'s* and *s'* (The possessive form)

Lernfeld: Die S können **Apostrophe** richtig verwenden und zwischen **-'s** (= Einzahl) und **-s'** (= Mehrzahl) unterscheiden.

a) Match the phrases to the pictures.   1 B, 2 C, 3 D, 4 A

1 the girl's trophies

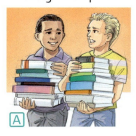

A

2 the girls' trophies

B

3 the boy's books

C

4 the boys' books

D

b) Draw pictures for these phrases:
  1 the student's pens   2 the students' pens

> **Language help**
>
> Singular nouns: Add **apostrophe + s** ('s):
> *Abby's house, the girl's room, ...*
>
> Plural nouns: Put an **apostrophe** (') after the **s**:
> *the Blackwells' house, the girls' rooms, ...*
> ➡ *GF 7: The possessive form (p. 162)*

➡ **Workbook** 13 (p. 27)

c) Read the sentences about Abby's family.

Partner A: Spell the missing word.
Partner B: Listen and write the word.

1 ... family name is Blackwell.
   Abby's: that's A - double B - Y - apostrophe S.
2 The ... house is in Wembury.
3 The ... name is Skip.
4 ... basket is near Abby's bed.
5 ... sailing trophies are in her bedroom.
6 Abby says: "My new ... name is Maya."

More help ➡ p. 130   2 Blackwells' · 3 dog's ·
4 Skip's · 5 Abby's · 6 friend's

More help: Die gesuchten Wörter sind (ohne Apostrophe) in einer Box vorgegeben.

Lernfeld S. 44–47: Die S verstehen Schaubilder und (Hör-/Lese-)Texte, in denen über die **Familie** gesprochen wird. Sie können über die Familie sprechen und beschreiben, wer mit wem verwandt ist.

1 👆 **Uncle** Amar comes to dinner

2 ▶ 14

It's Saturday evening. Uncle Amar is at Maya's flat. [ˈæmə, ˈʌmə]

Uncle:	So Mukesh, you go to a **sports** school!
Mukesh:	Yes, Uncle, Plymstock is a sports school **near here**.
5 Uncle:	And what's your favourite sport? Cricket?
Mukesh:	No, <u>I don't like</u> cricket, Uncle, I …
Uncle:	What? You're an Indian boy, and <u>you don't like</u> cricket!
10 Mukesh:	I'm not an **Indian** boy. I'm British.
Mr Sen:	Mukesh has lots of homework. <u>He **doesn't have time**</u> for sport, Amar.
Maya:	No, Uncle, he **only** has time for computer games.
15 Mrs Sen:	Maya! Ssshhh!
Uncle:	So, Mukesh goes to a sports school, but <u>he doesn't **do sport**</u>!
Mr Sen:	Maya does lots of sport, Amar.
Maya:	Yes, I **often** go sailing, and I like …
20 Uncle:	So Plymstock is the right school for you!
Mukesh:	<u>She doesn't go</u> to Plymstock, Uncle.
Maya:	No, I go to Coombe Dean. It's a maths and ICT school.
25 Uncle:	Maya is our next Albert Einstein.
Mukesh:	Ha, ha, ha …
Mrs Sen:	Mukesh! Ssshhh!
Maya:	Uncle, can I ask you a question?
Uncle:	A question?
30 Maya:	Yes, my English homework is: "Write about your family". But <u>I don't know</u> about our family. So, can you …?
Uncle:	Ah, Maya, I can **tell** you **all** about the Sens. We're a big family, **you know**.

35 Mr Sen:	And <u>we don't all live</u> in India and Britain. Your Uncle Dasan … [ˈdæsæn, ˈdʌsən]
Uncle:	Yes, your Uncle Dasan and Aunt Priya live in South Africa. And your **cousins** Dilip and Sanjay … [ˈpriːjaː ˈpriːjə]
40 Mukesh:	… live in South Africa too.
Uncle:	No, <u>they don't live</u> in South Africa now. Dilip lives in New York and Sanjay lives …

2 Who is it?

Find the information in 1 and say who it is.

1 This **person** doesn't like cricket.
2 This person plays computer games.
3 This person goes to a maths school.
4 This person goes sailing.
5 This person is Maya's uncle in South Africa.
6 This person lives in New York.

1 Mukesh · 2 Mukesh · 3 Maya · 4 Maya · 5 Dasan · 6 Dilip

3 Have a go

a) Mukesh says "I don't like cricket". Think of five things you don't like. Write them down.
– I don't like computer games.
– I don't like …

b) 👥 Tell your partner what you don't like.

c) Tell the class one thing about your partner.
– Alex doesn't like computer games.

Looking at language

a) Copy and finish the table.
The text on p. 44 can help you.

Singular	Plural
I don't like cricket.	We … all live in India.
You … like cricket.	You don't like maths.
He … do sport.	They … live in South Africa.
She … go to Plymstock.	
It doesn't play DVDs.	

➜ *GF 6 c: The simple present (p. 162)*

b) How do you make negative sentences?
When do you use don't?
When do you use doesn't?

---

1 Abby doesn't go to Coombe Dean (Simple present: negative sentences) ▪▫▫▫▫

a) Finish the dialogue. Use negative verbs.

Uncle: Is your friend Abby in your class at school?

Maya: No, Uncle, Abby (go) doesn't go to Coombe Dean.

Uncle: What about Abby's flat? Is it near here?

Maya: Abby (live) … in a flat. The Blackwells have a big house – in Wembury. They (live) … in Plymouth.

Uncle: Tell me about the Blackwells.

Maya: I (know) … Abby's family, Uncle.

Uncle: But she has brothers and sisters?

Maya: She (have) … a sister, but she has a brother, Tim. But he isn't so nice.

Uncle: You (like) … her brother!

Maya: I like Abby, Uncle. She's my friend. I (know) … Tim and he (know) … me.

Uncle: OK, Maya, what about your friend Lucy and her family?

doesn't live · don't live · don't know · doesn't have · don't like · don't know · doesn't know

2 ▶ 15 b) Listen and check.

c) 👥 Act out the dialogue.

---

2 EXTRA GAME I don't like cricket (Simple present: negative sentences) ▪▪▫▫▫

Play the game.

Ela

I don't like cricket.

Boris

Boris doesn't like cricket and I don't like Mondays.

Boris doesn't like cricket, Ela doesn't like Mondays and I don't like yoghurt.

Jan

Anne

Boris …

➜ **Workbook** *14–15 (p. 28)*

Box "grand-", Voc, S. 187

3 A weekend at Grandma's farm (Simple present: positive and negative statements) ■■■□□

Finish the dialogue. Use positive and negative verbs.

Lucy: My grandma has a farm. Holly and I often go there at weekends.

Sam: Tell me about a weekend there.

Lucy: We (wake up) wake up at 6 o'clock. Then we (feed) … the dogs and the rabbits.

Sam: You and your sister Holly?

Lucy: No, Holly (wake up) doesn't wake up at 6 o'clock, so she (feed) … the animals. I feed them with Grandpa.

Sam: Are there lots of animals?

Lucy: Well, we (have) … horses.

Sam: What about elephants?

Lucy: No, Sam. We (have) … elephants. The farm is in England, not in India.

Sam: OK, you (feed) … the animals – and then?

Lucy: Then Grandma (make) … breakfast. And after breakfast we (go) … for a walk.

Sam: You and your sister Holly?

Lucy: No, Holly (come) … with us. She (sleep) … **till** 12 o'clock. I (go) … with Grandma.

> More help → p. 131

> **More help:** Negative Verben sind rot, positive Verben sind grün gedruckt.

feed · doesn't feed · have · don't have · feed · makes · go · doesn't come · sleeps · go

4 A weekend in the library (Simple present: positive and negative statements) ■■■■□

2 ▶16 **a) Listen to Morph and correct the sentences.**

1 Morph lives in a house.

   He doesn't live in a house. He lives in a library.

2 Morph sits on chairs.

3 Morph has a bed.

4 The Plymstock students see Morph every day.

5 Morph sleeps at night.

6 The Plymstock students go to school at weekends.

7 Morph reads French books at weekends.

> More help → p. 131

Correct:
2 sits on books ·
3 has lots of books ·
4 see the teachers ·
5 sleeps in the day · 6 Monday to Friday · 7 reads English books

b) 🎥 **Compare and check your sentences.**

> **More help:** Vorschläge für korrekte Sätze sind vorgegeben; Verben müssen aus Box zugeordnet werden.

5 GAME At the weekend 💬 ■■■■□

a) 👥 **Play the game.**

2B.

2B? Justin doesn't go sailing at the weekend.

4G.

b) 👥 **Talk about your weekends.**

I watch TV at the weekend, but I don't …

		① Abby	② Justin	③ Lucy	④ Maya	⑤ Sam
do homework	A	✓	✗	✗	✓	✓
go sailing	B	✓	✗	✗	✓	✓
play basketball	C	✗	✗	✗	✗	✓
read a paper	D	✗	✓	✓	✓	✗
watch TV	E	✗	✓	✓	✓	✓
wear a uniform	F	✗	✗	✗	✗	✗
write emails	G	✗	✓	✓	✓	✗

→ **Workbook** 16–17 (pp. 28–29)

6 WORDS Families

THE TIZZARDS   ['tɪzəd]   Lucy Pascoe's **family tree**   THE PASCOES

Lewis   Lloyd   Holly   Lucy   Melissa

Lynn   Steve   Harry   Karen   Sam   Jim

Alternative: Die S festigen mit **KV 10** die *family words* in einer kommunikativen Übung.

Bill   Maggie   Helen   George

a) Look at Lucy's family tree:

Partner A: Point to a person and say the name.
Partner B: Say "That's Lucy's …".

grandfather · grandmother · father · mother ·
uncle · aunt · brother · sister · cousin

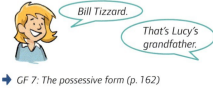

Bill Tizzard.

That's Lucy's grandfather.

➜ *GF 7: The possessive form (p. 162)*

b) Match the words to the symbols.

dead · divorced · married · single · twins

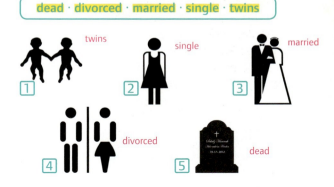

twins   single   married

1   2   3

divorced   dead

4   5

7 Lucy's family 💬 2 ▶ 17

Lucy talks to Sam about her family tree. Listen and choose the right answer.

1 Lucy's mum and dad are married / divorced.
2 Grandma Pascoe is / isn't dead.
3 Uncle Jim is single / married.
4 Uncle Jim lives / doesn't live in Plymouth.
5 Bill and Maggie Tizzard live / don't live near Plymouth.
6 Lewis and Lloyd are / aren't twins.

➜ **Workbook** *18–20 (pp. 29–30)*

EXTRA Make your family tree.
➜ *Wordbank 4 (p. 143)*

Draw people or use photos.
Tell other students about your family tree.

This is my grandma. Her name is … and she lives in …

You can put your family tree into your .

2 **Part C**

Lernfeld S. 48–50: Die S können Texte und Gespräche verstehen, in denen es um **Essen** geht.

1 Sunday lunch 2 ▷ 18

It's 12:45 on Sunday. The Bennett family is at home. Sam is in the kitchen with Mr Bennett.

Sam:	What's for lunch, Dad?
Mr B:	Your favourite.
Sam:	My favourite? Roast beef
5	with roast potatoes? Yummy!
Mr B:	And we start with your mother's yummy vegetable soup.
Sam:	Oh, no soup for me, thanks.
10	I don't like vegetable soup.
Mr B:	No soup, no roast beef.
Sam:	Oh, Dad! Well, what's for dessert?
Mr B:	Fruit salad.
15 Sam:	And ice cream, right?
Mr B:	No, wrong. No ice cream.
Sam:	Oh, Dad!
Mr B:	But we can make scones after lunch. And then we can have
20	°cream tea at 4 o'clock.
Sam:	Cream tea? Great!
Mr B:	Right. Take the soup into the dining room, please.
Sam:	Aye, aye, sir!

25 Mrs Bennett is in the dining room with Sam's sister, Lily. There's a song on the radio and Lily knows it.

Lily:	*Our house, in the middle of our street* …
30 Mr B:	OK, you two. It's time for your lunch. What would you like, Lily?
Lily:	*Our house* … Soup, soup, soup! I'd like soup.
Sam:	Er, Dad, the soup is …
35 Mr B:	Well, little girl, we have your mum's yummy vegetable soup here.
Sam:	Er, Mum, the soup …
Mr B:	Sam, put the soup on the table please!
Sam:	But Dad, …
40 Mrs B:	Hurry up, Sam. It's time for nice, hot soup.
Sam:	But that's it, Mum. The soup – it isn't hot. It's cold!

2 At the Bennetts' house

a) **What's for lunch at the Bennetts' house? What isn't for lunch?**

> scones · fruit salad · ice cream · roast beef · roast potatoes · vegetable soup

For lunch: fruit salad · roast beef · roast potatoes · vegetable soup
Not for lunch: scones · ice cream

b) **Sam says the soup is:**
   1 (cold)   2 hot   3 yummy.

c) **Imagine you're at the Bennetts' house. What would you like for lunch?**
   I'd like …

3 EXTRA Our house   `2 ⏵ 19`

a) Listen to the song and sing along with
the chorus:

*Father wears°his Sunday best
Mother's°tired, she°needs a°rest
°The kids are playing up downstairs
Sister's°sighing in her°sleep
Brother°'s got a date to keep
He can't°hang around
°Chorus: Our house, in the middle of our street
       Our house, in the middle of our …*

Bei dem Song geht
es nur ums Mitsingen
und Zuordnen. Der
Wortschatz sollte
kurz erklärt, aber
nicht gelernt werden.

b) Match the people in the song to the pictures.

Father – that's picture number 2.

1 sister
2 father
3 brother
4 kids
5 mother

 Grund-schule

c) Listen to the song again and point to
the people.

Background file

Cream tea

People in Britain **drink** lots of tea. It's always
time for a "nice cup of tea". And in the
afternoon, at 4 or 5 o'clock, people often have
their tea with **sandwiches**, **cake** or scones.
With a cream tea you have scones with **cream**
and **jam**.
You can make scones too, and have a cream tea
with your friends.

cream

jam

scone

---

4 EXTRA Let's make scones

°225g°flour
55g°sugar
3°teaspoons°baking powder
half teaspoon°salt
1 Put in a°bowl and°mix.

55g°butter
2°Rub in the butter.

°150ml°milk
1°egg
3°Add to the bowl and
mix.

4 Make the scones
and put them in the
°oven (220°C) for 12–15
minutes.

5 Take the scones°out
of the oven. Eat them
with jam and cream
and a nice cup of tea.

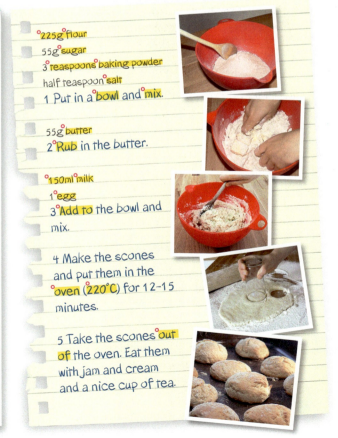

1 WORDS Food and drink

a) Match the words to the pictures.

> **biscuits** · **bread** · **cheese** · cornflakes · fruit ·
> **meat** · **milk** · pizza · potatoes · sandwich ·
> soup · spaghetti · vegetables · **water** · yoghurt

b) Put the words in groups.

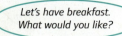

my breakfast
· cornflakes!

my lunch
·

my dinner
·

➡ *Wordbank 5 (pp. 144–145)*

c) 👥 Talk about what you would like.

> *Let's have breakfast.*
> *What would you like?*

> *I'd like bread*
> *and …*

➡ **Workbook** *21–22 (pp. 30–31)*

1 sandwich · 2 cornflakes · 3 milk · 4 yoghurt · 5 water · 6 cheese · 7 fruit · 8 bread ·
9 potatoes · 10 meat · 11 spaghetti · 12 pizza · 13 vegetables · 14 soup · 15 biscuits

2 I feed my bird *(my, your, his, …)*

a) Copy the rhyme.
Put in the words from the box.

> her · his · my · our · their · your · your

b) 👥 Learn the rhyme. Say it to your partner.

EXTRA Draw a picture for another line in
the rhyme.

> *I feed my bird*
> *You feed … cat*
> *He feeds … snake*
> *She feeds … rat*
>
> *We feed … frog*
> *You feed … horse*
> *They feed … dog*
> *With meat, of course.*

your · his · her · our · your · their

3 **EXTRA** There are 22 students in my class *(my, your, his, …)*

Sam and his family talk about people at
Plymstock school. Finish the sentences.

> her · his · my · our · their · your · your

1 Sam: "There are 22 students in my class."
2 Dad: "Is … class teacher OK?"
3 Sam: "We like … class teacher. … name is
   Miss Bell."
4 Mum: "What are … friends' names?"

5 Sam: "I have two good friends. … names are
   Justin and Lucy."
6 Sam: "Justin lives with … mum. … dad lives in
   Boston."
7 Sam: "Lucy lives with … mum too. And …
   grandma and grandpa have a farm. They have
   lots of animals on … farm."
8 Sam: "Lucy is sad. … best friend Maya goes to
   a different school."

More help ➡ p. 131   **More help:** Es sind je zwei
Optionen pro Lücke vorgegeben.

2 your · 3 our … Her · 4 your · 5 Their · 6 his … His · 7 her … her … their · 8 Her

1 My house, your house

a) Look at the picture. What time of day is it?
Does Lucy live in a house or a flat?

morning or afternoon · a small house

b) 👥 Watch the film.
Partner A: Find the photos of Ruby's home. 1, 5, 6
Partner B: Find the photos of Jack's home. 2, 3, 4

Then answer the questions for your photos.

1 What rooms can you see?
2 Is their home a house or a flat?

Jack's flat: bathroom, kitchen, Jack's room
Ruby's house: Ruby's room, kitchen, living room

c) Tell your partner about the photos.

I can see … in the …

2 EVERYDAY ENGLISH Time for lunch   2 ▶ 20

a) Watch the film. Match the names to the people (1–5): Katy, Luke, Oliver, Mrs White and Mr White.

1 Mrs White · 2 Luke · 3 Mr White · 4 Katy · 5 Oliver

b) Correct the sentences.
1 Katy likes fish.
2 There's only milk to drink.
3 There's only fruit salad for dessert.

1 lots of potatoes · 2 milk and water · 3 fruit salad and ice cream

c) Who says these things?
1 What's for lunch?
2 What would you like?
3 No fish for me, thanks.
4 What would you like to drink?
5 I'd like milk, please.
6 There's ice cream or fruit salad.

1 Oliver
2 Mrs White
3 Katy
4 Mr White
5 Luke
6 Mrs White

Watch the film again and check.

d) 👥 Make a dialogue like the one in the film.

Lernfeld S. 52–53: Die S können eine längere Geschichte verstehen und über ihren Inhalt sprechen.

Saturday in Plymouth

What places in Plymouth can you remember?

> I can **remember** the Hoe.

> Box "look", Voc, S. 189

2 ▶ 21 It's Saturday. Justin and his mum are at the Barbican in Plymouth. Justin has a new video camera – a **present** from his dad in Boston.

"OK, Justin, let's go to that nice **café**. Sarah is
5 there – and they have good cream teas."
"I don't like cream teas, Mum."
"That's OK, Justin. Then you can have an ice cream or a sandwich."
"But I don't like cafés. And you and Sarah talk,
10 talk, talk."
"OK, OK, Justin. You win. Let's meet here in an hour. Look at your watch. It's 3:45 now. So meet me here at 4:45. And don't be late! OK?"
"Thank you, Mum!"
15 Mrs Skinner goes to the café. Justin starts to film.
"Hi, Dad. It's 3:46 on Saturday, and I'm in town. I'm at the Barbican. Here you can see Sutton **Harbour**."
There are lots of **seagulls** at the harbour. Justin
20 starts to film them. "Can you see the seagulls, Dad?"

2 ▶ 22 Then he films a man near the harbour. The man **shouts**: "Boat tours! Boat tours! See all the navy **ships**! Next tour in 15 minutes …"
25 He films a boy and a girl. The girl has a big ice cream. **Suddenly**, a seagull comes **down** and takes it from her.
"Wow! That's so cool!" Justin says.
"Look! I have it on camera!"
30 The girl's friend doesn't think it's cool – he's angry. "Don't film us," he shouts. Justin runs away. There are lots of boats in the harbour. Justin starts to film them.
35 One is a big sailing boat.
"This is my favourite boat, Dad. **Maybe** it can take me to the USA – to Boston and to you."
Near it is an old sailing boat. Justin films
40 the boat and **its** name, *Blue Bird*. A small boy in a red T-shirt **jumps onto** the boat.
"Wow!" Justin thinks. "His family has a sailing boat."

Justin looks at his watch. "Time to go back to the **2 ▶ 23**
45 café," he thinks. Then he sees a group of people with a **police officer**. They **look worried**.
"Please find him!" a woman shouts. "He can't swim."
"How old is the boy?" the police officer asks.
50 "He's five years old. He has brown **hair**, and … he can't swim!"

> Box "plural words", Voc, S. 189

"And what about his **clothes**?"
"He has a red T-shirt, **jeans** and white trainers. Here's a picture of him," says the woman and
55 takes a photo from her bag. "His name is Tom."
"A red T-shirt … five years old … brown hair! Wait a minute …" Justin thinks. He finds the *Blue Bird* on his video camera.
"Is this Tom?" he asks.
60 The woman and the police officer look at the picture on Justin's video camera.
"Yes!" shouts the woman. "That's Tom."
"Can you take us to the boat, please?" asks the police officer.
65 Justin takes them to the *Blue Bird*. The woman shouts, "Tom! Tom, where are you?"
The police officer jumps onto the boat. After a minute or two, he comes back with the boy.

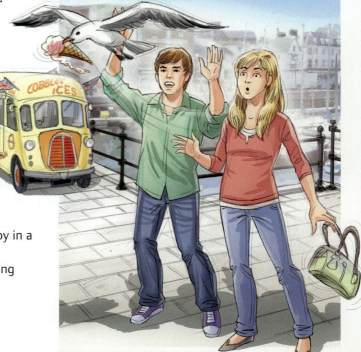

2 ▶ **24** "Oh, Tom!" the woman says.

70 "Hey, Mum," Tom answers. "This is a great boat.
It's so cool. <mark>Why</mark> is the police officer here?"
"<mark>Never</mark> do that again!" she says and°<mark>gives the boy a hug</mark>.
"Do what?" he asks.

75 Justin looks at his watch. "Uh-oh … it's 4:47!
I'm late!"
Then suddenly he sees his mother. Her friend
Sarah is with her. Mrs Skinner sees Justin with the
police officer.
80 "Oh, no, Sarah, Justin <mark>is in trouble</mark>. Hurry up!"
➡ *SF 8: Reading (p. 154)*

> **KV 11: Saturday in Plymouth** enthält einen Multiple-Choice-Quiz zum Text.

1 The <mark>story</mark> in pictures

B · C · D · A · F · E

a) 👥 Put the pictures in the right order. Check with your partner.

b) Find the six scenes in the text. Take turns and read them out.

A: ll.45–55 · B: ll. 1–14 · C: ll. 22–24 · D: ll. 39–43 · E: ll. 77–80 · F: ll. 69–74

2 Tom's mum

👥 Look at lines 44–73. Find sentences that show that Tom's mother is

a) worried   b) happy

*"Please find him!" shows **that** Tom's mother is …*

worried:
Please find him!
He can't swim.
Tom! Tom, where are you?

happy:
Oh, Tom!
Never do that again!

3 Act it out

Neigungsdifferenzierung: Die S haben die Wahl zwischen einer darstellenden Aufgabe und einer kreativen Schreibaufgabe.

You choose Do a) or b).

a) 👥 Act out one of these scenes.   Grund-schule
– Tom's mother talks to the police officer. Justin
shows them the picture on his video camera.
They run to the boat.
– The police officer takes Tom back to his
mother. Justin sees that he is late for his
mother.

b) What does Justin's mother say to him?
Write the rest of the story.

You can add information about the Plymouth
kids to the profiles in your 📖 *My Book*.

➡ **Workbook** *23 (p. 31)*

Workbook
Checkpoint 2
(pp.32–35)

Your task

A tour of my home 💬

Imagine one of the five Plymouth kids
visits you in Germany.
Give him or her a tour of your home and
speak about your family.

STEP 1[1]

Choose your Plymouth kid.

> Die unit-übergreifende Lernaufgabe führt
> die erworbenen Kenntnisse und
> Kompetenzen der Unit zusammen. Sie führt
> zu individuellen Ergebnissen der S, die
> stichprobenartig im Unterricht besprochen
> werden können. Die eigentliche Bearbeitung
> kann zu Hause stattfinden.

STEP 2

What can you say about the rooms in your
home? Your mind map from page 42 can help
you to find ideas and words.

> bedroom …
> small … sleep …
> do my homework …
> desk near window …
> kitchen … big …

STEP 3

What can you tell your friend about your family?
Your family tree from page 47 can help you.

STEP 4

👥 In front of your group, talk to your friend
from Plymouth about your home and the people
in it.

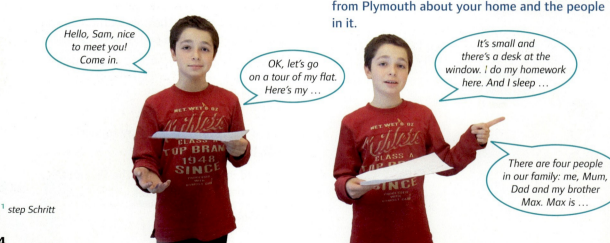

> Hello, Sam, nice
> to meet you!
> Come in.

> OK, let's go
> on a tour of my flat.
> Here's my …

> It's small and
> there's a desk at the
> window. I do my homework
> here. And I sleep …

> There are four people
> in our family: me, Mum,
> Dad and my brother
> Max. Max is …

[1] step Schritt

Diese Seite dient der Selbsteinschätzung durch die S, sollte aber bei diesem ersten Vorkommen zunächst im Unterricht besprochen werden. Das ist v.a. dann wichtig, wenn die S noch keine Erfahrung mit Selbsteinschätzung haben.

Das lief nicht gut, ich muss mehr üben.

Das war OK, aber ich könnte besser werden.

Das habe ich gut geschafft.

Red? I have to practise more.

Yellow? OK, but I can do better.

Green? Great!

Wie gut warst du?

Wie schätzt du dich selber ein? Schreibe *Words*, *Grammar*, *Mind map* und *Speaking* in dein Heft und ordne dir für jeden Bereich eine Ampelfarbe zu.

Words

· Fielen dir die meisten Wörter schnell ein oder gab es Lücken? Bei welchen Wortfeldern hattest du Schwierigkeiten?

Grammar

· Konntest du die Formen des *simple present* problemlos bilden? Hast du bei *he/she/it* das *s* immer angehängt?
· Wie oft hast du Fehler bei *my*, *your*, *his*, … gemacht?

Mind map

· Hat dir deine Mindmap bei der Vorbereitung geholfen?

Speaking

· Konntest du gut vor deiner Gruppe auf Englisch sprechen? Welche Probleme hattest du dabei?

Wie kannst du besser werden?

Wenn du dich eher rot oder gelb eingeschätzt hast, helfen dir folgende Tipps beim Wiederholen und Üben.

Words

Die wichtigsten Wörter von Unit 2 findest du hier:

➡ *S. 36–37, S. 42, S. 47*   ➡ *Wordbank 3 (S.143)*
➡ *Workbook S. 22, 29–30*

Grammar

Die Grammatik kannst du auf diesen Seiten wiederholen:

➡ *GF 6: The simple present (S. 160–162)*
➡ *LAL S. 40, S. 45, Übungen S. 40-41, S. 45, S.46, S. 50*
➡ *Workbook S. 25, 28*

Mind map

Hier im *Skills File* findest du alle wichtigen Angaben zu Mindmaps:

➡ *SF 2: Collecting information (S.149–150)*

TIP
Wenn du vor der Gruppe Englisch sprichst, atme tief durch und zähle bis 3, bevor du anfängst.

Clubs and hobbies

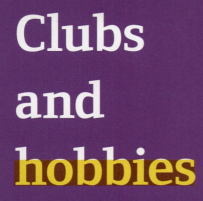

Film making. Cool!

Justin

Plymstock School
SPECIALIST SPORTS COLLEGE

Film Making with Mrs Hart

Where: TE9   When: Thur 3–4 **pm**
In our club you learn how you **edit** videos
on the computer.

Gardening Club   *trees :-)*

With Mrs Hobbs
Where: School garden
When: Wed after school

Come and work with us in the school
garden! We **grow** fruit and vegetables
and **sell** them.

1 Plymstock clubs

a) 👥 **Work in groups of five.**
Each student reads one text about a club.
Tell your group about your club.

– My club is the Samba / … club.
– It's on Monday/Tuesday / … / It's every day …
  at … / **from … to …**
– You can …

b) Now listen to the five clubs.
Match the sounds to the clubs.
👥 ✓ Check your answers with a partner.

2 ▶ 25–29

Grund-
schule

A: Number 1 is …
B: Yes, that's right. / No, that isn't right.
Number 1 is …

1 Quiet Reading · 2 Samba Club · 3 Basketball ·
4 Gardening Club · 5 Film Making

Lernfeld S. 56–57: Die S können wiedergeben, was jemand über seine **Freizeitaktivitäten** sagt oder schreibt. Sie können über ihre eigenen **Hobbys** oder **Schul-AGs** schreiben und sprechen. Sie können andere fragen, was sie in ihrer **Freizeit** machen.

– CLUBS FOR YEAR 7 STUDENTS –

Here are some of the great clubs at Plymstock School! Join one or more.
Look on the school website for information about more clubs, or talk to club teachers.

Basketball

With Miss Taylor
Where: Gym
When: Thur 3–4.30 pm
Play basketball and have fun with us in the gym. For boys and girls. Don't forget your PE kit!

Samba Club

Play an instrument, sing or dance.

With Mr Willis
Where: Music area
When: Mon lunchtime

It's like Rio here in Plymstock!

Quiet Reading

With Mr Wood
Where: Library
When: Mon–Fri lunchtime
We tell you about the best books for young people.
You choose one, find a chair and ... read, read, read.

There's a club in the library. So I can join a club too.

Einige der neuen Wörter auf diesem Aufschlag bringen eine hohe Komplexität in Bezug auf **Aussprache** mit sich (join, grow, quiet, choose). L sollte hier großen Wert auf Nachsprechen der Wörter legen.

2 Your clubs

Talk about a club at your school or in your area.
Tell the class what you can do there.

– There's a ... club at school/near our house.
– You can do sport/sing/play ... there.
– I go there every Tuesday/...

➡ Wordbank 6 (pp.146–147)
➡ **Workbook** 1–2 (p.36)

Your task

Am Ende dieser Unit wirst du ...
... für einen Gast aus Plymouth ein spannendes Programm für drei Nachmittage zusammenstellen.

Lernfeld S. 58–59: Die S können Lesetexten Informationen zum Thema *school clubs* entnehmen und sagen, wer was macht.

1 In the school canteen 2 ▷ 30

Sam: What's grey and never **gets wet**?
Abby: We don't know, Sam. Tell us.
Sam: An elephant with an **umbrella**.
Abby: Ha, ha – **very funny**.
5 Lucy: Do you know any good **jokes**, Sam?
Sam: Do I know any good jokes? Yes, of course. What's big and …
Lucy: Look, there's Justin!

Sam: Hey, Justin! Come and sit here.
10 Er … Abby, do you know Justin?
Abby: No, I don't. Hi Justin – I'm Abby.
Justin: Er … hi …
Sam: Hey, do you play basketball, Justin? I'm in the Basketball Club. You can come
15 with me.

Justin: Er … basketball?
Sam: Yes, on Thursday afternoons.
Justin: Sorry, I can't.
Sam: Why not?
20 Justin: **Because** I'm in the Film Making Club and it meets on Thursdays too.
Lucy: Film making? Cool! Do you have a camera?
Justin: Yes, I do.
25 Sam: That's soooo cool!
Lucy: What about you, Abby? Do you go to any clubs?
Abby: Yes, I do. I go to the Trampoline Club. And I'm in a sailing club too – at home in
30 Wembury.
Lucy: Wembury Sailing Club? My best friend Maya is in that club.
Abby: Oh, do you know Maya too? She's very nice. I often see her at weekends.
35 Lucy: **Really**?
Abby: Yes, she **sometimes** comes to my house.
Lucy: Oh?
Abby: And what about you, Lucy, are you in a club?
40 Lucy: No, I'm not. Er … I **have to** go now.
Sam: Why, Lucy? **What's the matter?**
Lucy: I have to do my maths homework.
Sam: What? Do we have maths homework?
Lucy: Sorry, but I have to go.

2 **Which** clubs are they in?

Copy and finish the table.

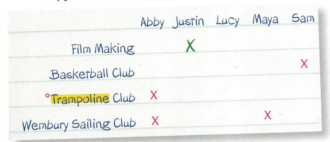

	Abby	Justin	Lucy	Maya	Sam
Film Making		X			
Basketball Club					X
°Trampoline Club	X				
Wembury Sailing Club	X			X	

Add the information to the character profile in your *My Book* .

Zur Zeitersparnis kann L ein Arbeitsblatt mit der Tabelle erstellen, damit die S diese nicht abschreiben müssen.

3 Do you play basketball?

👥 Make questions and ask a partner.

	football? tennis? …	
play		
know	Lukas? any good jokes? …	

Do you … — Yes, I do. / No, I don't.

➡ **Workbook** *3–4 (p. 37)*

Alternative: Die S füllen **KV 12: Do you play basketball?** aus und befragen in einer *Milling around activity* ihre Mit-S. Jede/r S sollte ca. 6 Mit-S befragen.

4 🖐 At Lucy's house [2] 31

Lucy: I have to join a club, Maya. **Everyone** at Plymstock is in a club.

Maya: Everyone?

5 Lucy: Yes, Sam goes to basketball. Justin is in the Film Making Club. And … and Abby is in the Trampoline Club.

Maya: Abby Blackwell? I know her.

Lucy: Yes, she's in your sailing club. **What's she like?**

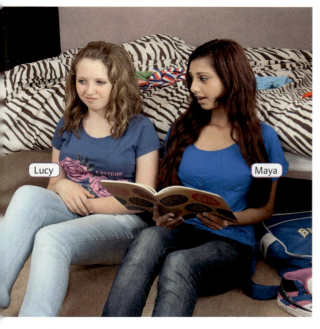

10 Maya: You know her too. She's at your school.

Lucy: Well, she isn't really my friend. But you **visit her** at weekends.

Maya: Yes, sometimes.

Lucy: <u>Does she live</u> in a nice house?

15 Maya: Yes, she does. It's great. You can see the sea from her window.

Lucy: Oh, nice. Er … what about her family? <u>Does she have</u> any brothers or sisters?

Maya: Yes, she does. Two brothers. And

20 she has a dog, a cat and …

Lucy: What about her brothers? <u>Do they go</u> sailing too?

Maya: Yes, they do. They all **love** the sea.

Lucy: And <u>does she visit</u> you at your house?

25 Maya: No, she doesn't … Hey, Luce, what's the matter? Why all the questions?

Lucy: **Nothing**, nothing. Let's forget it. I have to choose a club.

Maya: OK. Well, you like tennis. <u>Does Plymstock have</u> a tennis club?

30 Lucy: No, it doesn't.

Maya: Hmmm, there's a Computer Games Club on the **list**. My brother is in that.

Lucy: Mukesh? <u>Does he like</u> it?

35 Maya: Yes, he does. It's the best club, he says.

Lucy: But I don't like computer games so …

Maya: No, you don't. There's a Science Club …

Lucy: No! No science. I don't **want** more school **work**. **I want to** have fun.

40 Maya: Well, what about Quiet Reading, or the Samba Club …?

Lucy: Samba? That **sounds** fun. Maybe I can **make new friends** there.

5 Lucy, Maya and Abby

a) Are the sentences right or wrong? Correct the wrong sentences.

1 Lucy and Maya talk about Abby.
2 Lucy and Abby are good friends.
3 Lucy doesn't have any questions about Abby.
4 Maya helps Lucy to choose a club.

b) Is Lucy happy? Say what you think.

> *I think Lucy is happy because …*

> *I think Lucy isn't happy because …*

1 Right. · 2 Lucy and Abby aren't good friends. ·
3 Lucy has lots of questions about Abby. · 4 Right.

6 Have a go

Lucy asks questions about Abby:

Does she live in a nice house?
Does she have any brothers or sisters?
…

👥 **Think of more questions about Abby. Can your partner answer them?**

> *Does Abby go to Coombe Dean School?*

> *No, she doesn't.*

Lernfeld S. 60–61: Die S können andere zu ihren **Freizeitaktivitäten** befragen und solche **Fragen beantworten**.

Looking at language

a) Copy the table and finish the questions. The texts on pp. 58–59 can help you.

	Singular	Plural
1st person	Do I know any good jokes?	... we ... maths homework?
2nd person	... you ... any good jokes?	Do you all like the sea?
3rd person	... she ... in a nice house?	... they go sailing?

Early finisher Find more examples of the third person singular on p. 59.

b) What is different in the third person singular?

➡ GF 8 a: The simple present (p.163)

1 Yes or no? (Simple present: questions and short answers)

👥 Make six questions. Then ask your partner.

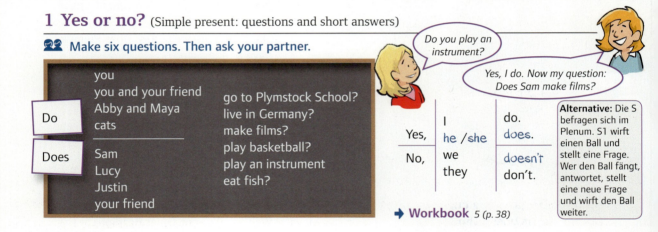

you
you and your friend
Abby and Maya
cats

Do

Does

Sam
Lucy
Justin
your friend

go to Plymstock School?
live in Germany?
make films?
play basketball?
play an instrument
eat fish?

Do you play an instrument?

Yes, I do. Now my question: Does Sam make films?

Yes,	I	do.
	he / she	does.
No,	we	doesn't
	they	don't.

Alternative: Die S befragen sich im Plenum. S1 wirft einen Ball und stellt eine Frage. Wer den Ball fängt, antwortet, stellt eine neue Frage und wirft den Ball weiter.

➡ **Workbook** 5 (p. 38)

2 WORDS Go, play or do?

Box "Sports and other activities (go/play/do)", Voc, S. 191

 Grund-schule

a) Match the words to the pictures.

basketball · **chess** · the **drums** · **gymnastics** ·
kung fu · sailing · **skating** · swimming · yoga

b) Make a table. Add the words from a).

go	play	do
swimming	...	...
riding	cards · football · the piano	judo

c) Add these words to your table:

cards · football · the **piano** · **riding** · **judo**

Early finisher ➡ p. 139

Early finisher: Die S können ein Rätsel lösen.

➡ **Workbook** 6–7 (pp. 38–39)

go	play	do
swimming	basketball	kung fu
1	2	3
skating	chess	yoga
4	5	6
sailing	the drums	gymnastics
7	8	9

| **Activities** with -ing | Team sports, games, instruments | **Other** sports and activities |

Alternative: Die S ordnen auf **KV 13: Go, play or do?** den entsprechenden Verben Wörter zu.

3 Find someone who ...

Use your activities table from exercise 2.
Find someone in your class for each activity on your table.
The winner is the first student with a "yes" for six different activities.

4 GAME Guess who!

a) Partner A: Choose a name from the list. Don't tell your partner the name.
   Partner B: Ask questions. Guess the name.

Abby	Morph
Justin	Sam
Lucy	Silky
Maya	

A: Guess who!
B: Is it a he?
A: Yes, it is.
B: Does he live in the library?
A: No, he doesn't.

B: Does he make films?
A: Yes, he does.
B: Then it's Justin!
A: Right! Now you choose a name.

More help ➔ p.132   More help: Als Hilfe sind einige weitere Fragen vorgegeben.

Zusatz: *Who am I?* Ein S überlegt sich einen Star. Die Mit-S müssen durch Erfragen von Eigenschaften den Namen erraten.

b) Play the game in groups of six. This time, think of a person in your group. Can the others guess who it is?

5 Sorry, but I have to clean my room (*have to*)

Lernfeld: Die S können sagen, was sie tun müssen und welche Pflichten und Aufgaben sie zu Hause haben.

a) Walk around the classroom. Ask and answer like this:

Do you want to go skating on Saturday?

Sorry, but I have to clean my room.

The ideas in the boxes can help you.

go swimming · play football · go to the club · play cards	do my homework · feed the cat · play with my little sister · visit my grandma

b) Write sentences like this:
   Maria can't go skating because she has to clean her room.
   Read one sentence to the class.

➔ **Workbook** 8 (p. 39)

Lernfeld S. 62: Die S können **Informationen** zu ihren Hobbys schriftlich so **zusammenstellen**, dass sie sie anschließend für einen **kurzen Vortrag** benutzen können.

6 Study skills: Collecting information

Maya has to talk about her free time in class. How can she collect information about her free-time activities? Her teacher asks her to try a mind map and a table.

2 ▷ 32 a) Look at Maya's mind map. What are the missing umbrella words?
Listen to Maya and check.

b) Copy Maya's table.
2 ▷ 33 Now listen to Maya and add the missing information.
Check with a partner.

	Monday	Tuesday	Wednesday	Thursday	Friday
activity	computer club	guitar lesson	skating	guitar lesson	sailing
time	3:15–4:00	5:00–6:00	3:30–5:00	5:00–6:00	4:00–6:00
place	at school	at home	the park	at home	Wembury beach
what I need	computer	guitar	inline skates	guitar	sailing boat

Neigungsdifferenzierung: Die S wählen zwischen Mindmap und Tabelle.

c) Collect information about your hobbies.
You choose Make a mind map or a table.
The study skills box can help with the table.

– Say what you do, where you do it and when you do it.
– Say what you need (clothes / skates / a ball / ...) for your hobby.
➜ *Wordbank 6 (pp.146–147)*

EXTRA Give a one-minute talk about your hobbies.
– Before class, practise with a partner.
– When you speak in class, use your mind map or your table.
– Show the class what you need (clothes / skates / a ball / ...).

➜ **Workbook** *9 (p.40)*

Study skills

Making a table

1 Überlege zuerst, wie du die Tabelle aufbaust:

– In die linke Spalte kommen die Überschriften für die waagerechten Tabellenzeilen (im Beispiel: **activity**, **time**, **place**, ...).
– In die obere Zeile kommen die Überschriften für die senkrechten Tabellenspalten (im Beispiel: die Namen der Wochentage).

2 Dann fülle die einzelnen Felder der Tabelle aus. Du kannst auch Symbole und Zeichnungen verwenden.

➜ *SF 2: Collecting information (pp.149–150)*

1 Plymstock school clubs

a) Who can you see in the photos? Oliver · Jack
What clubs are they in? Samba Club · Trampoline Club

b) Watch the film without sound and choose the right answer.

1 Oliver's club meets ⟨at lunchtime⟩ / after school.
2 They meet in the canteen / ⟨in the music area.⟩
3 Oliver plays the guitar / ⟨the drums.⟩
4 Jack's club meets ⟨at lunchtime⟩ / after school.
5 They meet ⟨in the gym⟩ / outside.
6 You can / ⟨can't⟩ wear trainers.
7 Jack and Abby do ⟨three⟩ / six different jumps.

c) Now watch the film with sound and check.

d) Which club does Ruby like?
Which club do you like? Why? Ruby likes the Samba Club because she likes music.

Oliver

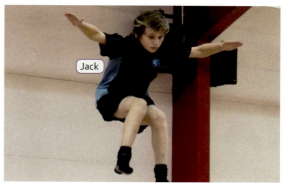

Jack

2 EVERYDAY ENGLISH |2 ▸34|
How can we join the club?

a) Watch part one of the film.
Where do Oliver and Luke want to go?
What do they want to do?
They want to go to the Life Centre. They want to go swimming.

b) Now watch part two and match the questions (1–5) to the right answers (A–E).

1 E · 2 D · 3 A · 4 B · 5 C

1 What can we do here?
2 When is the pool open?
3 Are there any kung fu classes?

4 Can we go swimming now?
5 How can we join the club?

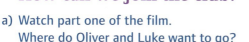

A No, sorry, we don't have kung fu classes, but you can do karate.

C We need a letter from your mum and dad.

E Well, we have lots of activities.

B Sorry, but you have to join the club before you go to the pool.

D It's open every day from 8 am to 10 pm.

c) Watch the film and check your answers.

d) 👥 You want to join a sports / music / ... club.
Make a dialogue like the one in the film.
Act it out for your class.

Lernfeld S. 64–65: Die S können von anderen **Informationen erfragen**, indem sie ihnen Fragen mit *when, where, what* und *do/does* stellen.

1 On Skype with Dad 2 35

Justin: Mum, Dad is on Skype. Can I talk to him?

Mum: OK, Justin, but don't forget to **finish** your homework.

Justin: **Come on**, Dad, answer … please.

5 Dad: Hey, Justin!

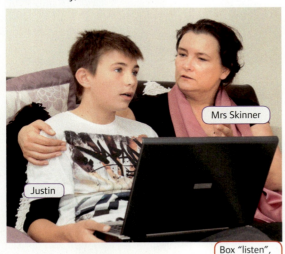

Mrs Skinner

Justin

Box "listen", Voc. S. 192

Justin: Hi, Dad. **How are you?**

Dad: **Listen**, Justin. This isn't a good time. I work in the afternoon. You know that.

Justin: Sorry, Dad.

10 Dad: And I don't have **much** time. I have a new **job**, you know, and …

Justin: A new job? <u>Where do you work</u> now?

Dad: Near Boston harbour. In a TV **studio**.

Justin: Wow! Er … <u>what do you do</u> there?

15 Dad: I edit TV **programmes**.

Justin: <u>What programmes</u> do you edit?

Dad: Justin, I really can't talk now. Let's talk **later**.

Justin: When do you finish work?

20 Dad: I finish at 7 o'clock, Justin. That's **midnight** in England – much **too** late.

Justin: OK, Dad. Maybe at the weekend?

Dad: Yes, the weekend is good.

Justin: When do you **get up**?

25 Dad: Try Saturday at 10 o'clock. That's 3 o'clock in England.

Justin: OK, Dad. Thanks. Oh, and thanks for the video camera.

Dad: Oh, yes, right. **How do you like it?**

30 Justin: It's great, Dad! I have a video for you. **It's about** a seagull.

Dad: OK, Justin, **send** it to me.

Justin: And I want to make a video about Plymouth for you.

35 Dad: Oh, good **idea**. You can tell me all about it at the weekend.

Justin: OK, Dad. I can tell you about school too. I'm in the Film Making Club now. And I have new friends – Lucy, Sam and …

40 Dad: Talk to you at the weekend, Justin.

Justin: Right, bye, Dad.

Mum: Justin, don't forget your homework.

Justin: Oh yes, my homework. Er … Mum, <u>why does Dad work</u> so much?

45 Mum: Because he loves his work, Justin.

2 Who is it?

Is it Justin or Justin's dad?
Finish the sentences.

1 … doesn't live in Plymouth.
2 … can't skype in the afternoon.
3 … has a new job.
4 … wants to know more about the new job.
5 … wants to skype at the weekend.
6 … has a new video camera.
7 … can skype at 10 am on Saturday.
8 … wants to make a film about Plymouth.
9 … wants to talk about his new friends.
10 … is sad.

1 Justin's dad · 2 Justin's dad · 3 Justin's dad · 4 Justin · 5 Justin ·
6 Justin · 7 Justin's dad · 8 Justin · 9 Justin · 10 Justin

3 Have a go

a) Justin asks his dad two questions with *when*.

When do you finish work, Dad?
When do you get up?

Write four questions for your partner with
When do you …?

b) Take turns and read out questions and answer them.

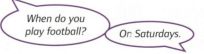

When do you play football?

On Saturdays.

Looking at language

a) Finish the questions. Use the right question word: what, when, where, why or how.
You can find the questions in the text on page 64.

Where do you work now?	Near Boston harbour.
... you do there?	I edit TV programmes.
... you finish work?	I finish at 7 o'clock.
... you like it?	It's great, Dad.
... Dad work so much?	Because he loves his work.

b) **What word do you use after the question word?**
What's different in the third person singular?

➡ *GF 8 b: The simple present (p.164)*

Box "listen · hear", Voc, S. 193

1 Where does Morph live? ▪ ▫ ▫ ▫ ▫
(Simple present: questions with question words)

Write questions.

1 does – where – live – Morph
   Where does Morph live?
2 work – does – Justin's father – where
3 Justin's father – do – does – what
4 next lesson – does – start – when – our
5 we – go to school – why – do – have to
6 at weekends – you – do – what – do

2 Where does J.'s father work? · 3 What does J.'s father do? · 4 When
does our next lesson start? ·
5 Why do we have to go to
school? · 6 What do you
do at weekends?

Early finisher Find a partner.
Ask and answer the questions.

2 Sorry, I can't **hear** you ▪ ▪ ▫ ▫ ▫
(Simple present: questions with question words)

👥 It's very noisy. You can't hear your partner.
Ask questions with what, when, where or why.

1 I play football.
   Sorry, what do you play?
2 On Saturday morning, I help my mum.
   Sorry, ...?
3 On Sundays I get up at 10 o'clock.
4 Then I go to the swimming pool.
5 I like it there because I meet my friends.
6 My friends all like swimming.

More help: Die Fragewörter
sind bereits angegeben.

More help ➡ *p.132* 2 ..., when do you help your mum? · 3 When do
you get up on Sundays? · 4 Where do you go
then? · 5 Why do you like it there? · 6 What do
your friends like?

3 What sport does Abby like? ▪ ▪ ▪ ▫ ▫

a) Read the answers. Then finish the questions.

Question	**Answer**
1 ... sport ... Abby ...?	She likes sailing.
What sport does Abby like?	
2 ... food ... Silky ...?	She eats fish and crabs.
3 ... games ... you ...?	I play computer games.
4 ... shoes ... Plymstock students ...?	They wear black shoes.
5 ... films ... you ...?	I watch James Bond films.
6 ... subjects ... you ...?	I like French and geography.

More help ➡ *p.132*

b) 👥 Ask and answer questions.

What books/films/food ...?

➡ **Workbook** *10 (p. 40)*

2 What food does Silky eat? · 3 What games do you play? ·
4 What shoes do Plymstock students wear? · 5 What films
do you watch? · 6 What subjects do you like?

TIP
German: *Was für Bücher liest du?*

English: *What books do you read?*

More help: Die Fragen sind als
Lückensätze vorgegeben, denen
die passenden Objekte aus einer
Box zugeordnet werden müssen.

Lernfeld S. 66: Die S können **Informationen über sich und andere** geben. Dabei können sie sagen und schreiben, was sie oder andere machen oder mögen.

4 Do you know your partner? (Simple present: mixed questions) ▪▪▪▪▫

a) Copy the table.
Add your ideas about your partner.

b) 👥 Ask your partner the questions.
Are your ideas right?

c) Write about your partner on a card.
Don't write his/her name.

This boy or girl lives in a house.
He/She has ...
His/Her mum ...
He/She goes ...
...

More help ➜ p.133

More help: Als Hilfe sind weitere Redemittel angegeben.

Questions	Your ideas about your partner	Your partner's answers
Do you live in a house or a flat?		
... have any brothers or sisters?		
Where ... your mum and dad come from?		
When ... go to bed?		
What music ... like?		
What hobbies ... have?		
What sports ... do?		

Alternative: Zur Zeitersparnis bearbeiten die S **KV 14: Do you know your partner?**

d) Take a card from another student.
Read it out loud.
Can the class guess the student's name?

5 Interview Morph ✏ ▪▪▪▪▪

a) You have a chance to interview Morph.
What questions do you want to ask him? Make a list of ideas:

home – family – favourite colour – food – hobbies – music – languages – ...

b) Write your questions on a big piece of paper.
Leave space for the answers.

Questions   Answers
1 Where do you come from? .
2 Do you have a family?
3 What's your favourite colour?
4 What food do you eat?
5 When ...

c) 👥 Swap your lists of questions.

Now you're Morph.
Think of answers to your partner's questions.
Write your answers on the piece of paper and give it back.

d) 👥 Ask and answer your questions.

EXTRA 👥 Act out one interview for the class.

➜ **Workbook** *11 (p. 41)*

FöFo 3.1, 3.6

Part B Practice 3

Lernfeld S. 67: Die S können **falsche und richtige Informationen** in Lesetexten **erfassen**.

6 In their free time ✏️

2 ▶ 36–37

a) Listen to two students, Molly and Adam.
In which photo can you see them? Say why.

Molly: 3
Adam: 1

I think Molly is in photo number … because …

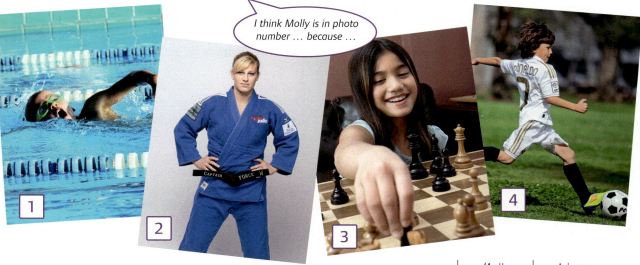

1
2
3
4

b) Copy the table and listen again.
Add the information to your table.
👥 Then compare with a partner.

Molly: 11 yrs, 9 mths · skating, judo, chess · Chess Club · Tuesdays and Fridays in the afternoon · Mr Short's classroom · best player in Year 7

Adam: 12 · watching football on TV, basketball, swimming · Wembury Swimming Club · Mondays, Thursdays, Saturdays, 7 to 9pm · Wembury · good and fast/200m in 3 mins

	Molly	Adam
age	…	…
free-time activities		
clubs		
when		
where		
how good		

c) Read these texts about Molly and Adam. Use your table to find the *wrong* information.

Molly
Molly is 9 years and 11 months old. In her free time she goes sailing and does yoga. She also plays chess. That's her favourite activity. She goes to the chess club at her school on Thursdays and Fridays in the lunch break. She's the best chess player in her school.

Adam
Adam is 12 years old. He often plays football in his free time. At school, he plays basketball and volleyball, but he isn't in a school team. His favourite sport is swimming. He goes to training two evenings every week. He's a good swimmer. He can swim 400 metres in three minutes.

Alternative: L kopiert die Texte, damit die S die Falschaussagen markieren können.

👥 Check with a partner.

d) Rewrite the text about Molly *or* the text about Adam.
Use the correct information.

Adam is twelve years old. He often watches …

EXTRA Write another text about your friend / your brother / your sister / …
Draw a picture of the person or add a photo.

Alternative: Diese Aufgabe kann als Hausaufgabe bearbeitet werden. L sollte diesen Aufwand auf jeden Fall wertschätzen und die Produkte in der Klasse positiv hervorheben. Die S können ihre Produkte dann in ihr *My Book* kleben.

➜ **Workbook** *12–14 (pp. 41–42)*

Lernfeld S. 68–69: Die S können **Texten** und Hörtexten **Informationen entnehmen**.

1 ✋ At the Hoe 2 ▶ 38

On Saturday afternoon, Lucy and Maya ride their bikes to the Hoe.

"Hey Lucy, wait for me," Maya shouts. But Lucy doesn't wait. She rides to Smeaton's Tower and
5 waits there.

"Let's stop for a minute," Maya says.

"Are you tired?" Lucy asks.

"I'm thirsty," Maya answers. "Would you like some water?"

10 "No, thank you," Lucy answers.

"I have some chocolate too," Maya says.

"No, thank you."

"Oh come on, Lucy! You usually love chocolate."

❖

Justin is at the Hoe too. He turns on his camera.
15 "Hi Dad, this is the Big Wheel at the Hoe. You can see all of Plymouth from here."

Box "Adverbs of frequency", Voc, S. 193

Suddenly someone is behind Justin. "Boo!" Justin jumps and turns around.

"It's OK, I'm not a ghost," says Sam.
20 "Hey, you can film me with your video camera." Sam does a kung fu°move and shouts, "Kung Fu Master Wu is ready for action."

❖

Lucy and Maya hear the two boys.

"They're very loud," Lucy says.
25 "Hey, they're your school friends!" Maya says.

"That's right – Sam and Justin."

Sam sees the girls and shouts, "Hey, Lucy, Maya – we're here! Justin wants to film me, Master Wu."

"I don't want to film you, Sam," Justin says.
30 "I want to make a video of Plymouth for my dad."

2 What's in the picture?

👥👥 Find sentences in the text for pictures 1–4. Read the sentences to a partner. Do you have the same sentences? Are they right?

1 ll. 20–23 ·
2 ll. 15–16 ·
3 ll. 3–5 ·
4 l. 17

1 — Sam / Justin

2 — Justin

3 — Maya

4 — Justin / Sam

3 A good idea 💬 2 ▷39

a) Listen to the rest of the story.
Which of these words do you hear?

> Barbican · film · ghost · harbour · monster ·
> scary · ship · snake · streets · time **travellers**

What is the good idea? a scary film about time travellers, with ghosts in it

b) Correct the wrong sentences.

1 All the kids like action films.
2 Maya wants to make a film about time travellers.
3 Justin wants to make a film about ghosts.
4 Lucy says Abby can be in the film.
5 Lucy says she has some ideas for a story.

Justin · Maya · Sam · Lucy

1 Sam likes action films. · 2 Right. · 3 Lucy wants to make a film about ghosts. · 4 Maya and Sam say Abby can be in the film. · 5 Right.

Lernfeld: Die S können anderen **Informationen über *Old Plymouth*** geben, indem sie ihnen mit Hilfe von **Notizen** davon erzählen.

Background file

Old Plymouth – the Barbican
The old **part** of Plymouth **is called** the Barbican. It has small streets and some very old houses. One of them, the Elizabethan House, is **over** 400 years old. It is now a **museum**, so you can visit its old bedrooms, dining room and kitchen. You don't need much **money** to go there. **Children's tickets** are only **£1**.
Can you **imagine life** in Plymouth in 1580?

Box "British money", Voc, S. 194

a) Read the text and take notes.
➡ *SF 5: Taking notes (p.152)*

b) 👥 Use your notes to tell your partner about old Plymouth.

➡ **Workbook** *15 (p. 42)*

69

> **Lernfeld:** Die S können **einem englischsprachigen Flyer Informationen entnehmen** und sie **auf Deutsch wiedergeben.**

1 The Elizabethan House

You and your grandparents are in Plymouth. You want to visit the Elizabethan House. Read the information and answer your grandma's questions.

1 Wo ist eigentlich das Elizabethan House?
2 Ist es überhaupt mittwochs auf?
3 Können wir es heute Mittag besichtigen oder ist es dann geschlossen?
4 Was gibt es denn da alles zu sehen?
5 Gibt es so etwas wie eine Familienermäßigung?
6 Wieviel würde es denn für uns drei kosten?

➔ *SF 10: Mediation (p.155)*

➔ **Workbook** *17 (p. 43)*

1 32 New Street, The Barbican · 2 Ja. 3 Ja. (Mo.: Nein.) · 4 Es ist ein altes Kapitänshaus aus dem 16. Jh. mit einer alten Einrichtung. Man kann z.B. die Küche, die Treppen und alte Möbel sehen. · 5 Ja. · 6 £4.50.

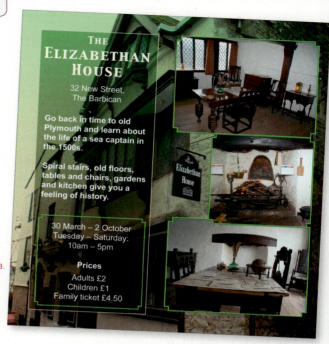

THE **ELIZABETHAN HOUSE**

32 New Street, The Barbican

Go back in time to old Plymouth and learn about the life of a sea captain in the 1500s.

Spiral stairs, old floors, tables and chairs, gardens and kitchen give you a feeling of history.

30 March – 2 October
Tuesday – Saturday:
10am – 5pm

Prices
Adults £2
Children £1
Family ticket £4.50

2 How often?

> **Lernfeld:** Die S können sagen, was sie **nie/manchmal/oft/gewöhnlich/immer** machen.

a) Copy the line. Then add the missing words: often, sometimes, usually.

```
                                                              always
                                               usually
                                    often
                    sometimes
    never
```

b) Put the words in the right order.

1 goes – always – Sam – on Thurdays. – to a club
Sam always goes to a club on Thursdays.
2 doesn't – Lucy – eat – always – in the canteen.
Lucy doesn't always eat in the canteen.
3 sometimes – Maya – Abby. – visits
4 doesn't – Justin – see – often – his dad.
5 goes – swimming – at the Lido. – often – Maya
6 does – kung fu – usually – Sam – at weekends.
7 in Plymstock Library. – Morph – sleeps – always
8 for breakfast. – eats – never – cornflakes – Silky

CORN FLAKES

Early finisher Write another sentence about Silky. Draw a picture for your sentence.

3 Maya sometimes visits Abby. · 4 Justin doesn't often see his dad. · 5 Maya often goes swimming at the Lido. · 6 Sam usually does kung fu at weekends. · 7 Morph always sleeps in Plymstock Library. · 8 Silky never eats cornflakes for breakfast.

c) 👥 Play this game.

Sometimes!

I sometimes play basketball.

Often!

I don't often eat fish.

Usually!

I usually …

TIP
English: I **sometimes** play chess.
German: Ich **spiele manchmal** Schach.

➔ *GF 9: Adverbs of frequency: word order (p.164)*
➔ **Workbook** *18 (p. 44)*

1 You say, you write ... [ɔː]

a) You hear the [ɔː]-sound in the word "sport".
Look at the six pictures.
Find five words with an [ɔː]-sound.
Then listen and check.

b) How many words with an [ɔː]-sound can you find in the box: 6, 7 or 8?   7

boat · (fall) · (floor) · food · (form) · group · hour · (small) · (talk) · (water) · (your)

Listen and check.

Can you spell "fall"?

Yes, I can. It's F – A – L – L.

c) Make a table. Write down the [ɔː]-words.

You say	You write
ɔː	fall
	... siehe Box b)

d) 👥 Ask your partner to spell the [ɔː]-words from b).

→ **Workbook** 19 (p. 44)

2 small °letters, °CAPITAL LETTERS

Lernfeld: Die S können erklären, wann man im Englischen **Groß- und Kleinschreibung** verwendet.

TIP

°Use small letters for nouns – **c**amera, **c**lub, **h**ouse, °etc.

an old **h**ouse
ein altes **H**aus

Read the tips about CAPITAL LETTERS. What's °the same in German? What's different?

Use **CAPITAL LETTERS** for
· the word "I": My friend and I like basketball.
· **names**: Abby, Justin, Morph, Uncle Amar, ...
· **days and months**: Monday, Tuesday, ... April, May, ...
· **names of clubs, schools, etc.**: Plymstock School, Wembury Sailing Club, ...
· °**cities**: Berlin, Boston, Plymouth, ...
· °**countries**: England, Scotland, ...
· **country adjectives**: an English cat, a German cat, ...

a) Read the text on the right and copy it.
Use capital letters where you need them.

Hi! My name is Tom. I come ...

More help → p.133

More help: Der Text enthält bereits alle Wortgrenzen, sodass nur noch die Groß- und Kleinschreibung zu korrigieren ist.

b) 👥 Check a partner's text.

Early finisher Think of a sentence with names, days of the week, etc. Read it out to your partner.

hi! mynameistom. icomefromwembury. that'snear plymouthinengland. ilikesport. everythursdayigoto judoandiplayfootballatwemburyfootballclubevery mondayandfriday. ilikegermanybecausemymotherisgerman. hernameissabineandshecomesfromfrankfurt. injulyoraugusteveryyearwevisitmygermanuncle nearfrankfurt.

→ **Workbook** 20 (p. 44)

Hi! My name is Tom. I come from Wembury. That's near Plymouth in England. I like sport. Every Thursday I go to judo, and I play football at Wembury Football Club every Monday and Friday. I like Germany because my mother is German. Her name is Sabine and she comes from Frankfurt. In July or August every year, we visit my German uncle near Frankfurt.

Lernfeld S. 72–73: Die S können einen Lesetext verstehen und einzelnen Textabschnitten Überschriften zuordnen. Sie können einen Lesetext in einen Dialog umschreiben und diesen dann vorspielen.

The captain's ghost

1 2 42

Abigail and her friend May are at Abigail's house.

"What's that funny **sound**?" asks May.

"Oh, it's Skipper," says Abigail. "My dog – he's in

5 the **attic**. He catches rats there."

"Let's go to the attic, then," says May. "It's **boring** here."

In the attic, they see Skipper. He has a book in his **mouth**.

10 "Here Skipper, give it to me!" says Abigail.

"What is it?" asks May.

"It looks like a **diary**. And there's a name and a year: Captain Justin Pascoe, 1581."

"1581. Wow! That's *old*," says May.

15 "And here's an **address**: New Street, Plymouth."

"Hey!" May shouts. "That's in the Barbican."

The two girls look at the diary.

"What's on that page there?" Abigail asks.

"It's a map – a map of a house," answers May.

20 "And look, it shows where Captain Pascoe has his gold."

"Gold!" Abigail shouts. "Wow!"

Then she sees a letter in the diary. She takes it and reads:

25 10th February 1581

Dear Father,

Mother is very **sick**. We don't have any money.

We can't eat. Please come home. Please help us!

Lucille

30 "How sad," says May. "I **hope** the girl finds her father's gold."

"Oh, no!" Abigail shouts. "Skipper has a **bottle** in his mouth!" She takes the bottle from him and opens it. "That **smells** funny, Abigail," says May.

35 "Oooh, I'm so tired …"

"Yes, **me too**," says Abigail.

2 2 43

May wakes up. She looks **out of** the attic window. There are horses, and people in strange clothes.

40 She **calls** Abigail and Skipper. "Look! The street looks different."

They all run out of the house. Abigail shouts to a boy, "Sorry, but are we in Plymouth?"

"Well, we aren't on the **moon**," says the boy.

45 "And what year is it?" asks May.

"What year? 1581, of course."

"The year of the diary!" Abigail shouts.

"Your clothes are very strange," the boy says.

50 "Sorry," says May, "but we have to find a girl. Her name is Lucille Pascoe. Do you know her?"

"Of course. Lucille is my friend. I can show you her house."

3 2 44

They **walk along** New Street. The boy stops at a house and shouts: "Lucille! Lucille!" Lucille opens the door. "**Oh, it's you**, Samuel," she says. "But who are they?"

60 "I'm May, and this is Abigail. Can we come in?"

"Er … yes, but what do you want?"

"We want to help you," says Abigail.

"Help me? How?" Lucille asks.

"Your father," May says. "We have his …"

65 "My father is dead. Now go, I have work to do."

"No, wait please," says May. "Look at this."

Lucille looks. "This is a map of my house!"

"Yes," says May. "And it shows where your father's gold is."

70 Suddenly, the door behind Lucille opens. Skipper **barks**. They hear loud **steps** and then a loud **voice**.

"Stop! **Thieves**!" it says. "Give me back my book!
You can't have my gold!"
A **hand** touches Abigail. It throws her onto the
75 floor.
"Help, a ghost!" she shouts. Skipper barks again.
"Come on, old ghost. I'm ready to **fight**!" shouts
Samuel.
"Luci-i-i-ille," the voice says.
80 "Father? Is that you?" asks Lucille.
"Yes, it's me. Stop them! They have the map."
"But they say they can help me," Lucille answers.
"Help you?" the voice asks. "But how?"
"Here, Lucille," May says. "The map is for you."
85 Lucille takes the map. "Father," she says. "Maybe
they're really our friends? … Father?"
But the ghost doesn't answer.

4   2   45

Lucille is quiet for a minute. Then she speaks:
90 "Let's go upstairs."
They all follow her.
"Here, this is the place," says Samuel. "There's a
little door in the floor. Open it, Lucille. Open it!"
Lucille opens the door. "Yes, it's here! The gold is
95 here!" she shouts. "Lots of gold **coins**." She takes
a coin. "This is for you, May."
"Hey! I'm thirsty," says Samuel.
"Let's go and drink some tea," Lucille says.
They go downstairs.

100 "This tea **tastes** funny," May says.
"Oh, no, I'm tired again … so tired."
"Yes, me too," says Abigail.

"Woof, woof!"
The girls wake up.
105 "Abigail," says May, "we're back in your attic!"
"What's that in your hand?" Abigail asks.
May looks in her hand and sees an old gold coin.

5   2   46

"And that's the **end** of my **dream**," says Lucy.
110 "Wow, that's a great story," says Sam.
"Yes, it's **perfect** for our film," says Maya.
"Let's tell Justin about it," says Sam.
"But we need Abby," says Maya. "Let's call her."
"Yes," says Lucy, "and we need her dog too!"

1 **Understanding** the story

Choose titles for the five parts of the story.
Or write your own titles.

It's 1581!
A great story   The sea captain's diary
Thieves or friends?   Lucille finds gold
Is this Plymouth?   Skipper finds an old book

2 New words

Find these new words in the story.
Is it easy to understand them? Why?

> **captain** *(l. 13)* · **gold** *(l. 21)* · **moon** *(l. 44)* ·
> **thieves** *(l. 72)* · **dream** *(l. 109)*

➜ *SF 4: Understanding and looking up new words (pp. 151–152)*

3 👥 The captain's ghost

> **Neigungsdifferenzierung:**
> Die S haben die Wahl zwischen einer künstlerischen Aufgabe und einer kreativen Schreibaufgabe.

You choose   Do a) or b).

a) Make a film poster for "The captain's ghost".
   Who is in the film? What are their roles?
– Draw one or more scenes from the film on your
   poster.
– Hang up the posters in your classroom. Walk
   around and look at the posters. Say what you
   like and don't like about them.

b) Write a dialogue for part 1, 2 or 3 of the story.
– Act it out for the class.

EXTRA 👥 Work with other groups and act out
the whole story as a play.

➜ **Workbook** *21 (p. 45)*

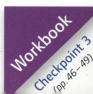

Workbook
Checkpoint 3
(pp. 46–49)

Your task

Step 1 und **2** können als vorbereitende Hausaufgabe bearbeitet werden. In der Folgestunde erfolgt dann die Gruppenarbeit in **Step 3**. **Step 4** und die **Selbsteinschätzung** können wieder zu Hause erfolgen.

What can we do this week? ✏️

Your friend from Plymouth has three more days in Germany. What can you do with him or her? Make plans for the three afternoons.

STEP 1

Work **alone**. What can you do with your friend? **Make a table** for three afternoons and add activities and times to it.
Maybe you can find some ideas on **pages 56–59**.

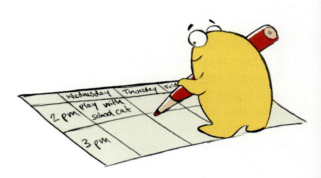

STEP 2

Get ready to talk about your ideas. What words do you need? Look at **2 on page 60** for useful words and phrases.

STEP 3

👥 Find other students with the same friend. Talk about the ideas in your table from Step 2. Then choose an activity for every afternoon.

We can play a game on Thursday.

Yes, that's a great idea – but I don't know any games.

STEP 4

Work alone. Text your British friend about your group's ideas.
Ask what your friend thinks of the ideas.

Why don't we find a good game on the internet?

Myfone.de   12:49

Hi Abby,
Here are our ideas for the next three days.
On Wednesday afternoon we can …

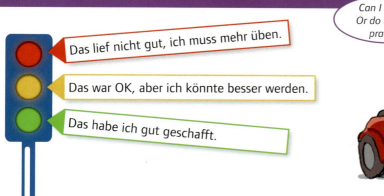

Das lief nicht gut, ich muss mehr üben.

Das war OK, aber ich könnte besser werden.

Das habe ich gut geschafft.

Can I do this? Or do I have to practise?

Wie gut warst du?

Wie schätzt du dich selber ein? Schreibe *Words*, *Speaking* und *Writing* in dein Heft und ordne dir für jeden Bereich eine Ampelfarbe zu.

Words

· Fielen dir die meisten englischen Wörter für Freizeitaktivitäten schnell ein? Wusstest du, wie man sie auf Englisch ausspricht?

Speaking

· Wie lief deine Vorbereitung auf das Gespräch? Wie viele nützliche Redewendungen kanntest du schon?
· Haben die anderen dich in dem Gespräch verstanden? Hast du sie verstanden?

Writing

· Konntest du gut Notizen zu den Ideen der Gruppe machen?
· Welche eigenen Ideen hast du in deiner SMS geschrieben?

Wie kannst du besser werden?

Dort, wo du dich rot oder gelb eingeschätzt hast, helfen dir folgende Tipps beim Wiederholen und Üben.

Words

Suche im Vocabulary zu Unit 3 und den Word-banks englische Wörter für Freizeitaktivitäten, Hobbys und Clubs. Bei der Aussprache hilft dir die phonetische Umschrift.

➜ *Wordbank 6, S. 146 – 147*

Speaking

Hier findest du nützliche Redewendungen, um Vorschläge zu machen, anzunehmen und abzulehnen. Schreibe sie auf.

➜ *U3, S. 58–59, S. 61, S. 68*

Writing

Tausche deine Nachricht mit einem Partner / einer Partnerin aus. Überprüfe:
· ob alle Gruppenentscheidungen erwähnt werden;
· ob andere wichtige oder interessante Informationen enthalten sind;
· ob alle Wörter richtig geschrieben sind.

Es gibt Wörter in dieser Geschichte, die du nicht kennst. Das macht nichts – versuch trotzdem erstmal, die Geschichte zu lesen und zu genießen. Vieles wirst du auch so verstehen. Und wenn's gar nicht geht: Einige Wörter findest du unten auf der Seite, alle anderen im Dictionary ab S. 206.

KV 15A: Animals in Stockbridge Zoo bietet ein leeres Raster zum Sammeln von Informationen über die Tiere in *My home, the zoo*. Eine Lösungsschablone mit gesammelten Informationen befindet sich auf **KV 15B**.

Die *Access story* ist ein fakultatives Angebot mit der Funktion des *Reading for fun*. Darüber hinaus zielt sie auf die zentrale Kompetenz des **extensiven Lesens**. Geübt werden u.a. **sinnentnehmendes Leseverstehen**, selbstständiger **Umgang mit Annotationen** und Strategien zum **Erschließen von unbekanntem Vokabular**. Die S können auch üben, eine Geschichte auf wesentliche Informationen zu Handlung und Hauptfiguren hin zu untersuchen.

My home, the zoo – Part 1

My home

I live in a zoo. No, I'm not a monkey and my mum and dad are people too. We live in a house – we don't live in a cage. But our house
5 is in the middle of Stockbridge Zoo. My name is Luke – Luke Miller – and I'm 11 years old. My dad is the director of the zoo. It isn't an easy job, but he loves animals. We have 75 different animals here. I love animals too …
10 but not all animals. I do *not* like wasps.

In the morning, I usually wake up when my mum comes into my room and touches my hair.

"Good morning, Luke," she says. "It's time to wake up!"

15 I stay in bed. It's so nice and warm. I listen to the different bird songs and match the right bird names to the songs. After ten minutes, Mum shouts: "Luke! Get up, now!"

After I get up, I look out of my bedroom
20 window through my binoculars.

---

l. 4 **cage** [keɪdʒ] Käfig · l. 10 **wasp** [wɒsp] Wespe · l. 20 **binoculars** *(pl)* [bɪˈnɒkjələz] Fernglas

The monkey area is right behind our house. We have twelve Rhesus monkeys, and they are always very active. They climb trees, they run around and around, they fight, and then
25 they're friends again. Really, they're like the kids at lunch break at my school.

There's also a baby monkey. Her name is Rosie. She usually rides on her mum's back to their little house. I watch them for a long time until
30 my mum shouts, "Come down, Luke! It's 8:15. You're late!"

I run downstairs to the kitchen. I eat my breakfast in 30 seconds. Then Mum takes me to school.

35 That's my routine every morning.

BUT, sometimes, King Tut wakes me up. No. Wrong. I don't wake up. I hear him and I jump out of bed. King Tut doesn't come into my room – he only roars. King Tut is our lion. We
40 have four lions here, but King Tut is – can you guess? – the king. Everybody listens to him. When he roars, my windows rattle. It's always a good day when he roars. I'm not late for school and Mum is happy.

45 My secret

I'm in Year 7 at Stockbridge School. Only my best friend Jeff knows my secret.

The other kids in my class don't know that I live in a zoo. Why? There are lots of reasons:

50 *1) When I say, "Hey, I live in a zoo with lions, tigers and bears," they usually say, "Yeah, right … and I live at Buckingham Palace and my mum is the Queen."*

2) I can't ask everybody in my class to come to
55 *my house. Mum and Dad need money for the*

zoo. Every visitor needs a ticket to see the animals.

3) I don't want the kids to tease me: "Luke Miller lives in a zoo. He looks like a monkey
60 *– and smells like one too!"*

4) I want true friends, kids who are my friends because they like me, not because they want to visit the zoo without a ticket.

After school, Mum takes me home. Sometimes
65 we meet Tom on the road to our house. Tom is a zookeeper. He takes care of the monkeys, the otters and the big cats. He feeds them, he

cleans their cages and takes care of them when they are sick.

70 Tom knows a lot and often tells me cool things about the animals. Here's an example: Rhesus monkeys put lots and lots of food into their mouths. But they don't eat it right away. They keep the extra food in their mouths and eat it
75 later on when they are alone.

---

l. 23 (to) **climb** [klaɪm] klettern · l. 28 (to) **ride** reiten · l. 28 **back** Rücken · l. 35 **routine** Routine · l. 39 (to) **roar** [rɔː] brüllen · l. 45 **secret** ['siːkrət] Geheimnis · l. 49 **reason** ['riːzn] Grund · l. 58 (to) **tease sb.** [tiːz] sich über jn. lustig machen · l. 66 (to) **take care of sth.** [keə] sich um etwas kümmern · l. 71 **example** Beispiel · l. 73 **right away** sofort

Every day I ask Mum, "Can I go with Tom today? Please?" She usually says, "What about your homework? Homework comes before the
80 animals, Luke."

Or she says, "OK, Luke, but not in your school uniform."

Tom smiles at me and says, "Meet me at the otters in 15 minutes."

85 Tom always wears a zookeeper uniform.

Dad says I'm part of the zoo team, and the visitors need to see that. So, I wear special clothes too. I wear a red "SZ" T-shirt and a black cap.

90 It's feeding time

We have four otters: there's Mickey, Minnie, Pip and Pop. There are otters in the rivers in Britain, but our otters are special. They are from Asia. When they see me, they make a
95 funny sound, a loud 'eeep-eeep, eeep-eeep'.

Then they jump out of their pool and roll around in the sand. Tom usually lets me feed the otters. They eat baby chicks and fish. I throw a baby chick into their pool and they
100 jump into the water and catch it. The otters are Megan's favourite animals.

Megan is my little sister. She's eight years old and is at a different school. Megan plays ball with the otters, but she doesn't like to feed
105 them. The baby chicks and the fish are dead and they don't smell very good. Megan doesn't like to touch dead animals. I don't have a problem with that. I hold my nose with one hand and get a chick with the other.

110 Then Tom and I go and feed the tigers – Sasha, Igor and Inga. Tom gets the meat and asks me to find a long stick. He puts a piece of meat onto the end of the stick and lets me push it through the fence. The tigers come and one of
115 them gets the meat from the stick.

Sometimes they fight for the food. We have to hurry up and give them more. We can't go over the fence, of course. Tigers have really big teeth. And we don't want to be their lunch.

120 Mum usually calls me on my mobile phone at five o'clock. She says it's time to come home. I say goodbye to Inga, Igor, Sasha and Tom of course, but before I go home every day, there is
125 one more animal family that I visit: the Indian elephants Raj, Sheba and their son Omar.

I love to watch them. They can suck up 15 litres of water with their trunks and they drink over 150 litres every day!

130 An elephant's trunk can do so many things: it can smell, pull up grass and trees, take fruit from trees, spray water, and hold another elephant's trunk – that's the way they give hugs. Elephants talk to each other in different
135 ways: they move their ears, they make little

---

l.96 **(to) roll** rollen · l.98 **chick** Küken · l.108 **(to) hold** halten · l.112 **stick** Stock · l.114 **through** [θruː] durch ·
l.114 **fence** [fens] Zaun · l.119 **teeth** *(pl)* [tiːθ] Zähne · l.127 **(to) suck up** aufsaugen · l.128 **trunk** Rüssel ·
l.131 **(to) pull up** herausreißen · l.132 **(to) spray** sprühen · l.134 **in different ways** auf verschiedene Weise

sounds we can't hear and they trumpet really loud with their trunks. Elephants are the biggest land animals in the world. They eat 250 kilos of food every day.

140 Dad calls me the elephant expert. One day I want to go to India and ride an elephant in the jungle.

Before my mobile rings again, I run home.

Weekends at the zoo

145 Sometimes, kids from my school come to the zoo at the weekend with their parents. I wear my red SZ T-shirt, cap and sunglasses all weekend. There's a lot of work to do.

I often help Mum at the Learning Centre. I hold 150 Suzie, our boa constrictor, and Mum tells visitors about her. She tells them what she eats (mice and rats), how she eats (a mouse or rat in one bite) and where she is from (Mexico).

Suzie is eight years old, is three metres long 155 and weighs twelve kilos. It's a bit scary to hold a snake, but I like it.

Then it's feeding time for me! When I help in the Learning Centre, I can have lunch at the restaurant. My favourite food is a roast beef 160 sandwich with salad and chocolate ice cream for dessert.

My birthday!

Kids sometimes have birthday parties at the zoo. They start in the Learning Centre. The 165 birthday kid can touch Suzie, and they learn about other snakes, scorpions and other insects. Tom gives a talk about the big cats. Then the group goes to the Children's Corner. There they can feed the goats and ponies. They 170 also get a yummy lunch at the restaurant and have cake and ice cream. After that, they play party games in the activity area near the restaurant or at the playground.

Today is my birthday. Every year I get a big 175 surprise. Let's see what it is this year.

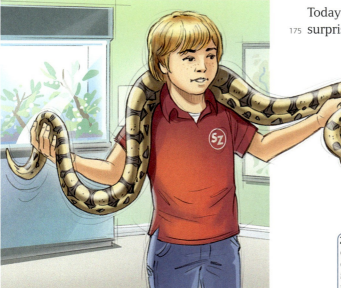

Die Fortsetzung dieser Geschichte findest du ab Seite 122.

Zusatz/Neigungsdifferenzierung: Die S können entweder eine Szene aus der Geschichte zeichnen oder ein Tierquiz für Mit-S entwerfen: *Draw a scene of the feeding of an animal at the zoo.* / *Make a quiz about the animals in the story for your classmates.*

---

l.135 (to) **move** [muːv] bewegen · l.135 **ear** [ɪə] Ohr · l.136 (to) **trumpet** [ˈtrʌmpɪt] tröten · l.147 **sunglasses** *(pl)* [ˈsʌnglɑːsɪz] Sonnenbrille · l.152 **mice** *(pl)* [maɪs] Mäuse · l.152 **in one bite** [baɪt] mit einem Bissen · l.155 (to) **weigh** [weɪ] wiegen · l.169 **goat** [gəʊt] Ziege · l.175 **surprise** [səˈpraɪz] Überraschung

Weekends

Lernfeld S. 80–83: Die S können Texte über Vergangenes verstehen, in denen **was** und **were** vorkommen. Sie können *was* und *were* auch selber benutzen und **sagen, wo sie und andere am Wochenende waren**.

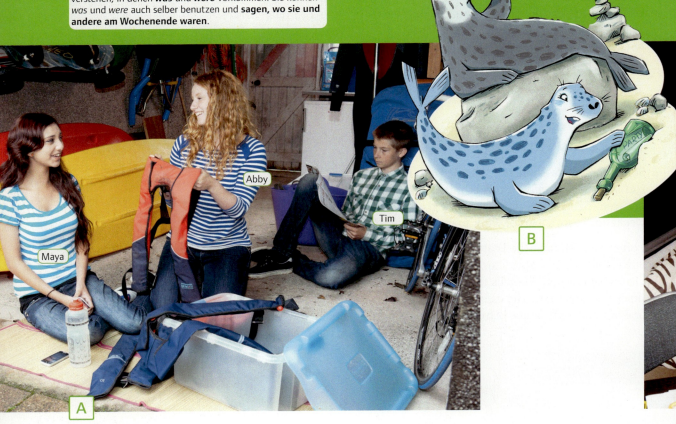

A · B

Abby · Maya · Tim

1 In the picture

a) ... and Spot are at the beach. · Lucy and Maya are in Lucy's room. · Sam and his dad are in the Bennetts' kitchen.

a) **Who is in the pictures? Where are they?**
Maya, Abby and Tim are in a garage.
Silky ...

b) **Find these things in the pictures.**

basketball · birthday invitation · bottle · box · life jacket · magazine · mobile phone · note · rock · sand · shorts · trainers

c) 👥 **Talk to your partner about what you see.**
A: I can see three life jackets in picture A.
B: And there's a mobile phone near Maya.
A: Yes, and there's ...

b) Picture A: bottle · box · life jacket · magazine · mobile phone · trainers
Picture B: bottle · note · rock · sand
Picture C: birthday invitation
Picture D: basketball · bottle · shorts · trainers

2 Weekend plans

 1–4

Grund-schule

a) **Listen and match the four dialogues to pictures A–D.** 1 D · 2 B · 3 A · 4 C

b) 👥 **Listen again. Which sentence is correct?**
Sam wants to ... win his basketball match.
help his dad in the kitchen.
Silky wants to ... break a bottle on a rock.
go to a seals' party.
Abby wants to ... phone her brother.
sail to Ivy Island.
Lucy wants to ... go to the Wheel of Plymouth.
play a game.

➤ **Workbook** *1 (p. 50)*

Mr Bennett

Sam

Lucy

Maya

C

D

Your task

Am Ende dieser Unit wirst du …
… ein Spiel anfertigen und mit deiner Gruppe spielen.

3 Your weekends

Zur Zeitersparnis erarbeiten die S die Übung anhand der Tabelle auf **KV 16: Your weekends.**

👥 What do you do at the weekend?
Where do you go?
Look at the boxes on the right for help. Talk to your classmates. Find somebody who goes to two of the same places or does two of the same things.

A: I often go to the zoo at the weekend and watch the animals. What do you do?
B: I never go to the zoo. I usually stay at home and do my homework. And we have a great Sunday lunch.
A: Oh, we always have Sunday lunch together too.

➡ **Workbook** 2–3 (p. 50)

PLACES
cinema · home · lake · library · museum · my friend's flat · my grandparents' garden · park · shopping mall · zoo · …

ACTIVITIES
go shopping · listen to … · see · play · read · ride a bike · visit · watch · …

Remember to add information about the Plymouth kids to the profiles in your My Book.

Lernfeld S. 82: Die S können einem Lesetext Informationen entnehmen und **sagen, wer was gemacht hat**.

1 Where **were** you? 3 ▸ 5

It's 9 am in Boston. Justin's dad is on Skype.

Dad: Justin? Are you there?
Justin: Hi, Dad! I'm here. Can you see me?
Dad: Wait a minute … Oh, yes, there you are.
5   Hi, Justin. How are you?
Justin: Well, I **was** sick **yesterday**.
Dad: Oh, I'm sorry.
Justin: But I'm OK **today**. What about you, Dad?
Dad: Oh, I'm fine.
10 Justin: Dad, where <u>were</u> you **last** weekend?
Dad: Er … **I'm sorry about** last Saturday,
         Justin. I **was busy** at the weekend, so I
         <u>wasn't</u> at home.
Justin: Yeah, you <u>weren't</u> on Skype.
15 Dad: No … sorry, I <u>was</u> at the studios all day.
         But listen, thank you for that video.
Justin: The video of the seagull, at Sutton
         Harbour?
Dad: Right.
20 Justin: <u>Was</u> it OK?
Dad: It <u>was</u> really good! And the part with the
         seagull and the ice cream <u>was</u> **fantastic**.
Justin: Thanks, Dad.
Dad: And where <u>were</u> you last weekend?
25 Justin: I <u>was</u> at the Barbican with my friends.
         We <u>were</u> in a film, Dad!
Dad: What film <u>was</u> it?
Justin: No, Dad, we <u>weren't</u> at the cinema. It
         <u>was</u> our film. We <u>were</u> the **actors**.
30 Dad: That sounds **exciting**.
Justin: Yes, it <u>was</u> about a girl in old Plymouth
         and her father's ghost.

Dad: So, <u>were</u> you the cameraman?
Justin: Yes, and **guess what**, Dad – I <u>was</u> the
35   ghost too!
Dad: Really? So, when can I see the film?
Justin: I **still** have to edit it, Dad.
Dad: OK, maybe I can help you **when** you
         come to Boston in the **summer**.

2 👥 Who was it?

Who was it: Justin or Justin's dad?
Finish the sentences.

1 … was sick yesterday.
  Justin was sick yesterday.
2 … was busy last weekend.
3 … wasn't on Skype last weekend.
4 … was the cameraman in a film about a ghost.
5 … was the ghost in the film.

2 Justin's dad · 3 Justin's dad · 4 Justin · 5 Justin

3 👥 **Chain** game

Grund-schule

Play the game.

I was at my grandpa's house at the weekend.

Jan was at his grandpa's house and I was at the park at the weekend.

Jan was at his grandpa's house, Ela was at the park and I was … at the weekend.

Zur Erhöhung der individuellen Sprechzeit empfiehlt es sich, die Übung in Kleingruppen (5–6 S) über mehrere Runden durchzuführen.

Justin
Justin's dad

Language help

The simple past of the verb *be*:

	Positive / Negative	Question	
I he she it	was / wasn't	Was	I he she it
you we they	were / weren't	Were	you we they

➡ *GF 10–11: The simple past (p.165)*

1 Dad wasn't at home

(Simple past of *be*: statements)

Finish the sentences.
Use positive (+) or negative (–) forms of *be*.

1 Justin: "Dad (–) at home last weekend. He (+) at the TV studios."
2 Lucy: "I (–) at home last Sunday. I (+) at Maya's flat. Mukesh (+) there, but Mr and Mrs Sen (+) at the cinema."
3 Sam: "I (–) at home yesterday afternoon. I (+) at my basketball club. It (+) great."
4 Mr and Mrs Bennett: "We (–) at home last Saturday. We (+) in London with Lily. But Sam (–) with us. He (+) at a basketball match."
5 Abby: "Maya, you (–) at home yesterday!"
Maya: "No, I (+) at Lucy's house."

1 Dad wasn't at home last weekend. He was at the TV studios. · 2 I wasn't at home last Sunday. I was at Maya's flat. Mukesh was there, but Mr and Mrs Sen were at the cinema. · 3 I wasn't at home yesterday afternoon. I was at my basketball club. It was great. · 4 We weren't at home last Saturday. We were in London with Lily. But Sam wasn't with us. He was at a basketball match. · 5 Maya, you weren't at home yesterday! – No, I was at Lucy's house.

2 Was it fun? 💬

a) Read the dialogue.
    Fill in the gaps with a word from the box.

> boring · cold · exciting · funny · long ·
> sad · scary · silly · strange · warm · wet

Ruby: I was at the pool on Saturday.
Jack: At the Lido? Was it fun?
Ruby: Yes, it was. The water was really (…). What about you?
Jack: I was at the cinema.
Ruby: Was the film good?
Jack: Yes, it was. It was really (…).

3 ▸ 6   **b) Listen to the dialogue.**
    👥 **Then practise with your partner.**

c) 👥 **Make your own dialogue about Saturday. You can use words from the box in a).**

More help ➡ *p.134* | **More help:** Ein Dialoggerüst und weitere Adjektive sind vorgegeben.

> **TIP**
> Remember how you make short answers:
> Was it fun? –   Yes, **it was.**
> Was it good? –   No, **it wasn't.**

Unit 4 bietet viele Partnerübungen. Mit Hilfe der **KV 17: Appointment partners** kann L die *Appointment*-Methode einführen und im Laufe der Unit immer wieder verwenden.

3 How was your weekend?

(Simple past of *be*: question words)

a) Read the dialogue between Jack and Oliver.
    Finish it with question words from the box
    and was or were.

> how · how · when · where · why · who

Jack: Hey, Oliver! How was your weekend?
Oliver: My weekend was great.
Jack: Oh, … you?
Oliver: I was at Katy's house.
Jack: Katy? Your cousin? … you there?
Oliver: I was there because it was her birthday. There was a big party.
Jack: A party! … it?
Oliver: On Sunday afternoon.
Jack: Oh, … there?
Oliver: Well, Abby was there with her friend Maya. And there were lots of other cousins.
Jack: That sounds fun.
Oliver: So, what about you? … your weekend?
Jack: It was OK, thanks.

where were · Why were · When was · who was · How was

More help ➡ *p.134* | **More help:** Textstellen, die auf das richtige Fragewort deuten, sind hervorgehoben.

b) Listen and check your answers.   3 ▸ 7

➡ **Workbook** *4 (p.51)*

Lernfeld S. 84–85: Die S können eine **Bildgeschichte/Texte über Vergangenes verstehen**, in denen *Simple past*-Verben mit *-ed* vorkommen. Sie können falsche Informationen korrigieren.

1 🔊 The basketball match   3 ▶ 8

On Saturday morning, Plymstock School played against Devonport°High School in the Plymouth Schools' Basketball Final. Sam was really excited.

❖

Later, on the way to Lucy's party, he talked to Justin about the match.

> Wörter wie *minibus*, *final* oder *half* sollten vor dem Lesen nicht semantisiert werden, sodass die S sie sich durch die Nähe zur deutschen Sprache oder den Kontext erschließen. Diese Strategien werden im Verlauf der Unit wieder aufgegriffen.

1

2 The match was at Devonport. We went there by minibus.

4 Our fans were great in the second half. They shouted and shouted. That helped us a lot.

5 In the last minute, it was 54 to 54 and we stopped Devonport's best player …

HOME 2 GUEST   54 54

6 … then I scored 2 points.

Justin

Sam

3

*Mr Tyler **came** too. He **had** a great **game plan** for us.*

*But in the first **half**, Devonport was really good. They **scored** 24 **points**. We only scored 16 …*

2 Right or wrong?

Correct the wrong sentences.
Check with a partner.

1 Sam played in a football match on Saturday.
   Wrong. He played in a basketball match.
2 Plymstock scored 24 points in the first half.
   Wrong. Plymstock …
3 In the second half, Plymstock was **better**.
4 In the last minute, Sam scored 3 points.
5 Sam showed Lucy his medal.

2 … scored 16 points. · 3 Right. · 4 Wrong. Sam scored 2 points. ·
5 Wrong. Sam showed his dad his medal.

3 Have a go

Look at the pictures of Morph.
Use the verbs to write about his Saturday morning.

cleaned · learned · listened · finished

7

*And so we **won** the match! Mr Tyler jumped **up** and **down** like a **madman**.*

8

Box "when",
Voc, S. 197

*When we **arrived** back at Plymstock, our fans were there.*

*Then I **saw** Dad in the car and showed him my **medal**. Do you want to see it too?*

9

On Saturday morning, Morph … English in bed.

Then he … his room.

Later he … to music.

Then he … his book.

learned · cleaned ·
listened · finished

Lernfeld S. 86: Die S können **Verben mit -*ed* selber verwenden** und sagen, was sie und andere gemacht haben. Sie können die **Aussprachevarianten [d], [t] und [ɪd] dieser Verben unterscheiden**. Sie kennen **einige unregelmäßige Verben**.

Looking at language

a) Look at the simple past form of the verb play.
   Then go to 1 on pages 84–85. Find the simple past forms of the other verbs. Make a table.

	Past
play	played
talk	...
score	...
shout	...

	Past
stop	...
jump	...
arrive	...

b) Look at the simple past form of the verb go.
   Then go to 1 on pages 84–85. Find the simple past forms of the other verbs. Make a table.

	Past
go	went
come	...
have	...
win	...
see	...

Uh-oh. I have to learn the past forms of irregular verbs.

went

What is the simple past ending of regular verbs?

➡ GF 12: The simple past (pp. 165–166)

1 Morph's Saturday evening (Simple past: positive statements, regular verbs) ▪▪▪▪

Say what Morph did on Saturday evening. Use the simple past form of the verbs.

After dinner I (walk) walked around the library.

I was happy. I (dance) ... between the shelves. danced

I (want) ... to find a new book. wanted

Suddenly a cat (arrive) ... in the library. arrived

She (look) ... at me – and she wasn't friendly. looked

"Help!" I (shout) .... shouted "She wants to eat me."

I (jump) ... onto a shelf between two books. jumped

I (wait) ... there till the waited silly cat (walk) ... away. walked

2 Pronunciation (The -*ed* sound: [d], [t] or [ɪd]) 3 ⏵ 9–10 ▪▪▪▫

a) Listen to the -ed sounds of the verbs in the story about Morph's Saturday evening. Put them in a table like this:

[d]	[t]	[ɪd]
arrived	walked	wanted
...	...	...

a) –
b) answered · called · listened · played · showed · turned

a) danced · looked · jumped
b) asked · touched · watched · liked

a) started · shouted · waited
b) visited · needed

b) Listen to the -ed sounds of these verbs. Add them to your table.

answered · arrived · asked · called · liked · listened · needed · played · showed · touched · turned · visited · watched

c) 👥 Compare your table with a partner. Read the verbs out loud.

Hier kann wieder **KV 17: Appointment partners** zum Einsatz kommen.

Part B Practice **4**

Lernfeld S. 87: Die S können **verstehen, was eine Person in der Vergangenheit gemacht hat,** und diese Informationen an andere weitergeben.

3 A **visit** from London (Simple past: positive statements, regular and irregular verbs) ■■■□

Tom is Sam's friend from London. Read about his visit to Plymouth.

a) Put the verbs into the simple past.

1 Last month Tom (come) came to Plymouth for a weekend.
2 He (arrive) … on Friday afternoon.
3 After dinner, Sam and Tom (play) … chess.
4 Tom (win) … two games; Sam (win) … one.
5 Then Sam (want) … to play computer games, but Tom was too tired.
6 So Tom (go) … to bed and Sam (watch) … a video.

Early finisher ➡ *p.139*

Early finisher: Die S lösen einige Rätsel.

➡ **Workbook** 5–6 (p. 52)

2 arrived · 3 played · 4 won (2x) · 5 wanted · 6 went … watched

b) Fill in the simple past forms of these verbs:

go · go · like · see · show · visit · walk · want

On Saturday, the boys … (1) into Plymouth by bus. Sam … (2) Tom the Hoe and then they … (3) swimming at the Lido. Later, Tom … (4) to see old Plymouth, so they … (5) around the Barbican for an hour. They … (6) lots of old houses and they … (7) the museum in the Elizabethan House. Tom really … (8) his day in Plymouth.

More help ➡ *p.134*

More help: Die Verben sind bereits im *Simple past* vorgegeben.

1 went · 2 showed · 3 went · 4 wanted · 5 walked · 6 saw · 7 visited · 8 liked

4 Dave's day in London 💬 ■■■■

👥 Partner B: Go to p.140.

Partner A:

a) Dave was in London. He talked to his grandma about his day there.
   Tell your partner your picture story: *Dave was in London last Saturday. In the morning he went to …*

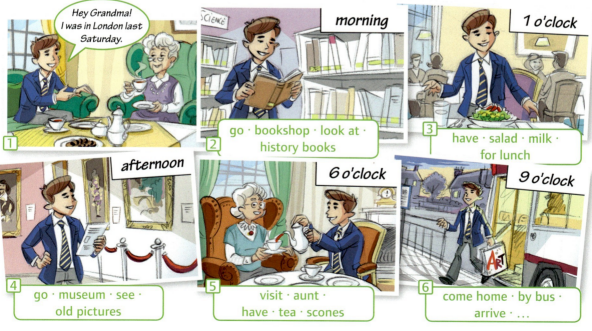

1 *Hey Grandma! I was in London last Saturday.*

2 go · bookshop · look at · history books — *morning*

3 have · salad · milk · for lunch — *1 o'clock*

4 go · museum · see · old pictures — *afternoon*

5 visit · aunt · have · tea · scones — *6 o'clock*

6 come home · by bus · arrive · … — *9 o'clock*

b) Listen to your partner's story.
   Then say how the two stories are different.
   A: In my story he talked to his grandma.
   B: In my story he talked to his classmates.
   And in my story he went …

c) Why do you think Dave's stories were different? Which story do you think is true?

EXTRA Write your "true" story about Dave's day in London.

Lernfeld S. 88: Die S können **verstehen**, wenn in Texten darüber berichtet wird, **was *nicht* passiert ist**.

1 🔊 Party at the Hoe 3 ▶ 11

Mum: Are you all ready to go on the Wheel?

Sam: I'm ready!

Justin: Yes, me too!

5 Lucy: Hey, Mum! We still have to wait for somebody. Remember?

Maya: Look, there's Abby!

Lucy: Hi, Abby. I'm … er … It's
10 great that you're here.

Abby: Hi – sorry I'm late! I **missed** the bus.

Lucy: That's OK. Let's go.

Lucy · Sam · Maya

Box "Unregelmäßige Vergangenheitsformen", Voc, S. 198

After the **ride**, Lucy, Maya, Justin and Abby ran
15 **over to** the birthday **picnic**. Sam **didn't run**. He walked. He **didn't look** happy.

Dad: Come on, everybody! **Sit down**. I want to hear all about your ride.

Lucy: It was really good, Dad! Plymouth Sound
20 looked fantastic …

Maya: … and we saw the Barbican and Sutton Harbour. The boats were really small.

Abby: I saw our school in Plymstock.

Lucy: *I didn't see* Plymstock School – it was
25 too **far** away.

Dad: What about you, Sam? Sam, are you **all right**?

Sam: I'm OK, Mr Pascoe.

Lucy: Sam didn't like the ride, Dad.
30 Dad: Oh, I'm sorry, Sam. What was the **problem**?

Lucy: It was too **high**.

Maya: Sam didn't like that.

Justin: And he didn't look out.

35 Mum: So you didn't see any **sights**. I'm sorry about that.

Box "this, that – these, those", Voc, S. 198

Sam: It's OK. I know all **those** places.

Dad: Yes, of course.

Sam: And today is a great day too. We won
40 our match against Devonport!

Maya: And it's Lucy's birthday!

Dad: Right. Where's the cake? It's time to **make a wish**, Lucy.

2 👥 The missing word

Can you remember the missing word? Who was the speaker?

1 "Sorry I'm late! I … the bus."
2 "The … were really small."
3 "I saw our … in Plymstock."
4 "Sam didn't like the …, Dad."
5 "Oh, I'm sorry, Sam. What was the …?"
6 "We won our … against Devonport!"

➜ **Workbook** *8–10 (pp. 53–54)*

1 missed (Abby) · 2 boats (Maya) · 3 school (Abby) ·
4 ride (Lucy) · 5 problem (Lucy's dad) · 6 match (Sam)

3 👥 Have a go

**Tell your partner what you *didn't* do last weekend.
You can use ideas from the box.**

*I didn't go on a big wheel last weekend.
I didn't …*

go on a big wheel · see my best friend ·
go to a birthday party · do my homework ·
get up **early** · play football

Box "Unregelmäßige Vergangenheitsformen", Voc, S. 198

KV 17 · LAS 4.2, 4.3

Part C Practice

4

Lernfeld S. 89: Die S können sagen, **was sie und andere in der Vergangenheit** *nicht* **gemacht haben**.

Looking at language

a) Finish these sentences from 1 on page 88.

Sam … run. He walked. He … look happy.
I … see Plymstock School – it was too far away.

b) Find more sentences with *didn't* in 1.
Write them down.

c) How do you make negative sentences in the simple past?

➡ GF 13: The simple past (p.166)

positive	negative
I *played* basketball.	I *didn't play* tennis.
He *went* swimming.	He *didn't go* sailing.

don't play
doesn't play
didn't play

Aha … after didn't you **use** *the infinitive too!*

1 Maya didn't read her book

(Simple past: negative statements) ∎∎∎

Last weekend Maya had a long list of things to do. But she only did three things.
Look at her list. Say what she *didn't* do.

Last weekend Maya didn't read her book. She didn't …

read my book
find a birthday present for Lucy ✓
go shopping
call Sam and Justin
do my maths homework
go to Lucy's party ✓
ride my bike
go sailing with Abby and Tim ✓
write to my cousin Dilip
visit Uncle Amar
watch a video

didn't read her book · didn't go shopping · didn't call · didn't do her maths homework · didn't ride her bike · didn't write to her cousin · didn't visit · didn't watch

2 I played … I didn't play …

(Simple past: positive and negative statements) ∎∎∎

a) Think about last week. Write two positive and two negative sentences about what you did.

More help ➡ *p.135*   **More help:** Enthält eine Anzahl von Anregungen/Redemitteln.

b) 👥 Make a double circle. Tell your partner what you did and what you didn't do. Then …

🔴 stay in your place.

🟢 move one place to a new partner.

I played with my cat. I didn't play with my dog.

I went to bed early. I didn't read in bed.

Hier kann wieder **KV 17: Appointment partners** zum Einsatz kommen.

3 👥 I think that's **true** 💬

∎∎∎

Make two sentences about your last weekend – one positive and one negative.
Only one sentence is true. Can the others guess the true sentence?

Last weekend I touched an elephant. I didn't go shopping.

You didn't go shopping: I think that's true.

➡ **Workbook** *11–13 (pp. 54–55)*

Lernfeld S. 90: Die S können einem Lesetext Informationen entnehmen und **sagen, ob auf den Text bezogene Aussagen korrekt sind**.

4 Seal saves hurt dog 📖

a) Read the story.
Are these sentences right or wrong?

1 On Saturday evening, Charles Hacker went swimming at the beach in Exmouth.
2 He saw a big black dog.
3 The dog was hurt.
4 When he saw the dog, Mr Hacker jumped into the water.
5 The dog °couldn't swim because it was hurt.
6 A seal helped Mr Hacker to swim back to the beach.
7 Mr Hacker called the police.
8 The seal was the °hero in this story.

b) Correct the wrong sentences.
👥 Compare your answers.

1 Wrong. He went for a walk. · 2 Wrong. He saw a small grey dog. · 3 Right. · 4 Wrong. The dog jumped into the water. · 5 Right. · 6. Wrong. The seal helped the dog to swim back to the beach. · 7 Right. · 8 Right.

Devon News

Seal saves dog in °South Devon

At 8:15 on Saturday evening, Charles Hacker went for a walk on the beach in Exmouth, Devon. Suddenly, he heard a strange sound. Then he saw a small grey dog, it was hurt. When Mr Hacker came °near, the dog jumped °off the rocks into the water. But because the dog was hurt, it couldn't swim. Mr Hacker saw that the dog had a problem. He wanted to help, but he didn't know how. Then he saw a seal in the water. The seal started to swim °around the dog. Then it swam behind the dog and °pushed it onto the beach. Mr Hacker called the police. The police came and took the dog to an animal help °centre.

"I didn't save the dog," said Mr Hacker later in an interview. "It was the seal."

Background file

Lernfeld: Die S verstehen einen **kurzen Sachtext** und können das **Wissen nutzen, um eine Entscheidung zu begründen**.

Devon – an English county
Devon is a county in the °south-west of England. Its °biggest city is Plymouth, with 260,000 people.

Dartmoor is the biggest area of °wild °country in the °south of Britain. It is the °setting for lots of °famous °detective stories.

DEVON
Plymouth

Devon's °north and south °coasts have lots of °sandy beaches. Swimming, °surfing and °fishing are very °popular with °holidaymakers.

Wild ponies on Dartmoor, Devon

Woolacombe Beach, Devon
['wʊləkəm]

Devon is one of the °warmest places in Britain. You can find lots of °palm trees there!

Torquay Gardens, Devon
[ˌtɔːˈkiː]

Write a short text. Say why you would / wouldn't like to go to Devon.
More help → p.135 **More help:** Sprachliche Hilfen werden strukturiert vorgegeben.

Zusatz: KV 18: Welcome to sunny Torquay! enthält einen weiteren Lesetext zu Devon – passend zur Kompetenzschulung Lesen.

1 You say, you write ... [iː]

3 ▶ 12–13

a) You hear the [iː]-sound in the word "week".
Look at the six pictures.
Find five words with an [iː]-sound.
Then listen and check.

green

cream

seal

tree

jeans

c) Make a chart. Write down the [iː]-words.

You say	You write
iː	cheese
	... siehe Box sowie a)

b) How many words with an [iː]-sound can you find: 6, 7 or 8?

> cheese · dead · dream · feed · list · meat ·
> people · red · ship · team · thief · wheel

Then listen and check.

d) Ask your partner to spell the [iː]-words from b).

Can you spell "cheese"?

Yes, I can. It's C - H - E - E - S - E.

2 Plurals (-s or -es?)

> **Lernfeld:** Die S können **Plurale bilden** und dabei **entscheiden, welche Endung** verwendet werden muss.

3 ▶ 14

a) Listen to the plurals of these words.
Do you spell them with -s or with -es?

> action · address · basket · beach · bed · box ·
> boy · bus · map · month · sandwich · watch

TIP

You usually °add **s** to a word to make the plural:
dog – dog**s**, seal – seal**s**, ...
You sometimes have to add -**es** to make it °easier to say the plural: beach – beach**es**.

-s: actions · baskets · beds · boys · maps · months
-es: addresses · beaches · boxes · buses · sandwiches · watches

b) 👥 Choose words from the box in a).
Ask your partner to spell the plural. Take turns.

Can you spell the plural of "basket"?

Can you spell the plural of "box"?

3 Plurals again (-s or -ies?)

TIP

Singular	Plural °ending
°consonant + y	ies
story	stories
°vowel + y	ys
boy	boys

➜ *GF 15: The plural of nouns (pp. 167–168)*

a) Which words have the plural ending -ies?

> birthday · boy · butterfly · day · family ·
> library · monkey · party · smiley · story ·
> toy · trophy

b) 👥 Choose words from the box in a).
Ask your partner to spell the plural. Take turns.

> **Alternative:** Schneeballverfahren im Plenum.

➜ **Workbook** 14 (p. 55)

Lernfeld S. 92–93: Die S können in Lesetexten
Informationen finden, die zu bestimmten Bildern passen.

1 🔊 Sailing on Sunday 3 🔘 15

Abby walked into the canteen and saw Lucy.
"Hi, Lucy. Can I sit with you?" she asked.
"Of course," said Lucy.
Abby sat down. "Hey, your party was great.
5 Thanks again for the invitation!"
Lucy smiled. "Did you have a good Sunday?"
"Yes, I did," Abby answered. "I went sailing with
Maya and my brother Tim. Did Maya tell you
about it?"
10 "No, she didn't. Where did you go?"
"Well, we sailed to a beach near Ivy Island."
"That's nice," Lucy said.
"Yes," said Abby. "And guess what we saw!"
"Tell me," Lucy said, "what did you see?"
15 "Seals!" said Abby. "There was a big group of
seals on the beach."
"Wow!" said Lucy. "That sounds exciting."
"Yes," said Abby. "But it was scary too. Seals can
bite, you know."
20 "So what did you do?" Lucy asked.
"We were very quiet," Abby answered. "We just
walked around the beach and looked. And then
we wanted to go back to the boat, but we
couldn't."
25 "Why not?"
"Because there was a big seal in front of it."
"Oh no!" said Lucy, "what did you do?"

"We waited, but the seal didn't go away. Then the
sea came in and took our boat."
30 "Oh no! What did you do then?"
"We went into the water and swam back to the
boat. Some of the seals followed us, but we were
OK."
"Seals can be scary. I didn't know that," said Lucy.
35 "Yes," said Abby. "Big seals can be scary, but not
baby seals."
"Did you see baby seals on Sunday too?" asked
Lucy.
"No, I didn't," said Abby. "But when I was nine …
40 oh, that's a long story."
"Tell me," said Lucy. "Please … "
"Well," said Abby, "I went sailing with my two
brothers – Tim and Will – and …"
"Uh-oh," said Lucy. "There's the bell."
45 "OK," said Abby. "I can tell you the story later."

Lernfeld: Die S können einen **kurzen Sachtext verstehen** und mit Hilfe des Textes **über ein Sachthema sprechen**.

Background file Grey seals

Grey seals are very big animals.
How much do you weigh? 30, 40, 50 kg?
Grey seals weigh between 150 and 230 kg!
They are grey or brown with dark spots.
They are also great swimmers.
They can swim 30 to 70 metres down into the sea.
Grey seals eat fish, crabs and sometimes birds.
A seal's first year is very hard. Seal mothers leave
their babies after only 17 to 19 days. Young seals
have to learn to find their way and how to catch
fish and crabs. They swim very far – 1,000 km or
more! Like kids, they have to practise, practise
and practise.

👥 **Close the book. Tell your partner three
things about seals.**

→ **Workbook** 15 (p. 56)

2 Abby's story

👥 Look at these scenes from Abby's story.
Find sentences in 1 for each picture.

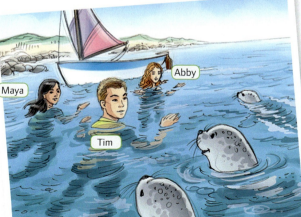

1 We went into the water and swam back to the boat. (ll. 31–32) /
Some of the seals followed us, but we were OK. (ll. 32–33)
2 I went sailing with Maya and my brother Tim. (ll. 7–8) /
Well, we sailed to a beach near Ivy Island. (l. 11)
3 There was a big group of seals on the beach. (ll. 15–16)

Early finisher

a) **Choose a sentence or two from the story in 1
and draw a picture.**

b) 👥 **Find a partner and show your picture.
Can he/she find the lines in the text?**

3 Lucy's questions

👥 Here are Abby's answers to some of Lucy's
questions.
Find the questions in 1 and write them down.

1 "Yes, I did," Abby answered. "I went sailing
with Maya and my brother Tim."

2 "Seals!" said Abby. "There was a big group of
seals on the beach."

3 "We waited, but the seal didn't go away. Then
the sea came in and took our boat."

4 "No I didn't," said Abby. "But when I was
nine ..."

1 Did you have a good Sunday? • 2 What did you see? • 3 What did you do? • 4 Did you see baby seals on Saturday too?

4 Your weekend

👥 Ask and answer these two questions:

1 Did you have a good weekend?
Yes, I did. / No, I didn't.

2 What did you do?
I went to ... / I saw ... / I played ... / ...

Lernfeld S. 94–95: Die S können fragen, wo andere **am Wochenende / in den Ferien** waren, und **Fragen anderer beantworten**.

Language help

In the simple present, you use *Do* or *Does* to make questions.
Do you **go** sailing in the summer?
Does Abby **go** sailing on Sundays?

In the simple past, you use *Did*.
Did you **go** sailing at the weekend?
Did Abby **go** sailing with Maya?

Remember how you make short answers:
Did you …?   Yes, I **did**. / No, I **didn't**.

➡ *GF 14: The simple past (p.167)*

1 Did you see an elephant yesterday? (Simple past: questions)

Ask questions from the table below and answer them. Take turns.

Did you	see	an elephant / the moon / …	yesterday?
	go	swimming / skating / … to the park / to a party / …	last week?
	play	football / tennis / chess / … the piano / the drums / …	last month?
	visit	your grandma / friend / …	last year?

Did you go to a party yesterday?

No, I didn't. But I went to a party last month.

Early finisher Think of more questions for your partner. Can you make funny questions too?

Hier kann wieder **KV 17: Appointment partners** zum Einsatz kommen.

2 Holidays

a) Make a double circle. Ask what your partner did in the last holidays.

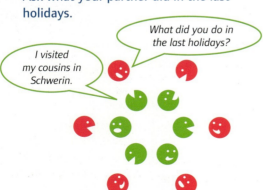

What did you do in the last holidays?

I visited my cousins in Schwerin.

b) What can you remember about your classmates' holidays?

Anne visited her cousins in Schwerin. Max stayed at home. Ela went to …

➡ **Workbook** *16–17 (pp. 56–57)*

Grund-
schule

3 How **many** did you count? `Box "much – many", Voc, S. 199`

a) Copy these words into a list.

> baskets · boxes · butterflies · guitars ·
> monkeys · **oranges** · scones · toys ·
> trophies · watches · **worms**

b) Count the things in the picture – and add
the numbers to your list.

3 baskets	2 guitars	8 scones	
4 boxes	5 monkeys	3 toys	3 watches
7 butterflies	6 oranges	5 trophies	6 worms

c) Cover the numbers on your list.
Then ask and answer like this. Take turns.

> How many baskets
> did you count?

> I counted three baskets.

> Right. I counted
> three baskets too.

➡ *GF 15: The plural of nouns (pp.167–168)*

4 Strange Devon sports

> **Lernfeld:** Die S können **zu einem englischen Text Notizen auf Deutsch anfertigen** und dabei **wesentliche Informationen auswählen** und weitergeben.

Partner B: Go to page 141.

a) Partner A: Read the information.
   Make notes in German.

Find out

– wann das nächste „orange rolling"stattfindet

– wo es stattfindet

– um was es beim „orange rolling" geht

b) 👥 In German, tell your partner about
   "orange rolling".

EXTRA Which event would you like to watch:
orange rolling or worm charming? Say why.

°I'd like to watch ... because it's fun /silly/...

Orange rolling: 25. August, 10 Uhr · in der High Street in Totnes · Es werden
Orangen die Straße herunter gekickt. Die Orangen dürfen nicht mit der Hand
berührt werden und dürfen hinterher nicht kaputt sein.

➡ **Workbook** *18 (p. 57)*

Worm charming: 11. Juni, 11 Uhr · in Blackawton, Devon · Die Spieler müssen in einem
Quadratmeter Gras ohne Spaten Würmer finden. Manche schütten Wasser oder Zucker auf das
Gras und hoffen, dass die Würmer rauskommen. Der Spieler mit den meisten Würmern gewinnt.

Orange°rolling

When?
25th August
at 10 am

Where?
High Street, Totnes,
Devon

What?
People°kick oranges down High Street. They
cannot touch the oranges with their hands.
At the end of the°race, the winner's orange
°must be°intact.
The°tradition started in the time of Sir
Francis Drake (1540–1596).°One day, Sir
Francis walked into a boy with a basket of
oranges. The basket°fell onto the street and
the oranges rolled down the hill.

> Die meisten unbekannten Wörter können aus dem
> Deutschen oder dem Kontext hergeleitet werden.

Lernfeld S. 96: Die S können Textabschnitte sinnvoll als **Einleitung, Hauptteil und Schluss** anordnen und einen **Text mit Bildern und Überschriften** so **gestalten**, dass er für andere interessant wird.

KV 19: Putting a page together enthält diese SB-Seite zum Ausschneiden, sodass die S die einzelnen Elemente hin- und herschieben können.

5 👥 Study skills: Putting a page together

Plymstock School News is the school paper at Plymstock. Imagine you work for it.
Last week you asked Abby for a story and now you have to put a nice page together.
Here are the four paragraphs from Abby's story, and two titles, two drawings and two captions.

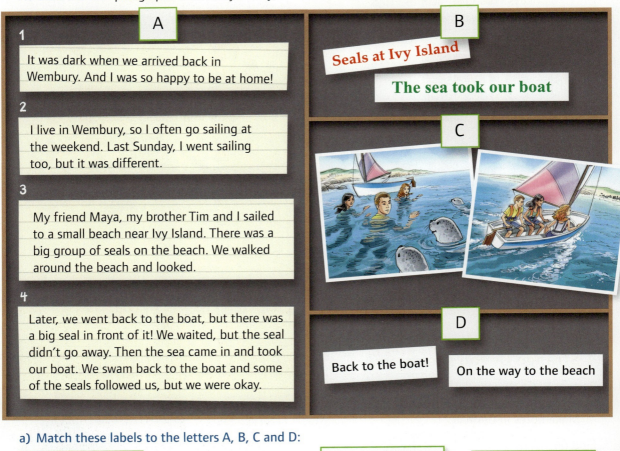

A

1 It was dark when we arrived back in Wembury. And I was so happy to be at home!

2 I live in Wembury, so I often go sailing at the weekend. Last Sunday, I went sailing too, but it was different.

3 My friend Maya, my brother Tim and I sailed to a small beach near Ivy Island. There was a big group of seals on the beach. We walked around the beach and looked.

4 Later, we went back to the boat, but there was a big seal in front of it! We waited, but the seal didn't go away. Then the sea came in and took our boat. We swam back to the boat and some of the seals followed us, but we were okay.

B Seals at Ivy Island / The sea took our boat

C

D Back to the boat! / On the way to the beach

a) Match these labels to the letters A, B, C and D:

Captions   D | Drawings   C | Paragraphs   A | Titles   B

b) Read the Study skills box. Then:
1 Put the paragraphs in the right order. 2 · 3 · 4 · 1
2 Choose one of the titles for the story, or think of another title.
3 Choose one of the drawings, or make another.
4 Choose one of the captions, or think of another caption.
5 Arrange all the parts of the text on a page and put it into your 📘 My Book .

c) Compare your page with another group.
– Are the paragraphs in the right order?
– Do the titles tell you what the story is about?
– Do the captions go with the pictures?

➜ SF 3: Putting a page together (pp. 150–151)

Study skills

Putting a page together

Wie gestaltet man eine gute Seite mit Text und Bild, z. B. für eine Schülerzeitung?
1 Ein guter **Text** hat eine kleine Einleitung, einen längeren Hauptteil und einen Schluss.
2 Der Text braucht eine **Überschrift** und evtl. auch Zwischenüberschriften. Überschriften verdeutlichen, worum es im Text geht.
3 **Bilder** liefern weitere Informationen – auch in den **Bildunterschriften**.

➜ **Workbook** 19–20 (p. 58)

1 Plymouth, my hometown

a) In the film, the girl shows us her hometown.
Watch the film. What did she show us?
Choose A or B.

In the film I saw ...

A	B
a gym	a swimming pool
an ice cream	a pizza
boats	buses
a museum	the Aquarium

b) Watch the film again.
What other things and places can you see in the film?
Make a list.   a girl · a restaurant · sailing boats · a police boat · a shopping mall · shops · the Hoe · ...

c) 👥 Compare your list with your partner.
Agree on three places or things for a weekend in Plymouth.
– My top place is ... I also like ...

2 EVERYDAY ENGLISH   A present for Ruby

a) Watch the film. What are Jack and Oliver's ideas for Ruby's present?
What do they give her?   Their ideas are: a bag, a T-shirt and a book. In the end they give her a bell for her bike.

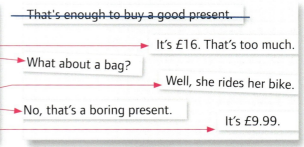

Jack   Oliver

b) Match the sentences below with sentences from the box.

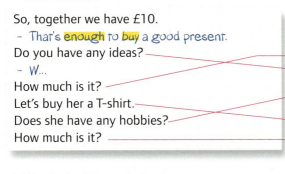

So, together we have £10.
– That's **enough** to **buy** a good present.
Do you have any ideas?
– W...
How much is it?
Let's buy her a T-shirt.
Does she have any hobbies?
How much is it?

~~That's enough to buy a good present.~~

It's £16. That's too much.

What about a bag?

Well, she rides her bike.

No, that's a boring present.

It's £9.99.

c) Watch the film and check.

d) 👥 What presents can you buy for a friend?
Talk to your partner and make a list.

e) 👥 Write a dialogue like in the film and act it out.

Hier kann wieder **KV 17: Appointment partners** zum Einsatz kommen.

Lernfeld S. 98–99: Die S können eine Geschichte auch verstehen, wenn sie nicht alle Wörter kennen. Sie verwenden dazu **verschiedene Worterschließungsstrategien**. Sie können eine Geschichte so **genau lesen**, dass sie Satzanfänge und -enden einander zuordnen können.

A baby seal

Der Text beschäftigt sich mit dem auf S. 93 bereits angedeuteten Segelausflug von Abby.

3 ▶17 **15 October, a beach near Ivy Island, not far from Wembury.**

A baby seal with bright eyes moved over the sand and into a small pool of water. Then another little
5 seal came … and another and another. But the pool was small, too small. So the seal with the bright eyes went back over the sand to the group of big seals on the rocks. She called and listened. She called again. Her mother called back. The
10 baby seal was hungry and pushed her head against her mother's body. She drank the milk. It was so good. The morning sun touched the baby seal's body, and she fell asleep. When she woke up, she called her mother again. But her
15 mother wasn't there.
The sun went down. The baby seal was hungry and called her mother. Her mother didn't come.

Box "Unregelmäßige Vergangenheitsformen", Voc, S. 200

The baby seal shouted at the sea. The sea didn't answer.
20 The morning came and the baby seals were ready to play after their milk breakfast. But not the seal with the bright eyes. She was too tired to play, and too tired to swim. When the sea came in, she moved back over the sand – away from the dark
25 water.

18 October, near Ivy Island **3 ▶18**
on the open sea.

Abby looked at her two brothers.
"Why can't I steer the boat?" she asked.
30 "Because you're only nine!" said Tim.
"Tim's right," said Will. "You're too young, Abby."
"That isn't fair," shouted the girl. She went to the front of the boat and sat down. "I can sail too! I won a trophy this year from Wembury Sailing
35 Club!"
"Yeah, yeah. We know, Abby. Everybody in Wembury knows that!" said Tim.
Abby looked away, over the water. There was a small beach not far away. She looked again and
40 saw something white.
"Hey look, what's that?" she asked.
Her brothers didn't look.
"Stop! I can see something," she shouted.
"We can't stop the boat, Abby," said her brother
45 Will.
"But it's an animal – maybe a seal!" she said.
"It's only a rock, Abby," said Tim.
"No, it isn't," she shouted. "You didn't look. Stop the boat! We have to go back. Please!"
50 "Oh, OK," said Will. "Let's turn around, Tim!"

1 Did you get it?

👥 **Choose the right ending for each sentence.**

1 The baby seal came out of the pool …	a she wasn't old enough.
2 She was too tired to swim …	b she looked very soft.
3 The boys didn't let Abby steer the boat …	c there were too many other seals there.
4 Abby wanted to sail back to the beach …	d she swam too near a ship.
5 Will called the rescue centre …	e she didn't get any milk from her mother.
6 The baby seal's mother is dead …	f she saw a seal there.
7 Abby called the baby seal Silky …	g the baby seal needed help.

because

1 c · 2 e · 3 a · 4 f · 5 g · 6 d · 7 b

"Aye, aye, Captain Blackwell!" They turned around and sailed to the beach.

"We're too near the rocks, Tim!" Will shouted.

"Steer the boat away."

55 But Tim was too **slow**. The boat **hit** the rocks and threw Will into the water.

"Will! Are you OK?" shouted Tim.

"Yeah, yeah – I'm wet, but I'm OK!" said Will.

He and Tim **pulled** the boat onto the sand. Abby

60 jumped down and ran to the animal.

"I *was* right! It *is* a seal!" she shouted.

"Be **careful**, Abby. Don't go too near it. Seals can bite."

"But I think it's sick," said Abby.

65 "Call Mum, please …"

"I can't. My phone is wet."

"Here, Will, take my phone," said Tim.

❖

19 "And don't touch the seal!" said Mum.

"Call the °**rescue centre**. Here's the number."

70 Will called the centre. The woman asked him lots of questions.

"Now just wait for us … and please, don't go too near the seal," said the woman.

They waited. Tim was hungry. Will **was cold**. Abby

75 watched the baby seal.

"Please don't **die**," she said again and again.

The rescue team came by boat. "They're here, they're here!" shouted Abby. Two men and a woman pulled their boat onto the sand. They had

80 a **cage**.

"**Poor** little seal," said the woman. "She needs food. She didn't **get** enough milk from her mother."

Box "get", Voc, S. 201

The two men put   the baby seal into the cage.

Abby   Tim   Will

85 "They usually fight," said the woman. "But this little baby is too tired and hungry."

"Where's her mother?" asked Abby.

"Well, yesterday, we found a dead seal not far from here."

90 "Oh, no!" said Abby.

"Yes, the poor girl swam too near a ship's °**propeller**."

"That isn't fair," said Abby.

"No, it isn't. But you found her baby **before** it was

95 too late. That's good."

"We're ready," said one of the men. "It's time to go." He looked at Abby and said, "You found her – so you can give her a name."

Abby thought for a minute. "She looks so **soft**,"

100 she said. "I know! Call her **Silky**."

2 New words

Here are some new words from the story:

> body *(l. 10)* · fair *(l. 32)* · front *(l. 33)* · steer *(l. 54)* ·
> cage *(l. 80)* · propeller *(l. 92)* · before *(l. 94)* · soft *(l. 99)*

Did you understand them

– from the pictures?

– because they are like German words?

– because they are like other English words?

Or did you check them in the Dictionary?

➜ *SF 4: Understanding and looking up new words (pp. 151–152)*

3 On the rescue team

👥 **Imagine you were on the rescue team. Make a short picture story about the rescue.**

You choose

One partner draws the pictures.
The other partner writes the captions.

Neigungsdifferenzierung: Die S arbeiten arbeitsteilig an einer kreativen Aufgabe und wählen ihren Teil je nach Neigung aus.

➜ **Workbook** *21 (p. 59)*

Workbook
Checkpoint 4
(pp. 60–63)

Your task

Step 1–4 sollten wegen der Gruppenarbeit im Unterricht durchgeführt werden. Es bietet sich aber auch an, die Selbsteinschätzung ausführlich mit den S im Plenum zu besprechen.

A memory game

 Make a memory game and play it in your group.

STEP 1

Make **12 name cards** for characters from your English book (Sam, Abby, Morph, Silky, …). You can use names more than once. Write the word **NAME** on one side and the **name** of the character on the other.

STEP 2

Now make **12 action cards**, one for each name card.
For example, think: "What did Sam do in Unit 4?" and write … played in a basketball match.
Write the word **ACTION** on one side and an **action** on the other.

STEP 3

Swap your cards with another group. Check their cards.
- Do all the action cards go with the name cards?
- Are the verb forms and spelling right? Write corrections and give them back to the group.

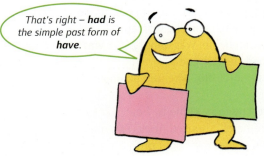

*That's right – **had** is the simple past form of **have**.*

STEP 4

Then swap cards with another group. Play the game. Choose one name card and one action card. If they go together, you get them. You can use these phrases:

> Whose turn is it?¹
> It's my/your/Maria's turn.²
> Yes, that's right.
> Those cards go together.
> No, that's wrong.
> They don't go together.
> Great, I get these two cards.
> That's the end of the game.
> Count your cards.
> Maria is the winner.

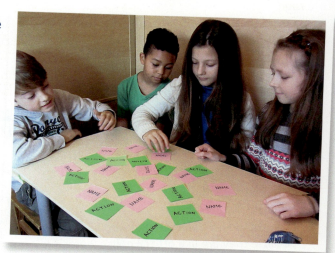

1 Whose turn is it? [huːz ˈtɜːn] – Wer ist dran?

2 It's my/your/Tina's turn. – Ich bin / Du bist / Tina ist dran.

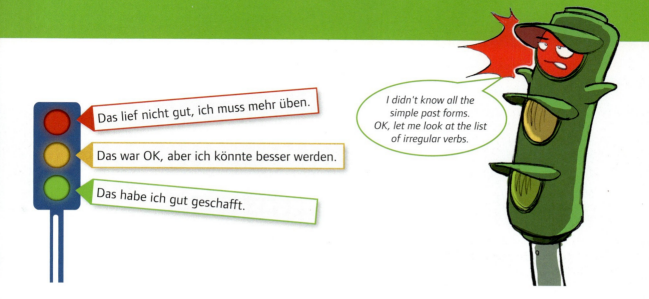

Das lief nicht gut, ich muss mehr üben.

Das war OK, aber ich könnte besser werden.

Das habe ich gut geschafft.

I didn't know all the simple past forms. OK, let me look at the list of irregular verbs.

Wie gut warst du?

Wie schätzt du dich selber ein? Schreibe *Ideas*, *Words* und *Grammar* in dein Heft und ordne dir für jeden Bereich eine Ampelfarbe zu.

Ideas
· Wie gut konntest du dich an Ereignisse im Buch erinnern? Wie einfach war es, die *action cards* zu schreiben?

Words
· Hattest du Probleme mit der Rechtschreibung?

Grammar
· Welche unregelmäßigen Verben haben dir Schwierigkeiten bereitet?

Wie kannst du besser werden?

Wenn du dich eher rot oder gelb eingeschätzt hast, helfen dir folgende Tipps beim Wiederholen und Üben.

Ideas
Schau dir nochmal die Profile der Lehrwerksfiguren in deinem MyBook an. Vervollständige sie, wenn nötig.

Words
Die Rechtschreibung kannst du im Dictionary überprüfen.
➡ *Workbook S. 55*

Grammar
Hilfe bei der Bildung und der Verwendung des *simple past* findest du hier.
➡ *GF 10–14: The simple past (S. 165–167)*
➡ *List of irregular verbs (S. 231)*
➡ *U4: LH S. 83, 1–3 S. 83,*
 LAL S. 86, 1–4 S. 86–87,
 LAL S. 89, 1–3 S. 89,
 LH S. 94, 1–3 S. 94–95
➡ *Workbook S. 51–52, 54–55*

By the sea

Cawsand Beach, near Plymouth

Silky

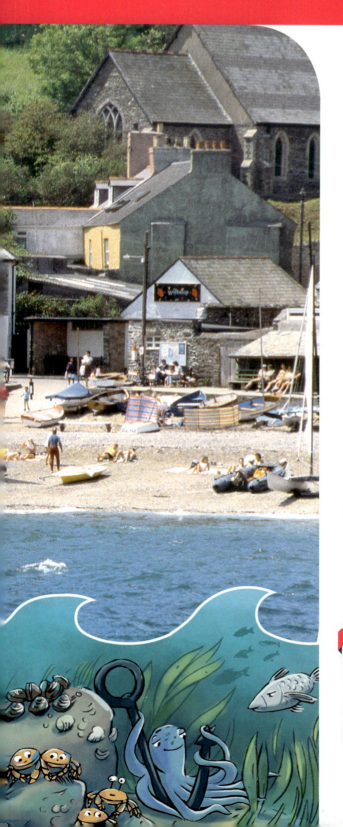

1 Cawsand Beach

a) Look at the photo of the beach.
   What can you see in it?
   Write down as many words as you can.

b) 👥 Compare your list with a partner's.
   Add words to your lists if you need to.

2 At the beach   3 ▶ 20

a) Now imagine you are at Cawsand Beach.
   Listen and write down what you hear.
   Think about what you can feel, and write that
   down too.
   I can hear a seagull. I can ==feel== the sun on my
   ==face==.

b) 👥 In a group, talk about Cawsand Beach.
   Say what you would like to do there.

A: I'd like to swim in the sea and ==look for== Silky.

B: I'd like to go sailing.   Box "Unregelmäßige Vergangen-
                              heitsformen", Voc, S. 201

3 °Octopus's garden   3 ▶ 21

 Grund-
schule

Listen to the song and sing along.

I'd like to be °under the sea
In an octopus's garden in the °shade.
°He'd let us in, knows °where we've been
In his octopus's garden in the shade.
I'd ask my friends to come and see
An octopus's garden with me.
I'd like to be under the sea
In an octopus's garden in the shade.

> **Your task**
>
> **Am Ende dieser Unit wirst du …**
> … Argumente für einen Urlaub in Plymouth
> sammeln.
> Dann wirst du in einem Rollenspiel versuchen,
> deine Eltern davon zu überzeugen.

➡ **Workbook** *1–2 (pp. 64–65)*

Lernfeld S. 104–107: Die S können zu Texten, Tonaufnahmen und Bildern sagen, was jemand gerade (nicht) macht. Sie benutzen dazu die Verlaufsform.

1 An afternoon in Cawsand

Last weekend, Justin, Lucy, Maya, Abby and Sam went to Cawsand Beach.
Justin made a film of their trip for his dad.

A [3] 22

Hi, Dad, it's Saturday, 11.36. I'm at Sutton Harbour with my friends. We want to take the ferry to Cawsand Beach. Lucy is late. Can you see her? She's wearing a pink top. And she's running. Maya and Sam are calling her. Abby is on the ferry too, but you can't see her. She's inside.

B [3] 23

Hey, Dad, we're at the beach now. It's 12.30. Sam is running after the girls. They're playing°tag and Sam is "it". But he's much too slow. Hey, come on Sam – you aren't running fast enough.

C [3] 24

Now it's time for a group photo. Look, here's Abby with her new camera. She's smiling at the others, but uh-oh – they aren't smiling at her. They're making silly faces.

D [3] 25

The others are swimming now. I'm not swimming. It's too cold for me. At the moment, I'm looking at °rock pools. You can see all kinds of sea life there. Hey, what's that sound?
It's coming from my rucksack. Oh, it's my mobile. Somebody is calling me. … Sorry, Dad, that was Lucy. It's time for our picnic.

E [3] 26

Hi, Dad. The picnic is over.
Hey, Maya! That's my …
Hi, Mr Skinner. This is Maya. Justin isn't filming now. I'm filming! So now you can see Justin with his friends – Sam, Lucy and Abby.

F [3] 27

Hey, Dad. We're on the ferry now. Look at the girls. They're all laughing. Sam is telling jokes again. It's almost 5 o'clock – we're going back home. It was a really great day.

2 Justin's film

Read text A. Match it to the right picture (1–6). Then read texts B–F and match each one to a picture.

A4 · B2 · C5 · D6 · E1 · F3

KV 20: Justin's film bietet *Right/wrong-statements* zur Überprüfung des Textverständnisses.

3 Have a go

a) What are the kids doing? Choose the right phrase from the box.

> making silly faces · playing tag with the girls · running to the ferry · ~~smiling at the camera~~ · telling jokes

In photo 1, Abby, Justin, Sam and Lucy are smiling at the camera.
In photo 2, Sam is …
In photo 3, Sam is …
In photo 4, Lucy is …
In photo 5, Maya, Sam and Lucy are …

2 … playing tag with the girls. ·
3 … telling jokes. ·
4 … running to the ferry. ·
5 … making silly faces.

b) Take turns. Ask and answer like this:

I spy a girl. She's wearing something red. Who is it?

It's Ela. My turn. I spy a boy. He's wearing something …

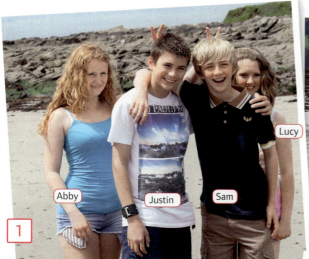

1

2

3

4

5

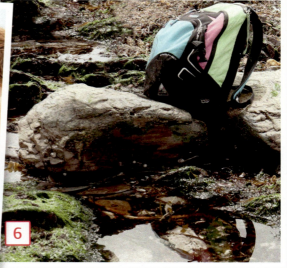

6

Looking at language

a) The table shows how you make the present progressive.
Copy and finish it. The text on p.104 can help you.

b) How do you make negative sentences in the present progressive?
Check p.104 for examples.

➡ *GF 16 a–b: The present progressive (p.168)*

Subject + form of *be*	-ing form	
I'm	look**ing**	for crabs
You're	eat**ing**	my sandwiches.
Sam is	tell…	jokes.
She's	wear…	a pink top.
It's	…	from my rucksack.
We're	…	back home.
Maya and Sam are	…	her.

1 At Cawsand Beach (Present progressive: positive statements)   ■ ■ ■ ■ ■

a) Lucy calls Sam on her mobile. Finish their dialogue. Use the right form of *be*.

Lucy: Hey, Sam! I'm waiting for you all. Our picnic is ready. Where is everybody?

Sam: Well, Maya and Abby … still swimming. No, sorry! They'… coming out of the water now. And I'… sitting on a rock.

Lucy: You'… sitting on a rock?

Sam: Yes, and I'… reading my kung fu book.

Lucy: What about Justin?

Sam: Oh, Justin … looking for crabs again. Or maybe he'… filming birds. Why don't you call him?

are · They're · I'm · You're · I'm · is · he's

b) Finish the sentences with the right form of *be* and the -ing form of the verb.

1 It's 4:50 Silky and Spot are swimming (swim) in the sea near Cawsand Beach.

2 They'… (look) for fish and crabs for dinner.

3 Silky: "Hey look, Spot. The ferry … (come)!"

4 Spot: "Yes, be careful! It'… (move) very fast."

5 Silky: "Hey, Spot. There's a boy with a video camera on the ferry. He'… (film) us."

6 Spot: "And there's a girl with red hair. She'… (eat) a sandwich."

7 Silky: "And we'… (talk) too much! I'm hungry. Come on, let's find some fish."

➡ **Workbook** *3–4 (pp. 65–66)*

They're looking · is coming · It's moving · He's filming · She's eating · we're talking

2 👥 After the picnic (Present progressive: positive statements)   ■ ■ ■ ■ ■

Say what is happening in the picture.
Take turns. You can use the verbs in the box.
The dog is ==smelling== …

eat · film · listen · play · read · sleep · ~~smell~~ · text · walk

➡ **Workbook** *5 (p. 66)*   The dog is smelling Justin's rucksack. · Justin is filming a seagull. · The seagull is eating a worm. · Maya is reading a book. · Maya is listening to music too. · Lucy is texting. · Abby and Sam are playing chess. · Three crabs are walking on the beach. · A seal is sleeping.

3 Reading, writing and running (-ing forms)

a) Look at the table. What is different about the spelling of the -ing form in groups 2 and 3?

Group 1	Group 2	Group 3
read > reading	write > writing	run > running
...	...	...

➜ *GF 16 b: The present progressive (p.168)*

> **KV 21: Reading, writing and running** enthält die Tabelle sowie ein Wimmelbild, das die S schriftlich beschreiben.

b) Copy the table from a).
Add these words to the right group:

> arrive · come · get · give · go · laugh · play · sit · sleep · swim · take · win · work

Early finisher ➜ *p.139* (Early finisher: Die S lösen Rätsel.)

Group 1 (unverändert): go, laugh, play, sleep, work · Group 2 (letzter Buchstabe verschwindet): arrive, come, give, take · Group 3 (letzter Buchstabe verdoppelt): get, sit, swim, win

4 I'm not laughing. I'm singing.

(Present progressive: positive and negative statements)

◐ 28 a) Listen. What sounds do you hear?
Make two sentences for each sound:
one positive and one negative.

1 I ... (laugh). I ... (sing).
 I'm not laughing. I'm singing.
2 He ... (read). He ... (sleep).
3 She ... (walk). She ... (run).
4 They ... (play) tennis. They ... (swim).
5 We ... (eat). We ... (watch) TV.
6 She ... (play) the guitar. She ... (play) the piano.
7 I ... (feed) the dog. I ... (feed) the cat.
8 They ... (speak) English. They ... (speak) German.

b) Make positive and negative sentences about the people in the picture.

More help ➜ *p.136* (More help: Die korrekten Verbformen müssen in Lückensätze eingetragen werden.)

a) 2 isn't reading / is sleeping · 3 isn't walking / is running · 4 aren't playing / are swimming · 5 aren't eating / are watching · 6 isn't playing / is playing · 7 I'm not feeding / I'm feeding · 8 aren't speaking / are speaking

5 Today is different (Simple present and present progressive)

Finish the sentences with the right form of the verbs in brackets.

1 Silky usually (eat) ... crabs for breakfast, but today she (eat) ... fish.
 Silky usually eats ..., but today she's ...
2 Justin often (drink) ... milk for breakfast, but this morning he (drink) ... tea.
3 Sam often (walk) ... to school, but today he (ride) ... his bike.
4 Sam and Justin usually (sit) ... together in the canteen, but today Sam (sit) ... with Oliver.
5 Silky almost always (play) ... in the afternoon, but this afternoon she (sleep) ... on her rock.
6 Lucy and Maya often (ride) ... their bikes to the Hoe, but today they (go) ... by bus.

➜ **Workbook** 6 (p.67)

> **Language help**
>
> Use the simple present to talk about **routines**.
> In the summer, Lucy often **swims** at the Lido.
> Sam **plays** basketball at 3 pm on Thursdays.
> Justin usually **talks** to his dad at the weekend.
>
> Use the present progressive to say what somebody is doing now.
> Lucy and Maya **are swimming** at the Lido now.
> At the moment, Sam **is playing** basketball.
> It's 3 o'clock on Saturday. Justin **is talking** to his dad on Skype.

1 eats / is eating · 2 drinks / is drinking · 3 walks / is riding · 4 sit / is sitting · 5 plays / is sleeping · 6 ride / are going

Lernfeld S. 108–110: Die S können **Fotos zu Textteilen zuordnen** und über die **Gefühle von Personen** in einem Text sprechen.

1 ✋ On Lucy's phone 3 🔊 29

Holly:	Hi, Luce, do you want to play cards?
Lucy:	I can't. I'm working on a mini-**talk** for school.
Holly:	No, you aren't. You're looking at your mobile.
Lucy:	Yes, silly. My talk is about the sleepover at the aquarium. And my **sleepover** photos are on my mobile.
Holly:	Let me see. Here, give me your mobile. Right. <u>Are those kids really sleeping?</u>
Lucy:	<u>Yes, they are.</u> They're sleeping in front of an aquarium window.
Holly:	What's this? <u>Are you watching</u> the fish?
Lucy:	<u>No, we aren't.</u> We're watching a film about fish.
Holly:	How was it?
Lucy:	It wasn't **bad**.
Holly:	But where are the **sharks**? At the sleepover, you sleep with sharks, right?
Lucy:	Right.
Holly:	But there aren't any sharks.
Lucy:	Of course there are sharks! Look.

5

10

15

20

Holly:	At last! A shark! <u>What's that °diver doing?</u>
Lucy:	It's feeding time, so he's feeding the sharks.
Holly:	That's a scary job! Now, wait a minute, what's this? <u>Why are you pushing</u> that boy?
Lucy:	What boy?
Holly:	That **blond** boy. <u>Are you fighting</u> with him?
Lucy:	<u>No, I'm not.</u> That's my friend Sam. Abby took that photo. We're …
Holly:	Is that at the sleepover?
Lucy:	No, it isn't. Give me back my phone!
Holly:	No, let me look at these photos **first**. Oh, now you're running away from that boy.
Lucy:	Give me back my phone, Holly.
Holly:	No, these photos are fun. Here you're running away from that *blond* boy. And then you're pushing him onto the floor. Mum! Come and look at Lucy's photos! They're really **interesting**!

25

30

35

40

2 Did you get it?

a) 👥 Find lines in the text that go with the photos on Lucy's mobile.

> I think **line** … goes with photo 76. That's "Are those kids really sleeping?".

> Yes. And line … goes with photo 76 too.

photo 58: l. 37 · photo: 64: l. 27 · photo 70: l. 23 · photo 75: l. 13 · photo 76: l. 10

b) 👥 Look at the photo of Lucy and Holly. Find a line in the text that goes with it.
l. 35 or l. 39

c) Does Lucy want to show Holly her photos? Why? / Why not?
How is she feeling: angry, happy, worried, …?

Background file

The aquarium in Plymouth

The National Marine Aquarium in Plymouth is the **UK**'s **biggest** aquarium.
It has four main zones:

▍ **Plymouth Sound:** Sea life in the Plymouth area

▍ **British Coasts:** Sea life in all parts of Britain

▍ **Atlantic Ocean:** Sharks and Caribbean sea life

▍ **Blue Planet:** Sea life from every ocean and from Australia's Great Barrier Reef

Children at the National Marine Aquarium

The aquarium has a learning **centre** for children. Students are welcome at the centre.

Children between 6 and 12 can have birthday parties at the aquarium.

There are four sleepovers (Sleeping with sharks) every year. The sleepovers are in the school holidays.

> You can visit the aquarium. What would you like to see and do?
> Would you like to go to the sleepover? Say why / why not.

Sleeping with sharks – the programme

· Arrive at 7 pm
· Watch a 4D film
· Aquarium tour – see what fish do at night
· Games
· Midnight **snacks**
· Breakfast in the aquarium café
· Sleepover finishes at 9 am
· **Price**: £35

3 The aquarium in Plymouth

After school you tell a friend about the aquarium. Finish your dialogue.

A: Es gibt vier Abteilungen, zum Beispiel über das Meeresleben in der Gegend um Plymouth.
B: Geht's da nur um Plymouth?
A: Nein, es gibt auch …
B: Bieten sie etwas Besonderes für Kinder?
A: Ja, sie haben dort … Und nachts …

More help ➜ p.136

➜ SF 10: Mediation (p.155)

More help: Die S finden hier deutschsprachige Hilfen.

B: Eine Übernachtung im Aquarium?
A: Ja, das heißt „Sleeping with sharks", weil …
B: Und das kann man jede Nacht machen?
A: Nein, …
B: Und was macht man da genau?
A: Du kannst …

➜ **Workbook** 7 (p.67)

… Abteilungen über den Atlantik, die britische Küste oder das Great Barrier Reef. · … ein Schülerzentrum und Geburtstagspartys. Und nachts kann man da schlafen. · … du da nachts Haie beobachten kannst. · …, nur in den Ferien. · … einen Film in 4D gucken oder eine Tour machen.

> **KV 22: Are you fighting?**
> bietet Bildkarten zu *Miming activities.*

Language help

In the present progressive, you use the verb *be* in questions and short answers.

Am I smiling?	Yes, **you are.** No, **you aren't.**	Are we working?	Yes, **we are.** No, **we aren't.**
Are you swimming?	Yes, **I am.** No, **I'm not.**	Are they singing?	Yes, **they are.** No, **they aren't.**
Is he/she/it drinking?	Yes, **he/she/it is.** No, **he/she/it isn't.**		

➡ *GF 16c: The present progressive (p.169)*

1 Is he drinking? (Present progressive: questions)

👥 Partner B: Go to page 141.
Partner A: Ask what's happening in pictures 1–3.
You can use verbs from the box.

A: In picture 1: is the boy drinking?
B: No, he isn't.
A: Well, is he …?

> dance · drink · eat · look for · make · play · read · sing · text · write

Partner A: Go to page 205.   Partner B: Ask what's happening in pictures 4–6.

2 Where is he going? (Present progressive: questions)

Sam and his sister Lily are watching a film. Lily has lots of questions. Finish them.
Use Where, What and Who.

Sam: That's Captain Goldfinger, Lily. He's bad! He's going to the harbour now.

Lily: Sorry Sam, (go) …? Where is he …?

Sam: To the harbour. And look! A policeman is following Goldfinger.

Lily: (follow) … Goldfinger?

Sam: A policeman. Hey, there's Goldfinger's team. They're meeting on that boat.

Lily: (meet) …?

Sam: On the green boat.

Lily: Oh no, it's Goldfinger, Sam. (give) … them?

Sam: A CD – with <mark>important</mark> information. Hey! The policeman is swimming to the boat.

Lily: (swim) …?

Sam: To the boat. Oh, Lily, it's 8 o'clock – time for you to go to bed.

Where is he going? · Who is following Goldfinger? · Where are they meeting? · What is he giving them? · Where is he swimming to?

➡ **Workbook** *8–9 (pp. 68–69)*

3 WORDS Adjectives

a) Make five pairs of opposites from the adjectives in the box.

> big · black · bright · dark · happy · long · sad · short · small · white

small – big · happy – sad ·
bright – dark · black – white ·
long – short

b) Match the adjective pairs to the picture.

c) Say what's happening in the pictures. Use adjectives.

A **small** shark is following a ... shark. ... big ... · A happy crab is talking to a sad crab. · A bright fish is dancing with a dark fish. · A black fish is jumping over a white fish. · A long fish is talking to a short fish.

➜ **Workbook** *10 (p. 69)*

4 Signs 🏴󠁧󠁢󠁥󠁮󠁧󠁿

a) 👥   You're on a visit to Plymouth. Some of your friends don't understand the signs. Explain in German what they mean. Take turns.

> Wenn vorhanden, kann L eigene Schilder oder Fotos von Schildern im Schulumfeld mitbringen.

1 This Way To *Fish Restaurant*

2 Big Wheel of Plymouth
Prices:
Adults: £8
Children under 16: £5
Infants (1 year and under): FREE

3 THE LIDO PLYMOUTH
Summer opening times
Mon–Sun: 10 am to 6 pm
Wed: 10 am to 7.30 pm

4 Shark feeding time 11 am

5 DO NOT FEED THE SEAGULLS

6 NO BICYCLES SKATEBOARDERS ROLLERBLADERS

1 Zum Fischrestaurant geht es da lang. · 2 Das Big Wheel kostet £8 für Erwachsene, £5 für Kinder (unter einem Jahr umsonst). · 3 Sommeröffnungszeiten des Lido: Mo.–So., 10–18 Uhr (Mi. bis 19:30 Uhr). · 4 Haifütterung: 11 Uhr. · 5 Möwen nicht füttern. · 6 Radfahren, Skateboarden und Rollschuhfahren verboten.

b) 👥   You have some English visitors. They don't understand the signs. Explain in English what they mean. Take turns.

TIP

When you don't know an English word, try to find another word. Like this:

You don't know *ausziehen*?
Schuhe ausziehen! is ==the same as==
Du darfst keine Schuhe tragen!
In English:
You can't wear your shoes.

7 Bitte Schuhe ausziehen! Danke!

8 Bitte ziehen Sie eine Nummer und warten Sie, bis Sie aufgerufen werden

9 Kein Trinkwasser

10 Tauben füttern verboten!

11 Fahrradabstellen ist verboten!

12 FOTO-VERBOT

13 Hände waschen nicht vergessen!

More help ➜ *p.137*

➜ **Workbook** *11 (p. 69)*

More help: Die S ordnen die Schilder vorgegebene Satzenden sowie *You can't / You have to* zu.

You can't: 7 ... wear your shoes. · 9 ... drink the water. · 10 ... feed the birds. ·
11 ... put your bike here. · 12 ... take pictures.
You have to: 8 ... take a number and wait. · 13 ... wash your hands.

5 Part C

Lernfeld S. 112: Die S können Lese- oder Hörtexten **einzelne Informationen entnehmen,** indem sie sagen können, was auf einer Listen von **Aussagen zum Text** wahr oder falsch ist.

1 ✋ Partners

Box "Unregelmäßige Vergangenheitsformen", Voc, S. 203

3 ▷ 30 After lunch on Thursday, Sam walked to the next lesson with Justin.

"What's your poster about?" he asked.

"Poster?" said Justin. "What poster?"

5 "We have to make a poster about our favourite place by the sea – and give a mini-talk! Remember?"

"Oh, that poster," Justin said. "Er … I do**n't** know **yet**."

10 "Miss Bell says we can work with a partner," Sam told him. "Do you want to be my partner?"

"OK. Let's give a talk about Cawsand then," Justin said. "I really liked it

15 there."

"Good idea," Sam **agreed**,

"Cawsand and **smugglers** …"

"Smugglers?" Justin asked.

"Yes, there were lots of smugglers

20 in Cawsand. I know that because I saw a sign about it in the **village**."

"But I know nothing about smuggling," Justin said.

"That's all right, Justin. I have a

25 book about smuggling at home," Sam said. "We can work at my house on Saturday."

"Saturday? Yes, why not?"

❖

3 ▷ 31 On Saturday, Justin and Sam looked at Sam's

30 book. Justin **pointed to** a picture of a woman.

"She looks funny. How can she be so **fat**?"

"She isn't really fat. She looks fat because she's smuggling something **under** her clothes," Sam **explained**.

35 "That's **clever**. Let's use that picture then," said Justin.

"Well, maybe," said Sam. "But what can we talk about? We have to know what our mini-talk is about before we make the poster."

40 "All right," said Justin. "But we have to use that picture on our poster. It's so good. Or **draw** a picture like it."

"OK," Sam said. "So let's work on our talk first. Then …"

45 "… then we make a poster for the talk," Justin **went on**, "and find more good pictures for it."

2 Right or wrong?

Are these statements right or wrong? Correct the wrong ones.

Alternative: Die S arbeiten mit einem Tandembogen, der in der Mitte gefaltet wird, in PA und können sich so gegenseitig korrigieren. Überprüfung im Plenum.

1 Justin and Sam have to give a mini-talk about Plymouth.

2 They have to make a poster for their mini-talk.

3 Sam asked Justin to be his partner.

4 It was Justin's idea to give a talk about Cawsand.

5 It was Justin's idea to talk about smugglers.

6 Justin said, "I know a lot about smuggling."

7 The two boys met at Justin's home on Saturday.

8 They looked for information in a book.

9 There was a picture of a fat woman in the book.

10 It was Sam's idea to use the picture of the woman for the poster.

1 They have to give a mini-talk about their favourite place by the sea. · 2–4 Right · 5 It was Sam's idea. · 6 He said: "But I know nothing about smuggling." · 7 They met at Sam's house. · 8 Right · 9 The woman wasn't fat. She smuggled something under her clothes. · 10 It was Justin's idea.

Lernfeld S. 113: Die S können anhand einer **Liste von Merkmalen** sagen, was ein **gutes Poster** ist und was noch verbessert werden kann.

3 The poster

CAWSAND

⌁ Our favourite place by the sea ⌁

- Cawsand is a village near Plymouth with a great beach.
- Lots of **tourists** go there by ferry. It's only 30 minutes from the Barbican.

Cawsand today

- 18th and 19th **centuries**: **lonely** villages like Cawsand were great places for smuggling.
- Smugglers' ships arrived with tea, pepper and other **expensive goods**.
- Smugglers sold their goods in Plymouth.

Cawsand – a really cool place!

Smugglers often **hid** goods in their clothes.

4 Poster **check**

a) 👥 Say what you like about Sam and Justin's poster.

b) 👥 Now use this list to check Sam and Justin's poster. What is good? How can they make it better? *Almost everything is there. They forgot the names of the authors.*

A good poster has:
- a title
- a **subtitle**
- important information only
- different colours
- pictures with captions
- names of **authors**

OK, there's a title.

Yes, the title is CAWSAND.

5 The mini-talk 🎧 3 ▸ 32

a) In their mini-talk, Sam and Justin give extra information about Cawsand. Listen. Which of these points do they talk about? Write down the numbers.
1. what you can see on Cawsand Beach
2. what tourists do at Cawsand
3. where you can eat at Cawsand
4. how often smugglers came to Cawsand
5. how smugglers took their goods to Plymouth
6. why smugglers smuggled tea and pepper

b) 👥 Say which numbers you wrote down and why.
Justin talks about number 1. He says …

Then listen again and check.

Lernfeld S. 114: Die S können in einer Textvorlage Substantive durch **Pronomina** ersetzen. Sie können Sätze in der richtigen **Wortreihenfolge** schreiben (SVO).

1 Sam showed him the book (Pronouns)

a) Copy the table and add the missing pronouns.

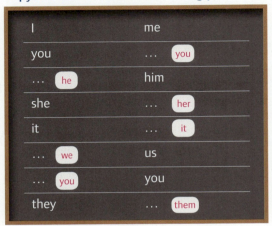

I	me
you	... you
... he	him
she	... her
it	... it
... we	us
... you	you
they	... them

b) Use pronouns for the <u>underlined</u> words.

1 Justin arrived at Sam's house at 10 o'clock.
Sam showed <u>Justin</u> the smuggling book.
Sam showed him the book.
2 Sam found some blue <mark>paper</mark> for their poster.
<u>Sam</u> put <u>the paper</u> on the kitchen table.
3 Mrs Bennett came into the kitchen.
Justin said good morning to <u>Mrs Bennett</u>.
4 Justin found some nice photos of Cawsand.
<u>Justin</u> looked at <u>the photos</u> with Sam.
5 Mr Bennett made some sandwiches.
"Are they for <u>Justin and me</u>?" Sam asked.
6 "Yes," said Mr Bennett.
"<u>The sandwiches</u> are for <u>Justin and you</u>."

2 He / it · 3 her · 4 He / them ·
5 us · 6 They / you

Early finisher Write three sentence pairs like in b). Leave out the pronouns.
Then find a partner. Can he/she write in the right pronouns?

➔ **Workbook** 12 (p. 70)

2 They smuggled pepper (Word order)

Language help

The word order in English sentences is:
S(ubject) – **V(erb)** – **O(bject)**
They   smuggled   pepper.

! **The word order in English sub-clauses is also S-V-O:**

They smuggled pepper because	they	needed	money.
Sie schmuggelten Pfeffer, weil	sie	Geld	brauchten.

S V O – that's like
Straßen**V**erkehrs**O**rdnung!

➔ *GF 17: Word order (pp.169–170)*

a) Join the sentences with the word in brackets.

1 Justin wanted to give a talk about Cawsand.
He really liked it there. (*because*)
Justin wanted to give a talk about Cawsand
because he really liked it there.
2 Sam knew a lot about smugglers.
He had a book about them at home. (*because*)
3 Justin went to Sam's house on Saturday.
They wanted to work on the poster. (*because*)
4 The students asked questions.
Sam and Justin finished their mini-talk. (*when*)
5 Sam and Justin were happy.
Their mini-talk was over. (*when*)

2 ... because he had a book about them at home. ·
3 ... because they wanted to work on the poster. ·
4 ... when Sam and Justin finished their mini-talk. ·
5 ... when their mini-talk was over.

b) Write the sentences in the right word order.

1 Morph – lives – in the library, – where – he – lots of books – read – can.
2 He – likes – English – because – it – a – cool language – is.
3 The Plymstock students – never see – Morph – because – he – in the day – sleeps.
4 He – gets up – when – the students – at home – are.
5 He hides – when – he – the school cat – sees.

Early finisher Write one more sentence in the wrong order. Then find a partner.
Can he/she put it in the right order?

➔ **Workbook** 13 (p. 70)

1 Morph lives in the library, where he can read lots of books. · 2 He likes English because it
a cool language. · 3 The Plymstock students never see Morph because he sleeps in the day
4 He gets up when the students are at home. · 5 He hides when he sees the school cat.

> **Lernfeld S. 115:** Die S können nach vorgegebenen Merkmalen ein **Poster erstellen** und dazu mit vorbereiteten Phrasen **einen kurzen Vortrag halten**.

3 Study skills: Preparing and giving a mini-talk

You have to prepare a mini-talk about your favourite character from this book. Follow these steps:

a) Collect information about your character.
   Use the profile in your MyBook and think about these things:
   - your character's home
   - age
   - family and friends
   - likes and dislikes
   - hobbies, activities, clubs
   - school
   ➜ SF 2: Collecting information (pp. 149–150)

b) Make a poster about your favourite character.
   - Give your poster a title.
   - Use the information from a) and write about your character (keywords only).
   - Write in big letters so that everyone can read the poster.
   - Look through the book. Choose and copy your favourite pictures of your character.
   - Write captions for your pictures.
   - Put the title, texts, pictures and captions on your poster.
   ➜ SF 3: Putting a page together (pp. 150–151)

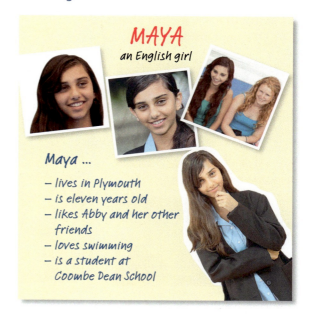

MAYA
an English girl

Maya ...
– lives in Plymouth
– is eleven years old
– likes Abby and her other friends
– loves swimming
– is a student at Coombe Dean School

c) 👥 Give a mini-talk for one minute about your favourite character to your group. Your poster and the box on the right can help you.

You can use these phrases:
   - My favourite character is …
   - I like him/her because …
   - It was funny/interesting/exciting/sad/… when he/she …
   - I was angry/happy when …

> **Study skills**
>
> ### Giving a (mini-)talk
>
> 1 Steh auf, atme tief durch und zähle bis 3, bevor du anfängst.
> 2 Schau deine Zuhörer an, wenn du sprichst.
> 3 Sprich langsam, laut und deutlich.
> 4 Wenn du den Faden verloren hast, fang nochmal neu an.
> ➜ SF 6: Giving a mini-talk (p.153)

d) 👥 Make a copy of the table and fill it with smileys: ☺ ☺ ☹. Say what you liked about the mini-talks and what your partners can do better next time. Then listen to your partners' feedback.

	You looked at us when you talked.	We could hear you.	Your talk was interesting.	Your talk was easy to understand.
Lukas	☹	☺	☺	☺
Cem	☺			
Lena				

e) Who is your group's favourite character? Tell the class.

➜ **Workbook** 14 (p. 71)

1 A ferry trip to Cawsand

a) You're on the ferry to Cawsand.
What can you see?

b) Watch the film and put photos A–F
in the right order. D · F · C · E · A · B

A · B · C · D · E · F

c) Match the photos with these captions:

D | Welcome to Cawsand ferry!   F | Buy your ticket on the ferry.   C | Cawsand Beach from the ferry

A | A walk in Cawsand village   B | Hello Plymouth!   E | Be careful when you get off!

2 EVERYDAY ENGLISH Making plans

a) Watch the film.
What are the children's ideas for a trip?
Where do they decide to go?

– Jack wants to go …
They decide to go to Wembury Beach.

Jack: Lido first, then Cawsand Beach; doesn't want to go to Wembury Beach · Ruby: Wembury Beach · Oliver: doesn't want to go to the Lido

Jack   Oliver   Ruby

3 ▸ 3

b) **Think**: Write the name of two fun places
in your hometown.

👥 **Pair**: Talk to a partner. Give reasons why you like or don't like the different places.
Agree on one place. Use the phrases in the box.

> What about …? · I agree. · I don't agree with you. · Yes, you're right. ·
> I like / love swimming / sailing / playing / … · How do we get there? · That isn't a good idea. ·
> That's a great idea. · OK, let's go to …

EXTRA 👥 **Share**: Work in groups of four. Agree on one place.
Tell the class where your group wants to go.

Lernfeld S. 117: Die S können **Wörter, die gleich klingen**, aber unterschiedlich geschrieben werden, **richtig schreiben**. Sie können Wörter, die zwar die **gleiche Buchstabenfolge enthalten**, aber unterschiedlich ausgesprochen werden, **richtig aussprechen**.

1 You say, you write ... [ðeə]

a) These words all sound the same.

their [ðeə]   there [ðeə]   they're [ðeə]

But they don't mean the same.
Finish these sentences with the right word.
You have to use one word twice.

1 Let's go to Cawsand. It's really exciting ...
2 Sam and Justin made a poster for ... mini-talk.
3 Tea and pepper were expensive in the 18th century but today ... cheap.
4 ... are four areas in the aquarium in Plymouth.

1 there · 2 their · 3 they're · 4 There

b) Finish the text. Put in their, there or they're.

Silky loves Plymouth Sound. She lives ... all year. Seals are very clever animals. In Britain, ... are two different kinds of seals: grey seals and <mark>common seals</mark>. Silky is a grey seal. Grey seals find ... food at sea and catch fish .... They use ... <mark>flippers</mark> to swim. ... very good swimmers – they can swim when ... only three or four hours old. When ... on <mark>land</mark>, they walk on ... flippers.

➡ **Workbook** 15 (p. 72)

there · there · their · there · their ·
They're · they're · they're · their

2 Spell with Morph

3 ▷ 34 **a)** Listen to Morph. He reads ten sentences. He asks you to write one word from each sentence.

group · students ·
book · boat · board ·
brother · floor · water ·
food · took

b) 👥 Check your words with your partner. Decide on the right spelling.

3 Same letters, different sounds

a) Finish the words in 1–6.

1 f_nd · w_n · T-sh_rt
   find, win, T-shirt
2 b_by · c_r · m_p · s_w
3 p_t · r_ler · _mbrella
4 f__r · gr__p · h__se · t__ch · y__r
5 br__kfast · gr__t · s__l · w__r
6 m_nkey · sh_p · t_wer · tr_phy

2 baby, car, map, saw ·
3 put, ruler, umbrella ·
4 four, group, house, touch, your ·
5 breakfast, great, seal, wear ·
6 monkey, shop, tower, trophy

More help ➡ p.137

More help: Die fehlenden Buchstaben sind in einer Box vorgegeben.

▷ 35 **b)** Now say the words.
Then listen and check.

Neigungsdifferenzierung: Die S wählen zwischen einer Übung für eher extrovertierte S und einer für S, die lieber still für sich arbeiten.

c) **You choose** Do i) or ii).

i) 👥 Choose two words from a).
Mime the words for the group.
Can they guess and spell the two words?

Umbrella?

Umbrella: That's U – M – ...

ii) Write a short story. Use ten words from a).

PLAY The pepper smugglers

Scene 1: [3] 36

The kitchen at the Red Lion, Cawsand.

Molly: Cook! Come and look! There are three smugglers in the dining room!

Cook: Don't be silly, Molly! They're just poor
5   farmers. I know them: that's Tom White, and the others are Jack Hill and Old Bill.

Molly: But look, they're drawing maps and plans. They're pepper smugglers, Cook, and my brother Flynn wants to work with
10   them.

Cook: They *were* farmers, Molly. But they had to sell their farms to Mr Collings.

Molly: Yes, but …

Cook: And then Mr Collings took away your
15   parents' farm too! Now he's rich and we're all poor.

Molly: But …

Cook: That isn't right, my girl. That isn't right.

(Flynn comes in. He looks excited.)

20 Flynn: Come, sister, dance with me! *(They dance.)* Soon you can have your new dress.

Molly: But I don't want a new dress! You can't go with those men, Flynn! Please …

25 Flynn: I have to go, Molly – I don't want to be poor all my life. We have a great plan. But there isn't much time. Please come and help me.

Molly: But …

30 Cook: Go and help your brother! I don't need you here. Good luck!

(Molly and Flynn go out.)

Scene 2: [3] 37

Cawsand Beach at night. Tom, Jack, Flynn and Old Bill wait for the ship with their pepper.
35 *Mr Collings watches from a hill.*

Flynn: Tom, someone is watching us.

Tom: *(He holds up his lamp.)* Where?

Flynn: On the hill there. *(He points.)*

Tom: Where? There's no one on the hill, Flynn.
40   Your eyes are playing games with you.

Jack: Look! Did you see the blue light from the sea?

Tom: Yes, that's the sign. The ship from France is here with our pepper.

45 Jack: Come on, then, let's go!

(They go to the ship in their boat. Men from the ship throw bags to Flynn and Tom.)

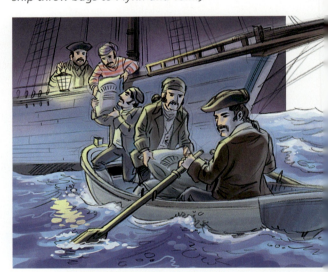

Tom: This is hard work, my boy. But we can sell the pepper for lots of money
50   in Plymouth.

Bill: Hurry up, boys! Put the bags in the cart.

(They take the bags of pepper to the cart.)

Jack: Come on, boys! Morning is coming.

Tom: OK, Jack, that's the last bag.
55 Bill: Good. Now to Tom's house!

Scene 3: [3] 38

In Tom's kitchen. Molly and Flynn put the bags of pepper into boxes.

Flynn: Now hide the pepper under these potatoes. Like that, yes.

60 Molly: *(She hides the bags.)* Mr Collings was at the Red Lion last night. And he knows about your plans.

Flynn: Oh, that's silly, Molly. Mr Collings never goes to the Red Lion.

65 Molly: But it's true! Collings wants to stop you. He's ==dangerous==, Flynn, and he has a ==sword==.

Flynn: Don't try to stop me, Molly, please!

(Jack arrives.)

70 Jack: The others are ready, my boy. Take the boxes outside.

(Five minutes later.)

Flynn: This is the last box. ==Goodbye==, Molly.

(He tries to give Molly a hug. Molly pushes him
75 *away and runs outside.)*

Scene 4:   3 ▶ 39

Tom's boat at Cawsand Beach. Molly arrives.
She hides in the boat. Flynn and Tom arrive.
They carry the boxes of potatoes onto the boat.

Tom: Flynn, are you ready? We're going to the
80 ==market== in Plymouth.

Flynn: I'm ready.

Tom: OK, let's go.

(Mr Collings arrives with his sword and ==points it at==
Flynn.)

85 Mr C: No, you can't go to Plymouth – it's ==prison== for you! I know what's in the boxes. You're smugglers! Now move! Out of the boat!

Flynn: Mr Collings! So, *you* were on the hill
90 yesterday! Tom, what can we do?

(Molly throws potatoes onto the deck. Mr Collings
==falls==. He gets up again. He still has his sword. Molly
gets up and throws pepper into his face.)

Molly: Your family took away our farm, but you
95 can't take more away.

Mr C: Ah – ah – aaaah – choo!

(Mr Collings ==sneezes== and Tom takes his sword.)

Flynn: Now you get off our boat!

(Mr Collings jumps off the boat. Tom throws the
100 *sword after him.)*

Tom: What you can't do with a sword, you can do with pepper.

(They all laugh. Flynn gives Molly a hug.)

Flynn: To the market! Let's go to Plymouth!

1 New words

Here are eight new words. Find them in the play.

> farmer · rich · good luck · light ·
> market · sword · deck · sneeze

l. 11 · l. 15 · l. 31 ·
l. 41 · ll. 80, 104 ·
ll. 67, 97, 100 ·
l. 91 · l. 97

Are they like any German words you know?
Farmer · reich · (viel) Glück · Licht · Markt · Schwert · Deck · niesen

2 The four scenes

a) Choose the best title for the first scene.
1 Look, Cook, look!
2 A new dress for Molly
3 At the Red Lion

b) Now write titles for the other three scenes.

c) Make a programme for the play. List your titles for each scene.

> **KV 23: A theatre programme** bietet eine Mustervorlage für ein Theaterprogramm.

3 Your play

> **Neigungsdifferenzierung:** Die S wählen zwischen zwei unterschiedlichen kreativen Übungen.

You choose   Do a) or b).

a) 👥 Make a group of seven students. Choose your actors. Learn the play.

Think about each scene. What can you use as a kitchen, the beach, the smugglers' boat, …?
Act out the play for your class.

b) Draw a comic strip for each scene in the play. Use speech bubbles and captions to show the story.

→ **Workbook** 16 *(p. 72)*

Workbook Checkpoint 5 *(pp. 74–77)*

> Es bietet sich an, im Anschluss an die Arbeit mit dem SB mit den S eine **Lektüre** zu lesen.

Your task

Step 1–4 können als vorbereitende Hausaufgabe durchgeführt werden, an die sich in der Folgestunde die Gruppenarbeit in **Step 5** anschließt. Es bietet sich aber auch an, die Selbsteinschätzung ausführlich mit den S im Plenum zu besprechen.

Yes, come and see us in Plymouth. Maybe you can find me in the school library.

Let's go to Plymouth

You want to go to Plymouth in the summer holidays.
In German, explain to your parents why it is a good idea.

STEP 1
Look at the flyer on this page.
What's interesting for your parents?

STEP 2
What other places in Plymouth are interesting for your parents?
Look back through your English book and find information.

STEP 3
Collect the information in a mind map or table and put it into your My Book.

STEP 4
Think about how you can tell your parents in German all about the great things to do in Plymouth. Don't translate word for word. Just explain the important information.

STEP 5
Imagine the students in your group are your parents. Explain in German why a trip to Plymouth is a great idea.

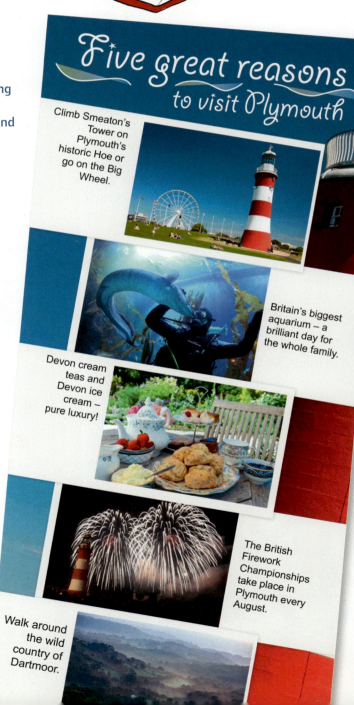

Five great reasons to visit Plymouth

Climb Smeaton's Tower on Plymouth's historic Hoe or go on the Big Wheel.

Britain's biggest aquarium – a brilliant day for the whole family.

Devon cream teas and Devon ice cream – pure luxury!

The British Firework Championships take place in Plymouth every August.

Walk around the wild country of Dartmoor.

OK, so I make mistakes. But I can learn from my mistakes.

Das lief nicht gut, ich muss mehr üben.

Das war OK, aber ich könnte besser werden.

Das habe ich gut geschafft.

Wie gut warst du?

Wie schätzt du dich selber ein? Schreibe *Ideas, Organizing information* und *Mediation* in dein Heft und ordne dir für jeden Bereich eine Ampelfarbe zu.

Ideas

· Wie viele Ideen hast du gefunden, die Plymouth für deine Eltern interessant machen würden – und nicht nur für dich?

Organizing information

· Welche Organisationsform hast du verwendet: Mindmap oder Tabelle?
Wie gut hat das geklappt?

Mediation

· Wie einfach war es, nur die wichtigsten Informationen auf Deutsch wiederzugeben? Oder hast du doch einfach alles übersetzt?

Wie kannst du besser werden?

Wenn du dich eher rot oder gelb eingeschätzt hast, helfen dir folgende Tipps beim Wiederholen und Üben.

Ideas

Blättere nochmal durch dein Englischbuch, um interessante Informationen über Plymouth zu finden.
Hör dir die Vorträge deiner Mitschüler und Mitschülerinnen an. Welche ihrer Ideen waren gut?

Organizing your information

Im *Skills File* findest du Hilfe, um Mindmaps und Tabellen zu erstellen.

➡ *SF 2: Collecting information (S. 149–150)*

Oder du schaust dir die *Study skills* in Unit 3 wieder an.

➡ *U3, S. 62*

Mediation

Tipps für Mediation findest du im *Skills File*.

➡ *SF 10: Mediation (S.155)*

Schau dir auch die Mediation-Aufgaben in Units 3–5 wieder an.

➡ *U3, 1 S. 70; U4, 5 S. 95; U5, 6 S. 111*

Hier findest du die Fortsetzung unserer Geschichte 'My home, the zoo'.

My home, the zoo – Part 2

My birthday party

Well, I did it. I asked twelve kids to my birthday party. I used the Stockbridge Zoo birthday invitation. It has a picture of King Tut
5 on the front and it says, "Come to my birthday party". Inside it says: "Let's have a roaring good time!"

Everybody arrived at 11 am. We met them at the gate. Then Dad took us on a special tour of
10 the zoo. We fed the otters and watched Tom the zookeeper feed the lions. At 12.30, we had lunch at the restaurant: pizza and cola. Tom came out of the kitchen with a big birthday cake. He sang "Happy birthday" and
15 everybody sang along. Then Tom gave me a hug. One of my friends asked, "Is he your uncle or something?"

At the Learning Centre, I held Suzie the boa constrictor without help from my mum. Suzie
20 kissed my face and wrapped her tail around my hand.

"Wow! That snake loves you!" said Jeff.

At the end of the day, I said goodbye to all the kids and gave them party bags with chocolate
25 and cards with photos of different animals.

A girl from my class asked me where I live.

Megan shouted, "We live here, of course! I was born in the zoo!"

Megan pointed to a building.

30 "See," she said, "that's our house there."

My friends heard her and looked at me in a strange way.

"So it's true," said one girl. "You live in the zoo. That's so cool!"

35 The surprise

That night Mum made my favourite dinner, beef curry. Tom was there too.

After dinner, Dad said, "Now it's time for your surprise, Luke. Somebody is waiting for you.
40 Come on, let's go."

The zoo wasn't open, but the lights were on. We took the "safari path" between King Tut and the monkeys.

Then I saw him – Raj had a black cloth on his
45 back. On his head were lines of red and gold paint.

We climbed over the fence. Next came the hard part: How could I climb onto Raj's back? It wasn't easy but Raj helped me. He went down
50 onto his knees, and I climbed up one of his legs and then moved over his back and sat just behind his ears. Raj knew I was ready and stood up. I was so high! Sheba stood by the small pool with Omar. Raj took a few steps and
55 I almost fell down!

"Hold onto his ears, Luke!" Tom shouted. Raj went to the pool and sucked water up through

---

l. 9 **gate** [geɪt] Tor · l. 20 (to) **kiss** [kɪs] küssen · l. 20 (to) **wrap** [ræp] wickeln · l. 20 **tail** [teɪl] Schwanz ·
l. 44 **cloth** [klɒθ] Tuch · l. 46 **paint** [peɪnt] Farbe · l. 50 **knee** [niː] Knie

his trunk. First he sprayed water on his son Omar. He sucked up more water and moved his
60 trunk to his mouth for a drink. But, suddenly he had a new idea. He moved his trunk up and sprayed the water onto his back – and onto me! I was wet from head to foot. But I loved it. This birthday present was the best in my whole life.

65 Everybody knows

I was at school early the next day. I went to my desk and got out my books for the first lesson. Usually everybody is noisy and tells jokes before the teacher comes, but that day, the kids
70 were quiet. They just watched me.

Then Jeff asked, "Can I hold Suzie the next time I come to the zoo?"

Then came more questions:
  "How old is the baby elephant?"
75 "Can I come to your house at the weekend?"
  "Yeah, me too?"
  "And can I feed the otters?"
  "Can you take animals into your house?"

I felt like a celebrity … and I didn't like it at all.
80 But then our teacher came in, and all the kids went back to their desks.

Things were really bad at lunchtime. Kids from other classes heard the news too, and there was a big group around me. They asked so
85 many questions that I had no time to eat my lunch.

The snake gang

The next week, everything was back to normal – or that's what I thought. On Friday afternoon, Mum was late. I played a game on
90 my mobile phone and waited for her at the school gate.

Then four Year 8 boys came towards me.

"Look, it's Tarzan," one of them said. "He lives in the zoo with all the other monkeys. Ha, ha,
95 ha."

I don't like it when people laugh at their own jokes. I knew that boy. It was Robbie, the brother of a girl in my class.

"He likes to hold snakes. Right, Tarzan?" said
100 Robbie.

"Everybody can do it," I said. "Boas don't hurt people. But you have to hold them in the right way, or …"

"Or what?"

105 "They can strangle you," I said.

"Oh, is that right? You mean … like this?"

Suddenly Robbie's hands were around my neck. A second boy took the mobile phone from me.

110 "Hey! That's my mobile! Give it back!" I shouted. But the boy threw it to one of his friends. Robbie let me go, but the mobile went from boy to boy.

---

l.64 **whole** [həʊl] ganze(r, s) · l.79 **celebrity** [sə'lebrəti] berühmte Persönlichkeit · l.92 **towards sb.** [tə'wɔːdz] jm. entgegen · l.96 **own** eigene(r, s) · l.101 (to) **hurt sb.** [hɜːt] jm. wehtun, jn. verletzen · l.105 (to) **strangle** erdrosseln

It was an old mobile. I walked away. But they
115 followed me.

"Hey, where are you going, Tarzan?"

"What do you want from me?" I asked.

"We want your s-snake … sss …" he said.

"Snake?" I asked.

120 "The big s-snake … Suzie … sss," he said.
Robbie was not only scary, he was also very
strange.

"Why?" I asked.

"For our gang," said one of the other boys.
125 Then they showed me their arms under their
jackets. All four boys had a handmade snake
tattoo.

"We're the Snakes and we want your snake as
our mascot."

130 "But Suzie isn't my snake. She belongs to the
zoo!" I shouted.

"Maybe you didn't hear what I said, Tarzan. We
want that snake, OK?"

Then he pushed me onto the ground. Just then,
135 I heard my mother's voice. I got up and cleaned
the dirt off my uniform.

Robbie touched me on the back.

"Is this yours? It was on the ground," he said
and held out my mobile phone. I took it from
140 him and got into the car.

"See you tomorrow, Luke," Robbie said with a
big smile.

"Are you OK?" said Mum. "You're as white as a
ghost!"

145 "I'm fine, Mum," I said.

Robbie and his friends didn't leave me alone.
The next day they took my schoolbag. On
Wednesday they tried to put worms into my
lunch. And on Thursday they took my PE kit.
150 They also left me a note that said, "Bring us
Suzie tomorrow, or you're in trouble."

I didn't know what to do, so in the afternoon, I
told Tom the whole story.

"He wants Suzie, does he?" said Tom.

155 Then Tom gave me a really good idea. He said,
"Let Robbie meet Suzie. Real snakes are scary.
You know all about Suzie, but Robbie doesn't.
We can give him a nice surprise."

So on Friday morning, I told Robbie to meet me
160 at the gate of Stockbridge Zoo at 8 pm. "I can
show you how to hold Suzie," I said.

"Oh yeah? I know all that already," said
Robbie. "I just want that snake."

But he *was* there at 8 pm, with a big box. We
165 went to the reptile room in the Learning Centre.
Tom was there too, but he didn't say much. He
let me do everything myself. First I took Suzie
out of her cage. I wrapped her around my neck.
Her tail moved around my hand and she gave
170 me a friendly squeeze. Then she pushed out her
black tongue near my face. It tickled.

---

l.134 **ground** [graʊnd] Boden · l.136 **dirt** [dɜːt] Dreck · l.167 **myself** [maɪˈself] selbst ·
l.170 (to) **give sb. a squeeze** [skwiːz] jn. drücken · l.171 **tongue** [tʌŋ] Zunge · l.171 (to) **tickle** [ˈtɪkl] kitzeln

"Hey, let me try that!" said Robbie. He tried to take Suzie from me. I moved back just before he got her.

175 "You can't just grab her," I said. "She doesn't like that. Boas sometimes bite!"

I put one hand near her tail and my other hand near her head. Then I said, "OK, Robbie, just put her around your neck like a scarf. Like 180 this." I put her around Robbie's neck. Her little black tongue went in and out near Robbie's face.

At first Robbie thought it was really cool to hold her. But then Suzie moved around Robbie 185 – front and back.

"Hey she's squeezing me! Help! She's squeezing me to death! Take her away from me!"

I went to Robbie and took Suzie back. "She's not really trying to hurt you. She just wants to 190 know that you're not going to let her fall to the ground. It just feels strange the first time. You can try it again."

"No, not now," said Robbie.

"Do you know what boas eat, Robbie?" asked 195 Tom.

"Salad?" said Robbie.

"No, they eat mice and rats," I said.

"We feed her live rats. She only needs one a week. And I have good news: today is feeding 200 day."

I took a rat out of its cage and held it by its tail in front of Suzie's open cage. Suzie waited and then suddenly moved towards it.

But she didn't get it and the rat fell to the 205 ground. I don't know why, but the rat ran up Robbie's leg, around his neck and onto his back. Robbie jumped and shouted and tried to get the rat off his back.

Then he called "Help!". I think it was scary for 210 the rat too because it stayed just there, on Robbie's back, behind his head.So I grabbed its tail and pulled it off.

"Are you all right, Robbie?" I asked.

"Yeah, of course I'm all right. But it's late, and I 215 need to go home. Maybe Mum is worried. And listen, I don't think that I can take Suzie. My room isn't big enough. I also didn't know about the rats. Mum doesn't like rats. She doesn't want them in the house. So, I have to go home 220 now. You can keep the box."

I walked back to the gate with Robbie and said goodbye. There was never any trouble from him again.

The end

> KV 24: **The snake gang** enthält *scrambled sentences* zur Sicherung des Textverständnisses.

---

l.175 (to) **grab** [græb] greifen · l.179 **scarf** [skɑːf] Schal · l.198 **live** [laɪv] lebend, lebendig

125

Welcome to the book rally!

Schnallt euch an – jetzt geht's los! Aber lest zuerst die Spielregeln. Dann wisst ihr, wie die book rally funktioniert.

S T A R T

Die Spielregeln

1. Arbeite mit einem Partner.
2. Ihr habt maximal 20 Minuten um das Ziel der Rally zu erreichen. Beginnt bei Frage 1, folgt der Straße bis Frage Nummer 14.
3. Schreibt eure Antworten auf ein Blatt Papier.
4. Nach 20 Minuten tauscht ihr euer Blatt mit einem anderen Paar.
5. Vergleicht die Ergebnisse mit den richtigen Lösungen. Für jede richtige Lösung gibt es einen Punkt.
6. Notiert die Punktzahl auf dem Blatt eurer Mitschüler und gebt das Blatt zurück.

Das Paar mit den meisten Punkten hat gewonnen!

1 Die Kapitel deines Englischbuches heißen "Units". Wie viele Units hat dieses Buch? *5 (mit Here we go = 6)*

3 Wie heißen die Seiten, wo du Grammatikregeln nachschlagen kannst? *Grammar file*

2 Jede Unit enthält mindestens ein Background file zu einem Thema der Unit. Unit 4 hat zwei Background files. Wie heißt das zweite? *Grey seals*

4 Auf einer Übungsseite von Unit 2 findest du das Bild einer Schulbibliothek. Welche Farbe haben die Luftballons dort? *grün*

I can spell "car". Can you?

5 In einem Teil jeder Unit geht es um die englische Rechtschreibung. Wie lang ist dieser Teil? *eine Seite (Spelling course)*

9 Wie heißt der Teil am Ende einer jeden Unit, der eine spannende oder lustige Geschichte enthält?

Text

10 Auf einer Seite jeder Unit dreht sich alles um Film. Welche Seite ist das in Unit 1?

S. 31 (The world behind the picture)

8 In einem Bild in Unit 2 steht ein Mann neben einer Uhr. Wie spät ist es dort?

4 o'clock

11 Wie heißt die Geschichte, die du nach den Units 3 und 5 findest?

My home, my zoo

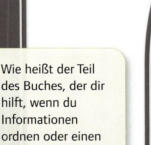

My mini-talk is …

7 Wie heißt der Teil des Buches, der dir hilft, wenn du Informationen ordnen oder einen kurzen Vortrag halten sollst?

Skills File

12 In welcher Unit kannst du lernen, etwas Englisches zu backen?

Unit 2 (Let's make scones)

What page are we on?

13 Auf einer Seite des Buches findest du Redewendungen für den Unterricht. Welche Seite ist das?

S. 236

Can you help me?

6 Welche Seiten des Buches enthalten die Wörter, die du von Unit 1 lernen sollst? Schreib die Seitenzahlen auf.

S. 178–184 (Vocabulary Unit 1)

What? Wrong? Oh, well – start again!

14 Nach Units 2 bis 5 gibt es jeweils 2 Seiten, auf denen du dich selbst einschätzen kannst. Wie heißen die Seiten?

Your task

F I N I S H

Part A Practice

7 Don't wear trainers

◀ p. 24

Make imperatives. Finish the sentences for the pictures.
Use the words from the box.

> forget · give · open · put ·
> talk · touch

1 ... ... the picture.

2 ... me the pen, please.

3 ... ... the rat in the bag.

4 ... ... the window.

5 ... ... your bag.

6 ... ... in the library.

Part B Practice

1 Yes, I am

◀ p. 27

b) Make questions for your partner.
   Use ideas from the box.

Is your mum at home?
Are you sad?

...

Is	your mum	from Berlin?
	your dad	friendly?
	your dog	at home?
	your ...	sad?
Are	you	British?
	your friends	in Year 5?
	...	...

6 A letter to Lucy

◄ *p. 28*

Copy the letter. Put in the right information.

Hi Lucy,
I'm at **<NAME OF YOUR SCHOOL>** – that's a school in **<YOUR TOWN>**.
The first lesson is at **<TIME>**.

There's a │ long │ break at **<TIME>**. There │ is │ a lunch break at our school.
          │ short │   │ isn't │

It's time to go home at **<TIME>**. Our school day │ is │ really long.
                                                     │ isn't │

My favourite subject is **<SUBJECT>** and I like **<SUBJECT>** too. School is │ nice │ .
Bye,   │ great │
<YOUR NAME>   │ cool │
                                                                              │ … │

┌─────────────────────┐
│ **Part C Practice** │
└─────────────────────┘

2 EVERYDAY ENGLISH Classroom English

◄ *p. 31*

a) Finish the sentences with the words from the box.

┌──────────────────────────────────────┐
│ can · do · go · open · page · sorry · spell · │
│ What's · window · work │
└──────────────────────────────────────┘

1 Please … your workbooks at page 15.
2 Can you … with Paul, please?
3 … I'm late.
4 What … are we on?

5 Miss, can I open the …?
6 I can't … number 3.
7 Paul, … you help Lisa, please?
8 Can I … to the toilet, please?
9 … for homework?
10 Can you … "Scotland", please?

4 GAME I can see …

◄ *p. 32*

Play the game.

Boris: I can see a yellow pencil.
Anne: Boris can see a yellow pencil and I can write English words.

Liu: Boris can see a yellow pencil, Anne can write English words and I can spell "cupboard".

You can use these ideas:

open the window	read a book	speak German	help my partner
ask questions	throw a ball	talk to my teacher	make appointments
catch a ball	sing a song	count to a hundred	write my profile

← p. 41

Part A Practice

4 Before school, after school (Simple present: positive statements)

b) Say what the kids do after school.

1 Abby (go) *goes* for a walk with Skip after school.
2 Maya (meet) … Lucy at the Broadway after school.
3 Sam (watch) … TV after school.
4 Justin (play) … computer games after school.
5 Lucy (help) … her mum in the kitchen after school.

5 A tour of Sam's house 💬

← p. 41

Sam shows Lucy his house. Finish his sentences and practise them with a partner.

> do · have (2x) · play · sit · throw · watch

1 Come into the kitchen. We have breakfast here.
2 This is the living room. Dad … TV here.
3 That's Mum's armchair. She … there in the evenings.
4 Look at the garden. My sister Lily … with her rabbit there.
5 Upstairs, now. That's Lily's room. Look, she … lots of toys.
6 And she always … them on the floor.
7 And this is my room. I … my homework here.

6 Study skills: Learning words with mind maps

← p. 42

b) Choose umbrella words for these word groups. 🎥 Check with a partner.

1 boy · girl · man · woman
2 blue · orange · purple · red
3 April · June · August · October
4 kitchen · bedroom · dining room · bathroom

> colours · house · months · people

Spelling course

2 Apostrophes again: 's and s' (The possessive form)

← p. 43

c) 🎥 Read the sentences about Abby's family.
Partner A: Choose the right word from the box. Spell it. Don't forget the apostrophe!
Partner B: Listen and write the word.

1 … family name is Blackwell.
  Abby's: that's A - double B - Y - apostrophe S.
2 The … house is in Wembury.
3 The … name is Skip.
4 … basket is near Abby's bed.

5 … sailing trophies are in her bedroom.
6 Abby says: "My new … name is Maya."

> Abby (2x) · Blackwells · friend · dog · Skip

3 A weekend at Grandma's farm (Simple present: positive and negative statements) ◀ p. 46

Finish the dialogue. Use positive and negative verbs.

Sam: Tell me about a weekend at your grandma's farm.
Lucy: Well, we (wake up) ... at 6 o'clock. Then we (feed) ... the dogs and the rabbits.
Sam: You and Holly?
Lucy: No, Holly (wake up) ... at 6 o'clock, so she (feed) ... the animals. I feed them with Grandpa.
Sam: Are there lots of animals?
Lucy: Well, we (have) ... horses.

Sam: What about elephants?
Lucy: No, Sam. We (have) ... elephants. The farm is in England, not in India.
Sam: OK, you (feed) ... the animals – and then?
Lucy: Then Grandma (make) ... breakfast. And after breakfast we (go) ... for a walk.
Sam: You and your sister Holly?
Lucy: No, Holly (come) ... with us. She (sleep) ... till 12 o'clock. I (go) ... with Grandma.

4 A weekend in the library

(Simple present: positive and negative statements)　　　　　　　　　◀ p. 46

a) Listen, copy and complete the sentences. Use the verbs in the box.

go · live · read · see · sit · sleep (2x)

1 Morph ... in a house. He ... in a library.
   He doesn't live in a house. He lives in a library.
2 Morph ... on a sofa. He ... on a shelf.
3 Morph ... in a bed. He ... on books.
4 The Plymstock students ... Morph every day. They ... the teachers.
5 Morph ... at night. He ... in the day.
6 The Plymstock students ... to school at weekends. They ... from Monday to Friday.
7 Morph ... French books at weekends. He ... English books.

3 There are 22 students in my class (my, your, his, …) ◀ p. 50

Sam and his family talk about people at Plymstock school.
Choose the right word to finish the sentences.

1 Sam: "There are 22 students in my class."
2 Dad: "Is my / your class teacher OK?"
3 Sam: "We like our / their class teacher. Your / Her name is Miss Bell."
4 Mum: "What are your / his. friends' names?"
5 Sam: "I have two good friends. Her / Their names are Justin and Lucy."
6 Sam: "Justin lives with his / our mum. His / My dad lives in Boston."
7 Sam: "Lucy lives with her / your mum too. And her / their grandma and grandpa have a farm. They have lots of animals on her / their farm."
8 Sam: "Lucy is sad. His / Her best friend Maya goes to a different school."

Part A Practice

4 GAME Guess who!

← Partner B (p. 61)

a) 👥 **Partner A:** Choose a name from the list. Don't tell your partner the name.
Partner B: Ask questions. The questions below can help you. Guess the name.

Abby	Morph
Justin	Sam
Lucy	Silky
Maya	

A: Guess who!
B: Is it a he?
A: Yes, it is.
B: Does he live in the library?
A: No, he doesn't.

B: Does he make video films?
A: Yes, he does.
B: Then it's Justin!
A: Right! Now you say a name.

Does she live in a big house?
Does she have piano lessons after school?
Does he film people and places?
Does he make jokes?

Does he live in the library?
Does she go to Coombe Dean School?
Does she have one brother?

Part B Practice

2 Sorry, I can't hear you (Simple present: questions with question words)

← p. 65

👥 It's very noisy. You can't hear your partner. Ask questions with what, when, where, or why.

1 I play football.
   A: Sorry, what do you play? B: Football!
2 On Saturday morning, I help my mum.
   A: Sorry, when …
3 On Sundays I get up at 10 o'clock.
   A: Sorry, when …

4 Then I go to the swimming pool.
   A: Sorry, where …
5 I like it there because I meet my friends.
   A: Sorry, why …
6 My friends all like swimming.
   A: Sorry, what …

3 What sport does Abby like?

← p. 65

a) Read the answers. Then finish the questions. Use words from the box.

food · films · games · shoes · sport · subjects

Question	Answer
1 What … does Abby like?	She likes sailing.
2 What … does Silky eat?	She eats fish and crabs.
3 What … do you play?	I play computer games.
4 What … do Plymstock students wear?	They wear black shoes.
5 What … do you watch?	I watch James Bond films.
6 What … do you like?	I like French and geography.

TIP
German: *Was für Bücher liest du?*
English: *What books do you read?*

b) 👥 Ask questions. *What books/films/food …?*

4 Do you know your partner? (Simple present: mixed questions)

← p. 66

a) Copy the table.
   Add your ideas about your partner.

b) 👥 Ask your partner the questions.
   Are your ideas right?

c) Write about your partner on a card.
   Don't write his/her name.

> This boy or girl lives in a house.
> He/She has ... brothers and ... sisters.
> His/Her mum/dad ... is from ...
> He/She goes to bed at ... o'clock.
> He/She likes ...
> His/Her hobbies are ... and ...
> He/She does ... and plays ...

Questions	Your ideas about your partner	Your partner's answers
Do you live in a house or a flat?		
... have any brothers or sisters?		
Where ... your mum and dad come from?		
When ... go to bed?		
What music ... like?		
What hobbies ... have?		
What sports ... do?		

Part C Practice

2 small letters, CAPITAL LETTERS

← p. 71

TIP

Use **small** letters for nouns – **c**amera, **c**lub, **h**ouse, etc.

an old **h**ouse
ein altes **H**aus

Read the tips about CAPITAL LETTERS. What's the same in German? What's different?

Use **CAPITAL LETTERS** for
- the word "I": My friend and I like basketball.
- **names:** Abby, Justin, Morph, Uncle Amar, ...
- **days and months:** Monday, Tuesday, ... April, May, ...
- **names of clubs, schools, etc.:** Plymstock School, Wembury Sailing Club, ...
- **cities:** Berlin, Boston, Plymouth, ...
- **countries:** England, Scotland, ...
- **country adjectives:** an English cat, a German cat, ...

a) Read the text and copy it.
   Use capital letters where you need them.

Hi! My name is Tom. I come ...

b) 👥 Check your partner's text.

hi! my name is tom. i come from wembury. that's near plymouth in england. i like sport. every thursday i go to judo and i play football at wembury football club every monday and friday. i like germany because my mother is german. her name is sabine and she comes from frankfurt. in july or august every year we visit my german uncle near frankfurt.

Part A Practice

2 💬 Was it fun?

← p. 83

c) 👥 Make your own dialogue about Saturday. Maybe you were at a castle, the cinema, a club, a farm, the gym, a museum, a shopping mall, ...

You can use these adjectives in your dialogue.

boring · cool · exciting · fantastic · funny · good · sad · scary · silly · strange · ...

A: I was at ... on Saturday.
B: Was it good/exciting/...?
A: Yes, it was. / No, it wasn't. It was ...
   Where were you on Saturday?
B: I was at ...
A: Was it ...?
B: Yes, ... / No, ...

TIP
Remember how you make short answers:
Was it fun? – Yes, it was.
Was it good? – No, it wasn't.

3 How was your weekend? (simple past of *be*: question words)

← p. 83

a) Read the dialogue between Jack and Oliver.
Finish it with question words from the box and was or were.

how · how · when · where · who · why

The words in blue can help you to find the right questions.

Jack: Hey Oliver! How was your weekend?
Oliver: My weekend was great.
Jack: Oh, ... you?
Oliver: I was at Katy's house.
Jack: Katy? Your cousin? ... you there?
Oliver: I was there because it was her birthday. There was a big party.
Jack: A party! ... it?

Oliver: On Sunday afternoon.
Jack: Oh, ... there?
Oliver: Well, Abby was there with her friend Maya. And there were lots of other cousins.
Jack: That sounds fun.
Oliver: So what about you? ... your weekend?
Jack It was OK, thanks.

Part B Practice

3 A visit from London (Simple past: positive statements, regular and irregular verbs)

← p. 87

b) Put in these verbs:

liked · saw · showed · visited · walked · wanted · went · went

On Saturday, the boys ... (1) into Plymouth by bus. Sam ... (2) Tom the Hoe and then they ... (3) swimming at the Lido. Later, Tom ... (4) to see old Plymouth, so they ... (5) around the Barbican for an hour. They ... (6) lots of old houses and they ... (7) the museum in the Elizabethan House. Tom really ... (8) his day in Plymouth.

Part C Practice

2 I played … I didn't play … (Simple past: positive and negative statements) ← p. 89

a) Think about last week. Write two positive and two negative sentences about what you did.
Here are some ideas:

> watch a film on TV · play cards · have ice cream for breakfast · fall asleep at school ·
> see my grandmother · forget my homework · help my dad · write a song · ride my bike to school ·
> text my grandpa · go to Berlin · say "I love you" · win some money · eat a book ·
> make a cake · talk to my brother · …

Background file

Devon – an English county

Devon is a county in the south-west of England.
Its biggest city is Plymouth, with 260,000 people.

Dartmoor is the biggest area of
wild country in the south of
Britain. It is the setting for lots of
famous detective stories

Devon's north and south coasts
have lots of sandy beaches.
Swimming, surfing and fishing are
very popular with holidaymakers.

Devon is one of the warmest
places in Britain. You can find lots
of palm trees there!

Wild ponies on Dartmoor, Devon

Woolacombe Beach, Devon

Torquay Gardens, Devon

Write a short text. Say why you would / wouldn't like
to go to Devon.

I would / wouldn't like to go to Devon because …	Plymouth Dartmoor the beaches …	looks look	great. scary. exciting. boring. …
I would / wouldn't like to go to …	Plymouth Dartmoor the beaches …	because	I like / don't like swimming and surfing. I want / don't want to see the palm trees. the wild country looks / doesn't look great. there's lots / there isn't much to do there. …

Part A Practice

4 I'm not laughing. I'm singing.

(Present progressive: positive and negative statements)

← p.107

b) Look at the picture on the right and fill in the gaps.

The man isn't wearing a yellow T-shirt.
He is wearing a green T-shirt.
The woman … a green T-shirt.
She … a blue T-shirt.
The man … a black watch. He … a yellow watch.
The woman … a white watch. She … a red watch.
The man … on a table. He … in an armchair.
The woman … on a chair. She … on the floor.
The man … to music. He … TV.
The woman … TV. She … a book.
The man … cake. He … a sandwich.
The woman … an apple. She … a biscuit.
The man … to music. He … with a cat.
The woman … with a cat. She … to music.

Part B

3 The aquarium in Plymouth

← p.109

After school you tell a friend about the aquarium. Finish your dialogue.
You can use the phrases in the box.

- Abteilungen über den Atlantik, die britische Küste oder das Great Barrier Reef
- du nachts die Haie beobachten kannst
- ein Schülerlernzentrum und Geburtstagspartys
- einen Film in 4D gucken, oder eine Tour durch das Aquarium machen
- kann man da schlafen
- nur in den Ferien
- vier Abteilungen

A: Es gibt vier Abteilungen, zum Beispiel über das Meeresleben in der Gegend um Plymouth.
B: Geht's da nur um Plymouth?
A: Nein, es gibt auch … .
B: Bieten sie etwas Besonderes für Kinder?
A: Ja, sie haben dort … . Und nachts … .

B: Eine Übernachtung im Aquarium?
A: Ja, das heißt „Sleeping with sharks", weil … .
B: Und das kann man jede Nacht machen?
A: Nein, … .
B: Und was macht man da genau?
A: Du kannst … .

➜ SF 10: Mediation (p.155)

Part B Practice

4 Signs

← p.111

b) 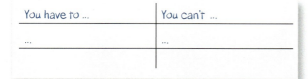 You have some English visitors.
They don't understand the signs.
You have to explain what they mean.
Match the phrases to the signs.

1   … take a number and wait.
2   … drink the water.
3   … put your bike here.
4   … wear your shoes.
5   … take pictures.
6   … wash your hands.
7   … feed the birds.

When you talk about signs, you can often say
You have to … or You can't …
Add the phrases from b) to the table.

You have to …	You can't …
…	…

7

8

10

9

11

12

13

Part C Practice

4 Same letters, different sounds

← p.117

a) Complete the words in 1–6. Use the letters from the box.

> a · ea · i · o · ou · u

1   f_nd · w_n · T-sh_rt
    find, win, T-shirt
2   b_by · c_r · m_p · s_w
3   p_t · r_ler · _mbrella
4   f__r · gr__p · h__se · t__ch · y__r
5   br__kfast · gr__t · s__l · w__r
6   m_nkey · sh_p · t_wer · tr_phy

Early finisher

Die S können ihre Antworten selbstständig mit den Lösungen auf S. 219 abgleichen.

1 Part B Practice

What is it?

← p. 29, exercise 10

The letters tell you the name of a place?

1 *Uhr* in English: the fourth letter.
2 Justin is from here: the fifth letter.
3 Do only what *he* says: the fourth letter.
4 Maya's brother: the first letter.
5 The third letter of the second month.
6 The sixth letter of Lucy's family name.
7 The pool in Plymouth: the third letter.
8 The seventh letter of the twelfth month.

9 Lucy's favourite animal: the second letter.
10 Sam's sport: the third letter.
11 The first letter of a two-year-old seal.
12 The fourth letter of the third month.
13 Lucy's sister: the first letter.
14 *Geschichte* in English: the fifth letter.
15 Sam is from here: the second letter.
16 The fourth letter of the class teacher's name.

2 Part A Practice

What's different?

← p. 40, exercise 2

These photos are different. Look at them for one minute. Then cover photo B with your exercise book.

A

B

Here are the things in photo A:

> 1 ball · 2 books · 3 cards · 1 CD · 1 clock ·
> 1 computer · 2 DVDs · 1 glue stick ·
> 1 lamp · 2 maps · 1 pen · 1 pencil ·
> 1 pencil case · 2 photos · 1 rubber · 1 ruler ·
> 1 sharpener · 2 telephones

What is different in photo B? What is the same?

3 | Part A Practice

Go, play or do?

← p. 60, exercise 2

Four children do four activities.
Copy the table.
Then use this information to find out who does what.

a) There is no "k" in Ann's activity.
b) There is no "g" at the end of Leo's activity.
c) Henry's activity has eight letters in it.
d) Leo's activity does not have four letters.

Leo	Henry	Maria	Ann	ACTIVITY
				football
				swimming
				skating
				judo

4 | Part B Practice

Think!

← p. 87, exercise 3

Can you solve these puzzles?

a) Mary's mum has four children: the first child is called April; the second is called June; the third is called August.
   What's the name of the fourth child?
b) You're the driver of a London-to-Plymouth bus. In London, 33 people get on the bus. In Oxford, 5 men get off and 10 women get on. In Bristol, 25 boys get off and 12 girls get on. In Exeter, 4 men get off and 10 boys get on.
   What's the driver's name?
c) Think of three days that start with the letter "t".
d) A boat goes from France to Plymouth at 20 km/h. 20 minutes later, a boat leaves Plymouth for France at 25 km/h. Plymouth is 200 km from France. When the two boats meet, which boat is nearer Plymouth?
e) On every day of the week, what's always in the middle of Plymstock?
f) You are in a room with three monkeys. One has a book, one has a bottle, one has nothing. Which animal in the room is the most intelligent?

5 | Part A Practice

Remember?

← p. 107, exercise 3

Read the sentences and write them down. Can you remember who said them?
Where were the sentences in the book?

1 ARE YOU A BOY OR A GIRL?
- Are you ...
2 I'M ORPH. I'M ORPH FROM LAWSTOCK SCHOOL.
3 Hey! Hey! Hey, here we go!
4 Go and find the yoghurt, little sister!
5 OAST EEF. ITH OAST OTATOES? UMMY!
6 What's grey and never gets wet?
7 Boat tours! See all the navy ships!
8 She looks so soft. Call her Silky.
9 Stop! Thieves! Give me back my book!
10 Help! I'm a sister and a naughty dog!

Answers (p. 219)

1 Part A Practice

5 Who's in the photo? (be)

Partner B:

a) Listen to your partner. Who is the boy in his/her photo?

b) Say as much as you can about *one* of these girls.
   Don't say her name.
   Can your partner guess who it is?

You can use these ideas to make sentences.
The girl in my photo is/isn't from Plymouth.
She's …
Her brother/sister is …

4 Part B Practice

4 Dave's day in London 💬

Partner B:

a) Listen to your partner's story about Dave's day in London.

b) Tell your partner your picture story: Dave was in London last Saturday. In the morning he went to …
   Then say how the two stories are different.
   A: In my story he talked to his grandma.
   B: In my story he talked to his classmates. And in my story he went …

Why do you think Dave's stories were different? Which story do you think is true?
EXTRA Write your "true" story about Dave's day in London.

4 | Part D Practice

4 Strange Devon sports

a) Partner B: Read the information.
Make notes in German.

Find out

- wann das nächste „worm charming" stattfindet

- wo es stattfindet

- um was es beim „worm charming" geht

b) In German, tell your partner about "worm charming".

EXTRA Which event would you like to watch: orange rolling or worm charming? Say why.

I'd like to watch … because it's fun/silly/…

Worm °charming

When?
11th June
at 11 am

Where?
Blackawton,
Devon

What?
Players have 1 °square metre of °grass. They have to find worms there, but they cannot use a °spade. Some people put °sugar or water in the grass and hope that the worms come out. The player with the °most worms is the winner.
The tradition started in 1984 when two people had nothing to do. Worm charming was their idea of fun.

5 | Part B Practice

1 Is he drinking? (Present progressive: questions)

Partner B: Answer Partner A's questions about pictures 1–3.
Use short answers (Yes, he is. / No, he isn't., etc.). Then go back to page 110.

A: In picture 1: is the boy drinking?   B: No, he isn't.
A: Well, is he …?

Wordbank 1: More animals and pets → *Here we go! (p.15)*

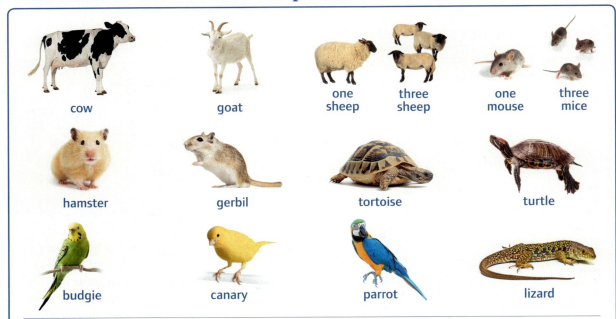

cow • goat • one sheep • three sheep • one mouse • three mice • hamster • gerbil • tortoise • turtle • budgie • canary • parrot • lizard

pet [pet] Haustier • **cow** [kaʊ] • **goat** [gəʊt] • **sheep,** *pl* **sheep** [ʃiːp] • **mouse,** *pl* **mice** [maʊs], [maɪs] •
hamster [ˈhæmstə] • **gerbil** [ˈdʒɜːbɪl] Rennmaus • **tortoise** [ˈtɔːtəs] Landschildkröte • **turtle** [ˈtɜːtl] Wasserschildkröte •
budgie [ˈbʌdʒi] • **canary** [kəˈneəri] • **parrot** [ˈpærət] • **lizard** [ˈlɪzəd] Eidechse •

Wordbank 2: My timetable → *Unit 1 (p. 28)*

biology • chemistry • physics • class assembly • Spanish • Italian • Latin • ethics • social studies • drama • extracurricular activities

biology [baɪˈɒlədʒi] • **chemistry** [ˈkemɪstri] • **physics** [ˈfɪzɪks] • **class assembly** [ˌklɑːs_əˈsembli] Klassenlehrerstunde,
Verfügungsstunde • **Spanish** [ˈspænɪʃ] • **Italian** [ɪˈtæliən] • **Latin** [ˈlætɪn] • **ethics** [ˈeθɪks] Ethik • **social studies** [ˌsəʊʃl
ˈstʌdiz] Gesellschaftskunde, Gemeinschaftskunde • **drama** [ˈdrɑːmə] darstellende Kunst, Schauspiel • **extracurricular**
activities [ˌekstrəkəˌrɪkjələr_ækˈtɪvətiz] Arbeitsgemeinschaften u.Ä

Wordbank 3: My bedroom ➜ *Unit 2 (p. 36)*

blinds *(pl)* [blaɪndz] • **cage** [keɪdʒ] • **carpet** ['kɑːpɪt] • **chest of drawers** [ˌtʃest_əv 'drɔːz] Kommode • **curtain** ['kɜːtn] • **cushion** ['kʊʃn] • **drawer** [drɔː] • **mirror** ['mɪrə] • **printer** ['prɪntə] • **radiator** ['reɪdieɪtə] Heizkörper • **wardrobe** ['wɔːdrəʊb]

Wordbank 4: Families ➜ *Unit 2 (p. 47)*

Me and my parents.

My uncle Philip. He's my dad's brother and Laura's husband. I'm his nephew.

Tim

My aunt Laura, Philip's wife.

Emma

Philip and Laura have two children, a son and a daughter – Tim and Emma. They're my cousins.

My sister Clara. She's Philip and Laura's niece.

My cousin Jasper with his dad and his stepmother.

My grandparents and my grandma's dad. He's my great-grandfather.

child, *pl* **children** [tʃaɪld], [tʃɪldrən] • **daughter** ['dɔːtə] • **grandparents** ['grænpeərənts] Großeltern • **great-grandfather/-mother** Urgroßvater/-mutter • **husband** ['hʌzbənd] Ehemann • **nephew** ['nefjuː] Neffe • **niece** [niːs] Nichte • **parents** ['peərənts] • **son** [sʌn] • **stepmother** ['stepmʌðə] • **wife** [waɪf] Ehefrau

Wordbank 5: Food → *Unit 2 (p. 50)*

FRUIT

apples

pears

oranges

strawberries

cherries

bananas

grapes

plums

VEGETABLES

carrots

tomatoes

peppers

peas

beans

mushrooms

broccoli

cauliflower

cucumber

lettuce

sweetcorn

MEAT AND FISH

grilled steak

lamb chops

roast chicken

sausages

salami

ham

cold cuts

fish fingers

fish filet

bean [biːn] • **carrot** [ˈkærət] • **cauliflower** [ˈkɒliflaʊə] • **cherry** [ˈtʃeri] • **cold cuts** *(pl)* [ˈkəʊld kʌts] Aufschnitt •
cucumber [ˈkjuːkʌmbə] • **fish fillet** [fɪʃ ˈfɪlət] • **fish finger** [fɪʃ ˈfɪŋgə] • **lamb chop** [ˈlæm tʃɒp] Lammkotelett •
lettuce [ˈletɪs] • **mushroom** [ˈmʌʃrʊm] • **pea** [piː] • **pear** [peə] • **plum** [plʌm] • **roast chicken** [ˌrəʊst ˈtʃɪkɪn] •
sausage [ˈsɒsɪdʒ] • **strawberry** [ˈstrɔːbəri] • **sweetcorn** [ˈswiːtkɔːn]

EGGS, POTATOES, PASTA, …

pasta

pasta salad

rice

boiled eggs

scrambled eggs

fried eggs

omelette

mashed potatoes

fried potatoes

chips

potato salad

DRINKS

coffee

hot chocolate

mineral water

orange juice

lemonade

DESSERTS / SWEETS

blancmange

fruit flan with whipped cream

jelly with custard

cupcakes

AND FOR BREAKFAST …

butter

honey

chocolate hazelnut spread

muesli

cereals

rolls

toast

blancmange [bləˈmɒnʒ] • **boiled egg** [ˌbɔɪld ˈeg] • **butter** [ˈbʌtə] • **cereals** (pl) [ˈsɪəriəlz] Getreideflocken, Frühstücksflocken •
chocolate hazelnut spread [ˌtʃɒklət ˌheɪzlnʌt ˈspred] • **custard** [ˈkʌstəd] • **fried egg** [ˌfraɪd ˈeg] • **honey** [ˈhʌni] • **jelly** [ˈdʒeli] •
lemonade [ˌleməˈneɪd] • **mashed potatoes** (pl) [ˌmæʃt pəˈteɪtəʊz] • **muesli** [ˈmjuːzli] • **orange juice** [ˈɒrɪndʒ dʒuːs] •
pasta [ˈpæstə] • **roll** [rəʊl] • **scrambled eggs** (pl) [ˌskræmbld ˈegz] • **whipped cream** [ˌwɪpt ˈkriːm]

Wordbank 6: Clubs and hobbies → *Unit 3 (p. 57 / p. 62)*

SPORTS

I play ...

| badminton | hockey | ice hockey | table tennis | volleyball |

I go ...

| canoeing | climbing | ice skating | riding | rowing |
| skateboarding | skating | skiing | snowboarding | windsurfing |

I do ...

| gymnastics | judo | yoga |

badminton racket, shuttlecocks   hockey stick   ice hockey stick, puck   table tennis bat   canoe, paddles

climbing gear, rope

skateboard

saddle, riding boots   (ice) skates   (in-line) skates   helmets   pads   skis, snowboard

badminton racket [ˈrækɪt] • **canoe** [kəˈnuː] • **climbing gear** [ˈklaɪmɪŋ ɡɪə] Kletterausrüstung • **gymnastics** [dʒɪmˈnæstɪks] • **helmets** [ˈhelmɪts] • **judo** [ˈdʒuːdəʊ] • **paddles** [ˈpædlz] • **pads** [pædz] (Schutz-)Polster, Schützer • **puck** [pʌk] • **riding boots** [buːts] • **rope** [rəʊp] • **rowing** [ˈrəʊɪŋ] • **saddle** [ˈsædl] • **shuttlecock** [ˈʃʌtlkɒk] • **skiing** [ˈskiːɪŋ] • **yoga** [ˈjəʊɡə]

MUSIC

I like ...
My hobby is ...

ballet dancing

listening to music

playing in a band

playing in the school orchestra

rapping

singing in a choir

I play the ...

clarinet

flute

recorder

cello

saxophone

trumpet

◄ Wind instruments

String ► instruments

violin

OTHER HOBBIES

I like ...
My hobby is ...

acting

drawing

making models

collecting stamps (comics, stickers, ...)

surfing the internet

taking photos

---

acting [ˈæktɪŋ] • **ballet dancing** [ˈbæleɪ] • **choir** [ˈkwaɪə] • **clarinet** [ˌklærəˈnet] • **drawing** [ˈdrɔːɪŋ] • **flute** [fluːt] Querflöte •
model [ˈmɒdl] • **orchestra** [ˈɔːkɪstrə] • **recorder** [rɪˈkɔːdə] Blockflöte • **saxophone** [ˈsæksəfəʊn] • **trumpet** [ˈtrʌmpɪt] •
violin [ˌvaɪəˈlɪn]

SF 1 Learning vocabulary

→ p. 24, p. 42

Vokabeln kann man auf unterschiedliche Weise lernen. Wir stellen dir hier ein paar Möglichkeiten vor. Probiere sie im Laufe des Schuljahres aus, dann kannst du herausfinden, welche Methode für dich die beste ist.

Vokabeln lernen mit dem Vocabulary

Dein erster Weg führt dich zum Vocabulary (S. 172–205). Die wichtigsten Dinge dazu hast du ja schon in Unit 1 gelernt (S. 24).
Und so lernst du damit:

1 Lies die Vokabeln
· Lies das englische Wort in der linken Spalte laut.
· Lies dann die deutsche Übersetzung und den Beispielsatz.

I'm a seal. [aɪm] (= **I am** a seal.)	Ich bin eine Robbe.	**!** Das englische Wort **I** (= „ich") wird immer großgeschrieben – auch wenn es nicht am Satzanfang steht.
a seal [ə ˈsiːl]	eine Robbe	[iː] ist ein langes „i" wie in „W**ie**n".

2 Teste dich Zeile für Zeile
· Decke die Spalte mit der deutschen Übersetzung ab. Sag die deutschen Wörter.
· Decke die linke und die rechte Spalte ab. Sag die englischen Wörter. Versuche auch immer noch die Beispielsätze aus der rechten Spalte zu nennen.

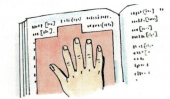

Und so kannst du dir eine Lernhilfe zum Abdecken der Spalten basteln:

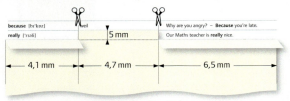

Englisch – Deutsch

Deutsch – Englisch

TIPP
· Lerne immer 7–10 Wörter und Wendungen zusammen.
· Lerne Vokabeln regelmäßig, am besten jeden Tag 5–10 Minuten.
· Wiederhole die gelernten Vokabeln einmal in der Woche.
· Lernen mit anderen macht Spaß – und ihr könnt euch gegenseitig abfragen.

Vokabeln lernen mit dem Vokabelheft

Manche lernen Vokabeln besonders gut, wenn sie sie aufschreiben: Dazu kannst du ein Vokabelheft mit drei Spalten anlegen. Schreibe das englische Wort in die linke Spalte, die deutsche Übersetzung in die mittlere Spalte und einen Beispielsatz (z. B. aus dem Vocabulary) in die rechte Spalte. Du kannst auch ein Bild malen. Lies die geschriebenen Wörter noch einmal laut.

Vokabeln lernen mit Merkzetteln

Du kannst Vokabeln, die du dir schwer merken kannst, auf kleine Notizzettel schreiben und zu Hause an Stellen kleben, wo du sie häufig siehst.

Du kannst auch Zettel an Gegenstände in deinem Zimmer kleben und so die englischen Wörter für diese Gegenstände lernen.

Vokabeln lernen mit Karteikarten

Manche können auch mit Karteikarten prima Vokabeln lernen. Und so geht das:

1 Schreib das englische Wort mit einem Beispielsatz (z. B. aus dem Vocabulary) und evtl. einem Bild auf die Vorderseite einer Karteikarte und die deutsche Übersetzung auf die Rückseite.

2 Lies das englische Wort laut und sage die deutsche Bedeutung dazu. Dann kontrollierst du, ob du richtig gelegen hast. Beim nächsten Durchgang liest du das deutsche Wort zuerst und sagst das englische Wort laut.

sweet

I don't like bananas. They're too sweet.

süß

Vorderseite   *Rückseite*

> **TIPP**
> • Vergiss nicht, auch regelmäßig die Wörter zu wiederholen, die du kannst. Erst wenn du die Wörter nach zwei oder drei Wochen immer noch weißt, kannst du die Karten aussortieren.

Vokabeln in Gruppen sammeln und ordnen: Mindmaps

Du kannst neue Vokabeln ordnen und in Gruppen lernen – zum Beispiel mit Mindmaps. Wie das geht, kannst du dir auf S. 150 noch mal ansehen.

Vokabeln lernen mit dem Computer

Vielleicht fällt dir das Vokabellernen auch leichter, wenn du am Computer übst. Du kannst dazu dein e-Workbook nutzen.

SF 2 Collecting information

➜ *p. 62*

Wenn du einen Text schreiben oder etwas vortragen sollst, hilft es, wenn du vorher alle wichtigen Ideen und Informationen sammelst und ordnest. Dafür gibt es verschiedene Möglichkeiten wie z. B. Listen, Tabellen oder Mindmaps.

Listen

Listen sind die einfachste Art, Ideen zu sammeln. Sie sind gut geeignet, wenn du z. B. nur ein paar Punkte notieren willst.

My favourite school subjects
- *English*
- *German*
- *Maths*
- *...*

Tabellen

Tabellen sind vor allem dann gut, wenn deine Informationen schon eine gewisse Struktur haben, z. B. wenn du darüber reden willst, wann du was machst. Wie du eine Tabelle aufbauen kannst und worauf du achten solltest, kannst du noch mal auf S. 62 nachlesen.

Monday	Tuesday	Wednesday
football	piano	-
...	...	...

Mindmaps

Mindmaps können dir beim Sammeln und Ordnen von Ideen helfen.

Stell dir vor, du sollst einen Text über deine Schule schreiben. Wenn du nur über deine Fächer reden möchtest, ist eine Liste eine gute Wahl. Wenn es mehr um deinen Stundenplan geht, ist das mit einer Tabelle vielleicht einfacher. Wenn du aber über alles rund ums Thema Schule reden willst, dann eignet sich am besten eine Mindmap.

1 Was brauchst du?
· Ein leeres Blatt Papier, das du quer vor dich legst.
· Stifte in verschiedenen Farben.

2 Wie erstellst du eine Mindmap?
· Schreib das Thema in die Mitte des Blattes und umrahme es mit einem Kreis oder einer Zeichnung.
· Überlege dir, welche Oberbegriffe (umbrella words) zu deiner Sammlung von Ideen passen. Verwende unterschiedliche Farben. Jetzt hat deine Mindmap Hauptäste.
· Ergänze jede Idee, die zu einem umbrella word passt, auf einem Nebenast.
· Du kannst statt Wörtern auch Zahlen oder Symbole eintragen und Bilder ergänzen.

SF 3 Putting a page together

➔ p. 96

Nimm an, du möchtest eine Seite gestalten, z.B. für die Schülerzeitung oder als Poster für einen kleinen Vortrag. Folgende Hinweise können dir dabei helfen.

Sammle und ordne deine Informationen
· Sortiere die Informationen, die auf der Seite stehen sollen. Wenn du dir nicht mehr ganz sicher bist, wie das geht, schau noch mal auf S. 62 nach.

Schreibe deinen Text
· Gib deinem Text eine klare Struktur. Die meisten Texte haben drei Teile, eine Einleitung, einen Hauptteil und einen Schluss.
· Beginne einen neuen Absatz für jeden neuen Gedanken, aber nicht für jeden Satz.
· Achte darauf, dass du dich nicht wiederholst und keine überflüssigen Informationen lieferst.

Wähle eine passende Überschrift
· Die Überschrift verdeutlicht, worum es in deinem Text geht. Sie kann auch lustig sein und den Leser neugierig machen auf das, was in deinem Text steht.
· Wenn es in deinem Text um mehrere Themen geht, dann kannst du für einzelne Abschnitte auch Zwischenüberschriften verwenden. Das gibt deinem Text eine klare Struktur und hilft dem Leser, sich schnell zu orientieren.

Suche oder zeichne Bilder für deinen Text

· Die Bilder sollten deinen Text näher erklären und interessant machen.
· Wähle Bildunterschriften, die das Bild kurz erläutern.

Sortiere Text und Bilder auf der Seite

· Achte darauf, dass die Seite nicht zu voll oder halbleer ist.
· Man muss erkennen, welches Bild zu welchem Textabschnitt gehört.

SF 4 Understanding and looking up new words

→ p. 73

Immer gleich nachschlagen?

Englische Texte enthalten oft Wörter, die du noch nicht kennst. Schlage sie nicht gleich im Wörterbuch nach, denn das kostet Zeit und nimmt dir vielleicht den Spaß am Lesen. Häufig kannst du die Bedeutung dieser Wörter selbst herausfinden. Folgende Punkte können dir dabei helfen.

Was hilft dir, unbekannte Wörter zu verstehen?

1 Sieh dir die Bilder an
Bilder sind eine große Hilfe. Oft zeigen sie Dinge, die du in einem Text nicht verstehst. Was könnte im folgenden Satz mit **leash** gemeint sein?

My dog Rocky has a new red leash.

2 Denke an ähnliche Wörter im Deutschen
Es gibt viele englische Wörter, die im Deutschen ähnlich geschrieben werden oder ähnlich klingen, so genannte „verwandte Wörter". Was bedeuten wohl die Wörter in der Box rechts auf Deutsch?

> balloon · brilliant · clarinet · combination · private · series · sharp · shine · spray · violin

3 Schau dir die Wörter genau an
Manchmal stecken in unbekannten Wörtern bekannte Teile.

> **sing**er · **friend**ly · un**happy** · **end**less

4 Schau dir den Satzzusammenhang an
Oft helfen dir auch die Wörter, die in der Nähe des unbekannten Wortes stehen. Kannst du im Beispiel rechts aus dem Zusammenhang heraus verstehen, was mit **building** gemeint ist?

> The Queen lives in Buckingham Palace. It's a big **building** with over 600 rooms.

Und wenn du doch nachschlagen musst?

Wenn du trotz allem das unbekannte Wort nicht herausfindest und dir der Text Probleme macht, hilft dir das Dictionary (S. 206–219). Es enthält alle Wörter und Wendungen, die im Buch vorkommen.

Das Dictionary zeigt dir zudem auch, wie man die Wörter ausspricht.

Let's see …

Wie benutzt du das Dictionary?

1 Die blau gedruckten Stichwörter (z. B. **fall**, **family**) sind alphabetisch angeordnet (also **f** vor **g**, **fa** vor **fe**, **fla** vor **flo**).

2 Längere Ausdrücke findest du oft unter mehr als einem Stichwort, z. B. **free-time activities** unter **free** und unter **activity**.

3 Aussprache und Betonung stehen in den eckigen Klammern. Du bist bei den Lautschriftzeichen unsicher? Dann schau dir *English sounds*, S. 233 an.

4 Es ist wichtig, den ganzen Eintrag nach dem Stichwort zu lesen. Oft findest du zusätzliche Hinweise, z. B. auf
   – besondere Pluralformen
   – längere Ausdrücke (z. B. **the first day**).

5 Die Ziffern 1., 2. usw. zeigen, dass das englische Stichwort mehrere Bedeutungen hat.

> ▶ **fall** [fɔːl], *simple past:* **fell** fallen, stürzen; hinfallen 5 (119) **fall asleep** einschlafen 1 (30)
> ▶ **family** [ˈfæməli] Familie 2 (36) **the Blackwell family** (die) Familie Blackwell 2 (36) °**family name** Familienname, Nachname **family tree** (Familien-)Stammbaum 2 (47)

> ▶ **free** [friː] frei 3 (62) **free time** Freizeit, freie Zeit 3 (62)▶ **free-time activities** Freizeitaktivitäten 3 (62)

> **first** [fɜːst] zuerst, als Erstes 5 (108) **the first day** der erste Tag 1 (18)
> ▶ S. 233 English numbers
> ▶ **fish** [fɪʃ], *pl* **fish** Fisch 2 (38)

> **get** [get], *simple past:* **got:**
> ▶ **1.** bekommen 4 (99) **Did you get it?** *(infml)* Hast du es verstanden? / Hast du es mitbekommen? 4 (98)
> ▶ **2.** gelangen, (hin)kommen 5 (116)

SF 5 **Taking notes** ➜ *p. 69*

Manchmal liest oder hörst du etwas und willst es dir merken, z. B. um anderen davon zu erzählen. Da hilft es, wenn du dir in Stichworten Notizen machst.

Wie machst du Notizen?

Am besten kannst du das an einem Beispiel sehen. Yasmin soll herausfinden, wie man in England Halloween feiert. Sie hat ihre englische Freundin Sophie gefragt. Schau dir an, wie sie in Sophies Antwort das Wichtige markiert und sich in Stichworten Notizen gemacht hat.

Dear Yasmin
Do I have a Halloween party? Yes, I do – every year. The party is only for girls – from my football team and from my class. There are no boys at this party. This year I'm a pirate.
The party usually starts at seven o'clock. We play games and then we eat pizza and chocolate cake. My mum always tells a ghost story at the end of the party.
Your friend
Sophie

> Sophie: Halloween party ✓
> only girls, ~~boys~~
> Sophie: pirate
> party starts: at 7
> play games, eat pizza + choc. cake
> end of party: Mum – ghost story

TIPP
· Verwende Ziffern (z. B. „7" statt „seven").
· Verwende Symbole und Abkürzungen, z. B. ✓ („Ja") und + („und") wie im Beispiel oben. Am besten erfindest du eigene Symbole.
· Verwende „not" oder ✕ bei Verneinungen.

SF 6 Giving a mini-talk

➡ p.115

Oft musst du Arbeitsergebnisse aus der Hausaufgabe, einem
Projekt oder einer Gruppenarbeit in einem kleinen Vortrag
präsentieren. Folgende Schritte helfen dir, dich gut
vorzubereiten und deinen *mini-talk* interessant zu gestalten.

Wie hältst du einen guten Vortrag?

1 Sammle deine Ideen
- Sammle alle wichtigen Ideen und Punkte und ordne sie, z. B. in einer Liste,
  Tabelle oder Mindmap. Wenn du Informationen aus einem Buch oder dem
  Internet benutzt, schreibe dir auf, woher sie stammen.
  ➡ *SF 2: Collecting information (p.149)*

2 Zeig deinen Zuhörern etwas
- Für deine Zuhörer ist es hilfreich, wenn sie nicht nur zuhören müssen,
  sondern etwas sehen (Bilder, Folien etc.) oder lesen können (Arbeitsblatt mit
  kleinen Texten). Wenn du z. B. ein Poster gestaltest, achte darauf, dass es gut
  lesbar und übersichtlich ist.
  ➡ *SF 3: Putting a page together (p.150)*

3 Übe deinen Vortrag
- Lerne deinen Vortrag nicht auswendig, lies ihn auch nicht ab, sondern
  schreibe dir einen kleinen Merkzettel.

4 Während des Vortrags
- Fang erst an, wenn es ruhig ist.
- Schau deine Zuhörer an.
- Nenn den Titel deines Vortrags und sag kurz, worüber du reden wirst.
- Sprich klar und deutlich und nicht zu schnell.
- Drück dich möglichst einfach aus.

5 Am Ende des Vortrags
- Erkundige dich, ob es Nachfragen gibt.
- Bedanke dich für die Aufmerksamkeit.

> *My presentation is about …*
> *First I'd like to talk about …*

> *Here's a new word.*
> *It is … in German.*

> *On my poster you can see*
> *a photo of …*
> *The mind map shows …*

> *That's the end of my presentation.*
> *Do you have any questions?*
> *Thank you very much.*

SF 7 Listening

➡ p.25

Wenn du Leute im Alltag reden hörst, hast du normalerweise eine Menge
Informationen, die dir helfen herauszufinden, worum es geht (Gesichtsausdruck,
Körpersprache usw.). Im Unterricht ist das schwieriger, weil das Gespräch aus
dem CD-Player kommt, und meistens musst du auch noch Aufgaben dazu
beantworten. Diese Hinweise können dir dabei helfen.

Vor dem Hören

- Guck dir die Aufgabenstellung vor dem Hören genau an. Was genau sollst du
  heraushören? Konzentrier dich darauf.

- Wenn es Überschriften und Bilder zu der Höraufgabe gibt, schau sie dir vorm
  Hören an und finde heraus, wer in der Aufnahme wohl mit wem spricht, wo
  die Leute sind und worum es geht.

- Überlege kurz, was du über das Thema schon weißt und welche englischen
  Begriffe wohl im Gespräch fallen werden.

Während des Hörens

- Höre nicht nur auf die Sprecher, sondern auch auf die Hintergrundgeräusche – ist das Gespräch in einem Laden, am Strand, in der Schule?

- „Hilfe – ich verstehe nicht alles!" – Keine Panik, das ist völlig normal. Mach dir lieber klar, was du alles verstanden hast; oft ergibt sich der Rest.

Nach dem Hören

- Wenn möglich, vergleiche kurz mit einem Partner, ob ihr das Gleiche verstanden habt. Vielleicht kannst du den Text auch noch ein zweites Mal hören.

SF 8 Reading

➜ p. 53

Vor dem Lesen

Ehe du anfängst, einen Text zu lesen, schau dir die Überschrift und die Bilder an, die dazu gehören. Was sagen sie dir über den Inhalt des Textes?

Während des ersten Lesens

- Lies den Text einmal am Stück durch und versuche, ihn insgesamt zu verstehen. Lass unbekannte Wörter erstmal beiseite.

Nach dem ersten Lesen

- Wenn du fertig bist, versuch, die fünf W-Fragen zum Text zu beantworten: „Wer? Wo? Wann? Was? Warum?" um sicher zu sein, dass du den Text verstanden hast. Noch besser ist es, mit einem Partner zusammen die Fragen zu beantworten.

Während des zweiten Lesens

- Geh den Text noch einmal genauer durch. Wenn du auf ein unbekanntes Wort triffst, versuch, die Bedeutung zu erschließen. Tipps dafür gibt es in Skills File 4 . ➜ *SF 4: Understanding and looking up new words, p.151*

- Was dir jetzt noch unbekannt ist, musst du nachschlagen oder erfragen.

SF 9 Writing – Check your spelling

➡ p. 33

Dein Text ist fertig – und jetzt?

Glückwunsch, du hast einen Text geschrieben! Leider bist du noch nicht ganz fertig, denn du solltest ihn noch einmal durchlesen, um Fehler zu korrigieren.

Wenn möglich, lies dir deinen Text laut vor. Das kann helfen, Fehler schneller zu finden. Noch besser: finde einen Partner, mit dem du Texte tauschen kannst. Fremde Fehler sind oft leichter zu erkennen als eigene.

Achte insbesondere auf folgende Dinge:

Laute, die gleich klingen, aber anders geschrieben werden	*their/there/they're* *your/you're*
Schreibung des Apostrophs	*the pupils' books, the pupil's books*
Bildung der Zeitformen der Verben	*stop* → *sto**pp**ing, try* → *tr**ies***
Groß- und Kleinschreibung	*Tom is **B**ritish, I am **G**erman.*
ungewöhnliche Buchstabenkombinationen	*thought, enough*
Wörter, die im Deutschen ähnlich, aber nicht ganz genau gleich sind	*Elefant* → *elephant* *Biologie* → *biology*
Wörter mit Buchstaben, die man nicht spricht	*walk, talk*

Immer die gleichen Fehler?

Versuche herauszufinden, welche Fehler du immer wieder machst. Sieh dir an, was bei deinen Texten oder Klassenarbeiten wiederholt angestrichen ist.

> **TIPP**
> Schreib diese Fehler auf kleine Zettel. Dann helfen sie dir vielleicht, wenn du wieder einen Text schreibst.

Meine Fehlerliste!
British → British
stop → stopping
try → tries
...

SF 10 Mediation

➡ p. 70

Was ist Mediation?

Wenn du zwischen zwei Sprachen vermittelst, also z. B. deutsche Informationen auf Englisch wiedergibst oder umgekehrt, nennt man das *mediation*.

Worauf muss ich achten?

- Übersetze nicht alles wörtlich, gib nur wichtige Informationen wieder. Du kannst Unwichtiges weglassen und Sätze anders formulieren.
- Verwende kurze und einfache Sätze.
- Wenn du ein Wort nicht kennst, umschreibe es oder ersetze es durch ein anderes mit ähnlicher Bedeutung.

Mama sagt, wir könnten eine Pizza zum Abendessen bestellen. Sie hätte jetzt aber auch noch Zeit, Spaghetti zu kochen. Was denkt ihr?

Do you want pizza or spaghetti for dinner, Ryan?

Grammar File – Inhalt

Seite

Das **Grammar File** (S. 156–171) fasst zusammen, was du in den fünf Units deines Englischbuches über die **englische Sprache** lernst.
Hier kannst du nachsehen,
– wenn du selbstständig etwas lernen oder etwas wiederholen möchtest,
– wenn du Übungen aus dem *Practice*-Teil deines Englischbuches oder aus dem *Workbook* bearbeitest,
– wenn du dich auf einen Test vorbereiten willst.

In der **linken Spalte** findest du **Beispielsätze** und **Übersichten**, z. B.

In der **rechten Spalte** stehen **Erklärungen** und nützliche Hinweise (auf Deutsch).

Besonders wichtig sind die Stellen mit den **roten Ausrufezeichen** (!). Sie zeigen, was im Deutschen anders ist, und machen dich auf besondere Fehlerquellen aufmerksam.

Verweise wie ➡ *p. 22, exercises 1–2* zeigen dir, wo du Übungen zum gerade behandelten grammatischen Thema findest.

Die grammatischen Fachbegriffe *(grammatical terms)* kannst du auf den Seiten 170–171 nachschlagen.

Am Ende der *Grammar-File*-Abschnitte stehen kleine **Aufgaben** zur **Selbstkontrolle**. Hier kannst du überprüfen, ob du das gerade behandelte Thema verstanden hast.
Auf S. 171 kannst du dann nachsehen, ob deine Lösungen richtig sind.

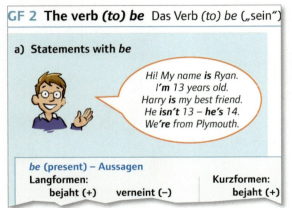

GF 2 The verb *(to) be* Das Verb *(to) be* („sein")

a) **Statements with *be***

> Hi! My name **is** Ryan.
> I**'m** 13 years old.
> Harry **is** my best friend.
> He **isn't** 13 – he**'s** 14.
> We**'re** from Plymouth.

be (present) – Aussagen
Langformen:		Kurzformen:
bejaht (+)	verneint (–)	bejaht (+)

Unit 1

GF 1 Personal pronouns Personalpronomen

Nomen:	*boy*	*girl*	*pencil*

Pronomen:	*he*	*she*	*it*

Nomen stehen für Lebewesen (*boy, girl, seal, cat*) und Gegenstände (*book, photo, pencil*), aber auch für alles, was man nicht sehen oder anfassen kann (*name, time, word, love*).

You are nice. = Du bist nett. / Ihr seid nett. / Sie sind nett.

Auch **Pronomen (Fürwörter)** können für Lebewesen, Gegenstände und Begriffe stehen.
Die Pronomen *I, you, he, she, it, we, you, they* nennt man **Personalpronomen**.

❗ Das englische Personalpronomen *you* kann *du* oder *ihr* oder *Sie* heißen.

Personal pronouns

Bei einer männlichen Person – *he*
Bei einer weiblichen Person – *she*
Bei einem Gegenstand oder Begriff – *it*
Bei einem Haustier – *he* oder *she*
Bei einem Tier, das keinen Namen hat – *it*
Bei mehreren Personen, Gegenständen, Tieren – *they*

What colour is …   **Welche Farbe hat …**

  … *the pencil?*   … **der** Bleistift?
  – *It's green.*   – **Er** ist grün.

 … *the bag?*   … **die** Tasche?
  – *It's blue.*   – **Sie** ist blau.

  … *the ruler?*   … **das** Lineal?
  – *It's brown.*   – **Es** ist braun.

❗ Das englische Personalpronomen *it* steht für alle Gegenstände und Begriffe, kann also *er* oder *sie* oder *es* heißen.

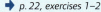

➡ p. 22, exercises 1–2

Möchtest du überprüfen, ob du alles verstanden hast? Dann löse jetzt diese beiden Aufgaben:

a) Wie viele Personalpronomen enthält diese Liste?

   boy · the · it · Silky · she · they · nice · your · you · we · green

b) *he*, *she*, *it* oder *they*?

   1 *Look, a snake. – …'s big.*
   2 *This is my cat Susie. – How old is …?*
   3 *And this is my dog Victor. – …'s nice.*
   4 *Where are your rabbits? – …'re in my room.*

(Auf S. 171 kannst du nachschauen, ob deine Antworten richtig sind.)

GF 2 The verb *(to) be* Das Verb *(to) be* („sein")

a) Statements with *be*

*Hi! My name is Ryan.
I'm 13 years old.
Harry is my best friend.
He isn't 13 – he's 14.
We're from Plymouth.*

Aussagen mit *be*

Das Verb *be* hat in der Gegenwart *(present)* drei Formen: *am*, *are* und *is*.

◀ Im Beispiel links siehst du einige Lang- und Kurzformen von *be*.

be (present) – Aussagen

Langformen:		Kurzformen:	
bejaht (+)	**verneint (−)**	**bejaht (+)**	**verneint (−)**
I am	I am not	I'm	I'm not
you are	you are not	you're	you aren't
he/she/it is	he/she/it is not	he's/she's/it's	he/she/it isn't
we are	we are not	we're	we aren't
you are	you are not	you're	you aren't
they are	they are not	they're	they aren't

Beim Sprechen und in persönlichen Briefen werden meist die Kurzformen von *be* verwendet.

➡ *p. 23, exercises 3 – 6*

b) Questions with *be*

***Are** you in Year 5?
Where are you from?*

Fragen mit *be*

Es gibt zwei Arten von Fragen:

– **ohne** Fragewort: ***Are** you 13?* · ***Is** she your friend?*
– **mit** Fragewort: ***Who** are you?* · ***Where** are you?*

Nach einem Fragewort wird *is* oft verkürzt:

***Who's** that?*
***Where's** my book?*
***What's** your name?*

be (present) – Fragen

Am I …?	Are we …?
Are you …?	Are you …?
Is he/she/it …?	Are they …?

➡ *p. 27, exercise 1*

c) Short answers with *be*

Are you 13? – **Yes, I am.**
Are you from Plymouth? – **No, I'm not.**
Is Emma your sister? – **Yes, she is. / No, she isn't.**

Kurzantworten mit *be*

Fragen ohne Fragewort werden meist nicht nur mit *Yes* oder *No* beantwortet – das wäre unhöflich. Du solltest eine Kurzantwort verwenden, z. B. **Yes, I am** oder **No, I'm not**.

be (present) – Kurzantworten:

+	Yes, I am.	–	No, I'm not.
	Yes, you are.		No, you aren't.
	Yes, he/she/it is.		No, he/she/it isn't.
	Yes, we/you/they are.		No, we/you/they aren't.

❗ In Kurzantworten mit **Yes** darfst du keine Kurzform verwenden.
Also nur
Yes, I am. / Yes, she is. / Yes, we are.
usw.

➡ *p. 27, exercise 1*

Alles verstanden? Dann kannst du jetzt diese Aufgabe lösen:
Wie antwortet man höflich auf die folgende Frage? (Zwei Antworten sind richtig.)

Are you eleven? – **1** *Yes.* · **2** *Yes, I'm.* · **3** *Yes, I am.* · **4** *No.* · **5** *No, I'm not.*

GF 3 *There is … / There are …*

There's a desk in my room.
In meinen Zimmer steht ein Schreibtisch.

There are books and school things on my desk.
Es liegen Bücher und Schulsachen auf meinem
Schreibtisch.

Is there a clock in your room?
– **Yes, there is.** / **No, there isn't.**

There aren't any cats in my picture.
Es gibt keine Katzen auf meinem Bild.

Are there any cats in your picture?
Sind Katzen auf deinem Bild?

➡ *p. 32, exercises 1–2*

Mit **There is …** (kurz: **There's …**) und **There are …**
drückst du aus, dass etwas vorhanden ist.

Im Deutschen benutzt man meist **Es gibt …**,
Es ist … / **Es sind …** oder Sätze mit **liegen** oder **stehen**.

Auf Fragen reagiert man mit einer Kurzantwort:
+ **Yes, there is.** / **Yes, there are.**
– **No, there isn't.** / **No, there aren't.**

❗ Beachte, dass nach **There aren't** und **Are there** in der
Regel das Wort **any** steht.

Schau dir das Bild an und vervollständige die Sätze.
(Vorsicht: In drei Sätzen brauchst du **any**!)

1 … a computer on the desk.
2 … books on the desk.
3 (pencils?) … on the desk? – Yes, …
4 (ball?)   … on the desk? – No, …
5 (CDs?)   … on the desk? – …
6 (ruler?)   … on the desk? – …

GF 4 **Imperatives** Aufforderungen, Befehle

Open the window, please.

Don't open the window.

➡ *p. 24, exercise 7*

Anders als im Deutschen gibt es im Englischen nur eine
Befehlsform, egal mit wem du sprichst:

Englisch: **Open** the window, please.
Deutsch: **Öffne / Öffnet / Öffnen Sie** bitte das Fenster.

Aus Höflichkeit solltest du **please** verwenden, wenn du
jemanden aufforderst, etwas zu tun.

Bei einer Aufforderung, etwas nicht zu tun (einem
verneinten Befehl), steht **don't** vor dem Infinitiv:

Don't open the window. (Langform: **Do not open …**)

*Don't open the window …
don't open the window …*

GF 5 *can* „können"

> I **can** spell my name.
> **Can** you spell your name?

> He **can't** spell his name.

I **can answer** your question.
Ich kann **deine Frage** beantworten.

We **can't help** you.
Wir können **dir** nicht helfen.

Can we watch a DVD, please?
– **Yes, you can. / No, you can't.**

➡ *p. 32, exercises 3 – 4*

Mit **can** drückst du aus, was jemand tun kann.

Mit **can't** (Langform: **cannot**) drückst du aus, was jemand nicht tun kann.

Die Formen **can** und **can't** gelten für alle Personen:

I/you/he/she/it/we/you/they **can** *spell.*
I/you/he/she/it/we/you/they **can't** *spell.*

❗ Anders als im Deutschen steht das Verb im Englischen direkt hinter **can** bzw. **can't**.

Auf Fragen reagiert man mit einer Kurzantwort:
+   **Yes, I can. / Yes, you can.** usw.
–   **No, I can't. / No, you can't.** usw.

Unit 2

GF 6 **The simple present (I)** Die einfache Form der Gegenwart (I)

a) Positive statements

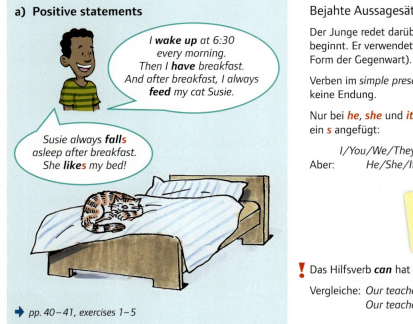

> I **wake up** at 6:30 every morning. Then I **have** breakfast. And after breakfast, I always **feed** my cat Susie.

> Susie always **falls** asleep after breakfast. She **likes** my bed!

➡ *pp. 40 – 41, exercises 1 – 5*

Bejahte Aussagesätze

Der Junge redet darüber, wie jeden Morgen sein Tag beginnt. Er verwendet das *simple present* (die einfache Form der Gegenwart).

Verben im *simple present* haben bei **I, you**, **we** und **they** keine Endung.

Nur bei **he**, **she** und **it** (der 3. Person Singular) wird ein **s** angefügt:

      I/You/We/They **like** *games.*
Aber: *He/She/It* **likes** *games.*

> **He, she, it –**
> das **s** muss mit!

❗ Das Hilfsverb **can** hat **kein s** bei *he/she/it*!

Vergleiche: *Our teacher* **can** *help us.*
            Our teacher always **helps** *us.*

Eine kleine Aufgabe? Wo fehlt ein **s**? Schreibe die korrekten Sätze in dein Übungsheft.

1 *I like_ card games.*
2 *My sister like_ football.*
3 *My dog always sleep_ in his basket.*
4 *Susie can_ sleep_ on my bed.*
5 *Seals eat_ fish.*
6 *Silky eat_ crabs too.*

b) 3rd person singular: pronunciation and spelling

1 [s] *Silky **eats** fish.*   [-ts]
    *Skip **sleeps** in a basket.*   [-ps]
    *Mr Blackwell **likes** games.*   [-ks]

2 [z] *Silky **lives** in Plymouth.*   [-vz]
    *Dad always **comes** home late.*   [-mz]
    *Abby **feeds** Skip in the morning.* [-dz]
    *Mink **plays** at night.*   [-eɪz]
    *Abby **knows** Maya.*   [-əʊz]

3 [ɪz] *Silky always **catches** lots of fish.* [-tʃɪz]
    *Maya **watches** TV at weekends.*   [-tʃɪz]
    *Our teacher **uses** red pens.*   [-zɪz]

*He's late for school, so he **hurries** up.*
Er ist spät dran für die Schule, daher beeilt er sich.

*Sam always **tries** to help his sister Lily.*
Sam versucht immer, seiner Schwester Lily zu helfen.

*Abby **has** a new friend.*

*Sam **goes** to Plymstock School.*

*Abby always **does** her homework in her room.* [dʌz]

*Simon **says**, "Put your pens on your desk."*   [sez]

➡ *p. 41, exercise 3*

3. Person Singular: Aussprache und Schreibung

Der Laut **vor** dem *s* bestimmt,
wie das *s* ausgesprochen wird:

◄ **1** Folgt das *s* auf einen **stimmlosen Konsonanten**, wird es wie das Zischen einer Schlange gesprochen: [s]. Stimmlose Konsonanten sind z.B. [t], [p], [k].

◄ **2** Folgt das *s* auf einen **stimmhaften Konsonanten** oder einen **Vokal**, wird es wie das Summen einer Biene gesprochen: [z]. Stimmhafte Konsonanten sind z.B. [v], [m], [d].

◄ **3** Folgt das *s* auf einen **Zischlaut**, wird es [ɪz] gesprochen. Zischlaute sind z.B. [s], [z], [ʃ], [tʃ], [dʒ]. Nach Zischlauten wird *es* oder *s* angehängt, je nach Schreibung des Infinitivs: *catch – catches* · *use – uses*.

◄ Bei Verben, die auf **Konsonant + y** enden, gibt es eine Besonderheit in der 3. Person Singular: ***y + s ⟶ ies***.

Beispiel: ***hurry* + *s* ⟶ *hurries*, *try* + *s* ⟶ *tries***

(Aber: **Vokal + y** bleibt unverändert: ***play* + *s* ⟶ *plays***)

❗ Auch bei den Verben ***have, go, do*** und ***say*** gibt es Besonderheiten in der 3. Person Singular:

* ***have* ⟶ *he/she/it* has**
* ***go* + *es* ⟶ *he/she/it* goes**
* ***do* + *es* ⟶ *he/she/it* does**
  Die Aussprache ändert sich: *do* [duː] – *does* [dʌz]
* Bei ***say*** ändert sich die Aussprache:
  I say [seɪ] – *he/she/it says* [sez]

Und hier wieder zwei kleine Aufgaben:

a) Bei welchen Verben musst du bei *he/she/it* die Endung **-es** (statt **-s**) anhängen?

watch · *write* · *think* · *touch* · *go* · *play* · *sleep* · *catch* · *put* · *do*

b) Welche Aussprache ist richtig? Ordne die Wörter den Buchstaben **A** bis **C** zu.

1 *helps* · 2 *watches* · 3 *answers* · 4 *goes* · 5 *follows*
6 *touches* · 7 *meets* · 8 *comes* · 9 *asks* · 10 *feeds*

A [s]   **B** [z]   **C** [ɪz]

c) Negative statements

*I **don't** like cricket.*   Ich mag Kricket nicht.

*He **doesn't** have time for sport.*   Er hat keine Zeit für Sport.

Verneinte Aussagesätze

So verneinst du Aussagesätze im *simple present*:

* bei *I, you, we, they* mit **don't** + Infinitiv

* bei *he, she, it* mit **doesn't** + Infinitiv.

❗ Das **s** der 3. Person Singular steckt im Wort **doesn't**: *He/She **doesn't** live in Britain.* (nicht: *He/She doesn't lives …*)

Simple present – verneinte Aussagen			
I	don't	live	
You	don't	live	
He/She/It	doesn't	live	in Britain.
We	don't	live	
You	don't	live	
They	don't	live	

➡ *pp. 45–46, exercises 1–5*

Vervollständige jetzt diese Sätze in deinem Übungsheft. Vorsicht – **don't** oder **doesn't**?
Beispiel: *We (watch TV)* don't watch TV *at weekends, we play games.*

1 *Dilip and Sanjay (live) … in South Africa.*
2 *Uncle Dasan (live) … in Britain.*
3 *He goes to a sports school, but he (do sport) …*
4 *Maya (go) … to Plymstock School.*
5 *My cats (sleep) … at night – they play.*
6 *I (have) … a cat, I have a rabbit.*

GF 7 The possessive form   Der *s*-Genitiv

English: ***Abby's** house*   ***Justin's** father*
German: **Abbys** Haus   **Justins** Vater

Singular: *The **dog's** basket is in **Abby's** room.*
Der Korb des Hundes steht in Abbys Zimmer.

Plural: *They meet at the **Blackwells'** house.*
Sie treffen sich im Haus der Blackwells.

Wenn du sagen willst, dass etwas jemandem gehört (oder zu jemandem gehört), benutzt du den **s-Genitiv**.

❗ Anders als im Deutschen steht im Englischen ein Apostroph: *Abby's house*.

◀ Im Singular wird **'s** angehängt.

◀ Wenn die Pluralform auf **s** endet, wird nur ein Apostroph angehängt.

➡ *p. 43, exercise 2*

Verstanden? Dann beantworte jetzt diese Fragen:
Wie viele Personen sind es? Sind es **ein** oder **mehrere** Brüder, Mädchen, Schüler/innen?

1 *my **brother's** room*
2 *my **brothers'** room*
3 *the **girls'** father*
4 *the **students'** teacher*
5 *the **student's** desk*
6 *the **girl's** family name*

Unit 3

GF 8 The simple present (II) Die einfache Form der Gegenwart (II)

a) Yes/No questions and short answers

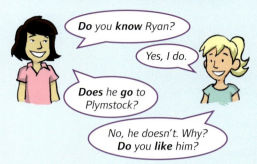

Do you **know** Ryan?

Yes, I **do**.

Does he **go** to Plymstock?

No, he doesn't. Why? **Do** you **like** him?

Does Lucy **know** Abby?
Does Abby **live** in a nice house?
Does Sam **go** to basketball?

Do you **like** sport? – **Yes, I do**. / **No, I don't**.
Does Justin **have** a camera? – **Yes, he does**.
Does Lucy **go** to any clubs? – **No, she doesn't**.
Do Abby's brothers **have** a hobby? – **Yes, they do**.

Entscheidungsfragen und Kurzantworten

Entscheidungsfragen sind Fragen, auf die man mit „Ja"
oder „Nein" antworten kann.

Fragen im *simple present* bildet man mit **do** oder **does**:

- **do** bei *I, you, we, they*
- **does** bei *he, she, it* (3. Person Singular).

Die Wortstellung in Entscheidungsfragen ist wie beim
Aussagesatz. Vergleiche:

Aussagesatz: They go sailing.   Sie gehen segeln.
Fragesatz: **Do** they go sailing?   Gehen sie segeln?

❗ Das **s** der 3. Person Singular steckt im Wort **does**:
Does she **live** in a nice house?
(nicht: *Does she lives …?*)

Entscheidungsfragen werden meist nicht nur mit *Yes* oder
No beantwortet, sondern mit einer Kurzantwort:
- **Yes, I do. / Yes, she does. / Yes, we do.** usw.
- **No, I don't. / No, she doesn't. / No, we don't.** usw.

Simple present – Entscheidungsfragen und Kurzantworten				
?			**+**	**−**
Do	I	know …?	Yes, you do.	No, you don't.
Do	you	know …?	Yes, I do.	No, I don't.
Does	he/she/it	know …?	Yes, he/she/it does.	No, he/she/it doesn't.
Do	we	know …?	Yes, you do.	No, you don't.
Do	you	know …?	Yes, we do.	No, we don't.
Do	they	know …?	Yes, they do.	No, they don't.

➡ *p. 60, exercise 1 · p. 61, exercises 3–4*

Möchtest du wieder überprüfen, ob du alles verstanden hast? Hier zwei Aufgaben:

a) Stelle Fragen. Frage nach den Personen in Klammern.
   Beispiel: *Justin has a camera. (Sam?)*   Does Sam have a camera too?

   1 *Sam plays basketball. (Lucy?)*
   2 *The Blackwells play games at weekends. (Maya?)*
   3 *Abby lives in a nice house. (Sam and Lily?)*
   4 *Maya visits Abby at weekends. (Lucy?)*
   5 *Justin makes video films. (Sam?)*
   6 *Abby goes sailing. (Abby's brothers?)*

b) Welche Kurzantwort ist richtig, **A**, **B** oder **C**?

   1 *Does Maya have a dog?*   **A** *Yes, she does.*   **B** *Yes, she don't.*   **C** *Yes, she do.*
   2 *Does your brother like cornflakes?* **A** *No, they don't.*   **B** *No, he doesn't.*   **C** *No, he don't.*
   3 *Do Maya's cousins live in Africa?*   **A** *No, she doesn't.*   **B** *No, they doesn't.*   **C** *No, they don't.*

b) Questions with question words

Justin: **Where do** you **work**, Dad?
And **what do** you **do** there?

Why does Dad **work** so much, Mum?

➡ pp. 65–66, exercises 1–5

Fragen mit Fragewörtern

Fragen mit Fragewörtern (When, Where, What, Why, How) bildest du wie Entscheidungsfragen.
Das Fragewort steht am Anfang der Frage, vor do bzw. does. Vergleiche:

	They **go** sailing.
Entscheidungsfrage:	**Do** they **go** sailing?
Frage mit Fragewort:	**Where do** they **go** sailing?

Sieh dir die Antwort an, finde das richtige Fragewort und bilde die Frage.
Beispiel: (… you – have breakfast?)   **At 7 o'clock.** ⟶ When do you have breakfast?

1 (… Maya – visit Abby?)   **At weekends.**
2 (… Abby – live?)   **In a nice house in Wembury.**
3 (… Abby's brothers – go sailing)?   **Because they love the sea.**
4 (… you – do in your free time?)   **I play hockey.**

GF 9 Adverbs of frequency: word order Häufigkeitsadverbien: Wortstellung

Lucy and Maya **often ride** their bikes.
Lucy und Maya fahren oft Rad.

They **usually ride** to Smeaton's Tower.
Sie fahren meistens zu Smeaton's Tower.

They **sometimes have** a picnic there.
Sie machen manchmal ein Picknick dort.

But they **don't always meet** the boys.
Aber sie treffen nicht immer die Jungen.

In simple present-Sätzen stehen oft sogenannte Häufigkeitsadverbien:
always, usually, often, sometimes, never.

Sie drücken aus, wie regelmäßig etwas geschieht oder nicht geschieht.

◀ Häufigkeitsadverbien stehen in der Regel **direkt vor dem Vollverb** (hier: ride, have, meet).
Vergleiche die Beispiele links mit ihren deutschen Übersetzungen.

	Objekt			Objekt
We **often play** cards.		But we	**never play** chess.	

Wir **spielen oft** Karten.   Aber wir **spielen nie** Schach.

❗ Anders als im Deutschen stehen Häufigkeitsadverbien **nie zwischen Verb und Objekt**.

On Saturdays, Lucy and Maya **are often** on the Hoe.
Sam **is always** nice to his sister Lily.

➡ p. 70, exercise 2

❗ Vorsicht bei den Formen von be:
Häufigkeitsadverbien stehen **hinter** am/are/is.

Füge die Häufigkeitsadverbien an der richtigen Stelle ein:

1 (usually)   Kids like ice cream.
2 (often)   It is very cold in Germany in January.
3 (always)   Sam goes to basketball on Thursdays.
4 (never)   I eat scones for breakfast.
5 (sometimes)   Morph plays cards in the evening.

Unit 4

GF 10   The simple past Die einfache Form der Vergangenheit

Girl: *How **was** your weekend?*

Boy: *It **was** OK. We **were** at my cousin's birthday party. What about you?*

Girl: *On Saturday, I **played** hockey with my friends. And on Sunday, we **visited** my grandma.*

Mit dem *simple past* kannst du über **Vergangenes** berichten.

Mit Zeitangaben wie *yesterday, last week, last summer, on Saturday morning* sagst du, wann etwas geschehen ist oder wann jemand etwas getan hat.

GF 11   The simple past of *(to) be* Die einfache Form der Vergangenheit von *(to) be*

Beim *simple past* von **be** gibt es nur zwei Formen:

> **I, he/she/it was**   **you, we, they were**

- Die verneinten Formen heißen **wasn't** und **weren't**.
- Fragen bildet man mit **Was I …?, Were you …?** usw.
- Die Kurzantworten lauten **Yes, I was., No, we weren't.** usw.
- Fragewörter stehen wie immer am Satzanfang.

➡ *p. 83, exercises 1–3*

GF 12   The simple past: positive statements

Die einfache Form der Vergangenheit: bejahte Aussagesätze

a) Regular verbs

*Last Saturday, Sam's team **played** against Devonport. Their fans **watched** the match. Later Sam **talked** to Justin about his day.*

*I/you/he/she/it/we/you/they **played, talked, …***

1 *Their fans were there when they **arrived**.*

2 *They **stopped** Devonport's best player.*

3 *In the second half, they **tried** to play better.*

4 *Their fans **shouted** and **shouted**.*

➡ *p. 86, exercises 1–2*

Regelmäßige Verben

Bei **regelmäßigen** Verben hängst du **ed** an den Infinitiv, um das *simple past* zu bilden:

play → played [pleɪd]   **film → filmed** [fɪlmd]
talk → talked [tɔːkt]   **watch → watched** [wɒtʃt]

◀ Es gibt für alle Personen nur eine Form.

❗ Beachte folgende Besonderheiten:

1 Ein stummes **e** fällt weg: **arrive → arrived**

2 Nach einem einzelnen, betonten Vokal wird der Konsonant verdoppelt: **stop → stopped**

3 Ein **y** nach Konsonant wird zu **ied**: **try → tried**

4 Nach **t** und **d** wird die **ed**-Endung [ɪd] ausgesprochen: **shouted** [ˈʃaʊtɪd], **needed** [ˈniːdɪd]

b) Irregular verbs

Last Saturday, Sam's team **went**
 to Devonport.
Their fans **came** too.
They **had** a great time.
Sam's team **won** the match.
When Sam **saw** his dad,
 he showed him his medal.

Infinitiv: **go**

come
have
win
see

➡ p. 87, exercises 3–4

Unregelmäßige Verben

Wie im Deutschen gibt es auch im Englischen eine Reihe von **unregelmäßigen** Verben.
Jedes unregelmäßige Verb hat eine eigene Form für das *simple past*, die du einzeln lernen musst.

◀ Links findest du einige Beispiele.

➡ *Liste der unregelmäßigen Verben, S. 231*

Wie werden die *simple past*-Formen dieser Verben gebildet?
Ordne die Verben den Buchstaben **A** bis **D** zu.

1 *ask* · **2** *dance* · **3** *hope*
4 *hurry* · **5** *like* · **6** *live*
7 *play* · **8** *score* · **9** *start*
10 *stay* · **11** *stop* · **12** *want*

A *call* ⟶ *called*
B *arrive* ⟶ *arrived*
C *plan* ⟶ *planned*
D *try* ⟶ *tried*

GF 13 The simple past: negative statements

Die einfache Form der Vergangenheit: verneinte Aussagesätze

Sam **didn't run**. He walked. And he **didn't look** happy.
Sam **didn't like** the ride on the Big Wheel.
And he **didn't see** any sights.

I/you/he/she/it/we/you/they **didn't play, go, ...**

Eine Aussage im *simple past* **verneinst** du mit
didn't + **Infinitiv** (Langform: *did not*).

Vergleiche: *Lucy* **looked** *happy.*
         Sam **didn't look** *happy.*
(nicht: *Sam didn't looked happy.*)

◀ Dies gilt für alle Personen und für regelmäßige und unregelmäßige Verben.

Verneinte Aussagen
Vergleiche:

	Simple present	Simple past
	I **don't like** the Big Wheel.	I **didn't like** the Big Wheel.
	Sam **doesn't like** the Big Wheel.	Sam **didn't like** the Big Wheel.

➡ p. 89, exercises 1–3

Sieh dir die Bilder an und vervollständige die Sätze in deinem Übungsheft.

1 I ...n't watch TV last night.

2 Justin ... film his friends last Friday.

3 Emily ... make ... this morning.

4 Sam ... basketball yesterday.

GF 14   The simple past: questions and short answers

Die einfache Form der Vergangenheit: Fragen und Kurzantworten

*Did Sam **like** the ride on the Big Wheel?*
*– No, he **didn't**.*

*Did you **have** a good Sunday?*
*– Yes, I **did**. / No, I **didn't**.*

***What did** you **do**? **Where did** you **go**?*

Fragen im *simple past* bildest du mit ***did***.

Vergleiche: *Lucy **looked** happy.*
            ***Did** Sam **look** happy?*
            (nicht: *Did Sam look̶e̶d̶ happy?*)

◄ Das Fragewort steht wie immer am Satzanfang.

Fragen
Vergleiche:

Simple present	Simple past
Do you **like** the Big Wheel?	**Did** you **like** the Big Wheel?
Does Sam **like** the Big Wheel?	**Did** Sam **like** the Big Wheel?
Why do you **like** the Big Wheel?	**Why did** you **like** the Big Wheel?

➡ *p. 94, exercises 1–2*

Frage nach den Personen in Klammern.
Beispiel: *Abby missed the bus. (Maya?)*   *Did Maya miss the bus?*

1 *Abby saw a group of seals on the beach. (Lucy?)*
2 *Justin made a video for his dad. (Sam?)*
3 *Abby and her brothers sailed to a beach near Ivy Island. (Sam and Lily?)*
4 *Devonport scored 24 points in the first half. (Plymstock?)*
5 *Morph walked around the library on Saturday. (Silky?)*

GF 15   The plural of nouns   Der Plural der Nomen

a bag
(Singular)

two bags
(Plural)

Du bildest den Plural (die Mehrzahl) eines Nomens, indem du **s** an das Nomen anhängst.

Singular + s ⟶ Plural

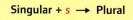

Wie beim **s** der 3. Person Singular (vgl. GF 6b auf S. 161) hängt die Aussprache des Plural-**s** vom **vorhergehenden Laut** ab:

1 [s] *baskets · biscuits · cups*
     groups · bikes · books

◄ 1 [s] nach **stimmlosen Konsonanten**.
     Stimmlose Konsonanten sind z.B. [t], [p], [k].

2 [z] *clubs · beds · bags*
     girls · rooms · cousins
     boys · trees · cameras

◄ 2 [z] nach **stimmhaften Konsonanten** und **Vokalen**.
     Stimmhafte Konsonanten sind z.B. [b], [d], [g], [l], [m].

3 [ɪz] *classes · places · buses*
      boxes · houses · wishes
      watches · pages

◄ 3 [ɪz] nach **Zischlauten**.
     Zischlaute sind z.B. [s], [z], [ʃ], [tʃ], [dʒ].
     Nach Zischlauten wird *es* oder *s* angehängt, je nach Schreibung des Singulars:
     beach – beaches · horse – horses

activity + s ⟶ activities   *diary + s ⟶ diaries*
family + s ⟶ families   *hobby + s ⟶ hobbies*
party + s ⟶ parties   *story + s ⟶ stories*

◄ Bei Nomen, die auf **Konsonant + *y*** enden, gibt es eine Besonderheit im Plural: ***y* + s ⟶ *ies***.

   (Aber **Vokal + *y*** bleibt unverändert: ***day* + s ⟶ *days***)

half [f] + **s** → **halves** [vz]   **life** + **s** → **lives**
shelf + **s** → **shelves**   **thief** + **s** → **thieves**

child → **children**   **fish** → **fish**
man → **men**   **woman** → **women**

◆ Nomen, die auf **-f** oder **-fe** enden, bilden den Plural meist mit **-ves**.

◆ Einige Nomen haben **unregelmäßige Pluralformen**.

➡ *p. 91, exercises 2–3 · p. 95, exercise 3*

Wie bildest du die Pluralform dieser Nomen?
Ordne die Nomen den Buchstaben **A** bis **C** zu.

1 *address* · **2** *animal* · **3** *ant* · **4** *bear*
5 *butterfly* · **6** *library* · **7** *match* · **8** *monkey*
9 *sandwich* · **10** *toy* · **11** *trophy* · **12** *way*

| A -s | B -es | C -ies |

Unit 5

GF 16 **The present progressive** Die Verlaufsform der Gegenwart

a) Simple present und present progressive

Simple present   *I* **get up** *at 6:30 every morning.*

My sister **plays** *hockey. She* **goes** *to training two afternoons every week.*

Present progressive

I'm cleaning my bike.

Einfache Form und Verlaufsform der Gegenwart

Du kennst bereits das *simple present* und weißt, dass man mit dem *simple present* über die **Gegenwart** spricht (vgl. GF 6 und GF 8 auf den Seiten 160–164).

Auch das *present progressive* bezieht sich auf die **Gegenwart**. Man verwendet es, wenn man sagen will, was **gerade passiert** oder was **jemand in diesem Moment gerade tut**.
(Daher der Name „**Verlauf**sform der Gegenwart": Man spricht damit über etwas, das **gerade im Verlauf** ist.)

Eine Verlaufsform gibt es im Deutschen nicht. Aber manchmal sagen wir „Ich bin gerade dabei, mein Rad zu putzen."

b) Positive and negative statements

It's 8 o'clock. Olivia **is watching** *TV.*
Es ist 8 Uhr. Olivia sieht (gerade) fern.

Her brother **isn't watching** *TV,* **he's cleaning** *his bike.*
Ihr Bruder sieht nicht fern, er putzt (gerade) sein Rad.

Their parents **are working** *in the garden.*
Ihre Eltern arbeiten (gerade) im Garten.

1 *Look, the ferry* **is arriving** *now.*

2 *Lucy* **is running**. *She doesn't want to miss the ferry.*

➡ *pp. 106–107, exercises 1–5*

Bejahte und verneinte Aussagesätze

Das *present progressive* wird mit **am/are/is** + **-ing**-Form des Verbs gebildet:
He's **cleaning** *his bike. He* **isn't watching** *TV.*

Die *-ing*-Form besteht aus **Infinitiv + ing**:
clean + ing → **cleaning** · **watch + ing** → **watching**

❗ Beachte folgende Besonderheiten:

1 Ein stummes *e* fällt weg: *arrive* → *arriving*

2 Nach einem einzelnen, betonten Vokal wird der Konsonant verdoppelt: **run** → **running**
forget → *forgetting*

c) Questions and short answers

> *What are you doing?*
> *Are you watching video clips?*

> *No, I'm not.*
> *I'm working.*

> *And where's Dad?*
> *Is he still working in the garden?*

> *Yes, he is.*

Fragen und Kurzantworten

In Fragen sind Subjekt *(you, he)* und *am/are/is* vertauscht.

Die Kurzantworten kennst du bereits vom Verb **be** (vgl. GF 2c auf S. 158).

Fragewörter stehen wie immer am Satzanfang.

Vergleiche:

	He **is working**.
Entscheidungsfrage:	**Is** he **working**?
Frage mit Fragewort:	**Why** **is** he **working**?

Present progressive		
+	**–**	**?**
I'm working	I'm not working	Am I working?
You're working	You aren't working	Are you working?
He's/She's/It's working	He/She/It isn't working	Is he/she/it working?
We're/You're/They're working	We/You/They aren't working	Are we/you/they working?

➡ *p. 110, exercises 1–2*

Löse jetzt diese beiden Aufgaben:

a) Wie bildest du die *-ing*-Form dieser Verben? Ordne die Verben den Buchstaben **A** bis **C** zu.

    1 *call* · 2 *clean* · 3 *dance* · 4 *get* · 5 *jump*
    6 *live* · 7 *make* · 8 *read* · 9 *sit* · 10 *sleep*
    11 *smile* · 12 *stop* · 13 *swim* · 14 *win* · 15 *write*

A	work	⟶ working
B	arriv**e**	⟶ arriving
C	run	⟶ ru**nn**ing

b) Welche Sätze drücken aus, dass Jay **gerade dabei** ist, etwas zu tun?
Welche Sätze drücken aus, dass Jay etwas **regelmäßig** tut?
Ordne die Sätze den Buchstaben **A** oder **B** zu.

> **A** *gerade jetzt*   **B** *regelmäßig*

    1 *Jay often has tea for breakfast.*
    2 *Today Jay isn't drinking tea. He's drinking milk.*
    3 *And look, he's eating sandwiches today.*
    4 *He doesn't usually eat sandwiches.*
    5 *He usually gets up too late!*

GF 17 **Word order** Wortstellung

Subject	**V**erb	**O**bject
Justin's father	has	a new job.
He	doesn't have	much time.
Justin	is making	a video.
You	can film	all your friends.

Die wichtigste Wortstellungsregel im Englischen ist **S–V–O**: *subject – verb – object*
                  (Subjekt – Prädikat – Objekt)

Das kannst du dir gut merken, wenn du an die **S**traßen**v**erkehrs**o**rdnung denkst.

❗ Es gibt einige wichtige Unterschiede zwischen dem Englischen und dem Deutschen. Sieh dir die Beispielsätze und die Übersetzungen gut an.

1 *"Justin, you **can film** me and my sister."*
„…, du **kannst** meine Schwester und mich **filmen**."

2 *Sam **plays basketball** every Saturday afternoon.*
Sam **spielt** jeden Samstagnachmittag **Basketball**.

oder

***Every Saturday afternoon** Sam **plays basketball**.*
Jeden Samstagnachmittag spielt Sam **Basketball**.

3 *Maya likes Plymouth because she **likes** **the sea**.*

Maya mag Plymouth, weil sie **das Meer mag**.

➡ *p.114, exercise 2*

1 Das Objekt (hier: *me and my sister*) kann **nicht** zwischen *can* und Vollverb (hier: *film*) stehen.

2 Zeitangaben (hier: *every Saturday afternoon*) können **nicht** zwischen Prädikat und Objekt stehen. Sie stehen am Ende oder am Anfang des Satzes.

3 In englischen Nebensätzen ist die Wortstellung genauso wie im Hauptsatz: **S – V – O**.

Schreibe die Sätze mit der richtigen Wortstellung in dein Übungsheft.

1 **We** … *(can – cards – play – when – you – home – come)*
2 **Today** … *(can – you – your homework – do – in the dining room)*
3 **My room** … *(is – too small – so – meet – we – usually – at Emily's house)*
4 **Justin** … *(live – doesn't – with his dad – because – his dad – a job – in Boston – has)*
5 **After breakfast** … *(I – feed – always – my cat)*

Grammatical terms (Grammatische Fachbegriffe)

adjective [ˈædʒɪktɪv]	Adjektiv (Eigenschaftswort)	*good, new, green, interesting, …*
adverb [ˈædvɜːb]	Adverb	*today, there, outside, very, …*
adverb of frequency [ˈfriːkwənsi]	Häufigkeitsadverb	*always, usually, often, sometimes, never*
article [ˈɑːtɪkl]	Artikel	*the, a, an*
conjunction [kənˈdʒʌŋkʃn]	Konjunktion	*and, but, …; because, when, …*
imperative [ɪmˈperətɪv]	Imperativ (Befehlsform)	*Open your books. Don't talk.*
infinitive [ɪnˈfɪnətɪv]	Infinitiv (Grundform des Verbs)	*(to) open, (to) go, …*
irregular verb [ɪˈreɡjələ]	unregelmäßiges Verb	*(to) go – went, (to) see – saw, …*
negative statement [ˈneɡətɪv]	verneinter Aussagesatz	*I don't like oranges.*
noun [naʊn]	Nomen, Substantiv	*Justin, girl, man, time, name, …*
object [ˈɒbdʒɪkt]	Objekt	*Justin has **a new camera**.*
past [pɑːst]	Vergangenheit	
personal pronoun [ˌpɜːsənl ˈprəʊnaʊn]	Personalpronomen (persönliches Fürwort)	*I, you, he, she, it, we, they; me, you, him, her, it, us, them*
plural [ˈplʊərəl]	Plural, Mehrzahl	
positive statement [ˈpɒzətɪv]	bejahter Aussagesatz	*I like oranges.*
possessive determiner [pəˌzesɪv dɪˈtɜːmɪnə]	Possessivbegleiter (besitzanzeigender Begleiter)	*my, your, his, her, its, our, their*
possessive form [pəˌzesɪv ˈfɔːm]	s-Genitiv	*Sam's sister, the Blackwells' house, …*
preposition [ˌprepəˈzɪʃn]	Präposition	*after, at, in, into, near, …*
present [ˈpreznt]	Gegenwart	
present progressive [ˌpreznt prəˈɡresɪv]	Verlaufsform der Gegenwart	*Olivia **is playing** cards.*
pronoun [ˈprəʊnaʊn]	Pronomen (Fürwort)	
pronunciation [prəˌnʌnsiˈeɪʃn]	Aussprache	
question [ˈkwestʃən]	Frage(satz)	
question word [ˈkwestʃn wɜːd]	Fragewort	*who?, what?, when?, where?, how?, …*
regular verb [ˈreɡjələ]	regelmäßiges Verb	*(to) help – helped, (to) look – looked, …*
short answer [ˌʃɔːt ˈɑːnsə]	Kurzantwort	*Yes, I am. / No, we don't. / …*

simple past [ˌsɪmpl ˈpɑːst]	einfache Form der Vergangenheit	Olivia **played** cards last Friday.
simple present [ˌsɪmpl ˈpreznt]	einfache Form der Gegenwart	Olivia **plays** cards every Friday evening.
singular [ˈsɪŋɡjələ]	Singular, Einzahl	
spelling [ˈspelɪŋ]	Schreibweise, Rechtschreibung	
statement [ˈsteɪtmənt]	Aussage(satz)	
sub-clause [ˈsʌbklɔːz]	Nebensatz	I like Plymouth **because I like the sea.**
subject [ˈsʌbdʒɪkt]	Subjekt	**Justin/He** has a new camera.
verb [vɜːb]	1. Verb;	go, help, look, see, …
	2. Prädikat	Reading **can be** fun.
word order [ˈwɜːd ˌɔːdə]	Wortstellung	
yes/no question	Entscheidungsfrage	Are you 14? Do you like oranges?

Lösungen der Grammar-File-Aufgaben

p. 157 a) it, she, they, you, we (5)

p. 157 b)
1 Look, a snake. – **It's** big.
2 This is my cat Susie. – How old is **she**?
3 And this is my dog Victor. – **He's** nice.
4 Where are your rabbits? – **They're** in my room.

p. 158 3, 5

p. 159
1 **There's** a computer on the desk.
2 **There aren't any** books on the desk.
3 **Are there any** pencils on the desk?
 – Yes, **there are.**
4 **Is there a** ball on the desk?
 – No, **there isn't.**
5 **Are there any** CDs on the desk?
 – No, **there aren't.**
6 **Is there a** ruler on the desk?
 – Yes, **there is.**

p. 160
1 I like card games.
2 My sister **likes** football.
3 My dog always **sleeps** in his basket.
4 Susie can sleep on my bed.
5 Seals eat fish.
6 Silky **eats** crabs too.

p. 161 a) watches, touches, goes, catches, does

p. 161 b) 1A, 2C, 3B, 4B, 5B, 6C, 7A, 8B, 9A, 10B

p. 162/1
1 Dilip and Sanjay **don't live** in South Africa.
2 Uncle Dasan **doesn't live** in Britain.
3 He goes to a sports school, but he **doesn't** do sport.
4 Maya **doesn't go** to Plymstock School.
5 My cats **don't sleep** at night – they play.
6 I **don't have** a cat, I have a rabbit.

p. 162/2
1 Singular (ein Bruder)
2 Plural (mehrere Brüder)
3 Plural (mehrere Mädchen)
4 Plural (mehrere Schüler/innen)
5 Singular (ein Schüler oder eine Schülerin)
6 Singular (ein Mädchen)

p. 163 a)
1 **Does** Lucy **play** basketball too?
2 **Does** Maya **play** games at weekends too?
3 **Do** Sam and Lily **live** in a nice house too?
4 **Does** Lucy **visit** Abby at weekends too?

p. 163 b) 1A, 2B, 3C
4 **Do** Abby's brothers go sailing too?
5 **Does** Sam make video films too?

p. 164/1
1 **When does** Maya visit Abby?
2 **Where does** Abby live?
3 **Why do** Abby's brothers go sailing?
4 **What do** you do in your free time?

p. 164/2
1 Kids **usually** like ice cream.
2 It is **often** very cold in Germany in January.
3 Sam **always** goes to basketball on Thursdays.
4 I **never** eat scones for breakfast.
5 Morph **sometimes** plays cards in the evenings.

p. 166/1 1A, 2B, 3B, 4D, 5B, 6B, 7A, 8B, 9A, 10A, 11C, 12A

p. 166/2
1 I **didn't** watch TV last night.
2 Justin **didn't** film his friends last Friday.
3 Emily **didn't** make her bed this morning.
4 Sam **didn't play** basketball yesterday.

p. 167
1 **Did** Lucy **see** a group of seals on the beach?
2 **Did** Sam **make** a video for his dad?
3 **Did** Sam and Lily **sail** to a beach near Ivy Island?
4 **Did** Plymstock **score** 24 points in the first half?
5 **Did** Silky **walk** around the library on Saturday?

p. 168 1B, 2A, 3A, 4A, 5C, 6C, 7B, 8A, 9B, 10A, 11C, 12A

p. 169/1 1A, 2A, 3B, 4C, 5A, 6B, 7B, 8A, 9C, 10A, 11B, 12C, 13C, 14C, 15B

p. 169/2 1B, 2A, 3A, 4B, 5B

p. 170
1 **We can play** cards when you come home.
2 **Today you can do** your homework in the dining room.
3 My room is too small so we usually meet at Emily's house.
4 Justin doesn't live with his dad because his dad has a job in Boston.
5 After breakfast I always feed my cat.

Vocabulary

Das **Vocabulary** (S. 172–205) enthält alle Wörter und Wendungen deines Englischbuches, die du lernen musst.
Sie stehen in der Reihenfolge, in der sie im Buch zum ersten Mal vorkommen.

Hier siehst du, wie das **Vocabulary** aufgebaut ist:

Diese Zahl gibt die **Seite** an, auf der die Wörter zum ersten Mal vorkommen.
p. 16 = Seite 16

Die **Lautschrift** zeigt dir, wie ein Wort ausgesprochen wird.
Eine Übersicht über alle **Lautschriftzeichen** findest du auf S. 233.
Die Lautschriftzeichen stehen auch unten auf den **Vocabulary**-Seiten.

Eingerückte Wörter lernst du am besten zusammen mit dem vorausgehenden Wort, weil die beiden zusammengehören.

Das **rote Ausrufezeichen** bedeutet: Vorsicht, hier macht man leicht Fehler!

Dies ist das „Gegenteil"-Zeichen: „**new** ist das Gegenteil von **old**".

Blau gedruckte Wörter kennst du wahrscheinlich schon aus dem Englischunterricht in der Grundschule.

Diese **Kästen** solltest du dir immer besonders gut ansehen: Hier sind Vokabeln zu einem bestimmten Thema zusammengestellt. Oder du erfährst mehr über ein Wort und wie es verwendet wird.

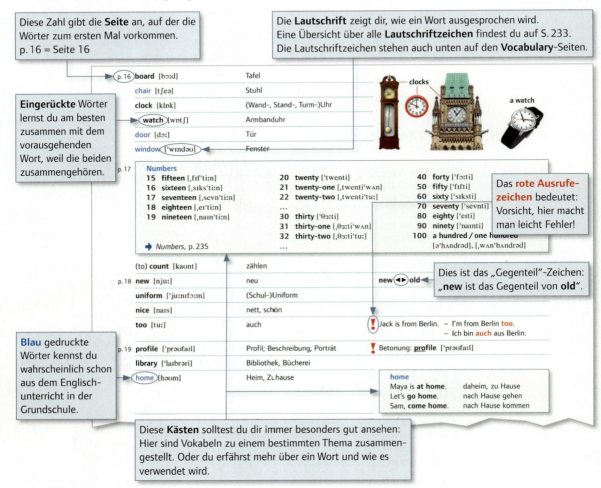

p. 16	board [bɔːd]	Tafel
	chair [tʃeə]	Stuhl
	clock [klɒk]	(Wand-, Stand-, Turm-)Uhr
	watch [wɒtʃ]	Armbanduhr
	door [dɔː]	Tür
	window ['wɪndəʊ]	Fenster

clocks · a watch

p. 17 **Numbers**

15	fifteen [ˌfɪf'tiːn]	20	twenty ['twenti]	40	forty ['fɔːti]
16	sixteen [ˌsɪks'tiːn]	21	twenty-one [ˌtwenti'wʌn]	50	fifty ['fɪfti]
17	seventeen [ˌsevn'tiːn]	22	twenty-two [ˌtwenti'tuː]	60	sixty ['sɪksti]
18	eighteen [ˌeɪ'tiːn]	…		70	seventy ['sevnti]
19	nineteen [ˌnaɪn'tiːn]	30	thirty ['θɜːti]	80	eighty ['eɪti]
		31	thirty-one [ˌθɜːti'wʌn]	90	ninety ['naɪnti]
		32	thirty-two [ˌθɜːti'tuː]	100	a hundred / one hundred
		…			[ə'hʌndrəd], [ˌwʌn'hʌndrəd]

➜ *Numbers, p. 235*

	(to) **count** [kaʊnt]	zählen
p. 18	**new** [njuː]	neu
	uniform ['juːnɪfɔːm]	(Schul-)Uniform
	nice [naɪs]	nett, schön
	too [tuː]	auch

new ◄►old

! Jack is from Berlin. – I'm from Berlin too.
– Ich bin auch aus Berlin.

p. 19	**profile** ['prəʊfaɪl]	Profil; Beschreibung, Porträt
	library ['laɪbrəri]	Bibliothek, Bücherei
	home [həʊm]	Heim, Zuhause

! Betonung: **profile** ['prəʊfaɪl]

home
Maya is **at home**.   daheim, zu Hause
Let's **go home**.   nach Hause gehen
Sam, **come home**.   nach Hause kommen

Tipps zum Wörterlernen findest du im **Skills File** auf den Seiten 148 und 149.

Im **Vocabulary** werden folgende **Abkürzungen** verwendet:
p. = page (Seite)   pp. = pages (Seiten)
sth. = something (etwas)   sb. = somebody (jemand)
jn. = jemanden   jm. = jemandem
pl = plural (Mehrzahl)
infml = informal (umgangssprachlich)

Wenn du **nachschlagen** möchtest, was ein englisches Wort bedeutet oder wie man es ausspricht, dann verwende das **English – German Dictionary** auf den Seiten 206–219.
Und wenn du vergessen hast, wie etwas auf Englisch heißt, dann kann dir das **German – English Dictionary** auf den Seiten 220–230 eine erste Hilfe sein.

[iː] green · [i] happy · [ɪ] big · [e] red · [æ] cat · [ɑː] class · [ɒ] song ·
[ɔː] door · [uː] blue · [ʊ] book · [ʌ] mum · [ɜː] girl · [ə] a partner

Here we go

p.8	**Here we go.** [ˌhɪə wi ˈgəʊ]	Los geht's. / Jetzt geht's los.	

Hello. [həˈləʊ]	Hallo. / Guten Tag.	

I'm a seal. [aɪm] (= **I am** a seal.)	Ich bin eine Robbe.	❗ Das englische Wort **I** (= „ich") wird immer großgeschrieben – auch wenn es nicht am Satzanfang steht.

a seal [ə ˈsiːl]	eine Robbe	[iː] ist ein langes „i" wie in „W**ie**n".

My name is Silky. [maɪ ˈneɪm‿ɪz]	Ich heiße Silky. (*wörtlich:* Mein Name ist Silky.)	[z] ist ein weiches „s" wie in „le**s**en".

I'm **two years** old. [ˌtuː jɪəz‿ˈəʊld]	Ich bin zwei Jahre alt.	[ɪə] klingt wie das „ier" in „h**ier**".

Numbers

1	**one** [wʌn]	5	**five** [faɪv]	9	**nine** [naɪn]	13	**thirteen** [ˌθɜːˈtiːn]
2	**two** [tuː]	6	**six** [sɪks]	10	**ten** [ten]	14	**fourteen** [ˌfɔːˈtiːn]
3	**three** [θriː]	7	**seven** [ˈsevn]	11	**eleven** [ɪˈlevn]		
4	**four** [fɔː]	8	**eight** [eɪt]	12	**twelve** [twelv]	➜ *Numbers,* p. 233

---

p.9	**I'm from** Plymouth. [frɒm], [frəm]	Ich bin aus Plymouth. / Ich komme aus Plymouth.	

in England [ɪn‿ˈɪŋglənd]	in England	❗ Ländernamen werden großgeschrieben: in **E**ngland

What about you? [əˈbaʊt]	Und du? / Und was ist mit dir? Und ihr? / Und was ist mit euch?	*Englisch:* **you** *Deutsch:* **du – dich – dir** **ihr – euch – euch** **Sie – Sie – Ihnen**

what? [wɒt]	was?	Der Laut [ɒ] klingt wie das „o" in „d**o**ch".

Silky's questions [ˈkwestʃənz]	Silkys Fragen	

What's your name?	Wie heißt du? / Wie heißt ihr?	

> Hello. My name is Ava. What's your name?

> My name is Jake.

your [jɔː], [jə]	dein/e; euer/eure; Ihr/e	

Are you ...? [ˈɑː ju]	Bist du ...?	**Are you** a boy or a girl?

boy [bɔɪ]	Junge	[ɔɪ] klingt ähnlich wie das „eu" in „H**eu**".

or [ɔː]	oder	

girl [gɜːl]	Mädchen	[ɜː] klingt etwa so wie der Laut in „T-Sh**ir**t".

How old are you? [haʊ]	Wie alt bist du?	

Where are you from? [weə]	Woher kommst du?	

where? [weə]	wo? / wohin?	[eə] kennst du aus dem Wort „f**air**".

Meet your classmates. [miːt]	Triff deine Mitschüler/innen. / Lerne deine Mitschüler/innen kennen.	

[eɪ] n**a**me · [aɪ] t**i**me · [ɔɪ] b**oy** · [əʊ] **o**ld ·
[aʊ] t**ow**n · [ɪə] **here** · [eə] **where** · [ʊə] t**our**

classmate [ˈklɑːsmeɪt]	Mitschüler/in, Klassenkamerad/in	[ɑː] ist ein langes „a" wie in „Kr**a**m".
card (to) [kɑːd]	Karte (an)	
and [ænd], [ənd]	und	[æ] kennst du aus „(Rock-, Pop-)B**a**nd"
I like … [laɪk]	Ich mag …	
the [ðə]	der, die, das; die	
colour [ˈkʌlə]	Farbe	
red [red]	rot	
tip [tɪp]	Tipp	
Let's go to England. [lets]	Lass(t) uns nach England gehen / fahren.	
to [tu], [tə]	zu, nach	
(to)* go [gəʊ]	gehen; fahren	[əʊ] kennst du aus dem Wort „Sh**ow**".
(to) come [kʌm]	kommen	
(to) see [siː]	sehen; besuchen	[s] ist ein hartes, scharfes „s" wie in „la**ss**en".
hometown [ˌhəʊmˈtaʊn]	Heimatstadt	
town [taʊn]	Stadt	

I like the colour red.

Welcome to Plymouth

p. 10 **Welcome to** Plymouth. [ˈwelkəm]	Willkommen in Plymouth.	Der Laut [ə] ist ein schwaches „e" wie am Ende von „bitt**e**".
Silky's tour of Plymouth [ˈtʊə‿əv]	Silkys Rundgang / Rundfahrt / Reise durch Plymouth	[ʊə] klingt ähnlich wie das „ur" in „K**ur**".
river [ˈrɪvə]	Fluss	[v] klingt wie „**V**ampir" – nicht wie „**V**ater"!
castle [ˈkɑːsl]	Burg, Schloss	
(swimming) pool [puːl]	Schwimmbad, Schwimmbecken	
tower [ˈtaʊə]	Turm	
hill [hɪl]	Hügel	
boat [bəʊt]	Boot	
sea [siː]	Meer	
big wheel [bɪg ˈwiːl]	Riesenrad	
big [bɪg]	groß	
can [kæn], [kən]	können	
on the map [ɒn ðə ˈmæp]	auf der Landkarte; auf dem Stadtplan	

tower   castle   boat

river   hill   sea

I can see a river on the map. And you?

p. 11 **Silky's song** [sɒŋ]	Silkys Lied, Silkys Song	[ŋ] ist wie „ng" in „Di**ng**".

* Mit dem vorangestellten **(to)** ist der Infinitiv (die Grundform des Verbs) gekennzeichnet.

[b] **b**oat · [p] **p**ool · [d] **d**ad · [t] **t**en · [g] **g**ood · [k] **c**at · [m] **m**um · [n] **n**o · [ŋ] so**ng** · [l] **h**ello · [r] **r**ed · [w] **w**e · [j] **y**ou

Is it Monday? [ˈɪz‿ɪt]   Ist es Montag?

> **The days of the week**
> **Monday** [ˈmʌndeɪ], [ˈmʌndi]   Montag   **Saturday** [ˈsætədeɪ], [ˈsætədi]   Samstag, Sonnabend
> **Tuesday** [ˈtjuːzdeɪ], [ˈtjuːzdi]   Dienstag   **Sunday** [ˈsʌndeɪ], [ˈsʌndi]   Sonntag
> **Wednesday** [ˈwenzdeɪ], [ˈwenzdi]   Mittwoch
> **Thursday** [ˈθɜːzdeɪ], [ˈθɜːzdi]   Donnerstag   ❗ Die Wochentage werden immer großgeschrieben.
> **Friday** [ˈfraɪdeɪ], [ˈfraɪdi]   Freitag

every day / colour / boat [ˈevri]   jeder Tag / jede Farbe / jedes Boot

great [greɪt]   großartig

A week in Plymouth

p.12 **at** [æt], [ət]   *(in Ortsangaben)* an, bei, in

near [nɪə]   in der Nähe von, nahe (bei)   Silky is **near** the boat.
❗ *Nicht:* … ~~in the near of~~ …

on Monday/Tuesday/…   am Montag/Dienstag/…

On Thursday I'm in the sea.

she's … [ʃiːz] **(= she is)**   sie ist …   [ʃ] klingt wie das „sch" in „**sch**ön".

p.13 **photo** [ˈfəʊtəʊ]   Foto   *Englisch:* **in** the photo
Deutsch: **auf** dem Foto

Look, … [lʊk]   Sieh mal, … / Schau mal, …

it's … [ɪts] **(= it is)**   er/sie/es ist …

Englisch:	**it**	*Deutsch:*	**er/sie/es**
the **river** …	**it's** big		**er** ist groß
the **town** …	**it's** old		**sie** ist alt
the **photo** …	**it's** great		**es** ist großartig

Where are you?

here [hɪə]   hier; hierher

I'm here.

Yes, that's right. [ˌjes ðæts ˈraɪt]   Ja, das ist richtig. / Ja, das stimmt.   [ð] klingt etwa wie ein gelispeltes „Wie**s**e".

No, that's wrong. [ˌnəʊ ðæts ˈrɒŋ]   Nein, das ist falsch. / Nein, das stimmt nicht.   ❗ Aussprache – das "w" wird nicht gesprochen: **wrong** [rɒŋ]

rhyme [raɪm]   Reim; Vers

There are … [ˈðeər‿ɑː]   Es sind … / Es gibt …   **There are** two boys and two girls in the boat.

There's … [ðeəz]   Es ist … / Es gibt …   **There's** a girl on the tower.

lots of … [ˈlɒts‿əv]   viel …, viele …   **lots of** books

[f] **f**ather · [v] ri**v**er · [s] **s**ister · [z] plea**s**e · [ʃ] **sh**op · [ʒ] televi**s**ion ·
[tʃ] **t**ea**ch**er · [dʒ] **G**ermany · [θ] **th**anks · [ð] **th**is · [h] **h**ere

animal [ˈænɪml]	Tier
Follow me. [ˈfɒləʊ miː]	Folg mir. / Folgt mir.
me [miː]	mich; mir

Englisch: **me**	*Deutsch:* **mich – mir**
Come and see **me**.	Besuch **mich**.
Follow **me**	Folg **mir**.

My favourite animal

pp. 14/15

my **favourite** animal [ˈfeɪvərɪt]	mein Lieblingstier
ant [ænt]	Ameise
bear [beə]	Bär
bird [bɜːd]	Vogel
butterfly [ˈbʌtəflaɪ], *pl* **butterflies** [ˈbʌtəflaɪz]	Schmetterling
cat [kæt]	Katze
dog [dɒg]	Hund
elephant [ˈelɪfənt]	Elefant
frog [frɒg]	Frosch
giraffe [dʒəˈrɑːf]	Giraffe
guinea pig [ˈgɪni pɪg]	Meerschweinchen
horse [hɔːs]	Pferd
lion [ˈlaɪən]	Löwe
monkey [ˈmʌŋki]	Affe
pig [pɪg]	Schwein
rabbit [ˈræbɪt]	Kaninchen
rat [ræt]	Ratte
snake [sneɪk]	Schlange
whale [weɪl]	Wal
an elephant [æn], [ən]	ein Elefant

elephant • butterfly • butterflies • giraffe • frog • birds • monkey • rabbit • pig • horse • whale • dog • rat • guinea pig • cat • bear • lion • snake • ants

❗ **an** <u>e</u>lephant, **an** <u>a</u>nt, **an** <u>a</u>nimal – **a** <u>b</u>ear, **a** <u>h</u>orse, **a** <u>m</u>onkey

picture [ˈpɪktʃə]	Bild

Englisch: **in** the picture
Deutsch: **auf** dem Bild

strange [streɪndʒ]	seltsam, komisch

[dʒ] kennst du aus „Jeans" und „Job".

Colours

red [red]	rot	brown [braʊn]	braun	purple [ˈpɜːpl]	violett, lila
yellow [ˈjeləʊ]	gelb	orange [ˈɒrɪndʒ]	orange	white [waɪt]	weiß
blue [bluː]	blau	grey [greɪ]	grau	black [blæk]	schwarz
green [griːn]	grün	pink [pɪŋk]	pink, rosa		

ruler [ˈruːlə]	Lineal
game [geɪm]	Spiel
with [wɪð]	mit
leg [leg]	Bein

[iː] green · [i] happy · [ɪ] big · [e] red · [æ] cat · [ɑː] class · [ɒ] song · [ɔː] door · [uː] blue · [ʊ] book · [ʌ] mum · [ɜː] girl · [ə] a partner

without [wɪˈðaʊt]	ohne	with ◄► without
now [naʊ]	nun, jetzt	[aʊ] klingt wie das „au" wie in „bl**au**".
time [taɪm]	Zeit; Uhrzeit	
for [fɔː], [fə]	für	
English [ˈɪŋglɪʃ]	Englisch; englisch	❗ Das englische Wort **English** wird immer großgeschrieben.
lesson [ˈlesn]	(Unterrichts-)Stunde	

Our English class

p. 16 **our** [ˈaʊə]	unser/e	
class [klɑːs]	(Schul-)Klasse	
Mr Schwarz [ˈmɪstə]	Herr Schwarz	
Mrs Schwarz [ˈmɪsɪz]	Frau Schwarz	
teacher [ˈtiːtʃə]	Lehrer/in	[tʃ] klingt wie „tsch" in „**tsch**üs".
school [skuːl]	Schule	
word [wɜːd]	Wort	
classroom [ˈklɑːsruːm]	Klassenzimmer	
cupboard [ˈkʌbəd]	Schrank	[ʌ] klingt wie das kurze „a" in „K**a**mm".
desk [desk]	Schreibtisch	
thing [θɪŋ]	Sache, Ding	
rubber [ˈrʌbə]	Radiergummi	
pen [pen]	Kugelschreiber, Stift, Füller	
board [bɔːd]	Tafel	
chair [tʃeə]	Stuhl	
clock [klɒk]	(Wand-, Stand-, Turm-)Uhr	
watch [wɒtʃ]	Armbanduhr	
door [dɔː]	Tür	
window [ˈwɪndəʊ]	Fenster	
This is … [ˈðɪs_ɪz]	Dies ist … / Das ist …	
school bag [ˈskuːl bæg]	Schultasche	
book [bʊk]	Buch	
exercise book [ˈeksəsaɪz bʊk]	Schulheft, Übungsheft	
pencil [ˈpensl]	Bleistift	
pencil case [ˈpensl keɪs]	Federmäppchen	
glue stick [ˈgluː stɪk]	Klebestift	
glue [gluː]	Klebstoff	
sharpener [ˈʃɑːpnə]	Anspitzer	
Let me show you …	Lass mich dir … zeigen.	
(to) **show** [ʃəʊ]	zeigen	**Show** me your hometown, Silky.

clocks

a watch

sharpener · pencil case · glue stick · pencil · rubber · pen · desk

[eɪ] n**a**me · [aɪ] t**i**me · [ɔɪ] b**oy** · [əʊ] **o**ld ·
[aʊ] t**ow**n · [ɪə] **here** · [eə] wh**ere** · [ʊə] t**our**

Simon **says** … [sez]	Simon sagt …	
(to) **put** [pʊt]	legen, stellen, (etwas wohin) tun	**Put** the photos in the box.
(to) **talk (to)** [tɔːk]	reden (mit), sich unterhalten (mit)	
(to) **open** [ˈəʊpən]	öffnen, aufmachen	
(to) **touch** [tʌtʃ]	berühren, anfassen	
(to) **give** [gɪv]	geben	Can you **give** me your rubber?

p. 17

Numbers

15	**fifteen** [ˌfɪfˈtiːn]		**20**	**twenty** [ˈtwenti]		**40**	**forty** [ˈfɔːti]	
16	**sixteen** [ˌsɪksˈtiːn]		**21**	**twenty-one** [ˌtwentiˈwʌn]		**50**	**fifty** [ˈfɪfti]	
17	**seventeen** [ˌsevnˈtiːn]		**22**	**twenty-two** [ˌtwentiˈtuː]		**60**	**sixty** [ˈsɪksti]	
18	**eighteen** [ˌeɪˈtiːn]			…		**70**	**seventy** [ˈsevnti]	
19	**nineteen** [ˌnaɪnˈtiːn]		**30**	**thirty** [ˈθɜːti]		**80**	**eighty** [ˈeɪti]	
			31	**thirty-one** [ˌθɜːtiˈwʌn]		**90**	**ninety** [ˈnaɪnti]	
			32	**thirty-two** [ˌθɜːtiˈtuː]		**100**	**a hundred / one hundred** [əˈhʌndrəd], [ˌwʌnˈhʌndrəd]	
	Numbers, p. 233			…				

(to) **count** [kaʊnt]	zählen	
them [ðem], [ðəm]	sie; ihnen	Look, there are the boys. Can you see **them**? Let's talk to **them**.

Die Betonungszeichen

Die **Betonungszeichen** [ˈ] und [ˌ] stehen immer vor der betonten Silbe. [ˈ] zeigt die Hauptbetonung, [ˌ] zeigt die Nebenbetonung.
Im Deutschen sagt man <u>neunzehn</u> (Hauptbetonung auf der ersten Silbe). Die englische Zahl **nineteen** hat die Hauptbetonung auf **-teen**: [ˌnaɪnˈtiːn].
Also Vorsicht bei der Aussprache:
19 nine<u>teen</u> [ˌnaɪnˈtiːn] – **90 <u>nine</u>ty** [ˈnaɪnti]

Der Bindebogen

Der **Bindebogen** [‿] in der Lautschrift zeigt an, dass zwei Wörter beim Sprechen aneinandergebunden und wie <u>ein</u> Wort gesprochen werden. Beispiele:

seven‿ants	[sevn‿ˈænts]
boys‿and girls	[ˌbɔɪz‿ənd ˈgɜːlz]
in‿our class	[ɪn‿aʊə ˈklɑːs]
12 years‿old	[twelv jɪəz‿ˈəʊld]

---

telephone [ˈtelɪfəʊn]	Telefon	
o [əʊ]	Null (in Telefonnummern)	❗ Du <u>schreibst</u>: 0166 204 …
double [ˈdʌbl]	Doppel-	Du <u>sagst</u>: **o** one **double** six two **o** four …
See you.	Bis gleich. / Bis bald.	

Unit 1   The first day at school

p. 18 **the first day** [fɜːst]	der erste Tag	
at school	in der Schule	*English:* **at school** *German:* **in der** Schule
kid [kɪd] (*infml*)	Kind; Jugendliche(r)	
her best friend [hɜː ˌbest ˈfrend]	ihr bester Freund / ihre beste Freundin	
they're … [ðeə] (= **they are** [ðeɪ‿ɑː])	sie sind …	
flat [flæt]	Wohnung	
their first day [ðeə]	ihr erster Tag	

[b] **boat** · [p] **pool** · [d] **dad** · [t] **ten** · [g] **good** · [k] **cat** · [m] **mum** · [n] **no** · [ŋ] **song** · [l] **hello** · [r] **red** · [w] **we** · [j] **you**

new [njuː]	neu	new ◄► old
uniform [ˈjuːnɪfɔːm]	(Schul-)Uniform	
nice [naɪs]	nett, schön	
too [tuː]	auch	❗ Jack is from Berlin. – I'm from Berlin **too**. – Ich bin **auch** aus Berlin.
(to) know [nəʊ]	wissen; kennen	
brother [ˈbrʌðə]	Bruder	
sister [ˈsɪstə]	Schwester	
student [ˈstjuːdənt]	Schüler/in; Student/in	❗ Betonung: **student** [ˈstjuːdənt]
but [bʌt], [bət]	aber	Luca is ten, **but** Jack is fourteen.
he/she/it isn't … [ˈɪznt] **(= he/she/it is not** [nɒt]**)**	er/sie/es ist nicht …; er/sie/es ist kein/e …	Maya **isn't** at Plymstock School. And **she isn't** a teacher – she's a student.
his mum [hɪz]	seine Mama	I – **my** name **we** – **our** names you – **your** name you – **your** names he – **his** name they – **their** names she – **her** name
mum [mʌm]	Mama, Mutti	
mother [ˈmʌðə]	Mutter	
dad [dæd]	Papa, Vati	
father [ˈfɑːðə]	Vater	
navy [ˈneɪvi]	Marine	
(to) **look at** [lʊk]	anschauen, ansehen	*Look at my poster. It's nice.*
dark [dɑːk]	dunkel	
Thank you. [ˈθæŋk juː]	Danke.	
please [pliːz]	bitte	Can you open the window, **please**?
You're late. [leɪt]	Du bist spät dran. / Du bist zu spät.	
(to) **wait (for)** [weɪt]	warten (auf)	*Wait for me, please.*
minute [ˈmɪnɪt]	Minute	❗ Betonung: **minute** [ˈmɪnɪt]
What time is it?	Wie spät ist es?	
p. 19 **profile** [ˈprəʊfaɪl]	Profil; Beschreibung, Porträt	❗ Betonung: **profile** [ˈprəʊfaɪl]
library [ˈlaɪbrəri]	Bibliothek, Bücherei	
home [həʊm]	Heim, Zuhause	**home** Maya is **at home**. daheim, zu Hause Let's **go home**. nach Hause gehen Sam, **come home**. nach Hause kommen

Part A

p. 20 **before** school/lessons [bɪˈfɔː]	vor der Schule (*vor Schul- beginn*) / vorm Unterricht	
you aren't … [ɑːnt] **(= you are not)**	du bist nicht …; du bist kein/e …; ihr seid nicht …; ihr seid kein/e …	**You aren't** at my school. And **you aren't** a student.

[f] **f**ather · [v] ri**v**er · [s] **s**ister · [z] plea**s**e · [ʃ] **sh**op · [ʒ] televi**s**ion ·
[tʃ] **t**ea**ch**er · [dʒ] **G**ermany · [θ] **th**anks · [ð] **th**is · [h] **h**ere

there [ðeə]	da, dort; dahin, dorthin	Let's go to the park. Let's meet our friends **there**. here ◄► there
sad [sæd]	traurig	
Don't go. [dəʊnt]	Geh nicht.	
Bye. [baɪ]	Tschüs.	**Hello.** ◄► **Bye.**
Watch out! [ˌwɒtʃ_'aʊt]	Pass auf! / Vorsicht!	
(I'm) sorry. ['sɒri]	Tut mir leid. / Entschuldigung.	

Hey, watch out!

So? [səʊ]	Und? / Na und?	
Nice **to** meet you.	Freut mich, dich/euch/Sie kennenzulernen.	

English "to" – German "zu"
Nice **to** meet you.   kennen**zu**lernen
It's time **to** go now.   **zu** gehen
It's nice **to** see you.   **zu** sehen

(to) hurry up [ˌhʌri_'ʌp]	sich beeilen	
who? [huː]	wer?	*English:* **who?** – *German:* **wer?**
English: **where?** – *German:* **wo? / wohin?**
friendly ['frendli]	freundlich	
p.21 shoe [ʃuː]	Schuh	
trainer ['treɪnə]	Turnschuh	
(to) forget [fə'get]	vergessen	
(to) wear [weə]	tragen *(Kleidung)*	**Wear** black shoes.
Don't **wear** trainers.
British ['brɪtɪʃ]	britisch	
different ['dɪfrənt]	verschieden; anders	The Coombe Dean uniform is **different**.
(to) have [hæv], [həv]	haben	I **have** one brother and two sisters.
I don't like green. [dəʊnt]	Ich mag Grün nicht. / Ich mag kein Grün.	**I like …** ◄► **I don't like …**
Have a go. [ˌhæv_ə 'gəʊ]	Versuch's mal.	
p.22 **language** ['læŋgwɪdʒ]	Sprache	
form (of) [fɔːm]	Form (von)	"am", "is" and "are" are **forms of** "be".
of [ɒv], [əv]	von	a map **of** Britain
long [lɒŋ]	lang	At German schools, a lesson is 45 minutes **long**.
short [ʃɔːt]	kurz	**long** ◄► **short**
people ['piːpl]	Leute, Menschen	The **people** in Plymouth are nice.
p.23 silly ['sɪli]	albern; blöd	
sentence ['sentəns]	Satz	
p.24 help [help]	Hilfe	
(to) help [help]	helfen	Can you **help** me, please?

■ England
■ Scotland
■ Wales

[iː] green · [i] happy · [ɪ] big · [e] red · [æ] cat · [ɑː] class · [ɒ] song · [ɔː] door · [uː] blue · [ʊ] book · [ʌ] mum · [ɜː] girl · [ə] a partner

p.25 **speaker** ['spiːkə]	Sprecher/in	
(to) **speak** [spiːk]	sprechen	Can you **speak** English?
about me/you/… [ə'baʊt]	über mich/dich/…	
at 1 o'clock [ə'klɒk]	um 1 Uhr / um 13 Uhr	It's **1 o'clock** now.
appointment [ə'pɔɪntmənt]	Verabredung, Termin	I have an **appointment** at 2 o'clock.

Part B

p.26 **Miss** Bell [mɪs]	Frau Bell (übliche Anrede von Lehrerinnen)	Can I open the window, **Miss**?
Good morning. [gʊd 'mɔːnɪŋ]	Guten Morgen.	
so [səʊ]	also; deshalb, daher	It's your first day at school, **so** let me show you the school.
(to) **come in**	hereinkommen	
(to) **start** [stɑːt]	anfangen, beginnen	
ball [bɔːl]	Ball	a **football**
(to) **throw** [θrəʊ]	werfen	
(to) **ask** [ɑːsk]	fragen	Can I start? – **Ask** Miss Bell. *English:* Can I **ask** you a **question**? *German:* Kann ich dir eine **Frage stellen**?
(to) **catch** [kætʃ]	fangen	(to) **throw a ball** ◄► (to) **catch a ball**
(to) **answer** ['ɑːnsə]	antworten; beantworten	(to) **ask** ◄► (to) **answer**
answer ['ɑːnsə]	Antwort	
about yourself [jɔː'self]	über dich selbst	
birthday ['bɜːθdeɪ]	Geburtstag	
September [sep'tembə]	September	❗ Monatsnamen werden großgeschrieben: in **S**eptember
(to) **do** [duː]	machen, tun	
(to) **live** [lɪv]	leben; wohnen	Justin and his mum **live** in Plymouth.
at 14 Dean Street [striːt]	in der Deanstraße 14	*English:* They live **at** 14 Dean Street. *German:* Sie wohnen **in** der Deanstraße 14.
then [ðen]	dann	Throw the ball. **Then** ask a question.
again [ə'gen]	wieder; noch einmal	Can you say that **again**, please?
timetable ['taɪmteɪbl]	Stundenplan	
p.27 **quarter past** ten ['kwɔːtə pɑːst]	Viertel nach zehn (10.15 / 22.15)	
half past ten ['hɑːf pɑːst]	halb elf (10.30 / 22.30)	
quarter to eleven ['kwɔːtə tʊ]	Viertel vor elf (10.45 / 22.45)	

(school) subject ['sʌbdʒɪkt]   Schulfach   ❗ Betonung: **subject** ['sʌbdʒɪkt]

School subjects

art [ɑːt]	Kunst	**ICT**[1] [ˌaɪ siː ˈtiː]	Informations- und Kommunikationstechnologie
design and technology [dɪˌzaɪn ‿ənd tekˈnɒlədʒi]	Design und Technik	**maths** [mæθs]	Mathematik
French [frentʃ]	Französisch	**music** ['mjuːzɪk]	Musik
geography [dʒiˈɒɡrəfi]	Geografie	**PE**[2] [ˌpiː ‿ˈiː]	Sportunterricht, Turnen
history ['hɪstri]	Geschichte	**religion** [rɪˈlɪdʒən]	Religion
		science ['saɪəns]	Naturwissenschaft

[1] *Information and Communication Technology*   [2] *Physical Education*

---

p. 28   **hour** ['aʊə]   Stunde   ❗ Das „h" wird nicht gesprochen: **hour** ['aʊə]

lunch [lʌntʃ]   Mittagessen

break [breɪk]   Pause

(to) learn [lɜːn]   lernen

p. 29   **month** [mʌnθ]   Monat

The months

2 February ['februəri] Februar

3 March [mɑːtʃ] März

1 January ['dʒænjuəri] Januar

4 April ['eɪprəl] April

12 December [dɪˈsembə] Dezember

5 May [meɪ] Mai

11 November [nəʊˈvembə] November

6 June [dʒuːn] Juni

10 October [ɒkˈtəʊbə] Oktober

7 July [dʒuˈlaɪ] Juli

9 September [sepˈtembə] September

8 August ['ɔːɡəst] August

❗ Monatsnamen werden immer großgeschrieben.

---

second ['sekənd]   zweite(r, s)

third [θɜːd]   dritte(r, s)

1	**one**	eins	**1st**	**first**	erste(r, s)
2	**two**	zwei	**2nd**	**second**	zweite(r, s)
3	**three**	drei	**3rd**	**third**	dritte(r, s)
4	**four**	vier	**4th**	**fourth**	vierte(r, s)
5	**five**	fünf	**5th**	**fifth**	fünfte(r, s)

➔ *Numbers*, p. 233

when? [wen]   wann?

Birthdays

My birthday **is** in May. **When's** your birthday?
– My birthday is in August. **On** 5th August.

Ich **habe** im Mai Geburtstag. **Wann hast** du Geburtstag?
– Ich habe im August Geburtstag. **Am** 5. August.

❗ Du <u>schreibst</u>: **on 5th August** – du <u>sagst</u>: **on the fifth of August**

(to) write [raɪt]   schreiben   ❗ Das „w" wird nicht gesprochen: **write** ['raɪt]

[b] **b**oat · [p] **p**ool · [d] **d**ad · [t] **t**en · [g] **g**ood · [k] **c**at ·
[m] **m**um · [n] **n**o · [ŋ] so**ng** · [l] **h**ello · [r] **r**ed · [w] **w**e · [j] **y**ou

Part C

p. 30 (to) **find** [faɪnd]	finden	

Max, find Nick!

Are there any …? [ˈeni]	Gibt es (irgendwelche) …?	**Are there any** English students at your school?
(to) **spell** [spel]	buchstabieren	
(to) **work** [wɜːk]	arbeiten	
(to) read [riːd]	lesen	
(to) **watch** [wɒtʃ]	*sich etwas* anschauen; beobachten	

> **look · see · watch**
> · **Look** at the picture.   (hin)schauen
> · Can you **see** the cat?   sehen
> · Can I **watch** a DVD?   anschauen
>   Let's **watch** the seals.   beobachten

(to) **fall asleep** [ˌfɔːl_əˈsliːp]	einschlafen	
place [pleɪs]	Ort, Platz, Stelle	Plymouth is a great **place**.
this place/break/subject	dieser Ort / diese Pause / dieses Fach	
I don't know.	Ich weiß (es) nicht.	
(to) eat [iːt]	essen	
What colour …?	Welche Farbe …?	
canteen [kænˈtiːn]	Kantine, (Schul-)Mensa	
gym [dʒɪm]	Turnhalle	
We're finished. [ˈfɪnɪʃt]	Wir sind fertig.	**We're finished.** What can we do now?
back [bæk]	zurück	
we **can't** … [kɑːnt]	wir können nicht …	I can speak English, but I **can't** speak French.
(to) **win** [wɪn]	gewinnen	
him [hɪm]	ihn; ihm	Look, there's Sam. Can you see **him**? Let's help **him**.
winner [ˈwɪnə]	Gewinner/in, Sieger/in	
p. 31 **everyday** [ˈevrideɪ]	Alltags-	
workbook [ˈwɜːkbʊk]	Arbeitsheft	
page [peɪdʒ]	Seite	*English:* What **page** are we **on**? *German:* **Auf** welcher **Seite** sind wir?
toilet [ˈtɔɪlət]	Toilette	❗ Betonung: **toilet** [ˈtɔɪlət]
What's for homework? [ˈhəʊmwɜːk]	Was haben wir als Hausaufgabe auf?	*English:* **Do your homework now.** *German:* **Mach jetzt deine Hausaufgaben.**
homework [ˈhəʊmwɜːk]	Hausaufgabe(n)	❗ **homework** hat keinen Plural: *English:* Where **is** your **homework**? *German:* Wo **sind** deine **Hausaufgaben**?
p. 32 **There aren't any …** [ˈeni]	Es gibt/sind keine …	

> **There are** two cats in my photo.
> **Are there any** cats in your photo?
> – No, **there aren't any** cats in my photo.

in German/English	auf Deutsch/Englisch	

---

[f] **f**ather · [v] ri**v**er · [s] **s**ister · [z] plea**s**e · [ʃ] **sh**op · [ʒ] televi**si**on ·
[tʃ] **t**ea**ch**er · [dʒ] **G**ermany · [θ] **th**anks · [ð] **th**is · [h] **h**ere

Chaos at the corner shop

p. 34	**chaos** [ˈkeɪɒs]	Chaos	
	corner shop [ˈkɔːnə ʃɒp]	Laden an der Ecke; Tante-Emma-Laden	
	master [ˈmɑːstə]	Meister/in	
	yoghurt [ˈjɒɡət]	Joghurt	*English:* **yoghurt** – *German:* **Joghurt**
	little [ˈlɪtl]	klein	This is Lily, my **little** sister.
p. 35	**always** [ˈɔːlweɪz]	immer	
	group (of) [ɡruːp]	Gruppe	*English:* a **group of** boys/girls *German:* eine **Gruppe** Jungen/Mädchen
	that group [ðæt], [ðət]	die Gruppe (dort), jene Gruppe	
	(to) swim [swɪm]	schwimmen	
	like boys [laɪk]	wie Jungen	
	swimmer [ˈswɪmə]	Schwimmer/in	
	(to) be good at kung fu	gut sein in Kung-Fu; gut Kung-Fu können	Are you **good at** football?
	feeling [ˈfiːlɪŋ]	Gefühl	
	angry [ˈæŋgri]	wütend	
	happy [ˈhæpi]	glücklich, froh	She's **happy.** 🙂 He isn't **happy.** 🙁
	surprised [səˈpraɪzd]	überrascht	
	(to) act out	vorspielen	
	the **next** picture/question [nekst]	das nächste Bild / die nächste Frage	
	man, *pl* **men** [mæn], [men]	Mann	❗ one **man** – two, three, four **men**
	woman, *pl* **women** [ˈwʊmən], [ˈwɪmɪn]	Frau	❗ one **woman** – two, three, four **women**

Unit 2   Homes and families

pp. 36/37	**family** [ˈfæməli], *pl* **families**	Familie	*English:* the Blackwell **family** *German:* **Familie** Blackwell
	road [rəʊd]	Straße (*Landstraße zwischen Orten; Straße in Orten*)	• ohne Hausnummer: **in Dean Street** / **in Beach Road** in der Dean Street / in der Beach Road • mit Hausnummer: **at 14 Dean Street** / **at 8 Beach Road** in der Dean Street 14 / in der Beach Road 8
	house [haʊs]	Haus	
	garden [ˈgɑːdn]	Garten	
	upstairs [ˌʌpˈsteəz]	oben; nach oben	upstairs
	downstairs [ˌdaʊnˈsteəz]	unten; nach unten	downstairs

[iː] green · [i] happy · [ɪ] big · [e] red · [æ] cat · [ɑː] class · [ɒ] song · [ɔː] door · [uː] blue · [ʊ] book · [ʌ] mum · [ɜː] girl · [ə] a partner

bedroom [ˈbedruːm]	Schlafzimmer	
bathroom [ˈbɑːθruːm]	Badezimmer, Bad	
dining room [ˈdaɪnɪŋ ruːm]	Esszimmer	
kitchen [ˈkɪtʃɪn]	Küche	
living room [ˈlɪvɪŋ ruːm]	Wohnzimmer	
armchair [ˈɑːmtʃeə]	Sessel	
bed [bed]	Bett	
lamp [læmp]	Lampe	
shelf [ʃelf], pl shelves [ʃelvz]	Regal	
sofa [ˈsəʊfə]	Sofa	
table [ˈteɪbl]	Tisch	
toy [tɔɪ]	Spielzeug	
TV [ˌtiːˈviː]	Fernsehen, Fernsehgerät	
watch TV	fernsehen	

bathroom   bedroom
kitchen   living room

❗ one shel**f** – two, three, four shel**ves**

My bedroom
desk
bed
lamp
TV   table   armchair

small [smɔːl]	klein	big ◄► small
task [tɑːsk]	Aufgabe	

Part A

p. 38 (to) wake up [ˌweɪk‿ˈʌp]	aufwachen	Wake up! It's time for school! (to) fall asleep ◄► (to) wake up
(to) have breakfast [ˈbrekfəst]	frühstücken	
a plate of … [pleɪt]	ein Teller …	
crab [kræb]	Krebs	

Silky's breakfast

a plate of crabs

after breakfast [ˈɑːftə]	nach dem Frühstück	after breakfast ◄► before breakfast
in the afternoon [ˌɑːftəˈnuːn]	nachmittags, am Nachmittag	
(to) play [pleɪ]	spielen	In the afternoon we always play football.
in the evening [ˈiːvnɪŋ]	abends, am Abend	

• in the morning	morgens, am Morgen
in the afternoon	nachmittags, am Nachmittag
in the evening	abends, am Abend

• on Monday	am Montag
on Mondays	montags, an Montagen

fish [fɪʃ], pl fish	Fisch	❗ one fish – two, three, four fish
dinner [ˈdɪnə]	Abendessen, Abendbrot	

(to) have breakfast	frühstücken
(to) have lunch	zu Mittag essen
(to) have dinner	zu Abend essen

[eɪ] n**a**me · [aɪ] t**i**me · [ɔɪ] b**oy** · [əʊ] **o**ld ·
[aʊ] t**ow**n · [ɪə] h**ere** · [eə] wh**ere** · [ʊə] t**our**

one hundred and eighty-five   **185**

(to) **sit** [sɪt]	sitzen; sich setzen	
rock [rɒk]	Fels, Felsen	
(to) **text** a friend [tekst]	einem Freund / einer Freundin eine SMS schicken	I wake up, I have breakfast, and then I **text** my friends.
p.39 **her** [hɜː]	sie; ihr	Look, there's Abby. Can you see **her**? Let's help **her**.
(to) **go sailing** [ˈseɪlɪŋ]	segeln; segeln gehen	Abby and Maya **go sailing** at Wembury Sailing Club.
into the kitchen [ˈɪntʊ]	in die Küche (hinein)	
(to) **make** [meɪk]	machen; herstellen	
a cup of … [kʌp]	eine Tasse …	
tea [tiː]	Tee	**a cup of tea**
paper [ˈpeɪpə]	Zeitung	
at the weekend [ˌwiːkˈend]	am Wochenende	
at night [ət ˈnaɪt]	nachts, in der Nacht	❗ **in** the morning/afternoon/evening **at** night, **at** the weekend
(to) **sleep** [sliːp]	schlafen	Our cat always **sleeps** on the sofa.
(to) **feed** [fiːd]	füttern	Can I **feed** the rabbits?
no … [nəʊ]	kein …, keine …	There's **no** school at weekends.
us [ʌs], [əs]	uns	We're here. Can you see **us**? Please help **us**.
of course [əv ˈkɔːs]	natürlich, selbstverständlich	
basket [ˈbɑːskɪt]	Korb	My dog Ben always sleeps in his **basket** on the **floor**.
floor [flɔː]	Fußboden	
trophy [ˈtrəʊfi], *pl* **trophies**	Pokal; Trophäe	**trophies**
away [əˈweɪ]	weg, fort	
mad [mæd]	verrückt	
(to) **think** [θɪŋk]	denken, glauben	I **think** Silky is nice.
so cool/nice/… [səʊ]	so cool/nett/…	
(to) **go for a walk** [wɔːk]	einen Spaziergang machen, spazieren gehen	
p.41 **pronunciation** [prəˌnʌnsiˈeɪʃn]	Aussprache	
(to) **run** [rʌn]	rennen, laufen	

Part B

p.44 **uncle** [ˈʌŋkl]	Onkel	your father's or your mother's brother
aunt [ɑːnt]	Tante	your father's or your mother's sister
sport [spɔːt]	Sport; Sportart	Plymstock is a **sports** school.
(to) **do sport**	Sport treiben	On Saturdays, I always **do sport**.
near here	(hier) in der Nähe	Is there a sports shop **near here**?
he doesn't have time	er hat keine Zeit	

[b] **b**oat · [p] **p**ool · [d] **d**ad · [t] **t**en · [g] **g**ood · [k] **c**at · [m] **m**um · [n] **n**o · [ŋ] so**ng** · [l] he**ll**o · [r] **r**ed · [w] **w**e · [j] **y**ou

only ['əʊnli]	nur, bloß	
often ['ɒfn], ['ɒftən]	oft	We **often** do sport on Saturdays.
(to) **tell (about)** [tel]	erzählen (von); berichten (über)	**Tell me about** your family.
all [ɔːl]	alles; alle	Can you tell me **all** about Plymstock School? I have five friends, and they **all** live near here.
..., you know. [nəʊ]	..., weißt du. / ..., wissen Sie.	We're a big family, **you know**.
cousin ['kʌzn]	Cousin, Cousine	❗ Betonung: <u>**cous**in</u> ['kʌzn]
person ['pɜːsn]	Person	❗ Betonung: <u>**per**son</u> ['pɜːsn] one **person** – two, three, four **people**

	grand-	Groß-
	grandfather, grandpa	Großvater, Opa
	grandmother, grandma	Großmutter, Oma

p. 46 **grandma** ['grænmɑː]	Oma	
farm [fɑːm]	Bauernhof, Farm	
Well, ... [wel]	Nun, ... / Also, ... / Na ja, ...	
till 12 o'clock [tɪl]	bis 12 Uhr	On Sundays I often sleep **till** 10 o'clock.

p. 47 **family tree**	(Familien-)Stammbaum	a **family tree**
tree [triː]	Baum	
dead [ded]	tot	
divorced [dɪ'vɔːst]	geschieden	
married (to) ['mærɪd]	verheiratet (mit)	*English:* **married to** *German:* **verheiratet mit**
single ['sɪŋgl]	ledig, alleinstehend	
twins *(pl)* [twɪnz]	Zwillinge	

Part C

p. 48 **What's for** lunch?	Was gibt es zum Mittagessen?	
roast beef [ˌrəʊst 'biːf]	Rinderbraten	roast beef
potato [pə'teɪtəʊ], *pl* **potatoes**	Kartoffel	roast potatoes
yummy ['jʌmi] *(infml)*	lecker	
vegetables *(pl)* ['vedʒtəblz]	Gemüse	*English:* **Vegetables are** good for you. *German:* **Gemüse ist** gut für dich.
soup [suːp]	Suppe	
dessert [dɪ'zɜːt]	Nachtisch, Nachspeise	vegetables fruit salad scones
fruit salad [ˌfruːt 'sæləd]	Obstsalat	
ice cream [ˌaɪs 'kriːm]	(Speise-)Eis	
scone [skɒn]	*kleines rundes Milchbrötchen, leicht süß, oft mit Rosinen*	soup

[f] **f**ather · [v] ri**v**er · [s] **s**i**s**ter · [z] plea**s**e · [ʃ] **sh**op · [ʒ] televi**si**on · [tʃ] **t**ea**ch**er · [dʒ] **G**ermany · [θ] **th**anks · [ð] **th**is · [h] **h**ere

(to) **take** [teɪk]	nehmen, mitnehmen; (weg-, hin)bringen	Thanks for the book. Can I **take** it with me? **Take** the chairs into the dining room, please.
on the radio [ˈreɪdiəʊ]	im Radio	*Englisch:* **on** the radio – *German:* **im** Radio
in the middle [ˈmɪdl]	in der Mitte	
What would you like? [wʊd]	Was hättest du gern? / Was möchtest du?	
I'd like … [ˌaɪd ˈlaɪk] (= **I would like …**)	Ich hätte gern … / Ich möchte …	
What would you like to eat?	Was möchtest du essen?	

There's ice cream or fruit salad. What would you like?

I'd like a scone. Can't I have a scone, Mum?

| hot [hɒt] | heiß | |
| cold [kəʊld] | kalt | |

hot   **cold**

p.49	(to) drink [drɪŋk]	trinken	
	drink [drɪŋk]	Getränk	
	sandwich [ˈsænwɪtʃ], [ˈsænwɪdʒ]	Sandwich, (zusammengeklapptes) belegtes Brot	
	cake [keɪk]	Kuchen	
	cream [kriːm]	Sahne	
	jam [dʒæm]	Marmelade	
p.50	food [fuːd]	Essen; Lebensmittel; Futter	
	biscuit [ˈbɪskɪt]	Keks, Plätzchen	*German* **Keks** – *English* **biscuit** *German* **Kuchen** – *English* **cake**
	bread [bred]	Brot	
	cheese [tʃiːz]	Käse	
	meat [miːt]	Fleisch	
	milk [mɪlk]	Milch	
	water [ˈwɔːtə]	Wasser	

cakes

sandwiches

cream   **jam**

My breakfast

cheese   **tea**

bread   **cornflakes**   **milk**

Saturday in Plymouth

p.52	(to) **remember** [rɪˈmembə]	sich erinnern (an)	*English:* Can you **remember** the name? *German:* Kannst du dich **an** den Namen **erinnern**?
	present [ˈpreznt]	Geschenk	a **present**
	café [ˈkæfeɪ]	Café	
	harbour [ˈhɑːbə]	Hafen	
	seagull [ˈsiːɡʌl]	Möwe	
	(to) **shout** [ʃaʊt]	schreien, rufen	
	ship [ʃɪp]	Schiff	
	suddenly [ˈsʌdnli]	plötzlich, auf einmal	

[iː] green · [i] happy · [ɪ] big · [e] red · [æ] cat · [ɑː] class · [ɒ] song · [ɔː] door · [uː] blue · [ʊ] book · [ʌ] mum · [ɜː] girl · [ə] a partner

down [daʊn]	hinunter, herunter; nach unten	
maybe ['meɪbi]	vielleicht	
its name [ɪts]	sein Name / ihr Name	This is my rabbit. **Its** name is Joe.

(to) **jump** [dʒʌmp]	springen	Can you **jump onto** your desk?
onto the boat ['ɒntʊ]	auf das Boot (hinauf)	
police officer [pə'liːs‿ˌɒfɪsə]	Polizist/in	
(to) **look** happy/angry/…	glücklich/wütend/… aussehen	

> **look**
> - **Look**, Sam. There's a seagull.
>   Schau mal, Sam. Da ist eine Möwe.
> - **Look at** the pictures.
>   Sieh dir die Bilder an.
> - Your school uniform **looks** great.
>   Deine Schuluniform sieht toll aus.

worried ['wʌrid]	besorgt, beunruhigt	
hair [heə]	Haar, Haare	*English:* Your **hair is** too long. *German:* Deine **Haare sind** zu lang.

clothes *(pl)* [kləʊðz]	Kleidung, Kleidungsstücke	
jeans *(pl)* [dʒiːnz]	Jeans	

> **clothes** und **jeans** sind <u>Plural</u>-Wörter:
> - All her **clothes are** red.
>   Ihre gesamte **Kleidung ist** rot.
> - My **jeans are** blue. **They're** new.
>   Meine **Jeans ist** blau. **Sie ist** neu.

p.53 **why?** [waɪ]	warum?	Lucy is sad. – **Why**? – Maya goes to a different school.
never ['nevə]	nie, niemals	My brother **never** feeds our dog. I always feed it. **always ◀▶ never**
(to) **be in trouble** ['trʌbl]	in Schwierigkeiten sein; Ärger kriegen	
story ['stɔːri], *pl* **stories**	Geschichte, Erzählung	❗ one **story** – two, three, four **stories**
it shows **that** … [ðæt], [ðət]	es zeigt, dass …	

Unit 3   Clubs and hobbies

56/57 **hobby** ['hɒbi], *pl* **hobbies**	Hobby	
some [sʌm], [səm]	einige, ein paar; etwas	There are **some** sandwiches for you on the table. And there's **some** milk too.
(to) **join a club** [dʒɔɪn]	in einen Klub eintreten; sich einem Klub anschließen	You like basketball? **Join** our basketball club!
more [mɔː]	mehr	For **more** help, go to page 56. Can you tell me **more** about the clubs at your school?
information (about) *(no pl)* [ˌɪnfə'meɪʃn]	Information(en) (über)	❗ Das englische Wort **information** hat keinen Plural: *English:* Here**'s** the **information** about our club. *German:* Hier **sind** die **Informationen** …

[eɪ] **name** · [aɪ] **time** · [ɔɪ] **boy** · [əʊ] **old** ·
[aʊ] **town** · [ɪə] **here** · [eə] **where** · [ʊə] **tour**

one hundred and eighty-nine   **189**

4 pm [ˌpiː ˈem]	4 Uhr nachmittags / 16 Uhr	❗ • Bei Uhrzeiten wird **pm** verwendet, wenn der Nachmittag oder Abend gemeint ist.
4 am [ˌeɪ ˈem]	4 Uhr morgens	• **am** wird verwendet, wenn der Morgen oder Vormittag gemeint ist.
		• **am** und **pm** stehen nie mit **o'clock** – also nur: **at 4 am / at 4 pm** (nicht: at 4 o'clock pm)
(to) **edit** [ˈedɪt]	bearbeiten; schneiden (Film, Video)	
gardening [ˈgɑːdnɪŋ]	Gärtnern, Gartenarbeit	Join the Gardening Club and have fun in our garden.
(to) **grow** [grəʊ]	anbauen, anpflanzen	
(to) **sell** [sel]	verkaufen	
(to) **have fun** [fʌn]	Spaß haben, sich amüsieren	
kit [kɪt]	Ausrüstung	
quiet [ˈkwaɪət]	ruhig, still, leise	Be **quiet**, please. I have lots of homework.
young [jʌŋ]	jung	**young** ◄► old
(to) **choose** [tʃuːz]	aussuchen, (aus)wählen; sich aussuchen	Look at the information on our school website. Then **choose** one or two clubs.
area [ˈeəriə]	Bereich; Gebiet, Gegend	The Samba Club meets in the Music **area**. I live in an **area** with lots of shops.
lunchtime [ˈlʌntʃtaɪm]	Mittagszeit	We can meet in the canteen **at lunchtime**. (German: … **mittags** …)
instrument [ˈɪnstrəmənt]	Instrument	❗ Betonung: **instrument** [ˈɪnstrəmənt]
(to) **sing** [sɪŋ]	singen	
(to) **dance** [dɑːns]	tanzen	
from … to …	von … bis …	The Film Making Club meets **from** 3 **to** 4 pm.

Part A

p. 58 (to) **get** angry/cold/… [get]	wütend/kalt/… werden	My dad is great. He never **gets** angry.
wet [wet]	nass	
umbrella [ʌmˈbrelə]	Schirm, Regenschirm	With an **umbrella**, you can't get wet.
funny [ˈfʌni]	witzig, komisch	
very funny/wet/… [ˈveri]	sehr witzig/nass/…	
joke [dʒəʊk]	Witz	
because [bɪˈkɒz]	weil	Why are you angry? – **Because** you're late.
really [ˈrɪəli]	wirklich	Our Maths teacher is **really** nice. I know some very good jokes. – **Really**?
sometimes [ˈsʌmtaɪmz]	manchmal	**never – sometimes – always** (nie – manchmal – immer) Mum **sometimes** comes home very late.
(to) **have to** go/work/… [ˈhæv tə]	gehen/arbeiten/… müssen	Look, it's late. We **have to** go now.
What's the matter? [ˈmætə]	Was ist denn? / Was ist los?	You look so sad. **What's the matter?**
Which clubs/jokes/…? [wɪtʃ]	Welche Klubs/Witze/…?	I like the Samba Club and the Film Making Club. **Which** clubs do you like?

[b] **b**oat · [p] **p**ool · [d] **d**ad · [t] **t**en · [g] **g**ood · [k] **c**at · [m] **m**um · [n] **n**o · [ŋ] so**ng** · [l] **h**ello · [r] **r**ed · [w] **w**e · [j] **y**ou

p.59	**everyone** ['evriwʌn] (or: **everybody** ['evribɒdi])	jeder; alle	**Everyone** knows that London is in England. (or: **Everybody** knows …)
	What's she like?	Wie ist sie? / Wie ist sie so?	You know Kristen Stewart? Really? **What's she like?**
	(to) visit ['vɪzɪt]	besuchen	Can we **visit** Grandma on Sunday?
	(to) love [lʌv]	lieben, sehr mögen	
	nothing ['nʌθɪŋ]	(gar) nichts	
	list [lɪst]	Liste	
	(to) want [wɒnt]	(haben) wollen	*I want that bike, Dad!*
	work [wɜːk]	Arbeit	
	(to) want to do	tun wollen	*English:* I **want to** dance. *German:* Ich **möchte** tanzen.
	(to) sound [saʊnd]	klingen, sich (*gut usw.*) anhören	A garden party? That **sounds** great.
	(to) make friends	Freunde finden	Join the Samba Club and **make** new **friends**.
p.60	**activity** [æk'tɪvəti], *pl* **activities**	Aktivität	❗ Betonung: ac**tiv**ity [æk'tɪvəti]
	other ['ʌðə]	andere(r, s)	The rabbits are in the garden. Where are the **other** animals?
	chess [tʃes]	Schach	
	drum [drʌm]	Trommel	*English:* (to) play **the drums** / **the** piano *German:* **Schlagzeug** spielen / **Klavier** spielen
	piano [pi'ænəʊ]	Klavier, Piano	
	gymnastics [dʒɪm'næstɪks]	Gymnastik, Turnen	
	skating ['skeɪtɪŋ]	Inlineskaten, Rollschuhlaufen	**skates**
	riding ['raɪdɪŋ]	Reiten	
	judo ['dʒuːdəʊ]	Judo	

Sports and other activities

You **do** …	You **play** …	You **go** …
judo, yoga, gymnastics, kung fu, sport, …	basketball, football, tennis, games, chess, cards, the drums, the piano, …	sailing, skating, swimming, riding, dancing, …

---

p.61	**Find someone who …**	Finde jemanden, der …	
	someone ['sʌmwʌn] (or: **somebody** ['sʌmbədi])	jemand	There's **someone/ somebody** at the door, I think.
	something ['sʌmθɪŋ]	etwas	Can I ask you **something**?
	(to) guess [ges]	raten, erraten	Can you **guess** how old I am?
	(to) clean [kliːn]	sauber machen, putzen	I can't go swimming now. I have to **clean** my room.
p.62	**(to) collect** [kə'lekt]	sammeln	My friend Jamie **collects** comics.
	free [friː]	frei	Can we meet at 1 o'clock? Are you **free**? *English:* **free time** · **free-time activities** *German:* **Freizeit** · **Freizeitaktivitäten**

---

[f] **f**ather · [v] ri**v**er · [s] **s**i**s**ter · [z] plea**s**e · [ʃ] **sh**op · [ʒ] televi**s**ion ·
[tʃ] **t**ea**ch**er · [dʒ] **G**ermany · [θ] **th**anks · [ð] **th**is · [h] **h**ere

(to) **ask** sb. **to do** sth.	jemanden bitten, etwas zu tun	You can always **ask** your teacher **to** help you.
(to) **try** [traɪ]	(aus)probieren; versuchen	**Try** a scone. They're really yummy. Sam always **tries** to help his sister Lily. ❗ I/you/we/they **try** • he/she/it **tries**
table ['teɪbl]	Tabelle	
(to) **need** [niːd]	brauchen, benötigen	*I think I need a new T-shirt.*
guitar [gɪ'tɑː]	Gitarre	*English:* (to) play **the guitar** *German:* **Gitarre** spielen
beach [biːtʃ]	Strand	**beach**
p. 63 **outside** [ˌaʊt'saɪd]	draußen; nach draußen	Where's the dog? – **Outside**, in the garden. It's hot in here. Let's go **outside**.
inside [ˌɪn'saɪd]	drinnen; nach drinnen	**inside** ◄► **outside**
jump [dʒʌmp]	Sprung	
letter ['letə]	Brief	

Part B

p. 64 (to) **finish** sth. ['fɪnɪʃ]	etwas beenden; mit etwas fertig werden/sein	**Finish** your homework, then you can go skating. Do you always **finish** school at 2 o'clock?
Come on, Dad.	Na los, Dad! / Komm, Dad!	
How are you? [haʊ_'ɑː ju]	Wie geht's? / Wie geht es dir/euch?	*How are you?* *Fine, thanks.*
Listen, Justin. ['lɪsn]	Hör zu, Justin.	
(to) **listen** ['lɪsn]	zuhören, horchen	**Listen**, please. Hör(t) zu, bitte. **Listen to** me. Hör(t) mir zu, bitte. **Listen to** the song. Hör dir/Hört euch den Song an.
much [mʌtʃ]	viel	Dad works so **much**. He doesn't have **much** time.
job [dʒɒb]	Job, (Arbeits-)Stelle	
studio ['stjuːdiəʊ]	Studio	
programme ['prəʊgræm]	Programm, (Radio-, Fernseh-)Sendung	❗ Betonung: **programme** ['prəʊgræm]
What programmes …?	Welche Programme …? / Welche Art von Programmen …?	**What TV programmes** do you watch and **what books** do you read?
later ['leɪtə]	später	I don't have much time now. Let's talk **later**.
midnight ['mɪdnaɪt]	Mitternacht	
too late/cold/big/… [tuː]	zu spät/kalt/groß/…	We can't go swimming. It's much **too** cold.
(to) **get up** [ˌget_'ʌp]	aufstehen	My mother **gets up** at 6 o'clock every morning.

[iː] green · [i] happy · [ɪ] big · [e] red · [æ] cat · [ɑː] class · [ɒ] song · [ɔː] door · [uː] blue · [ʊ] book · [ʌ] mum · [ɜː] girl · [ə] a partner

How do you like it?	Wie findest du es (sie/ihn)? / Wie gefällt es (sie/er) dir?	*How do you like my new watch?*
It's about a seagull.	Es geht um eine Möwe. / Es handelt von einer Möwe.	I can't go skating, I want to watch a video. **It's about** a kung fu master.
(to) **send** sth. **to** sb. [send]	jm. etwas schicken, senden	
idea [aɪˈdɪə]	Idee; Vorstellung	I have a great **idea** for a video about Plymouth. Justin has no **idea** about his dad's work.

p. 65 (to) **hear** [hɪə] — hören

> **listen · hear**
> **Listen.** Can you **hear** the dogs in the street?
> · (to) **listen (to)**   zuhören, horchen
> · (to) **hear**   hören (können)

p. 66 **partner** [ˈpɑːtnə]	Partner/in	
(to) **interview** sb. [ˈɪntəvjuː]	jn. interviewen, jn. befragen	
p. 67 **age** [eɪdʒ]	Alter	
also [ˈɔːlsəʊ]	auch	I play football, and I play basketball too. = I play football, and I **also** play basketball.
metre [ˈmiːtə]	Meter	

Part C

p. 68 **on Saturday afternoon**	am Samstagnachmittag	**!** **in** the morning/afternoon/evening *aber:* **on** Saturday afternoon / **on** Monday morning *usw.*
(to) **ride a bike** [ˌraɪd_ə ˈbaɪk]	Rad fahren	
bike [baɪk]	Fahrrad	
(to) **stop** [stɒp]	anhalten, stoppen	
tired [ˈtaɪəd]	müde	She's **tired**.
(to) **be thirsty** [ˈθɜːsti]	durstig sein, Durst haben	
chocolate [ˈtʃɒklət]	Schokolade	**!** Betonung: **choc**olate [ˈtʃɒklət]
usually [ˈjuːʒuəli]	meistens, normalerweise, gewöhnlich	never · sometimes · often · usually · always
(to) **turn** sth. **on** [ˌtɜːn_ˈɒn]	etwas einschalten	
all of Plymouth	ganz Plymouth, das ganze Plymouth	
behind [bɪˈhaɪnd]	hinter	**behind** the TV ◄► **in front of** the TV
in front of [ɪn ˈfrɒnt_əv]	vor	
(to) **turn around** [ˌtɜːn_əˈraʊnd]	sich umdrehen	
ghost [gəʊst]	Geist, Gespenst	
ready [ˈredi]	bereit, fertig	Are you **ready**? Can we go?
loud [laʊd]	laut	**loud** ◄► **quiet**

[eɪ] n**a**me · [aɪ] t**i**me · [ɔɪ] b**oy** · [əʊ] **o**ld ·
[aʊ] t**ow**n · [ɪə] h**ere** · [eə] wh**ere** · [ʊə] t**our**

p. 69 **scary** [ˈskeəri]	unheimlich, gruselig	I can tell you a **scary** story.
traveller [ˈtrævələ]	Reisende(r)	
(to) **travel** [ˈtrævl]	reisen	We always **travel** to Spain in June.
part [pɑːt]	Teil	
(to) **be called** [kɔːld]	heißen, genannt werden	Asterix has a very big friend. He**'s called** Obelix. (= His name is Obelix.)
over 400 years [ˈəʊvə]	über 400 Jahre; mehr als 400 Jahre	
museum [mjuˈziːəm]	Museum	
money [ˈmʌni]	Geld	
child [tʃaɪld], pl **children** [ˈtʃɪldrən]	Kind	❗ one **child** – two, three, four **children**
ticket [ˈtɪkɪt]	Eintrittskarte	
pound (£) [paʊnd]	Pfund (britische Währung)	

British money – pounds and pence		How much is the camera?	Was kostet die Kamera?
You **say**: You **write**:		How much are the DVDs?	Was kosten die DVDs?
fifty p [piː] / fifty pence [pens] 50p			
one pound / a pound £1		The camera **is** £165.	Die Kamera **kostet** …
five pounds £5		The DVDs **are** £12.95.	Die DVDs **kosten** …
two pounds fifty £2.50			

(to) **imagine** sth. [ɪˈmædʒɪn]	sich etwas vorstellen	**Imagine** you're Silky and tell your partner about Plymouth Sound.
life [laɪf], pl **lives** [laɪvz]	Leben	*English:* **Life** in Plymouth is fun. *German:* **Das** Leben in Plymouth …
in 1580	im Jahr 1580	

The captain's ghost

p. 72 **sound** [saʊnd]	Geräusch; Klang	
attic [ˈætɪk]	Dachboden	*English:* **in** the attic *German:* **auf** dem Dachboden
boring [ˈbɔːrɪŋ]	langweilig	
mouth [maʊθ]	Mund; Maul	
diary [ˈdaɪəri], pl **diaries**	Tagebuch; Kalender	
address [əˈdres]	Adresse, Anschrift	What's your **address**? – 14 New Street. *English:* **add**ress – *German:* **A**dresse
sick [sɪk]	krank	
(to) **hope** [həʊp]	hoffen	I **hope** you like my school uniform.
bottle [ˈbɒtl]	Flasche	
(to) **smell** [smel]	riechen	Can you **smell** the cake? It **smells** great!
Me too.	Ich auch.	*English:* I'm from Plymouth. – **Me** too. *German:* Ich bin aus Plymouth. – **Ich** auch.

[b] **b**oat · [p] **p**ool · [d] **d**ad · [t] **t**en · [g] **g**ood · [k] **c**at · [m] **m**um · [n] **n**o · [ŋ] so**ng** · [l] **h**ello · [r] **r**ed · [w] **w**e · [j] **y**ou

out of … [ˈaʊt_əv]	aus … (heraus/hinaus)	

into the house ◄► **out of** the house

(to) call [kɔːl]	rufen; anrufen; nennen	Please **call** your dog. It's in our garden. Can you **call** me at 6? Here's my phone number. Her name is Jessica, but we **call** her Jess.
moon [muːn]	Mond	
(to) walk [wɔːk]	(zu Fuß) gehen	
along the street/the river/… [əˈlɒŋ]	die Straße/den Fluss/… entlang	*English:* Go **along** the street. *German:* Geh **die Straße entlang**.
Oh, it's you.	Ach, du bist es.	
(to) bark [bɑːk]	bellen	
step [step]	Schritt	
voice [vɔɪs]	Stimme	
p. 73 **thief** [θiːf], *pl* **thieves** [θiːvz]	Dieb/in	
hand [hænd]	Hand	
(to) fight [faɪt]	kämpfen	
coin [kɔɪn]	Münze	some **coins**
(to) taste [teɪst]	schmecken	This soup smells nice, but it **tastes** funny.
end [end]	Ende, Schluss	
dream [driːm]	Traum	
perfect [ˈpɜːfɪkt]	perfekt, ideal	❗ Betonung: **perfect** [ˈpɜːfɪkt]
(to) understand [ˌʌndəˈstænd]	verstehen	Can you speak English, please? I don't **understand** German.

Unit 4   Weekends

80/81 **garage** [ˈɡærɑːʒ], [ˈɡærɪdʒ]	Garage	
invitation (to) [ˌɪnvɪˈteɪʃn]	Einladung (zu, nach)	
box [bɒks]	Kasten, Kiste, Kästchen	b[x]x
life jacket [ˈlaɪf dʒækɪt]	Schwimmweste	a **life jacket**
magazine [ˌmæɡəˈziːn]	Zeitschrift	
mobile phone [ˌməʊbaɪl ˈfəʊn] (*kurz auch:* **mobile**)	Mobiltelefon, Handy	❗ „Handy" klingt zwar englisch, ist es aber nicht. Auf Englisch heißt es immer **mobile** oder **mobile phone**.
note [nəʊt]	Notiz, Mitteilung	
sand [sænd]	Sand	

[f] **f**ather · [v] ri**v**er · [s] **s**ister · [z] plea**s**e · [ʃ] **sh**op · [ʒ] televi**s**ion ·
[tʃ] **t**ea**ch**er · [dʒ] **G**ermany · [θ] **th**anks · [ð] **th**is · [h] **h**ere

shorts *(pl)* [ʃɔːts]	Shorts, kurze Hose	
plan [plæn]	Plan	
match [mætʃ]	Spiel, Wettkampf, Match	
(to) **break** [breɪk]	zerbrechen, kaputt machen; brechen, kaputt gehen	Don't play football here. You don't want to **break** a window!
island [ˈaɪlənd]	Insel	
(to) **stay** [steɪ]	bleiben	Can we **stay** at home? Can I **stay** in bed?
together [təˈgeðə]	zusammen	We always have breakfast **together** on Sunday mornings.
cinema [ˈsɪnəmə]	Kino	
lake [leɪk]	(Binnen-)See	❗ the **lake** – der See • the **sea** – das Meer, die See
grandparents [ˈgrænpeərənts]	Großeltern	
parents [ˈpeərənts]	Eltern	
shopping mall [ˈʃɒpɪŋ mɔːl] (*kurz auch:* **mall**)	*(großes)* Einkaufszentrum	
zoo [zuː]	Zoo	❗ Aussprache: **zoo** [zuː] – Der Anfangslaut ist wie im deutschen Namen „Susie".
(to) **go shopping** [ˈʃɒpɪŋ]	einkaufen gehen	On Saturday mornings I **go shopping** with Mum.

Part A

p. 82 (we/you/they) **were** [wɜː], [wə]	*Vergangenheitsform von „be"*	
(I/he/she/it) **was** [wɒz], [wəz]	*Vergangenheitsform von „be"*	
yesterday [ˈjestədeɪ], [ˈjestədi]	gestern	**Yesterday** I was late for school. My teacher wasn't happy.
today [təˈdeɪ]	heute	
last weekend/Friday/… [lɑːst]	letztes Wochenende / letzten Freitag / …	**last** weekend – **this** weekend – **next** weekend
I'm **sorry about** …	Es tut mir leid wegen …	I'm **sorry about** your grandpa. He was a very nice man.
(to) **be busy** [ˈbɪzi]	beschäftigt sein; viel zu tun haben	I can't help you. I**'m busy**.
fantastic [fænˈtæstɪk]	fantastisch	
actor [ˈæktə]	Schauspieler/in	
exciting [ɪkˈsaɪtɪŋ]	aufregend, spannend	**exciting** ◄► **boring**
Guess what, Dad …	Stell dir vor, Dad … / Weißt du was, Dad …	
still [stɪl]	(immer) noch	My sister is seven, and she **still** can't read.
when [wen]	wenn	Can we play cards **when** you come home?
summer [ˈsʌmə]	Sommer	

spring   summer   autumn   winter

[iː] green · [i] happy · [ɪ] big · [e] red · [æ] cat · [ɑː] class · [ɒ] song · [ɔː] door · [uː] blue · [ʊ] book · [ʌ] mum · [ɜː] girl · [ə] a partner

chain [tʃeɪn]	Kette	a **chain**	

p. 83 **Was it fun?**	Hat es Spaß gemacht?	❗ Swimming **is fun**. That joke **was funny**.	Schwimmen **macht Spaß**. Der Witz **war lustig**.

warm [wɔːm]	warm	

cold   warm   too hot

Part B

p. 84/85 **against** [əˈgenst]	gegen	Sam's team played **against** Devonport.	
final [ˈfaɪnl]	Finale, Endspiel	❗ Betonung: **final** [ˈfaɪnl]	
excited [ɪkˈsaɪtɪd]	aufgeregt, gespannt	❗ Sam was **excited** about the final. It was an **exciting** day for Sam.	**aufgeregt** **aufregend**
on the way to … [weɪ]	auf dem Weg zu/nach …		
went [went]	*Vergangenheitsform von „go"*	Yesterday we **went** to Devonport.	
(to) go by minibus [baɪ ˈmɪnibʌs]	mit dem Kleinbus fahren	We went **by minibus** **by bus** **by car**.	
came [keɪm]	*Vergangenheitsform von „come"*	Uncle Amar **came** to dinner again last night.	
had [hæd]	*Vergangenheitsform von „have"*	Yesterday we **had** breakfast at 6 o'clock.	
half, *pl* **halves** [hɑːf], [hɑːvz]	Halbzeit		
(to) score [skɔː]	einen Treffer erzielen, ein Tor schießen		
point [pɔɪnt]	Punkt	Three **points** for the right answer!	
That helped us **a lot**. [ə ˈlɒt]	Das hat uns sehr geholfen.	He likes her **a lot**.	
won [wʌn]	*Vergangenheitsform von „win"*	Sam and his friends **won** the match last Saturday.	
up and down [ˌʌp‿ən ˈdaʊn]	auf und ab; rauf und runter		
up [ʌp]	hinauf, herauf; (nach) oben		
when [wen]	als		

> **when**
> 1. **When**'s your birthday?   **wann**
> 2. Call me **when** you're back, please.   **wenn**
> 3. He called me **when** he was back.   **als**

(to) arrive [əˈraɪv]	ankommen, eintreffen	The bus **arrived** at 6:20 pm.	
saw [sɔː]	*Vergangenheitsform von „see"*	I **saw** John yesterday. He looked sick.	
better [ˈbetə]	besser	Devonport was good, but Plymstock was **better**.	
p. 86 **past** [pɑːst]	Vergangenheit		
around the library/ the beach [əˈraʊnd]	in der Bücherei / auf dem Strand umher	We walked **around** the town for two hours and saw lots of nice things.	

[eɪ] n**a**me · [aɪ] t**i**me · [ɔɪ] b**oy** · [əʊ] **o**ld ·
[aʊ] t**ow**n · [ɪə] h**ere** · [eə] wh**ere** · [ʊə] t**ou**r

between [bɪ'twiːn]	zwischen	

between the rabbits

p.87 **visit** ['vɪzɪt]	Besuch	

Part C

p.88 (to) **miss** [mɪs]	verpassen	Sorry I'm late – I **missed** the bus.
ride [raɪd]	Fahrt	

Unregelmäßige Vergangenheitsformen (Irregular simple past forms)

(to) **do**	**did** [dɪd]	tun, machen	(to) **ride** a bike	**rode** a bike [rəʊd]	Rad fahren
(to) **eat**	**ate** [et], [eɪt]	essen	(to) **run**	**ran** [ræn]	laufen, rennen
(to) **fall** asleep	**fell** asleep [fel]	einschlafen	(to) **sing**	**sang** [sæŋ]	singen
(to) **forget**	**forgot** [fə'gɒt]	vergessen	(to) **write**	**wrote** [rəʊt]	schreiben

➡ *List of irregular verbs, p.231*

---

over to … ['əʊvə]	hinüber zu/nach …	
picnic ['pɪknɪk]	Picknick	
Sam **didn't run**. ['dɪdnt]	Sam rannte nicht.	he **ran/watched** ◄► he **didn't run** / **didn't watch**
(to) **sit down** [ˌsɪt 'daʊn], *simple past:* **sat down** [sæt]	sich hinsetzen	After the football match, the players **sat down** and had something to drink.
far [fɑː]	weit (entfernt)	
all right [ɔːl 'raɪt]	okay; in Ordnung	
problem ['prɒbləm]	Problem	❗ Betonung: **problem** ['prɒbləm]
high [haɪ]	hoch	
sights *(pl)* [saɪts]	Sehenswürdigkeiten	
those … [ðəʊz]	die … dort; jene …	*Singular:* **that book** – *Plural:* **those books**

---

this, that – these, those

- Wenn etwas näher beim Sprecher ist, verwendet man eher **this** und **these**.

- Wenn etwas weiter entfernt ist, verwendet man eher **that** und **those**.

I like this book and these DVDs.

I don't like that comic and those CDs.

(to) **make a wish** [wɪʃ]	sich etwas wünschen	
the **missing** words ['mɪsɪŋ]	die fehlenden Wörter	
early ['ɜːli]	früh	I have to get up very **early** on school days. **early** ◄► late

---

Unregelmäßige Vergangenheitsformen (Irregular simple past forms)

(to) **feed**	**fed** [fed]	füttern	(to) **say**	**said** [sed]	sagen
(to) **hear**	**heard** [hɜːd]	hören	(to) **swim**	**swam** [swæm]	schwimmen
(to) **make**	**made** [meɪd]	machen; herstellen	(to) **take**	**took** [tʊk]	nehmen; bringen
(to) **meet**	**met** [met]	(sich) treffen	(to) **think**	**thought** [θɔːt]	denken, glauben

➡ *List of irregular verbs, p.231*

---

p.89 (to) **use** [juːz]	benutzen, verwenden	Can I **use** your mobile, please?

[b] **b**oat · [p] **p**ool · [d] **d**ad · [t] **t**en · [g] **g**ood · [k] **c**at ·
[m] **m**um · [n] **n**o · [ŋ] so**ng** · [l] **h**ello · [r] **r**ed · [w] **w**e · [j] **y**ou

true [truː]	wahr	
p.90 (to) **save** [seɪv]	retten	
hurt [hɜːt]	verletzt	
county [ˈkaʊnti]	Grafschaft *(in Großbritannien)*	

Part D

p.92 (to) **smile** [smaɪl]	lächeln	
(to) **bite** [baɪt], *simple past:* **bit** [bɪt]	beißen	Don't feed the horses – they **bite**.
just [dʒʌst]	(einfach) nur, bloß	Don't **just** sit there. Come and help me.
We **couldn't** go back. [ˈkʊdnt]	Wir konnten nicht zurückgehen.	We **could** hear the dog, but we **couldn't** see it.
bell [bel]	Klingel, Glocke	
(to) **weigh** [weɪ]	wiegen	How much do you **weigh**?
kilogram [ˈkɪləɡræm], **kilo** [ˈkiːləʊ] **(kg)**	Kilogramm, Kilo	
spot [spɒt]	Fleck, Punkt	There's a **spot** on your T-shirt. – I know. It's chocolate.
hard [hɑːd]	schwer, schwierig; hart	This exercise isn't **hard**. You can do it. It's **hard** work to learn a language.
(to) **leave** [liːv], *simple past:* **left** [left]	verlassen; zurücklassen	Dad **leaves** the house at 8 am and starts work at 9. Don't **leave** your dog in the car when you go shopping.
kilometre [ˈkɪləmiːtə], [kɪˈlɒmɪtə] **(km)**	Kilometer	*English:* **kilometre** *German:* **Kilometer**
(to) **practise** [ˈpræktɪs]	üben, trainieren	
p.94 **holidays** *(pl)* [ˈhɒlədeɪz]	Ferien	
p.95 **many** [ˈmeni]	viele	

---

much („viel") – many („viele")

viel	**How much** tea do we need?	– We don't need **much** tea, but we need **lots of** milk.	
	Wie viel Tee …?	– … nicht **viel** Tee	… **viel** Milch
viele	**How many** scones do we need?	– We don't need **many** scones, but we need **lots of** sandwiches.	
	Wie viele Scones …?	– … nicht **viele** Scones	… **viele** Sandwiches

---

orange [ˈɒrɪndʒ]	Orange, Apfelsine	
worm [wɜːm]	Wurm	
p.96 **news** *(no pl)* [njuːz]	Nachrichten	❗ Das englische Wort **news** ist Singular: *English:* **That's** good news. *German:* **Das sind** gute Nachrichten.
paragraph [ˈpærəɡrɑːf]	Absatz *(in einem Text)*	❗ Betonung: **paragraph** [ˈpærəɡrɑːf]
title [ˈtaɪtl]	Titel, Überschrift	
drawing [ˈdrɔːɪŋ]	Zeichnung	
caption [ˈkæpʃn]	Bildunterschrift	
order [ˈɔːdə]	Reihenfolge	

---

[f] **f**ather · [v] ri**v**er · [s] **s**i**s**ter · [z] plea**s**e · [ʃ] **sh**op · [ʒ] televi**s**ion ·
[tʃ] **t**ea**ch**er · [dʒ] **G**ermany · [θ] **th**anks · [ð] **th**is · [h] **h**ere

(to) **think of** sth.	sich etwas ausdenken; an etwas denken	Read the story and **think of** a good title. I often **think of** our holidays in France last summer.
another [ə'nʌðə]	ein(e) andere(r, s); noch ein(e)	I don't like red. Can I use **another** colour? (= a different colour) Can I have **another** biscuit? They're yummy.
(to) **arrange** [ə'reɪndʒ]	anordnen	
What is the story about?	Wovon handelt die Geschichte? / Worum geht es in der Geschichte?	
(to) **go with** sth.	zu etwas passen; zu etwas gehören	Lot's of people say brown doesn't **go with** blue. The first text **goes with** the third picture.
p. 97 (to) **buy** [baɪ], *simple past:* **bought** [bɔːt]	kaufen	(to) **buy** ◄► (to) **sell**
enough [ɪ'nʌf]	genug	

A baby seal

p. 98 **bright** [braɪt]	strahlend, leuchtend, hell	**bright** ◄► **dark**
eye [aɪ]	Auge	
(to) **move** [muːv]	bewegen; sich bewegen	
over ['əʊvə]	über	She has a poster of a pop group **over** her desk. Can you jump **over** your chair?
(to) **be hungry** ['hʌŋgri]	hungrig sein, Hunger haben	
(to) **push** [pʊʃ]	drücken, schieben, stoßen	
head [hed]	Kopf	

body ['bɒdi]	Körper

Unregelmäßige Vergangenheitsformen (Irregular simple past forms)					
(to) **drink**	**drank** [dræŋk]	trinken	(to) **sit**	**sat** [sæt]	sitzen; sich setzen
(to) **find**	**found** [faʊnd]	finden	(to) **throw**	**threw** [θruː]	werfen
(to) **put**	**put** [pʊt]	legen, stellen, *(wohin)* tun	(to) **wake up**	**woke up** [wəʊk]	aufwachen
➡ *List of irregular verbs,* p. 231					

sun [sʌn]	Sonne	
(to) **go down** [ˌgəʊ 'daʊn]	untergehen *(Sonne)*	
(to) **steer** [stɪə]	steuern, lenken	
only ['əʊnli]	erst	My sister can't read – she's **only** four.
someone is right	jemand hat Recht	Jonathan says Aberdeen is in England. I think he**'s** **right**. – No, he**'s wrong**. Aberdeen is in Scotland!
someone is wrong	jemand irrt sich; jemand hat Unrecht	*English:* **You're right/wrong.** *German:* **Du hast Recht/Unrecht.**
front [frʌnt]	Vorderseite	

[iː] green · [i] happy · [ɪ] big · [e] red · [æ] cat · [ɑː] class · [ɒ] song ·
[ɔː] door · [uː] blue · [ʊ] book · [ʌ] mum · [ɜː] girl · [ə] a partner

Did you get it? *(infml)*	Hast du es verstanden? / Hast du es mitbekommen?	
p. 99 **slow** [sləʊ]	langsam	
(to) hit sth. [hɪt], *simple past:* **hit**	gegen etwas prallen, stoßen	John is hurt – his car **hit** a bus in Dean Street this morning.
(to) pull [pʊl]	ziehen	

(to) **push** ◄► (to) **pull**

careful ['keəfl]	vorsichtig	Be **careful** – seals can bite.
(to) be cold	frieren	*English:* **I'm cold.** *German:* **Mir ist kalt. / Ich friere.**
(to) die [daɪ]	sterben	
cage [keɪdʒ]	Käfig	
poor [pɔː], [pʊə]	arm	
(to) get [get], *simple past:* **got** [gɒt]	bekommen	

> **get**, *simple past:* **got**
> Did you **get** nice presents?   bekommen
> Mum **gets** angry when I'm late.   werden
> I always **get up** at 7 o'clock.   aufstehen

before [bɪ'fɔː]	bevor	Do your homework **before** you go out.
soft [sɒft]	weich	
silky ['sɪlki]	seidig	I love to touch my dog's ears – they are so **silky**.

Unit 5   By the sea

p. 102 **by** the sea [baɪ]	am Meer	
p. 103 **(to) feel** [fiːl], *simple past:* **felt** [felt]	fühlen; sich fühlen	Take my hand. Can you **feel** how cold it is? I always **feel** happy when I'm by the sea.
face [feɪs]	Gesicht	
(to) look for sth. ['lʊk fɔː]	etwas suchen	

I can feel the sun on my face.

> **Unregelmäßige Vergangenheitsformen (Irregular simple past forms)**
>
> | | | | | | | |
> |---|---|---|---|---|---|---|
> | (to) **break** | **broke** [brəʊk] | (zer)brechen | | (to) **send** | **sent** [sent] | schicken, senden |
> | (to) **catch** | **caught** [kɔːt] | fangen | | (to) **sleep** | **slept** [slept] | schlafen |
> | (to) **fight** | **fought** [fɔːt] | kämpfen | | (to) **understand** | **understood** | verstehen |
> | (to) **grow** | **grew** [gruː] | anbauen, anpflanzen | | | [ˌʌndə'stʊd] | |
> | (to) **read** | **read** [red] | lesen | | (to) **wear** | **wore** [wɔː] | tragen *(Kleidung)* |
>
> ➡ *List of irregular verbs, p. 231*

Part A

p. 104 **trip** [trɪp]	Ausflug; Reise	
ferry ['feri]	Fähre	
(to) run after sb. [ˌrʌn_'ɑːftə]	hinter jm. herrennen	"Come back," he shouted when he ran **after** his dog.

[eɪ] name · [aɪ] time · [ɔɪ] boy · [əʊ] old ·
[aʊ] town · [ɪə] here · [eə] where · [ʊə] tour

fast [fɑːst]	schnell	fast ◄► slow
at the moment [ˈməʊmənt]	gerade, im Moment	❗ Betonung: **moment** [ˈməʊmənt]
a kind of ... [kaɪnd]	eine Art (von) …	I like all **kinds of** music, but I never listen to jazz.
rucksack [ˈrʌksæk]	Rucksack	
(to) **be over** [ˈəʊvə]	vorbei sein, zu Ende sein	They looked sad. The holidays **were over**.
(to) **laugh** [lɑːf]	lachen	
almost [ˈɔːlməʊst]	fast, beinahe	It's **almost** six.
(**It's**) **my turn.** [tɜːn]	Ich bin dran / an der Reihe.	I'm finished. Now it's **your turn**.
p. 106 (to) **smell** sth. [smel]	an etwas riechen	Look, the dog is **smelling** the school bag.

Part B

p. 108 **talk** [tɔːk]	Vortrag, Referat, Rede	*English:* (to) **give** a talk (about) *German:* einen Vortrag/eine Rede **halten** (über)
sleepover [ˈsliːpəʊvə]	Schlafparty	
bad [bæd]	schlecht, schlimm	**good** ◄► **bad**
shark [ʃɑːk]	Hai	
at last [ət ˈlɑːst]	endlich, schließlich	We waited for a long time. **At last**, the bus arrived.
blond (*bei Frauen oft:* **blonde**) [blɒnd]	blond	
(to) **take photos**	fotografieren, Fotos machen	
first [fɜːst]	zuerst, als Erstes	You can watch TV later, but do your homework **first**.
interesting [ˈɪntrəstɪŋ]	interessant	
p. 109 **line** [laɪn]	Zeile	❗ Abkürzungen: **l.** 15 = **line** 15 (Zeile 15) **ll.** 15–18 = **lines** 15–18 (Zeilen 15–18)
the UK [ˌjuː ˈkeɪ] (**the United Kingdom** [juˌnaɪtɪd ˈkɪŋdəm])	das Vereinigte Königreich	**the UK** = **Great Britain** (England, Scotland, Wales) and **Northern Ireland** (*Nordirland*)
the biggest ... [ˈbɪgɪst]	der/die/das größte …	
coast [kəʊst]	Küste	
planet [ˈplænɪt]	Planet	❗ Betonung: **planet** [ˈplænɪt]
ocean [ˈəʊʃn]	Ozean	
centre [ˈsentə]	Zentrum; Mitte	
snack [snæk]	Snack, Imbiss	
price [praɪs]	(Kauf-)Preis	
p. 110 **important** [ɪmˈpɔːtnt]	wichtig	

[b] **b**oat · [p] **p**ool · [d] **d**ad · [t] **t**en · [g] **g**ood · [k] **c**at ·
[m] **m**um · [n] **n**o · [ŋ] so**ng** · [l] **h**ello · [r] **r**ed · [w] **w**e · [j] **y**ou

p.111 **sign** [saɪn]	Schild; Zeichen	The **sign** says it's only ten minutes to the zoo.
the same as …	der-/die-/dasselbe wie …	English is not **the same as** Scottish.

Part C

p.112

> **Unregelmäßige Vergangenheitsformen (Irregular simple past forms)**
>
> | | | | | | | |
> |---|---|---|---|---|---|---|
> | (to) **choose** | **chose** [tʃəʊz] | aussuchen, auswählen | | (to) **sell** | **sold** [səʊld] | verkaufen |
> | (to) **give** | **gave** [geɪv] | geben | | (to) **speak** | **spoke** [spəʊk] | sprechen |
> | (to) **know** | **knew** [njuː] | wissen; kennen | | (to) **tell** | **told** [təʊld] | erzählen, berichten |
>
> ➜ List of irregular verbs, p.231

not … yet [jet]	noch nicht	Are you ready? – No, I'm **not** ready **yet**. I can't find my mobile. (oder kurz: No, **not yet**. I can't find my mobile.)
(to) **agree with** sb. [əˈgriː]	jm. zustimmen	English: I **agree with you**. German: Ich **stimme dir zu**.
(to) **agree on** sth.	sich auf etwas einigen	We have to **agree on** a day for our party.
(to) **smuggle** [ˈsmʌgl]	schmuggeln	(to) **smuggle** · **smuggler** (Schmuggler/in) · **smuggling** (der Schmuggel, das Schmuggeln)
village [ˈvɪlɪdʒ]	Dorf	
(to) **point to** sth. [pɔɪnt]	auf etwas zeigen, deuten	He **pointed to** the clock. "We're late," he said.
fat [fæt]	dick, fett	
under [ˈʌndə]	unter	Where are my shoes? – **Under** your desk.
(to) **explain** sth. **to** sb. [ɪkˈspleɪn]	jm. etwas erklären, erläutern	English: Can you **explain** that **to me**? German: Kannst du **mir** das **erklären**?
clever [ˈklevə]	klug, schlau	
(to) **draw** [drɔː], simple past: **drew** [druː]	zeichnen	He's **drawing** a picture of his mum.
(to) **go on** [ˌgəʊ_ˈɒn], simple past: **went on**	weiterreden, fortfahren; weitermachen	She stopped in the middle of her sentence, smiled, then **went on**. That's enough for now. Let's **go on** after lunch.
p.113 **tourist** [ˈtʊərɪst]	Tourist/in	
century [ˈsentʃəri]	Jahrhundert	
lonely [ˈləʊnli]	einsam	
pepper [ˈpepə]	Pfeffer	
expensive [ɪkˈspensɪv]	teuer	£60 for a T-shirt? That's too **expensive**.
cheap [tʃiːp]	billig, preiswert	**cheap** ◄► **expensive**
goods (pl) [gʊdz]	Waren, Güter	
(to) **hide** [haɪd], simple past: **hid** [hɪd]	(sich) verstecken	Can you **hide** this box for me? It's a present for my mother. My little sister often **hides** under her bed.

---

[f] **f**ather · [v] ri**v**er · [s] **s**ister · [z] plea**s**e · [ʃ] **sh**op · [ʒ] televi**s**ion ·
[tʃ] **t**ea**ch**er · [dʒ] **G**ermany · [θ] **th**anks · [ð] **th**is · [h] **h**ere

check [tʃek]	Überprüfung, Kontrolle	
(to) **check** [tʃek]	(über)prüfen, kontrollieren	
subtitle ['sʌbtaɪtl]	Untertitel	
author ['ɔːθə]	Autor/in	
p. 114 **paper** ['peɪpə]	Papier	I need glue and some **paper** for our poster.
word order ['wɜːd_ɔːdə]	Wortstellung	
sub-clause ['sʌbklɔːz]	Nebensatz	
p. 115 (to) **prepare** sth. [prɪ'peə]	etwas vorbereiten	
character ['kærəktə]	Figur, Person (in Roman, Film, Theaterstück usw.)	
likes and dislikes (pl) [dɪs'laɪks]	Vorlieben und Abneigungen	Tell me about your **likes and dislikes**. – Well, I like football and hip hop, but I don't like tennis.
keyword ['kiːwɜːd]	Schlüsselwort	
letter ['letə]	Buchstabe	
through [θruː]	durch	I can't see **through** the window – it's too dark.
(to) **copy** ['kɒpi]	kopieren, abschreiben	
phrase [freɪz]	Ausdruck, (Rede-)Wendung	
easy ['iːzi]	leicht, einfach	Her talk was **easy** to understand.
p. 116 (to) **get off (the bus/boat)** [ˌget_'ɒf], simple past: **got off**	(aus dem Bus/Boot) aussteigen	**Get off the bus** at Green Road. I live in the white house.
(to) **get** [get], simple past: **got**	gelangen, (hin)kommen	Excuse me, how do I **get** to the zoo, please?

The pepper smugglers – a play

p. 118 **play** [pleɪ]	Theaterstück	
scene [siːn]	Szene	❗ Aussprache – das "c" wird nicht gesprochen: **scene** [siːn]
farmer ['fɑːmə]	Bauer/Bäuerin, Landwirt/in	
rich [rɪtʃ]	reich	**rich** ◄► **poor**
soon [suːn]	bald	It's my birthday **soon**. Can I have a party?
dress [dres]	Kleid	
Good luck! [lʌk]	Viel Glück!	
(to) **hold** [həʊld], simple past: **held** [held]	halten	Can you **hold** my bag, please? I can't open the door.
no one ['nəʊ wʌn] (or: **nobody** ['nəʊbədi])	niemand	Everyone remembered my birthday. = **No one** (or: **Nobody**) forgot my birthday. **everyone** ◄► **no one**
light [laɪt]	Licht	It's dark. Can you turn on a **light**, please.
cart [kɑːt]	Karren	
like that	so (auf diese Weise)	Don't do it **like that**. Look, do it like I'm doing.

[iː] green · [i] happy · [ɪ] big · [e] red · [æ] cat · [ɑː] class · [ɒ] song · [ɔː] door · [uː] blue · [ʊ] book · [ʌ] mum · [ɜː] girl · [ə] a partner

p.119 **dangerous** [ˈdeɪndʒərəs]	gefährlich	
sword [sɔːd]	Schwert	❗ Aussprache – das "w" wird nicht gesprochen: **sword** [sɔːd]
Goodbye. [ˌɡʊdˈbaɪ]	Auf Wiedersehen.	
market [ˈmɑːkɪt]	Markt	
(to) **point** sth. **at** sb. [pɔɪnt]	etwas auf jn. richten	She **pointed** her camera **at** him.
prison [ˈprɪzn]	Gefängnis	
(to) **fall** [fɔːl], *simple past:* **fell** [fel]	fallen, stürzen; hinfallen	Yesterday my brother **fell** into our swimming pool.
(to) **sneeze** [sniːz]	niesen	

Partner A

1 Unit

5 Who's in the photo? *(be)*

Partner A:

a) Say as much as you can about *one* of these boys.
   Don't say his name.
   Can your partner guess who it is?
   You can use these ideas to make sentences.
   The boy in my photo is/isn't from Plymouth.
   He's …
   His dad …

b) Listen to your partner. Who is the girl in his/her photo?

5 Unit

1 Is he singing? (Present progressive: questions)

Partner A:
Answer Partner B's questions about pictures 4–6. Use short answers (Yes, he is. / No, he isn't., etc.).

Dictionary

Das **Dictionary** besteht aus **zwei alphabetischen Wörterlisten**:
English – German (S. 206 – 219)   und   **German – English** (S. 220 – 230)

Im **English – German Dictionary** kannst du nachschlagen, wenn du wissen möchtest,
was ein englisches Wort bedeutet, wie man es ausspricht oder wie es geschrieben wird.

Im **Dictionary** werden folgende **Abkürzungen und Symbole** verwendet:

sth. = something (etwas)   sb. = somebody (jemand)   jn. = jemanden   jm. = jemandem
pl = plural (Mehrzahl)   *infml* = informal (umgangssprachlich)
° Mit diesem Kringel sind Wörter markiert, die nicht zum Lernwortschatz gehören.

► Der Pfeil weist auf Kästen im **Vocabulary** (S. 172 – 205) hin, in denen du weitere Informationen zu diesem Wort findest.

Die **Fundstellenangaben** zeigen, wo ein Wort zum ersten Mal in *English G Access 1* vorkommt.
Die Ziffern in Klammern bezeichnen Seitenzahlen: (3) = Seite 3   HWG (8) = Here we go, Seite 8   1 (19) = Unit 1, Seite 19

Tipps zur Arbeit mit einem Wörterbuch findest du im Skills File auf Seite 152.

A

a [ə] ein, eine HWG (8)

about [ə'baʊt]: **about me/you/...** über mich/dich/... 1 (25) **about yourself** über dich selbst 1 (26) **It's about a seagull.** Es geht um eine Möwe. / Es handelt von einer Möwe **What about you?** Und du? / Und was ist mit dir?; Und ihr? / Und was ist mit euch? HWG (9) **What is the story about?** Wovon handelt die Geschichte? Worum geht es in der Geschichte? 4 (96)

access ['ækses] Zugang, Zutritt (3)

act out [ˌækt_'aʊt] vorspielen 1 (35)

action ['ækʃn] Action; Handlung, Tat 3 (68)

°**active** ['æktɪv] aktiv

activity [æk'tɪvəti] Aktivität 3 (60) **free-time activities** Freizeitaktivitäten 3 (62)

actor ['æktə] Schauspieler/in 4 (82)

°**add (to)** [æd] hinzufügen, ergänzen, addieren (zu)

address [ə'dres] Adresse, Anschrift 3 (72)

after ['ɑːftə]:
1. after breakfast nach dem Frühstück 2 (38)
2. run after sb. hinter jm. herrennen 5 (104)

afternoon [ˌɑːftə'nuːn] Nachmittag 2 (38) **in the afternoon** nachmittags, am Nachmittag 2 (38) **on Saturday afternoon** am Samstagnachmittag 3 (68)

again [ə'gen] wieder; noch einmal 1 (26)

against [ə'genst] gegen 4 (84/85)

age [eɪdʒ] Alter 3 (67)

agree [ə'griː]: **agree with sb.** jm. zustimmen 5 (112) **agree on sth.** sich auf etwas einigen 5 (112)

all [ɔːl] alles; alle 2 (44) **all of Plymouth** ganz Plymouth, das ganze Plymouth 3 (68)

all right [ɔːl 'raɪt] okay; in Ordnung 4 (88)

almost ['ɔːlməʊst] fast, beinahe 5 (104)

°**alone** [ə'ləʊn] allein

along [ə'lɒŋ]: **along the street / the river / ...** die Straße / den Fluss / ... entlang 3 (72) °**sing along** mitsingen

°**alphabet** ['ælfəbet] Alphabet

°**already** [ɔːl'redi] schon

also ['ɔːlsəʊ] auch 3 (67)

always ['ɔːlweɪz] immer 1 (35)

am: 4 am [ˌeɪ_'em] 4 Uhr morgens 3 (56/57)

an [æn, ən] ein, eine HWG (14)

and [ænd, ənd] und HWG (9)

angry ['æŋgri] wütend 1 (35)

animal ['ænɪml] Tier HWG (13) **my favourite animal** mein Lieblingstier HWG (14)

another [ə'nʌðə]:
1. ein(e) andere(r, s) 4 (96)
2. noch ein(e) 4 (96)

answer ['ɑːnsə]:
1. antworten; beantworten 1 (26)
2. Antwort 1 (26)

ant [ænt] Ameise HWG (14)

any ['eni]: **Are there any ...?** Gibt es (irgendwelche) ...? 1 (30) **There aren't any ...** Es gibt keine / Es sind keine ... 1 (32)

°**apostrophe** [ə'pɒstrəfi] Apostroph, Auslassungszeichen

appointment [ə'pɔɪntmənt] Verabredung, Termin 1 (25)

April ['eɪprəl] April 1 (29)

aquarium [ə'kweəriəm] Aquarium; Aquarienhaus 5 (108)

are ['ɑː] bist; sind; seid HWG (9) **Are you ...?** Bist du ...? HWG (9) **The DVDs are ...** Die DVDs kosten ... 3 (69)

area ['eəriə] Bereich; Gebiet, Gegend 3 (56/57)

aren't [ɑːnt]: **you aren't** du bist nicht ...; du bist kein/e ...; ihr seid nicht ...; ihr seid kein/e ... 1 (20)

armchair ['ɑːmtʃeə] Sessel 2 (36)

around [ə'raʊnd]
1. around the library / the beach in der Bücherei / auf dem Strand umher 4 (86)
°**2.** um ... herum **run around** herumrennen

arrange [ə'reɪndʒ] anordnen 4 (96)

arrive [ə'raɪv] ankommen, eintreffen 4 (84/85)

art [ɑːt] Kunst 1 (27)

°**as** [æz, əz] während

°**as much as** [əz 'mʌtʃ_əz] so viel wie

ask [ɑːsk] fragen 1 (26) **ask a question** eine Frage stellen 1 (26) **ask sb. to do sth.** jemanden bitten, etwas zu tun 3 (62) °**ask sb. for sth.** jn. um etwas bitten

at [æt, ət] an, bei, in HWG (12) **at 14 Dean Street** in der Deanstraße 14 1 (26) **at home** daheim, zu Hause 1 (19) **at last** endlich, schließlich 5 (108) **at lunchtime** mittags 3 (56/57) **at the moment** gerade, im Moment 5 (104) **at night** nachts, in der Nacht 2 (39) **at school** in der

Schule 1 (18)   **at the weekend** am Wochenende 2 (39)

ate [et, eɪt] *simple past of* **eat**

attic ['ætɪk] Dachboden 3 (72)
   in the attic auf dem Dachboden 3 (72)

August ['ɔːgəst] August 1 (29)

aunt [ɑːnt] Tante 2 (44)

author ['ɔːθə] Autor/in 5 (113)

autumn ['ɔːtəm] Herbst 4 (82)

away [ə'weɪ] weg, fort 2 (39)

B

back [bæk]
   1. zurück 1 (30)
   °**2.** Rücken

background file ['bækgraʊnd ˌfaɪl] Hintergrundinformation(en) (3)

bad [bæd] schlecht, schlimm 5 (108)

bag [bæg] Tasche, Beutel, Tüte HWG (16)   **school bag** Schultasche HWG (16)

°**baking powder** ['beɪkɪŋ ˌpaʊdə] Backpulver

ball [bɔːl] Ball 1 (26)

bark [bɑːk] bellen 3 (72)

basket ['bɑːskɪt] Korb 2 (39)

basketball ['bɑːskɪtbɔːl] Basketball 2 (47)

bathroom ['bɑːθruːm] Badezimmer 2 (36)

be [bi], *simple past:* **was, were:**
   1. sein 1 (22)
   °**2.** werden

beach [biːtʃ] Strand 3 (62)

bear [beə] Bär HWG (14)

because [bɪ'kɒz] weil 3 (58)

bed [bed] Bett 2 (36)

bedroom ['bedruːm] Schlafzimmer 2 (36)

beef [biːf]: **roast beef** Rinderbraten 2 (48)

°**been** [biːn]: **where we've been** wo wir gewesen sind

before [bɪ'fɔː]:
   1. bevor 4 (99)
   2. vor 1 (20)   **before school/ lessons** vor der Schule *(vor Schulbeginn)* / vorm Unterricht 1 (20)

behind [bɪ'haɪnd] hinter 3 (68)

bell [bel] Klingel, Glocke 4 (92)

°**below** [bɪ'ləʊ] unterhalb (von)

best [best]: **the best ...** der/die/das beste ...; die besten ... 1 (18)   °**his Sunday best** *etwa:* sein Sonntagsanzug

better ['betə] besser 4 (84/85)

between [bɪ'twiːn] zwischen 4 (86)

big [bɪg] groß HWG (10)   °**big cat** Großkatze   **big wheel** Riesenrad HWG (10)   **the biggest ...** ['bɪgɪst] der/die/das größte ... 5 (109)

bike [baɪk] Fahrrad 3 (68)   **ride a bike** Fahrrad fahren 3 (68)

°**binoculars** *(pl)* [bɪ'nɒkjələz] Fernglas

bird [bɜːd] Vogel HWG (14)

birthday ['bɜːθdeɪ] Geburtstag 1 (26)
   My birthday is in May. Ich habe im Mai Geburtstag. 1 (29)   **My birthday is on 5th August.** Ich habe am 5. August Geburtstag. 1 (29)   **When's your birthday?** Wann hast du Geburtstag? 1 (29)
   ▶ S.182 Birthdays

biscuit ['bɪskɪt] Keks, Plätzchen 2 (50)

bite [baɪt]:
   1. *(simple past:* **bit***)* beißen 4 (92)
   °**2. in one bite** mit einem Bissen

black [blæk] schwarz HWG (15)

blond *(bei Frauen oft:* **blonde***)* [blɒnd] blond 5 (108)

blue [bluː] blau HWG (15)

°**boa constrictor** ['bəʊə kənstrɪktə] Abgottschlange, *Boa constrictor*

board [bɔːd] (Wand-)Tafel HWG (16)

boat [bəʊt] Boot, Schiff HWG (10)

body ['bɒdi] Körper 4 (98)

book [bʊk] Buch HWG (16)

bookshop ['bʊkʃɒp] Buchladen, Buchhandlung 4 (87)

boring ['bɔːrɪŋ] langweilig 3 (72)

bottle ['bɒtl] Flasche 3 (72)

bought [bɔːt] *simple past of* **buy**

°**bowl** [bəʊl] Schüssel

box [bɒks] Kasten, Kiste, Kästchen 4 (80)

boy [bɔɪ] Junge HWG (9)

°**bracket** ['brækɪt] Klammer *(in Texten)*

bread [bred] Brot 2 (50)

break [breɪk] Pause 1 (28)

break [breɪk], *simple past:* **broke:**
   1. zerbrechen, kaputt machen 4 (80)
   2. brechen, kaputt gehen 4 (80)

breakfast ['brekfəst] Frühstück 2 (38)   **have breakfast** frühstücken 2 (38)

bright [braɪt] strahlend, leuchtend, hell 4 (98)

British ['brɪtɪʃ] britisch 1 (21)

broke [brəʊk] *simple past of* **break**

brother ['brʌðə] Bruder 1 (18)

brown [braʊn] braun HWG (15)

°**bubble** ['bʌbl]: **speech bubble** Sprechblase

bus [bʌs] Bus 4 (84/85)   **go by bus** mit dem Bus fahren 4 (84/85)

busy ['bɪzi]: **be busy** beschäftigt sein; viel zu tun haben 4 (82)

but [bʌt, bət] aber 1 (18)

°**butter** ['bʌtə] Butter

butterfly ['bʌtəflaɪ] Schmetterling HWG (14)

buy [baɪ], *simple past:* **bought** kaufen 4 (97)

by [baɪ]:
   1. by the sea am Meer 5 (102)
   2. go by car/minibus/... mit dem Auto/Kleinbus/... fahren 4 (84/85)

Bye. [baɪ] Tschüs. 1 (20)

C

café ['kæfeɪ] Café 2 (52)

cage [keɪdʒ] Käfig 4 (99)

cake [keɪk] Kuchen 2 (49)

call [kɔːl] rufen; anrufen; nennen 3 (72)

called [kɔːld]: **be called** heißen, genannt werden 3 (69)

came [keɪm] *simple past of* **come**

camera ['kæmərə] Kamera, Fotoapparat 3 (58)

cameraman ['kæmərəmæn], *pl* **cameramen** ['kæmrəmen] Kameramann 4 (82)

can [kæn, kən] können HWG (10)   **we cannot** ['kænɒt], **we can't** [kɑːnt] ... wir können nicht ... 1 (30)

canteen [kæn'tiːn] Kantine, (Schul-)Mensa 1 (30)

°**cap** [kæp] Mütze, Kappe

°**capital (letter)** ['kæpɪtl] Großbuchstabe

captain ['kæptɪn] Kapitän/in 3 (72)

caption ['kæpʃn] Bildunterschrift 4 (96)

car [kɑː] Auto 4 (84/85)   **go by car** mit dem Auto fahren 4 (84/85)

card (to) [kɑːd] Karte (an) HWG (9)

°**care** [keə]: **take care of sb./sth.** sich um etwas/jn. kümmern

careful ['keəfl] vorsichtig 4 (99)

cart [kɑːt] Karren 5 (118)

castle ['kɑːsl] Burg, Schloss HWG (10)

cat [kæt] Katze HWG (14)   °**big cat** Großkatze

catch [kætʃ], *simple past:* **caught** fangen 1 (26)

caught [kɔːt] *simple past of* **catch**

°**Celsius (C)** ['selsiəs] Celsius

°**celebrity** [sə'lebrəti] berühmte
Persönlichkeit

centre ['sentə] Zentrum; Mitte 5 (109)
°**rescue centre** Rettungsstation

century ['sentʃəri] Jahrhundert
5 (113)

chain [tʃeɪn] Kette 4 (82)

chair [tʃeə] Stuhl HWG (16)

°**chance** [tʃɑːns] Chance

°**change** [tʃeɪndʒ] (sich) (ver-)ändern

°**change** [tʃeɪndʒ] wechseln

chaos ['keɪɒs] Chaos 1 (34)

character ['kærəktə] Figur, Person
(in Roman, Film, Theaterstück) 5 (115)

°**charm** [tʃɑːm] bezaubern,
beschwören

cheap [tʃiːp] billig, preiswert 5 (113)

check [tʃek]:
1. Überprüfung, Kontrolle 5 (113)
2. (über)prüfen, kontrollieren 5 (113)

°**checklist** [tʃek] Checkliste, Prüfliste

cheese [tʃiːz] Käse 2 (50)

chess [tʃes] Schach 3 (60)

°**chick** [tʃɪk] Küken

child [tʃaɪld], pl **children** ['tʃɪldrən]
Kind 3 (69)

chocolate ['tʃɒklət] Schokolade
3 (68)

choose [tʃuːz], simple past: **chose**
aussuchen, (aus)wählen; sich aussuchen 3 (56/57)

°**chorus** ['kɔːrəs] Refrain

chose [tʃəʊz] simple past of **choose**

cinema ['sɪnəmə] Kino 4 (81)

°**circle** ['sɜːkl] Kreis

°**city** ['sɪti] Stadt, Großstadt

class [klɑːs] (Schul-)Klasse HWG (16)
°**in class** im Unterricht

classmate ['klɑːsmeɪt] Mitschü-
ler/in, Klassenkamerad/in HWG (9)

classroom ['klɑːsruːm] Klassenzimmer HWG (16)

clean [kliːn] sauber machen,
putzen 3 (61)

clever ['klevə] klug, schlau 5 (112)

°**climb** [klaɪm] klettern **climb a
tree** auf einen Baum klettern

clock [klɒk] (Wand-, Stand-, Turm-)
Uhr HWG (16)

°**close** [kləʊz] schließen, zumachen

°**cloth** [klɒθ] Tuch

clothes (pl) [kləʊðz] Kleidung,
Kleidungsstücke 2 (52)
▶ S.189 Plural-Wörter

club [klʌb] Klub 2 (39) **join a club**
[dʒɔɪn] in einen Klub eintreten; sich
einem Klub anschließen 3 (56/57)

coast [kəʊst] Küste 5 (109)

coin [kɔɪn] Münze 3 (73)

cola ['kəʊlə] Cola 4 (87)

cold [kəʊld] kalt 2 (48) **be cold**
frieren 4 (99)

collect [kə'lekt] sammeln 3 (62)

colour ['kʌlə] Farbe HWG (9)
▶ S.176 Colours

°**column** ['kɒləm] Spalte

come [kʌm], simple past: **came**
kommen HWG (9) **come home** nach
Hause 1 (19) **come in** hereinkommen 1 (26) **Come on, Dad.**
Na los, Dad! / Komm, Dad! 3 (64)

°**comic strip** ['kɒmɪk ˌstrɪp] Comic-
strip

°**common seal** [ˌkɒmən 'siːl] Seehund
(Phoca vitulina)

°**communication** [kəˌmjuːnɪ'keɪʃn]
Kommunikation **Information and
Communications Technology** Infor-
mations- und Kommunikationstechnologie 1 (27)

°**compare** [kəm'peə] vergleichen

computer [kəm'pjuːtə] Computer
1 (30)

°**consonant** ['kɒnsənənt] Konsonant,
Mitlaut

cool [kuːl] cool 1 (20)

copy ['kɒpi] kopieren, abschreiben
5 (115)

corner ['kɔːnə] Ecke 1 (34) **corner
shop** Laden an der Ecke; Tante-
Emma-Laden 1 (34)

°**cornflakes** ['kɔːnfleɪks]
Cornflakes 2 (50)

°**correct** [kə'rekt] korrigieren,
verbessern

°**correction** [kə'rekʃn] Korrektur,
Berichtigung

could [kʊd]: **he could …** er konnte
… 4 (92) **we couldn't …** ['kʊdnt]
wir konnten nicht … 4 (92)

count [kaʊnt] zählen HWG (17)
count to ten bis zehn zählen
▶ S.233 English numbers

°**country** ['kʌntri] Land (auch als
Gegensatz zur Stadt), Landstrich,
Gegend

county ['kaʊnti] Grafschaft (in Großbritannien) 4 (90)

course [kɔːs] Kurs, Lehrgang (3)

cousin ['kʌzn] Cousin, Cousine 2 (44)

crab [kræb] Krebs 2 (38)

cream [kriːm] Sahne 2 (49) °**cream
tea** [ˌkriːm 'tiː] Mahlzeit mit Tee,
Scones, Marmelade und Sahne

cricket ['krɪkɪt] Cricket 2 (44)

cup [kʌp]: **a cup of tea** eine Tasse
Tee 2 (39)

cupboard ['kʌbəd] Schrank HWG (16)

°**curry** ['kʌri] Curry

D

dad [dæd] Papa, Vati 1 (18)

dance [dɑːns] tanzen 3 (56/57)

dangerous ['deɪndʒərəs] gefährlich
5 (119)

dark [dɑːk] dunkel 1 (18)

°**date** [deɪt] Verabredung, Date

day [deɪ] Tag HWG (11) **day of the
week** Wochentag HWG (11) °**one
day** eines Tages
▶ S.175 The days of the week

dead [ded] tot 2 (47)

December [dɪ'sembə] Dezember
1 (29)

deck [dek] Deck (eines Schiffes)
5 (119)

design and technology [dɪˌzaɪn_ənd
tek'nɒlədʒi] Design und Technik
1 (27)

desk [desk] Schreibtisch HWG (16)

dessert [dɪ'zɜːt] Nachtisch, Nachspeise 2 (48)

°**detective** [dɪ'tektɪv] Detektiv/in

°**dialogue** ['daɪəlɒg] Dialog

diary ['daɪəri] Tagebuch; Kalender
3 (72)

dictionary ['dɪkʃənri] alphabetisches
Wörterverzeichnis, Wörterbuch (3)

did [dɪd] simple past of **do**
he didn't run ['dɪdnt] Er rannte
nicht. 4 (88)

die [daɪ] sterben 4 (99)

different ['dɪfrənt] verschieden;
anders 1 (21) °**different from**
anders als °**in different ways**
auf verschiedene Weise

dining room ['daɪnɪŋ ruːm]
Esszimmer 2 (36)

dinner ['dɪnə] Abendessen, Abendbrot 2 (38) **have dinner** zu Abend
essen 2 (38)

°**director** [də'rektə] Direktor/in

°**dirt** [dɜːt] Dreck

°**discovery** [dɪ'skʌvəri] Entdeckung

dislikes [dɪs'laɪks]: **likes and
dislikes** (pl) Vorlieben und
Abneigungen 5 (115)

°**diver** ['daɪvə] Taucher/in

divorced [dɪ'vɔːst] geschieden 2 (47)

do [duː], simple past: **did** machen,
tun 1 (26) **do sport** Sport treiben
2 (44) **Don't go.** [dəʊnt] Geh nicht.
1 (20) **he doesn't have time** er hat
keine Zeit 2 (44)

dog [dɒg] Hund HWG (14)

door [dɔː] Tür HWG (16)

°**dot** [dɒt] Punkt, Pünktchen

double ['dʌbl] Doppel- HWG (17)

down [daʊn] hinunter, herunter; nach unten 2 (52) °**down to the ground** nach unten auf den Boden **up and down** auf und ab; rauf und runter 4 (84/85)

downstairs [ˌdaʊn'steəz] unten; nach unten *(im Haus)* 2 (36)

drank [dræŋk] *simple past of* **drink**

draw [drɔː], *simple past:* **drew** zeichnen 5 (112)

drawing ['drɔːɪŋ] Zeichnung 4 (96)

dream [driːm] Traum 3 (73)

dress [dres] Kleid 5 (118)

drew [druː] *simple past of* **draw**

drink [drɪŋk]:
  1. *(simple past:* **drank***)* trinken 2 (49)
  2. Getränk 2 (49)

drum [drʌm] Trommel 3 (60) **drums** *(pl)* Schlagzeug 3 (60) **play the drums** Schlagzeug spielen 3 (60)

DVD [ˌdiːviː'diː] DVD 1 (29)

E

°**each** [iːtʃ] jede(r, s) (einzelne)

ear [ɪə] Ohr 4 (98)

early ['ɜːli] früh 4 (88)

°**easier** ['iːziə] leichter, einfacher

easy ['iːzi] leicht, einfach 5 (115)

eat [iːt], *simple past:* **ate** essen 1 (30)

edit ['edɪt] bearbeiten; schneiden *(Film, Video)* 3 (56/57)

°**egg** [eg] Ei

eight [eɪt] acht HWG (8)
  ▶ S. 233 English numbers

elephant ['elɪfənt] Elefant HWG (14)

eleven [ɪ'levn] elf HWG (8)
  ▶ S. 233 English numbers

°**Elizabethan** [ɪˌlɪzə'biːθn] elisabethanisch *(aus dem Zeitalter der Königin Elisabeth I., 1558–1603)*

email ['iːmeɪl] E-Mail 2 (41)

end [end] Ende, Schluss 3 (73) °**in the end** schließlich, am Ende, zum Schluss

°**ending** ['endɪŋ] Ende, Endung

English ['ɪŋglɪʃ] Englisch; englisch HWG (15) **in English** auf Englisch 1 (32)

enough [ɪ'nʌf] genug 4 (97)

°**etc. (et cetera)** [et'setərə] usw. (und so weiter)

evening ['iːvnɪŋ] Abend 2 (38) **in the evening** abends, am Abend 2 (38)

every day/colour/boat ['evri] jeder Tag / jede Farbe / jedes Boot HWG (11)

everybody ['evribɒdi] jeder; alle 3 (59)

everyday ['evrideɪ] Alltags- 1 (31)

everyone ['evriwʌn] jeder; alle 3 (59)

°**example** [ɪg'zɑːmpl] Beispiel **for example** zum Beispiel

excited [ɪk'saɪtɪd] aufgeregt, gespannt 4 (84/85)

exciting [ɪk'saɪtɪŋ] aufregend, spannend 4 (82)

exercise ['eksəsaɪz] Aufgabe, Übung HWG (16)

exercise book ['eksəsaɪz bʊk] Schulheft, Übungsheft HWG (16)

expensive [ɪk'spensɪv] teuer 5 (113)

°**expert** ['ekspɜːt] Experte, Expertin, Fachmann, Fachfrau

explain sth. to sb. [ɪk'spleɪn] jm. etwas erklären, erläutern 5 (112)

eye [aɪ] Auge 4 (98)

F

face [feɪs] Gesicht 5 (103)

fair [feə] fair, gerecht 4 (98)

fall [fɔːl], *simple past:* **fell** fallen, stürzen; hinfallen 5 (119) **fall asleep** einschlafen 1 (30)

family ['fæməli] Familie 2 (36) **the Blackwell family** (die) Familie Blackwell 2 (36) °**family name** Familienname, Nachname **family tree** (Familien-)Stammbaum 2 (47)

°**famous** ['feɪməs] berühmt

fan [fæn] Fan, Anhänger/in 4 (84/85)

fantastic [fæn'tæstɪk] fantastisch 4 (82)

far [fɑː] weit (entfernt) 4 (88)

farm [fɑːm] Bauernhof, Farm 2 (46)

farmer ['fɑːmə] Bauer/Bäuerin, Landwirt/in 5 (118)

fast [fɑːst] schnell 5 (104)

fat [fæt] dick, fett 5 (112)

father ['fɑːðə] Vater 1 (18)

favourite ['feɪvərɪt]: **my favourite animal** mein Lieblingstier HWG (14)

February ['februəri] Februar 1 (29)

feed [fiːd], *simple past:* **fed** füttern 2 (39) **feeding time** Fütterungszeit 5 (108)

feel [fiːl], *simple past:* **felt** fühlen; sich fühlen 5 (103)

feeling ['fiːlɪŋ] Gefühl 1 (35)

fell [fel] *simple past of* **fall**

felt [felt] *simple past of* **feel**

°**fence** [fens] Zaun

ferry ['feri] Fähre 5 (104)

fight [faɪt], *simple past:* **fought** kämpfen 3 (73) °**fight for sth.** um etwas kämpfen

file [faɪl]: **background file** Hintergrundinformation(en) (3) **grammar file** Zusammenfassung der Grammatik jeder Unit (3) **skills file** Übersicht über Lern- und Arbeitstechniken (3)

film [fɪlm]:
  1. filmen 2 (52)
  2. Film 3 (56/57)

final ['faɪnl] Finale, Endspiel 4 (84/85)

find [faɪnd], *simple past:* **found** finden 1 (30) **Find someone who …** Finde jemanden, der … 3 (61)

fine [faɪn]: **Fine, thanks.** Gut, danke. 3 (64)

°**finger** ['fɪŋgə] Finger

finish ['fɪnɪʃ]:
  1. enden 5 (109)
  2. finish sth. etwas beenden; mit etwas fertig werden/sein 3 (64)
  °**3.** vervollständigen; abschließen

finished ['fɪnɪʃt]: **We're finished.** Wir sind fertig. 1 (30)

first [fɜːst] zuerst, als Erstes 5 (108) **the first day** der erste Tag 1 (18)
  ▶ S. 233 English numbers

fish [fɪʃ], *pl* **fish** Fisch 2 (38)

°**fishing** ['fɪʃɪŋ] Angeln, Fischen

five [faɪv] fünf HWG (8)
  ▶ S. 233 English numbers

flat [flæt] Wohnung 1 (18)

°**flipper** ['flɪpə] Flosse

floor [flɔː] Fußboden 2 (39)

°**flour** ['flaʊə] Mehl

°**flyer** ['flaɪə] Flyer, Flugblatt

follow ['fɒləʊ] folgen HWG (13) **Follow me.** Folg(t) mir. HWG (13)

food [fuːd] Essen; Lebensmittel; Futter 2 (50)

football ['fʊtbɔːl] Fußball 1 (26)

for [fɔː, fə] für HWG (15) **What's for lunch?** Was gibt es zum Mittagessen? 2 (48) **What's for homework?** Was haben wir als Hausaufgabe auf? 1 (31)

forget [fə'get], *simple past:* **forgot** vergessen 1 (21)

form (of) [fɔːm] Form (von) 1 (22)

fought [fɔːt] *simple past of* **fight**

found [faʊnd] *simple past of* **find**

four [fɔː] vier HWG (8)
  ▶ S. 233 English numbers

free [friː] frei 3 (62) **free time** Freizeit, freie Zeit 3 (62) **free-time activities** Freizeitaktivitäten 3 (62)

French [frentʃ] Französisch 1 (27)

Friday ['fraɪdeɪ, 'fraɪdi] Freitag HWG (11)

friend ['frend] Freund/in 1 (18)

friendly ['frendli] freundlich 1 (20)

frog [frɒg] Frosch HWG (14)

from [frɒm, frəm] aus, von HWG (9)
 from ... to ... von ... bis ... 3 (56/57)

front [frʌnt] Vorderseite 4 (98) **in front of** vor (räumlich) 3 (68) °**to the front** nach vorn

fruit [fruːt] Obst, Früchte; Frucht 2 (48) **fruit salad** Obstsalat 2 (48)

fun [fʌn] Spaß 3 (56/57) **have fun** Spaß haben, sich amüsieren 3 (56/57) °**a fun place** ein Ort, an dem man Spaß haben kann **That sounds fun.** Das klingt nach Spaß. 3 (59) **Was it fun?** Hat es Spaß gemacht? 4 (83)

funny ['fʌni] witzig, komisch 3 (58)

G

game [geɪm] Spiel HWG (15)

°**game plan** ['geɪm plæn] Strategie, Schlachtplan

°**gang** [gæŋ] Gruppe

garage ['gærɑːʒ, 'gærɪdʒ] Garage 4 (80)

garden ['gɑːdn] Garten 2 (36)

gardening ['gɑːdnɪŋ] Gärtnern, Gartenarbeit 3 (56/57)

°**gate** [geɪt] Tor

gave [geɪv] simple past of **give**

geography [dʒiˈɒgrəfi] Geografie 1 (27)

German ['dʒɜːmən] Deutsch; deutsch 1 (23) **in German** auf Deutsch 1 (32)

get [get], simple past: **got:**
 1. bekommen 4 (99) **Did you get it?** (infml) Hast du es verstanden? / Hast du es mitbekommen? 4 (98)
 2. gelangen, (hin)kommen 5 (116)
 3. get off (the bus/boat) (aus dem Bus/Boot) aussteigen 5 (116)
 4. get angry/cold/... wütend/kalt/... werden 3 (58) °**get ready (for)** sich fertig machen (für), sich vorbereiten (auf)
 5. get up aufstehen 3 (64)
 °**6.** holen **Get more words if you need them.** Hol dir mehr Wörter, wenn du sie brauchst.

ghost [gəʊst] Geist, Gespenst 3 (68)

giraffe [dʒəˈrɑːf] Giraffe HWG (14)

girl [gɜːl] Mädchen HWG (9)

give [gɪv], simple past: **gave:**
 1. geben HWG (16) °**Give me a hug.**

Umarme mich. °**give sb. a squeeze** jn. drücken
 2. give a talk (about) einen Vortrag / eine Rede halten (über) 5 (108)

glue [gluː] Klebstoff HWG (16)

glue stick ['gluː stɪk] Klebestift HWG (16)

go [gəʊ], simple past: **went:**
 1. gehen; fahren HWG (9) **go by car/minibus/...** mit dem Auto/Kleinbus/... fahren 4 (84/85) **go down** untergehen (Sonne) 4 (98) **go for a walk** spazieren gehen, einen Spaziergang machen 2 (39) **go home** nach Hause gehen 1 (19) °**go marching** marschieren **go on** weiterreden, fortfahren; weitermachen 5 (112) **go sailing** segeln; segeln gehen 2 (39) **go shopping** einkaufen gehen 4 (81) **go with sth.** zu etwas gehören, zu etwas passen 4 (96) **Here we go.** Los geht's. / Jetzt geht's los. HWG (8)
 2. Have a go. Versuch's mal. 1 (21)

°**goat** [gəʊt] Ziege

gold [gəʊld] Gold 3 (72)

good [gʊd] gut 1 (26) **be good at kung fu** gut sein in Kung-Fu; gut Kung-Fu können 1 (35) **Good luck!** Viel Glück! 5 (118) **Good morning.** Guten Morgen. 1 (26)

Goodbye. [ˌgʊdˈbaɪ] Auf Wiedersehen. 5 (119)

goods (pl) [gʊdz] Waren, Güter 5 (113)

got [gɒt]:
 1. simple past of **get**
 °**2. he's got** er hat

°**grab** [græb] greifen

°**gram (g)** [græm] Gramm

grammar file ['græmə ˌfaɪl] Zusammenfassung der Grammatik (3)

grandfather ['grænfɑːðə] Großvater 2 (46)

grandma ['grænmɑː] Oma 2 (46)

grandmother ['grænmʌðə] Großmutter 2 (46)

grandpa ['grænpɑː] Opa 2 (46)

grandparents (pl) ['grænpeərənts] Großeltern 4 (81)

°**grass** [grɑːs] Gras

great [greɪt] großartig HWG (11)

green [griːn] grün HWG (15)

grew [gruː] simple past of **grow**

grey [greɪ] grau HWG (15)

°**grey seal** [ˌgreɪ ˈsiːl] Kegelrobbe (Halichoerus grypus)

°**ground** [graʊnd] Boden **down to the ground** nach unten auf den Boden

group (of) [gruːp] Gruppe 1 (35) °**group word** Oberbegriff

grow [grəʊ], simple past: **grew** anbauen, anpflanzen 3 (56/57)

guess [ges] raten, erraten 3 (61) **Guess what, Dad ...** Stell dir vor, Papa ... / Weißt du was, Papa ... 4 (82)

guinea pig ['gɪni pɪg] Meerschweinchen HWG (14)

guitar [gɪˈtɑː] Gitarre 3 (62) **play the guitar** Gitarre spielen 3 (62)

gym [dʒɪm] Turnhalle 1 (30)

gymnastics [dʒɪmˈnæstɪks] Gymnastik, Turnen 3 (60)

H

had [hæd] simple past of **have**

hair [heə] Haar, Haare 2 (52)

half [hɑːf], pl **halves** [hɑːvz] Halbzeit 4 (84/85) **half past ten** halb elf (10.30 / 22.30) 1 (27)
▶ S. 233 English numbers

hand [hænd] Hand 3 (73)

°**handmade** [ˌhændˈmeɪd] von Hand gefertigt

°**hang** [hæŋ]: **hang around** rumhängen **hang up** aufhängen

°**happen** ['hæpən] passieren, geschehen

happy ['hæpi] glücklich, froh 1 (35)

harbour ['hɑːbə] Hafen 2 (52)

hard [hɑːd] schwer, schwierig; hart 4 (92)

has [hæz]: **he/she has** er/sie hat 2 (39)

have [hæv, həv], simple past: **had** haben 1 (21) **Have a go.** Versuch's mal. 1 (21) **have breakfast** frühstücken 2 (38) **have dinner** zu Abend essen 2 (38) **have fun** Spaß haben, sich amüsieren 3 (56/57) **have lunch** zu Mittag essen 2 (38) **have to do** tun müssen 3 (58) °**Just have a look.** Schau einfach mal.

he [hiː] er 1 (18)

head [hed] Kopf 4 (98)

hear [hɪə], simple past: **heard** hören 3 (65)
▶ S. 193 listen · hear

heard [hɜːd] simple past of **hear**

held [held] simple past of **hold**

Hello. [həˈləʊ] Hallo. / Guten Tag. HWG (8)

help [help]:
1. Hilfe 1 (24)
2. helfen 1 (24)
her [hɜː, hə]:
1. ihr, ihre 1 (18)   **her best friend**
ihr bester Freund / ihre beste Freundin 1 (18)
2. sie; ihr 2 (39)
here [hɪə] hier; hierher HWG (13)
Here we go. Los geht's. / Jetzt
geht's los. HWG (8)   **near here** (hier)
in der Nähe 2 (44)
°**hero** ['hɪərəʊ] Held/in
hid [hɪd] *simple past of* **hide**
hide [haɪd], *simple past:* **hid** sich
verstecken, etwas verstecken 5 (113)
high [haɪ] hoch 4 (88)   °**High**
School ['haɪ skuːl] *Schule für 11-
bis 18-Jährige*
hill [hɪl] Hügel HWG (10)
him [hɪm] ihn; ihm 1 (30)
his [hɪz]: **his friend** sein Freund /
seine Freundin 1 (18)
history ['hɪstri] Geschichte 1 (27)
hit [hɪt], *simple past:* **hit** prallen,
stoßen gegen 4 (99)
hobby ['hɒbi] Hobby 3 (56/57)
hold [həʊld], *simple past:* **held**
halten 5 (118)   °**hold onto sth.** sich
an etwas festhalten   °**hold sth. up**
etwas aufhalten
°**holidaymaker** ['hɒlədeɪˌmeɪkə]
Urlauber/in
holidays (pl) ['hɒlədeɪz] Ferien 4 (94)
home [həʊm] Heim, Zuhause 1 (19)
at home daheim, zu Hause 1 (19)
come/go home nach Hause
kommen/gehen 1 (19)
▶ S.179 home
hometown [ˌhəʊm'taʊn]
Heimatstadt HWG (9)
homework ['həʊmwɜːk]
Hausaufgabe(n) 1 (31)   **Do your
homework.** Mach deine Hausaufgaben. 1 (31)   **What's for homework?** Was haben wir als Hausaufgabe auf? 1 (31)
hope [həʊp] hoffen 3 (72)
horse [hɔːs] Pferd HWG (14)
hot [hɒt] heiß 2 (48)
hour ['aʊə] Stunde 1 (28)
house [haʊs] Haus 2 (36)
how [haʊ] wie HWG (9)   **How are
you?** Wie geht's? / Wie geht es dir/
euch? 3 (64)   **How do you like it?**
Wie findest du es (sie/ihn)? / Wie
gefällt es (sie/er) dir? 3 (64)   **How
many?** Wie viele? 4 (95)   **How
much?** Wie viel? 4 (95)   **How much**

are ...? Was kosten ...? 3 (69)   **How
much is ...?** Was kostet ...? 3 (69)
How old are you? Wie alt bist du?
HWG (9)
▶ S.199 much – many
°**hug** [hʌg]: **give sb. a hug** jn.
umarmen
hundred: a/one hundred
[ə'hʌndrəd, ˌwʌn'hʌndrəd]
einhundert HWG (17)
▶ S.233 English numbers
hungry ['hʌŋgri]: **be hungry**
hungrig sein, Hunger haben 4 (98)
°**hurrah** [hə'rɑː] hurra
hurry up [ˌhʌriˈ_'ʌp] sich beeilen
1 (20)
hurt [hɜːt]:
1. verletzt 4 (90)
°**2. hurt sb.** jm. wehtun, jn.
verletzen

I

I [aɪ] ich HWG (8)   **I'm a seal. (= I am
a seal.)** Ich bin eine Robbe. HWG (8)
I'm from Plymouth. Ich bin aus
Plymouth. / Ich komme aus Plymouth.
HWG (9)   **I'm two years old.** Ich bin
zwei Jahre alt. HWG (8)   °**I spy with
my little eye** *entspricht dem Spiel*
"Ich sehe was, was du nicht siehst"
ice cream [ˌaɪs 'kriːm] (Speise-)
Eis 2 (48)
ICT [ˌaɪ siː 'tiː] Informations- und
Kommunikationstechnologie 1 (27)
idea [aɪ'dɪə] Idee; Vorstellung 3 (64)
°**if** [ɪf] wenn, falls
imagine sth. [ɪ'mædʒɪn] sich etwas
vorstellen 3 (69)
important [ɪm'pɔːtnt] wichtig 5 (110)
in [ɪn] in HWG (9)   **come in** hereinkommen 1 (26)   **in 1580** im Jahr
1580 3 (69)   °**in class** im Unterricht
°**in different ways** auf verschiedene
Weise   **in England** in England
HWG (9)   **in front of** vor (räumlich)
3 (68)   **in German/English** auf
Deutsch/Englisch 1 (32)   **in the
afternoon** nachmittags, am Nachmittag 2 (38)   **in the attic** auf dem
Dachboden 3 (72)   °**in the end**
schließlich, am Ende, zum Schluss   **in
the evening** abends, am Abend 2 (38)
in the middle in der Mitte 2 (48)   **in
the morning** morgens, vormittags,
am Morgen/Vormittag 2 (38)   **in the
photo** auf dem Foto HWG (13)   **in
the picture** auf dem Bild HWG (14)

°**Indian** ['ɪndiən] indisch; Inder/in
information (about/on) (no pl)
[ˌɪnfə'meɪʃn] Information(en) (über)
3 (56/57)   **Information and Communications Technology** Informations-
und Kommunikationstechnologie 1 (27)
°**insect** ['ɪnsekt] Insekt
inside [ˌɪn'saɪd] drinnen; nach
drinnen 3 (63)
instrument ['ɪnstrəmənt]
Instrument 3 (56/57)
°**intact** [ɪn'tækt] intakt, ganz
interesting ['ɪntrəstɪŋ]
interessant 5 (108)
interview sb. ['ɪntəvjuː] jn.
interviewen, jn. befragen 3 (66)
into ['ɪntʊ]: **into the kitchen** in die
Küche (hinein) 2 (39)
invitation (to) [ˌɪnvɪ'teɪʃn]
Einladung (zu, nach) 4 (80)
is [ɪz]: **Is it Monday?** Ist es Montag?
HWG (11)   **Is that you?** Bist du's? /
Bist du das? 3 (72)   **The camera is
...** Die Kamera kostet ... 3 (69)
island ['aɪlənd] Insel 4 (80)
isn't ['ɪznt]: **he/she/it isn't (= is
not)** er/sie/es ist nicht ... 1 (18)
it [ɪt] er, sie, es HWG (13)   °**Sam is
it** Sam ist Fänger (beim Fangenspie-
len)
it's ... (= it is) [ɪts] er/sie/es ist ...
HWG (13)
its name [ɪts] sein Name / ihr Name
2 (52)

J

°**jacket** ['dʒækɪt] Jacke
jam [dʒæm] Marmelade 2 (49)
January ['dʒænjuəri] Januar 1 (29)
jeans (pl) [dʒiːnz] Jeans 2 (52)
▶ S.189 Plural-Wörter
job [dʒɒb] Job, (Arbeits-)Stelle 3 (64)
join a club [dʒɔɪn] in einen Klub eintreten; sich einem Klub anschließen
3 (56/57)
joke [dʒəʊk] Witz 3 (58)
judo ['dʒuːdəʊ] Judo 3 (60)
July [dʒu'laɪ] Juli 1 (29)
jump [dʒʌmp]:
1. springen 2 (52)
2. Sprung 3 (63)
June [dʒuːn] Juni 1 (29)
°**jungle** ['dʒʌŋgl] Dschungel
just [dʒʌst] (einfach) nur, bloß 4 (92)
°**Just have a look.** Schau einfach
mal.

Dictionary

K

°**karate** [kə'rɑːti] Karate

°**keep** [kiːp]: **keep a date** eine Verabredung einhalten

keyword ['kiːwɜːd] Schlüsselwort 5 (115)

°**kick** [kɪk] treten

kid [kɪd] Kind 1 (18) °**the kids are playing up** hier: die Kinder machen Unsinn

kilogram, kilo (kg) ['kiːləʊ, 'kɪləgræm] Kilogramm, Kilo 4 (92)

kilometre (km) ['kɪləmiːtə, kɪ'lɒmɪtə] Kilometer 4 (92)

kind [kaɪnd]: **a kind of ...** eine Art (von) ... 5 (104)

°**king** [kɪŋ] König

°**kiss** [kɪs] küssen

kit [kɪt] Ausrüstung 3 (56/57)

kitchen ['kɪtʃɪn] Küche 2 (36)

°**knee** [niː] Knie

knew [njuː] simple past of **know**

know [nəʊ], simple past: **knew** wissen; kennen 1 (18) **I don't know.** Ich weiß (es) nicht. 1 (30) **..., you know.** ..., weißt du. / ..., wissen Sie. 2 (44)

kung fu [ˌkʌŋ 'fuː] Kung Fu 1 (35)

L

°**label** ['leɪbl] beschriften, beschildern

°**ladder** ['lædə] (die) Leiter

lake [leɪk] (Binnen-)See 4 (81)

lamp [læmp] Lampe 2 (36)

°**land** [lænd]: **on land** auf dem Land **land animal** Landtier

language ['læŋgwɪdʒ] Sprache 1 (22)

last [lɑːst]:
1. last weekend/Friday letztes Wochenende / letzten Freitag 4 (82)
2. at last endlich, schließlich 5 (108)

late [leɪt] spät 1 (18) **You're late.** Du bist spät dran. / Du bist zu spät. 1 (18)

later ['leɪtə] später 3 (64)

laugh [lɑːf] lachen 5 (104)

learn [lɜːn] lernen 1 (28)

leave [liːv], simple past: **left** verlassen; zurücklassen 4 (92) °**leave space** Platz lassen

left [left] simple past of **leave**

leg [leg] Bein HWG (15)

lesson ['lesn] (Unterrichts-)Stunde HWG (15) **before lessons** vorm Unterricht 1 (20)

let [let], simple past: **let:** lassen HWG (16) **Let me show you ...** Lass mich dir ... zeigen. HWG (16) **Let's ...** Lass(t) uns ... HWG (9) **Let's go to England.** Lass(t) uns nach England gehen/fahren. HWG (9)

letter ['letə]:
1. Brief 3 (63)
2. Buchstabe 5 (115)

library ['laɪbrəri] Bibliothek, Bücherei 1 (19)

life [laɪf], pl **lives** [laɪvz] Leben 3 (69)

life jacket ['laɪf dʒækɪt] Schwimmweste 4 (80)

light [laɪt] Licht 5 (118)

like [laɪk]:
1. mögen, gernhaben HWG (9) **I like ...** Ich mag ... HWG (9) **I don't like ...** Ich mag ... nicht. / Ich mag kein ... 1 (21) **I'd like ...** Ich hätte gern ... / Ich möchte ... 2 (48) **I'd like to go** Ich möchte gehen / Ich würde gern gehen 5 (103) °**like sth. about sth.** etwas an etwas mögen
2. like boys wie Jungen 1 (35) **like that** so (auf diese Weise) 5 (118) °**like this** so **What's she like?** Wie ist sie? / Wie ist sie so? 3 (59)

likes and dislikes (pl) [ˌlaɪks ən 'dɪslaɪks] Vorlieben und Abneigungen 5 (115)

line [laɪn]:
1. Zeile 5 (109)
°**2.** Reihe
°**3.** Linie

lion ['laɪən] Löwe HWG (14)

list [lɪst] Liste 3 (59)

listen ['lɪsn] zuhören, horchen 3 (64) **listen to sb.** jm. zuhören 3 (64) **listen to sth.** sich etwas anhören 3 (64) **Listen, Justin.** Hör zu, Justin. 3 (64)
▶ S. 193 listen · hear

°**litre** ['liːtə] Liter

little ['lɪtl] klein 1 (34) °**the little one** der/die/das Kleine

live [lɪv] leben; wohnen 1 (26)

°**live** [laɪv] lebend, lebendig

living room ['lɪvɪŋ ruːm] Wohnzimmer 2 (36)

lonely ['ləʊnli] einsam 5 (113)

long [lɒŋ] lang 1 (22)

look [lʊk]:
1. schauen 1 (18): **Look, ...** [lʊk] Sieh mal, ... / Schau mal, ... HWG (13) **look at** anschauen, ansehen 1 (18) **look happy/angry/...** glücklich/wütend/... aussehen 2 (52) **look for sth.** etwas suchen 5 (103)

°**2. Just have a look.** Schau einfach mal.
▶ S. 189 look
▶ S. 183 look · see · watch

lot [lɒt]: **a lot** viel 5 (112) **That helped us a lot.** Das hat uns sehr geholfen. 4 (84/85) **lots of ...** ['lɒts əv] viel ..., viele ... HWG (13)
▶ S. 199 much · many

loud [laʊd] laut 3 (68) °**read sth. out loud** etwas vorlesen

love [lʌv] lieben, sehr mögen 3 (59)

luck [lʌk]: **Good luck!** Viel Glück! 5 (118)

lunch [lʌntʃ] Mittagessen 1 (28) **have lunch** zu Mittag essen 2 (38) **What's for lunch?** Was gibt es zum Mittagessen? 2 (48)

lunchtime ['lʌntʃtaɪm] Mittagszeit 3 (56/57) **at lunchtime** mittags 3 (56/57)

M

mad [mæd] verrückt 2 (39)

made [meɪd] simple past of **make**

°**madman** ['mædmən] Irrer, Verrückter

magazine [ˌmægə'ziːn] Zeitschrift 4 (80)

make [meɪk], simple past: **made:**
1. machen; herstellen 2 (39) **make a wish** sich etwas wünschen 4 (88) **make friends** Freunde finden 3 (59) °**make sth. better** etwas verbessern
°**2.** bilden

mall [mɔːl] (großes) Einkaufszentrum 4 (81)

man [mæn], pl **men** [men] Mann 1 (35)

many ['meni] viele 4 (95) **How many?** Wie viele? 4 (95)

map [mæp] Landkarte; Stadtplan HWG (10) **on the map** auf der Landkarte; auf dem Stadtplan HWG (10)

March [mɑːtʃ] März 1 (29)

°**marching** ['mɑːtʃɪŋ]: **go marching** marschieren

market ['mɑːkɪt] Markt 5 (119)

married (to) ['mærɪd] verheiratet (mit) 2 (47)

°**mascot** ['mæskət] Maskottchen

master ['mɑːstə] Meister/in 1 (34)

match [mætʃ]:
1. Spiel, Wettkampf, Match 4 (80)
°**2. match sth. (to sth.)** etwas (zu etwas) zuordnen

maths [mæθs] Mathematik 1 (27)

matter: What's the matter? ['mætə] Was ist denn? / Was ist los? 3 (58)

May [meɪ] Mai 1 (29)

maybe ['meɪbi] vielleicht 2 (52)

me [miː] mich; mir HWG (13) **Me too.** Ich auch. 3 (72)

°**mean** [miːn] bedeuten

meat [miːt] Fleisch 2 (50)

°**medal** ['medl] Medaille

mediation [ˌmiːdi'eɪʃn] Sprachmittlung, Mediation (3)

meet [miːt], *simple past:* **met:**
  1. treffen; kennenlernen HWG (9) **Meet your classmates.** Triff deine Mitschüler/innen. / Lerne deine Mitschüler/innen kennen. HWG (9) **Nice to meet you.** Freut mich, dich/euch/Sie kennenzulernen. 1 (20)
  2. sich treffen 1 (25)

°**memory** ['meməri] Erinnerung, Gedächtnis

men [men] *plural of* **man** 1 (35)

met [met] *simple past of* **meet**

metre ['miːtə] Meter 3 (67) °**square metre** Quadratmeter

°**mice** [maɪs] *plural of* **mouse**

middle ['mɪdl] Mitte 2 (48) **in the middle** in der Mitte 2 (48)

midnight ['mɪdnaɪt] Mitternacht 3 (64)

milk [mɪlk] Milch 2 (50)

°**millilitre (ml)** ['mɪliliːtə] Milliliter

°**mime** [maɪm] vorspielen, pantomimisch darstellen

°**mind map** ['maɪnd mæp] Mindmap

minibus ['mɪnibʌs] Kleinbus 4 (84/85) **go by minibus** mit dem Kleinbus fahren

minute ['mɪnɪt] Minute 1 (18) **wait a minute** Warte einen Moment. / Moment mal. 1 (18)

miss [mɪs] verpassen 4 (88)

Miss [mɪs]: **Miss Bell** Frau Bell *(übliche Anrede von Lehrerinnen)* 1 (26)

missing ['mɪsɪŋ]: **the missing words** die fehlenden Wörter 4 (83)

°**mistake** [mɪ'steɪk] Fehler

°**mix** [mɪks] anmischen, anrühren

mobile (phone) [ˌməʊbaɪl 'fəʊn] Mobiltelefon, Handy 4 (80)

moment ['məʊmənt] Moment 5 (104) **at the moment** gerade, im Moment 5 (104)

Monday ['mʌndeɪ, 'mʌndi] Montag HWG (11) **on Monday** am Montag HWG (12)

money ['mʌni] Geld 3 (69)
▶ S.194 British money

monkey ['mʌŋki] Affe HWG (14)

monster ['mɒnstə] Monster 1 (32)

month [mʌnθ] Monat 1 (29)
▶ S.182 The months

moon [muːn] Mond 3 (72)

more [mɔː] mehr 3 (56/57) °**more than once** mehr als einmal

morning ['mɔːnɪŋ] Morgen, Vormittag 1 (26) **Good morning.** Guten Morgen. 1 (26) **in the morning** morgens, vormittags, am Morgen/Vormittag 2 (38)

°**most** [məʊst]: **the most** die meisten

mother ['mʌðə] Mutter 1 (18)

°**mouse** [maʊs], *pl* **mice** [maɪs] Maus

mouth [maʊθ] Mund; Maul 3 (72)

move [muːv]:
  1. bewegen; sich bewegen 4 (98)
  °2. Bewegung

MP3 player [ˌem piː 'θriː ˌpleɪə] MP3-Spieler 1 (29)

Mr Schwarz ['mɪstə] Herr Schwarz HWG (16)

Mrs Schwarz ['mɪsɪz] Frau Schwarz HWG (16)

much [mʌtʃ] viel 3 (64) **How much ...?** Wie viel ...? 4 (95) **How much are ...?** Was kosten ...? 3 (69) **How much is ...?** Was kostet ...? 3 (69)
▶ S.199 much – many

mum [mʌm] Mama, Mutti 1 (18)

museum [mju'ziːəm] Museum 3 (69)

music ['mjuːzɪk] Musik 1 (27)

°**must** [mʌst] müssen

my [maɪ] mein/e HWG (8) **My birthday is in May.** Ich habe im Mai Geburtstag. 1 (29) **My birthday is on 5th August.** Ich habe am 5. August Geburtstag. 1 (29) **my favourite animal** mein Lieblingstier HWG (14) **My name is Silky.** Ich heiße Silky. HWG (8)
▶ S.182 Birthdays

°**myself** [maɪ'self] selbst

N

name [neɪm] Name HWG (8) **My name is Silky.** Ich heiße Silky. HWG (8) **What's your name?** Wie heißt du? / Wie heißt ihr? HWG (9)

navy ['neɪvi] Marine 1 (18)

near [nɪə] in der Nähe von, nahe (bei) HWG (12) **near here** (hier) in der Nähe 2 (44)

°**neck** [nek] Hals, Nacken

need [niːd] brauchen, benötigen 3 (62)

°**negative** ['negətɪv] negativ

never ['nevə] nie, niemals 2 (53)

new [njuː] neu 1 (18)

news *(no pl)* [njuːz] Nachrichten 4 (96)

next [nekst]: **the next picture/question** das nächste Bild / die nächste Frage 1 (35) °**What's next?** Was kommt als Nächstes?

nice [naɪs] nett, schön 1 (18) **Nice to meet you.** Freut mich, dich/euch/Sie kennenzulernen. 1 (20)

night [naɪt] Nacht 2 (39) **at night** nachts, in der Nacht 2 (39)

nine [naɪn] neun HWG (8)
▶ S.233 English numbers

no [nəʊ]:
  1. nein HWG (13) **No, that's wrong.** Nein, das ist falsch. / Nein, das stimmt nicht. HWG (13)
  2. kein, keine 2 (39)

nobody ['nəʊbədi] niemand 5 (118)

°**noisy** ['nɔɪzi] laut, unruhig

no one ['nəʊ wʌn] niemand 5 (118)

°**north** [nɔːθ] nördlich, Nord-

nose [nəʊz] Nase 4 (98)

not [nɒt] nicht 1 (18) **he/she/it is not** [nɒt] er/sie/es ist nicht ... 1 (18) **not ... yet** noch nicht 5 (112)

note [nəʊt] Notiz, Mitteilung 4 (80)

nothing ['nʌθɪŋ] (gar) nichts 3 (59)

November [nəʊ'vembə] November 1 (29)

now [naʊ] nun, jetzt HWG (15)

number ['nʌmbə] Zahl, Nummer, Ziffer HWG (8)

O

o [əʊ] Null *(in Telefonnummern)* HWG (17)

ocean ['əʊʃn] Ozean 5 (109)

o'clock: at 1 o'clock [ə'klɒk] um 1 Uhr / um 13 Uhr 1 (25)

October [ɒk'təʊbə] Oktober 1 (29)

°**octopus** ['ɒktəpəs] Krake

of [ɒv, əv] von 1 (22)

of course [əv 'kɔːs] natürlich, selbstverständlich 2 (39)

°**off sth.** [ɒf] von etwas herunter

often ['ɒfn, 'ɒftən] oft 2 (44)

oh [əʊ]: **Oh, it's you.** Ach, du bist es. 3 (72)

old [əʊld] alt HWG (8) **How old are you?** Wie alt bist du? HWG (9)
▶ S.233 English numbers

on [ɒn] auf HWG (10) **on Monday** am Montag HWG (12) **on Monday afternoon** am Montagnachmittag

3 (68) **on the map** auf der Landkarte; auf dem Stadtplan HWG (10) **on the radio** im Radio 2 (48) °**on the road to** auf der Straße nach

°**once** [wʌns]: **more than once** mehr als einmal

one [wʌn] eins HWG (8) °**one by one** einzeln; einer nach dem anderen °**one day** eines Tages °**the little one** der/die/das Kleine
▶ S. 233 English numbers

only [ˈəʊnli]:
1. nur, bloß 2 (44)
2. erst 4 (98)

onto [ˈɒntʊ] auf (... hinauf) 2 (52)

open [ˈəʊpən]:
1. öffnen, aufmachen HWG (16); sich öffnen 3 (72)
2. geöffnet, offen 1 (30)

°**opposite** [ˈɒpəzɪt] Gegenteil

or [ɔː] oder HWG (9)

orange [ˈɒrɪndʒ]:
1. orange HWG (15)
2. Orange, Apfelsine 4 (95)

order [ˈɔːdə] Reihenfolge 4 (96)

other [ˈʌðə] andere(r, s) 3 (60)

°**otter** [ˈɒtə] Otter

our [aʊə] unser/e HWG (16)

out [aʊt]: **out of ...** [ˈaʊt_əv] aus ... (heraus/hinaus) 3 (72) °**read sth. out loud** etwas vorlesen

outside [ˌaʊtˈsaɪd] draußen; nach draußen 3 (63)

°**oven** [ˈʌvn] Ofen

over [ˈəʊvə]:
1. über 4 (98) **over to ...** hinüber zu/nach ... 4 (88)
2. **over 4 years** über 4 Jahre; mehr als 4 Jahre 3 (69)
3. **be over** vorbei sein, zu Ende sein 5 (104)

°**own** [əʊn] eigene(r, s)

P

p [piː] Abkürzung für „pence", „penny" 3 (69)
▶ S. 194 British money

page [peɪdʒ] Seite 1 (31) **What page are we on?** Auf welcher Seite sind wir? 1 (31)

°**paint** [peɪnt] Farbe

°**pair** [peə] Paar

°**palm tree** [ˈpɑːm triː] Palme

paper [ˈpeɪpə]:
1. Zeitung 2 (39)
2. Papier 5 (114) °**piece of paper** Stück Papier

paragraph [ˈpærəgrɑːf] Absatz (in einem Text) 4 (96)

parents (pl) [ˈpeərənts] Eltern 4 (81)

park [pɑːk] Park 2 (40)

part [pɑːt] Teil 3 (69)

partner [ˈpɑːtnə] Partner/in 3 (66)

party [ˈpɑːti] Party 1 (29)

past [pɑːst]:
1. Vergangenheit 4 (86)
2. **half past ten** halb elf (10.30 / 22.30) 1 (27) **quarter past ten** Viertel nach zehn (10.15 / 22.15) 1 (27)
▶ S. 233 English numbers

PE [ˌpiːˈiː] Sportunterricht, Turnen 1 (27)

pen [pen] Kugelschreiber, Stift, Füller HWG (16)

pence [pens] Pence (plural of **penny**) 3 (69)
▶ S. 194 British money

pencil [ˈpensl] Bleistift HWG (16)

pencil case [ˈpensl keɪs] Federmäppchen HWG (16)

people [ˈpiːpl] Leute, Menschen 1 (22)

pepper [ˈpepə] Pfeffer 5 (113)

perfect [ˈpɜːfɪkt] perfekt, ideal 3 (73)

person [ˈpɜːsn] Person 2 (44)

phone [fəʊn] Telefon 4 (80)

photo [ˈfəʊtəʊ] Foto HWG (13) **in the photo** auf dem Foto HWG (13) **take photos** fotografieren, Fotos machen 5 (108)

phrase [freɪz] Ausdruck, (Rede-)Wendung 5 (115)

Physical Education [ˌfɪzɪkl_ˌedʒuˈkeɪʃn] Sportunterricht, Turnen 1 (27)

piano [piˈænəʊ] Klavier, Piano 3 (60) **play the piano** Klavier spielen 3 (60)

°**pick up** [ˌpɪk_ˈʌp] aufheben

picnic [ˈpɪknɪk] Picknick 4 (88)

picture [ˈpɪktʃə] Bild HWG (14) **in the picture** auf dem Bild HWG (14)

°**piece** [piːs]: **a piece of paper** ein Stück Papier

pig [pɪg] Schwein HWG (14)

pink [pɪŋk] pink, rosa HWG (15)

pizza [ˈpiːtsə] Pizza 2 (50)

place [pleɪs] Ort, Platz, Stelle 1 (30)

plan [plæn] Plan 4 (80)

planet [ˈplænɪt] Planet 5 (109)

plate [pleɪt]: **a plate of ...** ein Teller ... 2 (38)

play [pleɪ]:
1. spielen 2 (38) °**play ball** mit dem Ball spielen **play the drums** Schlagzeug spielen 3 (60) **play the guitar** Gitarre spielen 3 (62) **play the piano** Klavier spielen 3 (60) °**the kids are playing up** die Kinder machen Unsinn
2. abspielen (CD, DVD) 2 (40)
3. Theaterstück 5 (118)

player [ˈpleɪə] Spieler/in 3 (67)

°**playground** [ˈpleɪgraʊnd] Spielplatz

please [pliːz] bitte 1 (18)

pm: 4 pm [ˌpiːˈem] 4 Uhr nachmittags / 16 Uhr 3 (56/57)

°**poem** [ˈpəʊɪm] Gedicht

point [pɔɪnt]:
1. Punkt 4 (84/85)
2. **point to sth.** auf etwas zeigen, deuten 5 (112)
3. **point sth. at sb.** etwas auf jn. richten 5 (112)

police officer [pəˈliːs_ˌɒfɪsə] Polizist/in 2 (52)

policeman [pəˈliːsmən] Polizist 5 (110)

°**pony** [ˈpəʊni] Pony

pool [puːl]:
1. Schwimmbad, Schwimmbecken HWG (10)
°**2.** Gezeitentümpel

poor [pɔː, pʊə] arm 4 (99)

°**popular** [ˈpɒpjələ] populär, beliebt

poster [ˈpəʊstə] Poster HWG (16)

potato [pəˈteɪtəʊ], pl **potatoes** Kartoffel 2 (48) **roast potatoes** (pl) im Backofen in Fett gebackene Kartoffeln 2 (48)

pound [paʊnd] Pfund (britische Währung) 3 (69)
▶ S. 194 British money

practice [ˈpræktɪs] Übung (3)

practise [ˈpræktɪs] üben, trainieren 4 (92)

prepare sth. [prɪˈpeə] etwas vorbereiten 5 (115)

°**preposition** [ˌprepəˈzɪʃn] Präposition

present [ˈpreznt] Geschenk 2 (52)

price [praɪs] (Kauf-)Preis 5 (109)

prison [ˈprɪzn] Gefängnis 5 (119)

problem [ˈprɒbləm] Problem 4 (88)

profile [ˈprəʊfaɪl] Profil; Beschreibung, Porträt 1 (19)

programme [ˈprəʊgræm] Programm (auch im Theater usw.); (Radio-, Fernseh-)Sendung 3 (64) **What programmes ...?** Welche Programme ...? / Welche Art von Programmen ...? 3 (64)

pronunciation [prəˌnʌnsiˈeɪʃn] Aussprache 2 (41)

°**propeller** [prəˈpelə] Propeller

pull [pʊl] ziehen 4 (99) °**pull up** herausreißen

purple ['pɜːpl] violett, lila HWG (15)

push [pʊʃ] drücken, schieben, stoßen 4 (98)

put [pʊt], *simple past:* **put** legen, stellen, *(etwas wohin)* tun HWG (16)
  °**Put up your hand.** Melde dich. / Heb deine Hand.

Q

quarter ['kwɔːtə]: **quarter past ten** Viertel nach zehn (10.15 / 22.15) 1 (27)   **quarter to eleven** Viertel vor elf (10.45 / 22.45) 1 (27)
  ▶ S. 233 English numbers

°**queen** [kwiːn] Königin

question ['kwestʃən] Frage HWG (9)

quiet ['kwaɪət] ruhig, still, leise 3 (56/57)

quiz [kwɪz] Quiz, Ratespiel 1 (30)

R

rabbit ['ræbɪt] Kaninchen HWG (14)

°**race** [reɪs] Rennen, (Wett-)Lauf

radio ['reɪdiəʊ] Radio 2 (48)   **on the radio** im Radio 2 (48)

°**rain** [reɪn] Regen

°**rally** ['ræli] Rallye

ran [ræn] *simple past of* **run**

rat [ræt] Ratte HWG (14)

°**rattle** ['rætl] klappern

read [riːd], *simple past:* **read** [red] lesen 1 (30)   °**read sth. out loud** etwas vorlesen

ready ['redi] bereit, fertig 3 (68)

really ['rɪəli] echt, wirklich 3 (58)

°**reason** ['riːzn] Grund

red [red] rot HWG (9)

religion [rɪ'lɪdʒən] Religion 1 (27)

remember sth. [rɪ'membə] sich an etwas erinnern 2 (52)

°**reptile** ['reptaɪl] Reptil

°**rescue centre** ['reskjuː ˌsentə] Rettungsstation

°**rest** [rest]:
  1. Pause
  2. Rest

°**restaurant** ['restrɒnt] Restaurant

°**rewrite** [ˌriː'raɪt] neu schreiben, umarbeiten

°**Rhesus monkey** ['riːsəs ˌmʌŋki] Rhesusaffe

rhyme [raɪm] Reim; Vers HWG (13)

rich [rɪtʃ] reich 5 (118)

ride [raɪd]:
  1. Fahrt 4 (88)
  °2. *(simple past:* **rode***)* reiten

ride a bike [ˌraɪd_ə 'baɪk], *simple past:* **rode** Fahrrad fahren 3 (68)

riding ['raɪdɪŋ] Reiten 3 (60)

right [raɪt] richtig HWG (13)   **sb. is right** jemand hat Recht 4 (98)   **Yes, that's right.** Ja, das ist richtig. / Ja, das stimmt. HWG (13)

°**right away** [ˌraɪt_ə'weɪ] sofort

river ['rɪvə] Fluss HWG (10)

road [rəʊd] Straße 2 (36)   **at 8 Beach Road** in der Beach Road (Nummer) 8 2 (36)   **in Beach Road** in der Beach Road 2 (36)   °**on the road to** auf der Straße nach

°**roar** [rɔː] brüllen

roast beef [ˌrəʊst 'biːf] Rinderbraten 2 (48)

roast potatoes *(pl)* [ˌrəʊst pə'teɪtəʊz] *im Backofen in Fett gebackene Kartoffeln* 2 (48)

rock [rɒk] Fels, Felsen 2 (38)

°**rock pool** ['rɒk puːl] Gezeitentümpel

rode [rəʊd] *simple past of* **ride**

°**role** [rəʊl] Rolle

°**roll** [rəʊl] rollen, kugeln

room [ruːm] Zimmer, Raum HWG (16)

°**routine** [ruː'tiːn] Routine

°**rub in** [rʌb] einreiben

rubber ['rʌbə] Radiergummi HWG (16)

rucksack ['rʌksæk] Rucksack 5 (104)

ruler ['ruːlə] Lineal HWG (15)

run [rʌn], *simple past:* **ran** rennen, laufen 2 (41)   **run after sb.** hinter jm. herrennen 5 (104)   °**run around** herumrennen

S

sad [sæd] traurig 1 (20)

°**safari path** [sə'fɑːri pɑːθ] Safaripfad

said [sed] *simple past of* **say**

sailing ['seɪlɪŋ]: **go sailing** segeln; segeln gehen 2 (39)   **sailing boat** Segelboot 2 (52)   °**sailing club** Segelclub

salad ['sæləd] Salat *(als Gericht oder Beilage)* 2 (48)   **fruit salad** Obstsalat 2 (48)

°**salt** [sɔːlt] Salz

samba ['sæmbə] Samba 3 (56/57)

same [seɪm]: **the same as …** der-/ die-/dasselbe wie … 5 (111)

sand [sænd] Sand 4 (80)

sandwich ['sænwɪtʃ, 'sænwɪdʒ] Sandwich, (zusammengeklapptes) belegtes Brot 2 (49)

°**sandy** ['sændi] sandig

sang [sæŋ] *simple past of* **sing**

sat [sæt] *simple past of* **sit**

Saturday ['sætədeɪ, 'sætədi] Samstag, Sonnabend HWG (11)   **on Saturday afternoon** am Samstagnachmittag 3 (68)

save [seɪv] retten 4 (90)

saw [sɔː] *simple past of* **see**

say [seɪ], *simple past:* **said** sagen 1 (26)   **Simon says …** [sez] Simon sagt … HWG (16)

°**scarf** [skɑːf] Schal

scary ['skeəri] unheimlich, gruselig 3 (69)

scene [siːn] Szene 5 (118)

school [skuːl] Schule HWG (16)   **at school** in der Schule 1 (18)   **before school** vor der Schule *(vor Schulbeginn)* 1 (20)   **in front of the school** vor der Schule *(vor dem Schulgebäude)* 1 (20)   **school bag** Schultasche HWG (16)

science ['saɪəns] Naturwissenschaft 1 (27)

scone [skɒn] *kleines rundes Milchbrötchen, leicht süß* 2 (48)

score [skɔː] einen Treffer erzielen, ein Tor schießen 4 (84/85)

°**scorpion** ['skɔːpiən] Skorpion

sea [siː] Meer HWG (10)   °**sea life** Meeresleben

seagull ['siːgʌl] Möwe 2 (52)

seal [siːl] Robbe HWG (8)

second ['sekənd] zweite(r, s) 1 (29)
  ▶ S. 233 English numbers

°**secret** ['siːkrət] Geheimnis

see [siː], *simple past:* **saw** sehen; besuchen HWG (9)   **See you.** ['siː ju, 'siː jə] Bis gleich. / Bis bald. HWG (17)
  ▶ S. 183 look · see · watch

sell [sel], *simple past:* **sold** verkaufen 3 (56/57)

send [send], *simple past:* **sent: send sth. to sb.** jm. etwas schicken, senden 3 (64)

sent [sent] *simple past of* **send**

sentence ['sentəns] Satz 1 (23)

September [sep'tembə] September 1 (26)

°**setting** ['setɪŋ] Schauplatz

seven ['sevn] sieben HWG (8)
  ▶ S. 233 English numbers

°**shade** [ʃeɪd] Schatten *(von der Sonne geschützt)*

°**shape** [ʃeɪp] Form, Gestalt

shark [ʃɑːk] Hai 5 (108)

sharpener ['ʃɑːpnə] Anspitzer HWG (16)

she [ʃiː] sie HWG (12)

shelf [ʃelf], *pl* **shelves** [ʃelvz] Regal 2 (36)

ship [ʃɪp] Schiff 2 (52)

shoe [ʃuː] Schuh 1 (21)

shop [ʃɒp] Laden 1 (34) **corner shop** Laden an der Ecke; Tante-Emma-Laden 1 (34)

shopping [ˈʃɒpɪŋ]: **go shopping** einkaufen gehen 4 (81) **shopping mall** (großes) Einkaufszentrum 4 (81)

short [ʃɔːt] kurz 1 (22) °**short form** Kurzform

shorts (pl) [ʃɔːts] Shorts, kurze Hose 4 (80)

shout [ʃaʊt] schreien, rufen 2 (52)

show [ʃəʊ] zeigen HWG (16)

sick [sɪk] krank 3 (72)

°**side** [saɪd] Seite

°**sigh** [saɪ] seufzen

sights (pl) [saɪts] Sehenswürdigkeiten 4 (88)

sign [saɪn] Schild; Zeichen 5 (111)

silky [ˈsɪlki] seidig 4 (99)

silly [ˈsɪli]:
1. albern; blöd 1 (23)
2. Dummerchen 5 (108)

sing [sɪŋ], *simple past:* **sang** singen 3 (56/57)

°**singer** [ˈsɪŋə] Sänger/in

single [ˈsɪŋɡl] ledig, alleinstehend 2 (47)

sister [ˈsɪstə] Schwester 1 (18)

sit [sɪt], *simple past:* **sat** sitzen; sich setzen 2 (38) **sit down** sich hinsetzen 4 (88)

six [sɪks] sechs HWG (8)
▶ S. 233 English numbers

skates [skeɪts] Inlineskates 3 (60)

skating [ˈskeɪtɪŋ] Inlineskaten, Rollschuhlaufen 3 (60)

skills (pl) [skɪlz]: **skills file** Übersicht über Lern- und Arbeitstechniken (3) **study skills** Lern- und Arbeitstechniken (3)

°**skype** [skaɪp] per Skype telefonieren

sleep [sliːp]:
1. (simple past: **slept**) schlafen 2 (39)
°2. Schlaf

sleepover [ˈsliːpəʊvə] Schlafparty 5 (108)

slept [slept] *simple past of* **sleep**

slow [sləʊ] langsam 4 (99)

small [smɔːl] klein 2 (36)

smell [smel] riechen 3 (72) **smell sth.** an etwas riechen 5 (106)

smile [smaɪl] lächeln 4 (92) **smile at sb.** jn. anlächeln 5 (104)

smiley [ˈsmaɪli] Smiley 1 (35)

smuggle [ˈsmʌɡl] schmuggeln 5 (112)

smuggler [ˈsmʌɡlə] Schmuggler/in 5 (112)

smuggling [ˈsmʌɡlɪŋ] der Schmuggel, das Schmuggeln 5 (112)

snack [snæk] Snack, Imbiss 5 (109)

snake [sneɪk] Schlange HWG (14)

sneeze [sniːz] niesen 5 (119)

so [səʊ]:
1. also; deshalb, daher 1 (26)
2. **so cool/nice** so cool/nett 2 (39)
3. **So?** Und? / Na und? 1 (20)

sofa [ˈsəʊfə] Sofa 2 (36)

soft [sɒft] weich 4 (99)

sold [səʊld] *simple past of* **sell**

some [sʌm] einige, ein paar; etwas 3 (56/57)

somebody [ˈsʌmbədi] jemand 3 (61)

someone [ˈsʌmwʌn] jemand 3 (61)

something [ˈsʌmθɪŋ] etwas 3 (61)

sometimes [ˈsʌmtaɪmz] manchmal 3 (58)

song [sɒŋ] Lied, Song HWG (11)

soon [suːn] bald 5 (118)

sorry [ˈsɒri]: **(I'm) sorry.** Tut mir leid. / Entschuldigung. 1 (20) **I'm sorry about …** Es tut mir leid wegen … 4 (82)

sound [saʊnd]:
1. klingen, sich anhören 3 (59)
2. Geräusch; Klang 3 (72)
°3. Laut **sound group** Lautgruppe

°**sound** [saʊnd] Meerenge, Sund

soup [suːp] Suppe 2 (48)

°**south** [saʊθ] südlich, Süd-

°**south-west** [ˌsaʊθˈwest] Südwesten

°**space** [speɪs] Platz

°**spade** [speɪd] Spaten

spaghetti [spəˈɡeti] Spagetti 2 (50)

speak [spiːk], *simple past:* **spoke** sprechen 1 (25)

speaker [ˈspiːkə] Sprecher/in 1 (25)

°**special** [ˈspeʃl] besondere(r, s)

°**speech bubble** [ˈspiːtʃ bʌbl] Sprechblase

spell [spel] buchstabieren 1 (30)

spoke [spəʊk] *simple past of* **speak**

sport [spɔːt] Sport; Sportart 2 (44) **do sport** Sport treiben 2 (44)
▶ S. 191 Sports and other activities

spot [spɒt] Fleck, Punkt 4 (92)

°**spray** [spreɪ] sprühen

spring [sprɪŋ] Frühling 4 (82)

°**spy** [spaɪ]: **I spy with my little eye** *entspricht dem Spiel „Ich sehe was, was du nicht siehst"*

°**square metre** [ˌskweə ˈmiːtə] Quadratmeter

°**squeeze** [skwiːz]: **give sb. a squeeze** jn. drücken

°**stand** [stænd] stehen **stand up** aufstehen

star [stɑː] (Film-, Pop-)Star 2 (39)

start [stɑːt] anfangen, beginnen 1 (26)

stay [steɪ] bleiben 4 (81)

steer [stɪə] steuern, lenken 4 (98)

step [step] Schritt 3 (72)

°**stick** [stɪk] Stock

still [stɪl] (immer) noch 4 (82)

stop [stɒp] anhalten, stoppen 3 (68)

story [ˈstɔːri] Geschichte, Erzählung 2 (53)

°**strange** [streɪndʒ] seltsam, komisch HWG (14)

°**strangle** [ˈstræŋɡl] erdrosseln

street [striːt] Straße 1 (26) **at 14 Dean Street** in der Deanstraße 14 **in Dean Street** in der Dean Street 2 (36)

°**stripe** [straɪp] Streifen

student [ˈstjuːdənt] Schüler/in; Student/in 1 (18)

studio [ˈstjuːdiəʊ] Studio 3 (64)

study skills [ˈstʌdi ˌskɪlz] Lern- und Arbeitstechniken (3)

sub-clause [ˈsʌbklɔːz] Nebensatz 5 (114)

subject [ˈsʌbdʒɪkt] Schulfach 1 (27)
▶ S. 182 School subjects

subtitle [ˈsʌbtaɪtl] Untertitel 5 (113)

°**suck up** [ˌsʌk ˈʌp] aufsaugen

suddenly [ˈsʌdnli] plötzlich, auf einmal 2 (52)

°**sugar** [ˈʃʊɡə] Zucker

summer [ˈsʌmə] Sommer 4 (82)

sun [sʌn] Sonne 4 (98)

Sunday [ˈsʌndeɪ, ˈsʌndi] Sonntag HWG (11)

°**sunglasses** (pl) [ˈsʌnɡlɑːsɪz] Sonnenbrille

°**surfing** [ˈsɜːfɪŋ] Wellenreiten, Surfen

°**surprise** [səˈpraɪz] Überraschung

surprised [səˈpraɪzd] überrascht 1 (35)

swam [swæm] *simple past of* **swim**

°**swap** [swɒp] tauschen

swim [swɪm], *simple past:* **swam** schwimmen 1 (35)

swimmer [ˈswɪmə] Schwimmer/in 1 (35)

swimming pool [ˈswɪmɪŋ puːl] Schwimmbad, Schwimmbecken HWG (10)

sword [sɔːd] Schwert 5 (119)

°**symbol** [ˈsɪmbl] Symbol

T

table [ˈteɪbl]:
1. Tisch 2 (36)
2. Tabelle 3 (62)
°**tag** [tæg] Fangen *(Spiel)*
take [teɪk], *simple past:* **took** nehmen, mitnehmen; (weg-, hin)bringen 2 (48) **take photos** fotografieren, Fotos machen 5 (108) °**take care of sb./sth.** sich um etwas/jn. kümmern °**take turns** sich abwechseln
talk [tɔːk]:
1. Vortrag, Referat, Rede 5 (108)
give a talk (about) einen Vortrag / eine Rede halten (über) 5 (108)
2. talk (to) reden (mit), sich unterhalten (mit) HWG (16)
°**tall** [tɔːl] hoch, groß
task [tɑːsk] Aufgabe 2 (36)
taste [teɪst] schmecken 3 (73)
°**tattoo** [təˈtuː] Tätowierung
tea [tiː] Tee 2 (39)
teacher [ˈtiːtʃə] Lehrer/in HWG (16)
team [tiːm] Team, Mannschaft 1 (23)
°**tease sb.** [tiːz] sich über jn. lustig machen
°**teaspoon** [ˈtiːspuːn] Teelöffel
°**technology** [tekˈnɒlədʒi] Technologie **Information and Communications Technology** Informations- und Kommunikationstechnologie 1 (27)
°**teeth** [tiːθ] *plural of* **tooth**
telephone [ˈtelɪfəʊn] Telefon HWG (17)
tell [tel], *simple past:* **told: tell sb. about sth.** jm. von etwas erzählen; jm. über etwas berichten 2 (44)
ten [ten] zehn HWG (8)
▶ S. 233 English numbers
tennis [ˈtenɪs] Tennis 3 (58)
text [tekst]:
1. text sb. jm. eine SMS schicken 2 (38)
2. Text (3)
°**than** [ðən]: **more than once** mehr als einmal
Thank you. [ˈθæŋk juː] Danke. 1 (18)
Thanks. [ˈθæŋks] Danke. 2 (39)
that [ðæt, ðət]:
1. it shows that ... es zeigt, dass ... 2 (53)
2. that group die Gruppe (dort), jene Gruppe 1 (35)
3. that's das ist HWG (13)
▶ S. 198 this, that – these, those
the [ðə] der, die, das; die HWG (9)
their [ðeə] ihr 1 (18) **their first day** ihr erster Tag 1 (18)
them [ðem, ðəm] sie; ihnen HWG (17)

then [ðen] dann 1 (26)
there [ðeə] da, dort; dahin, dorthin 1 (20) **There are ...** [ˈðeər_ɑː] Es sind ... / Es gibt ... HWG (13) **There's ...** [ˈðeəz] Es ist/gibt ... HWG (13)
these [ðiːz] diese, die (hier) 4 (88)
▶ S. 198 this, that – these, those
they [ðeɪ] sie *(Plural)* 1 (18) **they're (= they are)** sie sind ... 1 (18)
thief [θiːf], *pl* **thieves** [θiːvz] Dieb/in 3 (73)
thing [θɪŋ] Sache, Ding, Gegenstand HWG (16)
think [θɪŋk], *simple past:* **thought** denken, glauben 2 (39) **think of sth.** sich etwas ausdenken; an etwas denken 4 (96)
third [θɜːd] dritte(r, s) 1 (29)
▶ S. 233 English numbers
thirsty [ˈθɜːsti]: **be thirsty** durstig sein, Durst haben 3 (68)
this [ðɪs]:
1. This is ... Dies ist ... / Das ist ... HWG (16)
2. this place/break/subject dieser Ort / diese Pause / dieses Fach 1 (30) °**this time** diesmal
▶ S. 198 this, that – these, those
those [ðəʊz] die ... dort; jene ... 4 (88)
▶ S. 198 this, that – these, those
thought [θɔːt] *simple past of* **think**
three [θriː] drei HWG (8)
▶ S. 233 English numbers
threw [θruː] *simple past of* **throw**
through [θruː] durch 5 (115)
throw [θrəʊ], *simple past:* **threw** werfen 1 (26)
Thursday [ˈθɜːzdeɪ, ˈθɜːzdi] Donnerstag HWG (11)
ticket [ˈtɪkɪt]:
1. Eintrittskarte 3 (69)
2. Fahrkarte 5 (116)
°**tickle** [ˈtɪkl] kitzeln
°**tiger** [ˈtaɪɡə] Tiger
till [tɪl]: **till 1 o'clock** bis 1 Uhr 2 (46)
time [taɪm] Zeit; Uhrzeit HWG (15)
feeding time Fütterungszeit 5 (108)
free time Freizeit, freie Zeit 3 (62)
free-time activities Freizeitaktivitäten 3 (62) °**time traveller** Zeitreisende(r) **What time is it?** Wie spät ist es? 1 (18)
timetable [ˈtaɪmteɪbl] Stundenplan 1 (26)
tip [tɪp] Tipp HWG (9)
tired [ˈtaɪəd] müde 3 (68)
title [ˈtaɪtl] Titel, Überschrift 4 (96)

to [tu, tə]:
1. zu, nach HWG (9) **count to ten** bis zehn zählen **from ... to ...** von ... bis ... 3 (56/57)
2. Nice to meet you. Freut mich, dich/euch/Sie kennenzulernen. 1 (20)
3. quarter to eleven Viertel vor elf (10.45 / 22.45) 1 (27)
▶ S. 233 English numbers
today [təˈdeɪ] heute 4 (82)
together [təˈɡeðə] zusammen 4 (81)
toilet [ˈtɔɪlət] Toilette 1 (31)
told [təʊld] *simple past of* **tell**
°**tongue** [tʌŋ] Zunge
too [tuː]:
1. auch 1 (18)
2. too late/cold/big/... zu spät/kalt/groß/... 3 (64)
took [tʊk] *simple past of* **take**
°**tooth** [tuːθ], *pl* **teeth** [tiːθ] Zahn
top [tɒp]:
1. Spitzen-, oberste(r, s) 4 (97)
2. Top, Oberteil 5 (104)
touch [tʌtʃ] berühren, anfassen HWG (16)
tour (of) [ˈtʊər_əv] Rundgang, Rundfahrt, Reise (durch) HWG (10)
tourist [ˈtʊərɪst] Tourist/in 5 (113)
°**towards sb.** [təˈwɔːdz] jm. entgegen
tower [ˈtaʊə] Turm HWG (10)
town [taʊn] Stadt HWG (9)
toy [tɔɪ] Spielzeug 2 (36)
°**tradition** [trəˈdɪʃn] Tradition
trainer [ˈtreɪnə] Turnschuh 1 (21)
training [ˈtreɪnɪŋ] Training(sstunde) 3 (67)
°**trampoline** [ˈtræmpəliːn] Trampolin
°**translate** [trænsˈleɪt] übersetzen
travel [ˈtrævl] reisen 3 (69)
traveller [ˈtrævələ] Reisende(r) 3 (69) °**time traveller** Zeitreisende(r)
tree [triː] Baum 2 (47)
trip [trɪp] Ausflug; Reise 5 (104)
trophy [ˈtrəʊfi] Pokal; Trophäe 2 (39)
trouble [ˈtrʌbl]: **be in trouble** in Schwierigkeiten sein; Ärger kriegen 2 (53)
true [truː] wahr 4 (89)
°**trumpet** [ˈtrʌmpɪt] tröten
°**trunk** [trʌŋk] Rüssel
try [traɪ] (aus)probieren; versuchen 3 (62)
T-shirt [ˈtiːʃɜːt] T-Shirt 2 (52)
Tuesday [ˈtjuːzdeɪ, ˈtjuːzdi] Dienstag HWG (11) **on Tuesday** am Dienstag HWG (12)
turn around [ˌtɜːn_əˈraʊnd]:
1. sich umdrehen 3 (68)
2. wenden, umdrehen 4 (98)

turn sth. on [ˌtɜːn ˈɒn] etwas einschalten 3 (68)

turn [tɜːn]: **(It's) my turn.** Ich bin dran / an der Reihe. 5 (104) °**take turns** sich abwechseln (etwas zu tun) °**Whose turn is it?** Wer ist dran / Wer ist an der Reihe?

TV [ˌtiːˈviː] Fernsehen, Fernsehgerät 2 (36)

twelve [twelv] zwölf HWG (8)
▶ S. 233 English numbers

°**twice** [twaɪs] zweimal

twins (pl) [twɪnz] Zwillinge 2 (47)

two [tuː] zwei HWG (8) °**two by two** zu zweit; in Zweiergruppen
▶ S. 233 English numbers

U

umbrella [ʌmˈbrelə] Schirm, Regenschirm 3 (58)

uncle [ˈʌŋkl] Onkel 2 (44)

under [ˈʌndə] unter 5 (112)

°**underlined** [ˌʌndəˈlaɪnd] unterstrichen

understand [ˌʌndəˈstænd], simple past: **understood** verstehen 3 (73)

uniform [ˈjuːnɪfɔːm] Uniform 1 (18)

unit [ˈjuːnɪt] Kapitel, Lektion (3)

up [ʌp] hinauf, herauf; (nach) oben 4 (84/85) **up and down** auf und ab; rauf und runter 4 (84/85)

upstairs [ˌʌpˈsteəz] oben; nach oben (im Haus) 2 (36)

us [ʌs, əs] uns 2 (39)

use [juːz] benutzen, verwenden 4 (89)

°**useful** [ˈjuːsfl] nützlich

usually [ˈjuːʒuəli] meistens, normalerweise, gewöhnlich 3 (68)

V

vegetables (pl) [ˈvedʒtəblz] Gemüse 2 (48)

very [ˈveri] sehr 3 (58)

video [ˈvɪdiəʊ] Video 3 (56/57)

video camera [ˈvɪdiəʊ ˌkæmərə] Videokamera 2 (52)

village [ˈvɪlɪdʒ] Dorf 5 (112)

visit [ˈvɪzɪt]:
1. besuchen 3 (59)
2. Besuch 4 (87)

°**visitor** [ˈvɪzɪtə] Besucher/in

vocabulary [vəˈkæbjələri] Vokabelverzeichnis, Wörterverzeichnis (3)

voice [vɔɪs] Stimme 3 (72)

volleyball [ˈvɒlibɔːl] Volleyball 3 (67)

°**vowel** [ˈvaʊəl] Vokal, Selbstlaut

W

wait (for) [weɪt] warten (auf) 1 (18)

wait a minute Warte einen Moment. / Moment mal. 1 (18)

wake up [ˌweɪk ˈʌp], simple past: **woke up:**
1. aufwachen 2 (38)
°2. **wake sb. up** jn. wecken

walk [wɔːk]:
1. Spaziergang 2 (39) **go for a walk** spazieren gehen, einen Spaziergang machen 2 (39)
2. (zu Fuß) gehen 3 (72) °**walk around** herumlaufen

want [wɒnt]: **want sth.** etwas (haben) wollen 3 (59) **want to do sth.** etwas tun wollen 3 (59)

warm [wɔːm] warm 4 (83)
°**warmest** [ˈwɔːmɪst] wärmste(r, s)

was [wɒz, wəz] simple past of **be**

°**wasp** [wɒsp] Wespe

watch [wɒtʃ]:
1. Armbanduhr HWG (16)
2. sich etwas anschauen; beobachten 1 (30) **watch TV** fernsehen 2 (36)
Watch out! Pass auf! / Vorsicht! 1 (20)
▶ S. 183 look · see · watch

water [ˈwɔːtə] Wasser 2 (50)

way [weɪ]:
1. Weg 4 (84/85) **on the way to …** auf dem Weg zu / nach … 4 (84/85)
°2. Art, Weise **in different ways** auf verschiedene Weise

we [wiː] wir 1 (18)

wear [weə], simple past: **wore** tragen (Kleidung) 1 (21)

website [ˈwebsaɪt] Website 3 (56/57)

Wednesday [ˈwenzdeɪ, ˈwenzdi] Mittwoch HWG (11)

week [wiːk] Woche HWG (11)
▶ S. 175 The days of the week

weekend [ˌwiːkˈend] Wochenende 2 (39) **at the weekend** am Wochenende 2 (39)

weigh [weɪ] wiegen 4 (92)

Welcome to Plymouth. [ˈwelkəm] Willkommen in Plymouth. HWG (10)

Well, … [wel] Nun, … / Also, … / Na ja, … 2 (46)

went [went] simple past of **go**

were [wɜː, wə] simple past of **be**

wet [wet] nass 3 (58)

whale [weɪl] Wal HWG (14)

what? [wɒt] was? HWG (9) **What about you?** Und du / ihr? / Und was ist mit dir / euch? HWG (9) **What colour …?** Welche Farbe …? 1 (30) **What is the story about?** Wovon handelt die Geschichte? Worum geht es in der Geschichte? 4 (96) **What page are we on?** Auf welcher Seite sind wir? 1 (31) **What programmes …?** Welche Programme …? / Welche Art von Programmen …? 3 (64) **What time is it?** Wie spät ist es? 1 (18) **What would you like to eat?** Was möchtest du essen? 2 (48) **What's your name?** Wie heißt du? / Wie heißt ihr? HWG (9) **What's for lunch?** Was gibt es zum Mittagessen? 2 (48) **What's for homework?** Was haben wir als Hausaufgabe auf? 1 (31) °**What's next?** Was kommt als Nächstes? **What's she like?** Wie ist sie? / Wie ist sie so? 3 (59)

wheel [wiːl]: **big wheel** Riesenrad HWG (10)

when [wen]:
1. wenn 4 (82)
2. als 4 (84/85)
3. **when?** wann? 1 (29) **When's your birthday?** Wann hast du Geburtstag? 1 (29)
▶ S. 182 Birthdays

where? [weə] wo? / wohin? HWG (9) **Where are you from?** Woher kommst du? HWG (9)

which? [wɪtʃ] welche(r, s)? **Which clubs / jokes …?** Welche Klubs / Witze / …? 3 (58)

white [waɪt] weiß HWG (15)

who? [huː] wer? 1 (20)

°**whole** [həʊl] ganze(r, s), gesamte(r, s)

why? [waɪ] warum? 2 (53)

°**wild** [waɪld] wild

win [wɪn], simple past: **won** gewinnen 1 (30)

window [ˈwɪndəʊ] Fenster HWG (16)

winner [ˈwɪnə] Gewinner / in, Sieger / in 1 (30)

winter [ˈwɪntə] Winter 4 (82)

wish [wɪʃ] Wunsch 4 (88) **make a wish** sich etwas wünschen 4 (88)

with [wɪð]
1. mit HWG (15)
2. bei 2 (53)

without [wɪˈðaʊt] ohne HWG (15)

woke [wəʊk] simple past of **wake**

woman [ˈwʊmən], pl women [ˈwɪmɪn] Frau 1 (35)

won [wʌn] simple past of **win**

°**woof** [wʊf] wau, wau

word [wɜːd] Wort HWG (16) °**group word** Obergriff **word order** Wortstellung 5 (114)

wordbank ['wɜːd‚bæŋk] „Wortspeicher" (3)

wore [wɔː] *simple past of* **wear**

work [wɜːk]
1. arbeiten 1 (30)
2. Arbeit 3 (59)

workbook ['wɜːkbʊk] Arbeitsheft 1 (31)

worm [wɜːm] Wurm 4 (95)

worried ['wʌrid] besorgt, beunruhigt 2 (52)

would [wʊd]: **What would you like to eat?** Was möchtest du essen? 2 (48) ° **he'd (= he would) let us in** er würde uns hereinlassen **I'd (= I would) like …** Ich möchte … 2 (48)

°**wrap** [ræp] wickeln

write [raɪt], *simple past:* **wrote** schreiben 1 (29) °**write down** aufschreiben

wrong [rɒŋ]:
1. falsch, verkehrt HWG (13) **No, that's wrong.** Nein, das ist falsch. / Nein, das stimmt nicht. HWG (13)
2. **sb. is wrong** jemand irrt sich; jemand hat Unrecht 4 (98)

wrote [rəʊt] *simple past of* **write**

Y

year [jɪə]:
1. Jahr HWG (8)
2. Jahrgang(sstufe) 1 (18)

yellow ['jeləʊ] gelb HWG (15)

yes [jes] ja HWG (13) **Yes, that's right.** Ja, das ist richtig. / Ja, das stimmt. HWG (13)

yesterday ['jestədeɪ, 'jestədi] gestern 4 (82)

yet [jet]: **not … yet** noch nicht 5 (112)

yoga ['jəʊgə] Yoga 3 (60)

yoghurt ['jɒgət] Joghurt 1 (34)

you [juː] du; Sie; ihr; dir; dich; euch; Ihnen HWG (9)

young [jʌŋ] jung 3 (56/57)

your [jɔː, jə] dein/e; euer/eure; Ihr/ Ihre HWG (9)

yourself [jɔːˈself]: **about yourself** über dich selbst 1 (26)

yummy *(infml)* ['jʌmi] lecker 2 (48)

Z

zoo [zuː] Zoo 4 (81)

°**zookeeper** ['zuːkiːpə] Zoowärter/in

Early finisher – answers

1 *Coombe Dean School*

2 Photo B:
0 ball · 3 books · 5 cards · 2 CD · 1 clock · 0 computer · 1 DVD · 1 glue stick · 1 lamp · 1 map · 4 pens · 2 pencils · 0 pencil case · 2 photos · 2 rubbers · 1 ruler · 0 sharpener · 1 telephone

3 a) *There is no "k" in Ann's activity, so she doesn't go **skating**.*
   b) *There is no "g" at the end of Leo's activity, so he plays **football** or does **judo**.*
   c) *Henry's activity has eight letters in it, so he plays **football** or goes **swimming**.*
   d) *Leo's activity does not have four letters (**judo**), so he plays **football**.*
   *Henry doesn't play **football**, so he goes **swimming**.*
   *So Ann does **judo**.*
   *And Maria goes **skating**.*
   Leo plays football, Henry goes swimming, Maria goes skating and Ann does judo.

4 a) *Not October but **Mary**. ("Mary's mum …")*
   b) *It's **your** name: "You're the driver …"*
   c) *Tuesday, Thursday and **today**.*
   d) *No boat is nearer, because the two boats **meet**.*
   e) *The letter **S**: Plym**S**tock.*
   f) *You are the most intelligent animal.*

5 1 *Silky, page 9: Are you a boy or a girl?*
   2 *Morph, page 19: I'm Morph, I'm Morph from Plymstock School.*
   3 *Silky, page 11: Hey, hey Hoe, here we go!*
   4 *Sam, page 34: Go and find the yoghurt, little sister!*
   5 *Sam, page 48: Roast beef with roast potatoes? Yummy!*
   6 *Sam, page 58: What's grey and never gets wet?*
   7 *A man near the harbour, page 52: Boat tours! See all the navy ships!*
   8 *Abby, page 99: She looks so soft. Call her Silky.*
   9 *The captain's ghost, page 72: Stop! Thieves! Give me back my book!*
   10 *Tim Blackwell, page 39: Help! A mad sister and a mad dog!*

Das **German – English Dictionary** enthält den **Lernwortschatz** von *English G Access 1*.
Es kann dir eine erste Hilfe sein, wenn du vergessen hast, wie etwas auf Englisch heißt.

Wenn du wissen möchtest, wo das entsprechende englische Wort zum ersten Mal in *English G Access 1* vorkommt,
dann kannst du im **English – German Dictionary** (S. 206 – 219) nachschlagen.

Im **German – English Dictionary** werden folgende **Abkürzungen** verwendet:

sth. = something (etwas)	sb. = somebody (jemand)	jn. = jemanden	jm. = jemandem
pl = plural (Mehrzahl)	*infml* = informal (umgangssprachlich)		

▶ Der Pfeil weist auf Kästen im **Vocabulary** (S. 172 – 205) hin, in denen du weitere Informationen zu diesem Wort findest.

A

ab: auf und ab up and down [ˌʌp_ən
'daʊn]

Abend evening ['iːvnɪŋ] **am Abend**
in the evening **zu Abend essen**
have dinner ['dɪnə]

Abendbrot, Abendessen dinner
['dɪnə]

abends in the evening ['iːvnɪŋ]

aber but [bʌt], [bət]

**Abneigungen: Vorlieben und Ab-
neigungen** likes and dislikes *(pl)*
[ˌlaɪks_ən 'dɪslaɪks]

Absatz *(in einem Text)* paragraph
['pærəgrɑːf]

abschreiben copy ['kɒpi]

abspielen *(CD usw.)* play [pleɪ]

acht eight [eɪt]
▶ S. 233 English numbers

Adresse address [ə'dres]

Affe monkey ['mʌŋki]

Aktivität activity [æk'tɪvəti]

albern silly ['sɪli]

alle all [ɔːl]; *(jeder)* everyone
['evriwʌn], everybody ['evribɒdi]

alleinstehend *(ledig)* single ['sɪŋgl]

alles all [ɔːl]

Alltags- everyday ['evrideɪ]

als **1.** *(zeitlich)* when [wen]
2. als Erstes first [fɜːst]

also **1.** *(deshalb, daher)* so [səʊ]
2. Also, … Well, … [wel]

alt old [əʊld] **Ich bin zwei Jahre
alt.** I'm two years old. **Wie alt bist
du?** How old are you?

Alter age [eɪdʒ]

am **1.** *(in Ortsangaben)* at [æt], [ət]
am Meer by the sea [baɪ]
2. *(in Zeitangaben)* **am Abend** in the
evening **am Montag/Dienstag/…**
on Monday/Tuesday/… **am Morgen** in the morning **am Nachmittag** in the afternoon **am Samstag-
morgen** on Saturday afternoon **am
Wochenende** at the weekend

Ameise ant [ænt]

amüsieren: sich amüsieren have fun
[fʌn]

an *(in Ortsangaben)* at [æt], [ət] **an
britischen Schulen** at British
schools

anbauen *(anpflanzen)* grow [grəʊ]

andere(r, s) other ['ʌðə] **ein anderer …/eine andere …/ein anderes
…** another … [ə'nʌðə]

anders *(verschieden)* different
['dɪfrənt]

anfangen start [stɑːt]

anfassen touch [tʌtʃ]

anhalten stop [stɒp]

anhören **1. sich etwas anhören**
listen to sth. ['lɪsn] **Hör dir/Hört
euch den Song an.** Listen to the
song.
2. sich gut anhören *(gut klingen)*
sound good [saʊnd]
▶ S. 193 listen · hear

ankommen arrive [ə'raɪv]

anlächeln: jn. anlächeln smile at sb.
[smaɪl]

anordnen *(in eine bestimmte Ordnung
bringen)* arrange [ə'reɪndʒ]

anpflanzen grow [grəʊ]

anrufen call [kɔːl]

anschauen: sich etwas anschauen
watch sth. [wɒtʃ]; look at sth. [lʊk]
▶ S. 183 look · see · watch
▶ S. 189 look

**anschließen: sich einem Klub an-
schließen** join a club [dʒɔɪn]

Anschrift address [ə'dres]

ansehen: sich etwas ansehen watch
sth. [wɒtʃ]; look at sth. [lʊk]
▶ S. 183 look · see · watch
▶ S. 189 look

Anspitzer sharpener ['ʃɑːpnə]

Antwort answer ['ɑːnsə]

antworten answer ['ɑːnsə]

Apfelsine orange ['ɒrɪndʒ]

April April ['eɪprəl]

Aquarienhaus aquarium [ə'kweəriəm]

Aquarium aquarium [ə'kweəriəm]

Arbeit work [wɜːk]; *(Job, Stelle)* job
[dʒɒb]

arbeiten work [wɜːk]

Arbeitsheft workbook ['wɜːkbʊk]

Ärger kriegen/haben be in trouble
['trʌbl]

arm poor [pɔː], [pʊə]

Armbanduhr watch [wɒtʃ]

Art: eine Art (von) … a kind of …
[kaɪnd]

auch: auch aus Berlin from Berlin
too [tuː]; also from Berlin ['ɔːlsəʊ]
Ich auch. Me too.

auf on [ɒn] **auf das Boot (hinauf)**
onto the boat ['ɒntʊ] **auf dem Bild**
in the picture **auf dem Dachboden**
in the attic **auf einmal** suddenly
['sʌdnli] **auf dem Foto** in the
photo **auf dem Weg zu/nach …**
on the way to … **auf der Land-
karte/dem Stadtplan** on the map
auf Deutsch/Englisch in German/
English **auf und ab** up and down
Auf welcher Seite sind wir? What
page are we on? **Auf Wiedersehen.**
Goodbye.

Aufgabe task; exercise ['eksəsaɪz]

aufgeregt *(gespannt)* excited
[ɪk'saɪtɪd]

aufmachen open ['əʊpən]

aufregend *(spannend)* exciting
[ɪk'saɪtɪŋ]

aufstehen get up [ˌget_'ʌp]

aufwachen wake up [ˌweɪk_'ʌp]

Auge eye [aɪ]

Augenblick moment ['məʊmənt]

August August ['ɔːgəst]

aus from [frɒm], [frəm] **aus … her-
aus/hinaus** out of … ['aʊt_əv]
Ich bin aus/komme aus Plymouth.
I'm from Plymouth.

ausdenken: sich etwas ausdenken
think of sth. [θɪŋk]

Ausdruck *(Redewendung)* phrase
[freɪz]

Ausflug trip [trɪp]
ausprobieren try [traɪ]
Ausrüstung kit [kɪt]
aussehen: glücklich/wütend/...
aussehen look happy/angry/...
▶ S. 189 look
Aussprache pronunciation
[prə,nʌnsi'eɪʃn]
aussteigen get off [,get_'ɒf] **aus dem Bus/Boot aussteigen** get off the bus/boat
aussuchen: (sich) etwas aussuchen choose sth. [tʃuːz]
auswählen: etwas auswählen choose sth. [tʃuːz]
Auto car [kɑː] **mit dem Auto fahren** go by car
Autor/in author ['ɔːθə]

B

Bad, Badezimmer bathroom ['bɑːθruːm]
bald soon [suːn] **Bis bald.** See you.
Ball ball [bɔːl]
Bär bear [beə]
Basketball basketball ['bɑːskɪtbɔːl]
Bauer/Bäuerin farmer ['fɑːmə]
Bauernhof farm [fɑːm]
Baum tree [triː]
beantworten answer ['ɑːnsə]
bearbeiten (Texte, Videos) edit ['edɪt]
beeilen: sich beeilen hurry up [,hʌri_'ʌp]
beenden: etwas beenden finish sth. ['fɪnɪʃ]
befragen: jn. befragen interview sb. ['ɪntəvjuː]
beginnen start [stɑːt]
bei (in Ortsangaben) at [æt], [ət] **bei den Blackwells zu Hause** at the Blackwells' house **bei jm. sein** be with sb. [wɪð]
Bein leg [leg]
beinahe almost ['ɔːlməʊst]
beißen bite [baɪt]
bekommen get [get]
bellen bark [bɑːk]
benötigen need [niːd]
benutzen use [juːz]
beobachten watch [wɒtʃ]
▶ S. 183 look • see • watch
Bereich area ['eəriə]
bereit ready ['redi]
berichten: jm. etwas berichten tell sb. about sth. [tel]
berühren touch [tʌtʃ]

beschäftigt sein (viel zu tun haben) be busy ['bɪzi]
besorgt worried ['wʌrid]
besser better ['betə]
beste(r, s) best [best] **ihr bester Freund / ihre beste Freundin** her best friend
Besuch visit ['vɪzɪt]
besuchen: jn. besuchen visit sb. ['vɪzɪt]; see sb. [siː]
Bett bed [bed]
beunruhigt worried ['wʌrid]
Beutel bag [bæg]
bevor before [bɪ'fɔː]
bewegen; sich bewegen move [muːv]
Bibliothek library ['laɪbrəri]
Bild picture ['pɪktʃə] **auf dem Bild** in the picture
Bildunterschrift caption ['kæpʃn]
billig cheap [tʃiːp]
bis (zeitlich) till [tɪl] **bis zwölf Uhr** till twelve o'clock **Bis gleich. / Bis bald.** See you. **bis zehn zählen** count to ten **von ... bis ...** from ... to ...
bitte please [pliːz]
bitten: jemanden bitten, etwas zu tun ask sb. to do sth. [ɑːsk]
blau blue [bluː]
bleiben stay [steɪ]
Bleistift pencil ['pensl]
blöd (albern) silly ['sɪli]
blond blond (bei Frauen oft: blonde) [blɒnd]
bloß only ['əʊnli]; (einfach nur) just [dʒʌst]
Boot boat [bəʊt]
brauchen need [niːd]
braun brown [braʊn]
brechen (kaputt gehen) break [breɪk]
Brief letter ['letə]
bringen (weg-, hinbringen) take [teɪk]
britisch British ['brɪtɪʃ]
Brot bread [bred]
Bruder brother ['brʌðə]
Buch book [bʊk]
Bücherei library ['laɪbrəri]
Buchhandlung bookshop ['bʊkʃɒp]
Buchstabe letter ['letə]
buchstabieren spell [spel]
Burg castle ['kɑːsl]
Bus bus **mit dem Bus fahren** go by bus

C

Café café ['kæfeɪ]
Chaos chaos ['keɪɒs]

Cola cola ['kəʊlə]
Computer computer [kəm'pjuːtə]
cool cool [kuːl]
Cornflakes cornflakes ['kɔːnfleɪks]
Cousin, Cousine cousin ['kʌzn]

D

da, dahin (dort, dorthin) there [ðeə]
Dachboden attic ['ætɪk] **auf dem Dachboden** in the attic
daheim at home [ət 'həʊm]
▶ S. 179 home
daher (deshalb) so [səʊ]
Danke. Thank you. ['θæŋk juː]; Thanks. [θæŋks] **Danke, gut.** Fine, thanks.
dann then [ðen]
das (Artikel) the [ðə]
das (dort) (Singular) that [ðæt]; (Plural) those [ðəʊz] **das (dort) ist ...** that's ... **das (dort) sind ...** those are ... **das Auto dort** that car
▶ S. 198 this, that – these, those
dass that [ðæt], [ðət] **es zeigt, dass ...** it shows that ...
dasselbe wie ... the same as ... [seɪm]
Deck deck [dek]
dein(e) ... your ... [jɔː], [jə]
denken think [θɪŋk] **an etwas denken** think of sth.
denn: Was ist denn? What's the matter? ['mætə]
der (Artikel) the [ðə]
der ... (dort) (Singular) that ... [ðæt]; (Plural) those ... [ðəʊz] **der ... (hier)** (Singular) this ... [ðɪs]; (Plural) these ... [ðiːz]
▶ S. 198 this, that – these, those
der (Relativpronomen): **Finde jemanden, der ...** Find someone who ...
derselbe wie ... the same as ... [seɪm]
deshalb so [səʊ]
Design design [dɪ'zaɪn]
deuten: auf etwas deuten (zeigen) point to sth. [pɔɪnt]
Deutsch; deutsch German ['dʒɜːmən]
Dezember December [dɪ'sembə]
dich you [juː]
dick fat [fæt]
die (Artikel) the [ðə]
die ... (dort) (Singular) that ... [ðæt]; (Plural) those ... [ðəʊz] **die ... (hier)** (Singular) this ... [ðɪs]; (Plural) these ... [ðiːz]
▶ S. 198 this, that – these, those

dieselbe(n) wie ... the same as ... [seim]

Dieb/in thief [θi:f], *pl* thieves [θi:vz]

Dienstag Tuesday ['tju:zdeɪ, 'tju:zdi]

dies (hier) *(Singular)* this [ðɪs]; *(Plural)* these [ði:z] **dies (hier) ist ...** this is ... **dies (hier) sind ...** these are ...

▶ S.198 this, that – these, those

diese(r, s): dieser Ort / diese Pause / dieses Fach this place/ break/subject **diese Leute** these people

▶ S.198 this, that – these, those

Ding thing [θɪŋ]

dir you [ju:]

Donnerstag Thursday ['θɜ:zdeɪ, 'θɜ:zdi]

Doppel- double ['dʌbl]

Dorf village ['vɪlɪdʒ]

dort, dorthin there [ðeə]

dran: Ich bin dran. (It's) my turn. [tɜ:n]

draußen outside [,aʊt'saɪd] **nach draußen** outside

drei three [θri:]

▶ S.233 English numbers

drinnen inside [,ɪn'saɪd] **nach drinnen** inside

dritte(r, s) third [θɜ:d]

▶ S.233 English numbers

drücken *(schieben, stoßen)* push [pʊʃ]

du you [ju:]

Dummerchen silly ['sɪli]

dunkel dark [dɑ:k]

durch through [θru:]

Durst haben be thirsty ['θɜ:sti]

durstig sein be thirsty ['θɜ:sti]

DVD DVD [,di:vi:'di:]

E

Ecke corner ['kɔ:nə] **Laden an der Ecke** *(„Tante-Emma-Laden")* corner shop ['kɔ:nə ʃɒp]

ein(e) *(Artikel)* a, an [ə], [ən] **ein anderer .../eine andere .../ein anderes ...** another ... [ə'nʌðə]

ein paar *(einige)* some [sʌm], [səm]

einfach 1. *(nicht schwierig)* easy ['i:zi]

2. einfach nur just [dʒʌst]

einhundert a hundred, one hundred ['hʌndrəd]

▶ S.233 English numbers

einige some [sʌm], [səm]

einigen: sich auf etwas einigen agree on sth. [ə'gri:]

einkaufen gehen go shopping ['ʃɒpɪŋ]

Einkaufszentrum shopping mall ['ʃɒpɪŋ mɔ:l], *(kurz auch:)* mall

Einladung (zu, nach) invitation (to) [,ɪnvɪ'teɪʃn]

einmal: auf einmal *(plötzlich)* suddenly ['sʌdnli] **noch einmal** again [ə'gen]

eins one [wʌn]

▶ S.233 English numbers

einsam lonely ['ləʊnli]

einschalten: etwas einschalten turn sth. on [,tɜ:n_'ɒn]

einschlafen fall asleep [,fɔ:l_ə'sli:p]

eintreffen arrive [ə'raɪv]

eintreten: in einen Klub eintreten join a club [dʒɔɪn]

Eintrittskarte ticket ['tɪkɪt]

Eis *(Speiseeis)* ice cream [,aɪs 'kri:m]

Elefant elephant ['elɪfənt]

elf eleven [ɪ'levn]

▶ S.233 English numbers

Eltern parents ['peərənts]

E-Mail email ['i:meɪl]

Ende end [end] **zu Ende sein** be over ['əʊvə]

enden finish ['fɪnɪʃ]

endlich *(schließlich)* at last [ət 'lɑ:st]

Endspiel final ['faɪnl]

Englisch; englisch English ['ɪŋglɪʃ]

entlang: die Straße/den Fluss/... entlang along the street/the river/ ... [ə'lɒŋ]

Entschuldigung. *(Tut mir leid.)* (I'm) sorry. ['sɒri]

er 1. *(männliche Person)* he [hi:] **2.** *(Ding; Tier)* it [ɪt]

erinnern: sich an etwas erinnern remember sth. [rɪ'membə]

erklären: jm. etwas erklären explain sth. to sb. [ɪk'spleɪn]

erläutern: jm. etwas erläutern explain sth. to sb. [ɪk'spleɪn]

erraten guess [ges]

erst only ['əʊnli]

erste(r, s) first [fɜ:st] **als Erstes** first **der erste Tag** the first day

▶ S.233 English numbers

erzählen (von) tell (about) [tel]

Erzählung story ['stɔ:ri]

erzielen: einen Treffer erzielen score [skɔ:]

es it [ɪt] **es ist ... / es gibt ...** there's ... **es sind ... / es gibt ...** there are ... **Ach, du bist es.** Oh, it's you. **Bist du es?** Is that you?

essen eat [i:t] **zu Abend essen** have dinner **zu Mittag essen** have lunch

Essen *(Lebensmittel)* food [fu:d]

Esszimmer dining room ['daɪnɪŋ ru:m]

etwas 1. something ['sʌmθɪŋ] **2.** *(ein bisschen)* some [sʌm], [səm]

euch you [ju:]

euer .../eure ... your ... [jɔ:], [jə]

F

Fähre ferry ['feri]

fahren go [gəʊ] **mit dem Bus/ Auto fahren** go by bus/car **Rad fahren** ride a bike [,raɪd_ə 'baɪk]

Fahrkarte ticket ['tɪkɪt]

Fahrrad bike [baɪk]

Fahrt ride [raɪd]

fair fair [feə]

fallen *(stürzen)* fall [fɔ:l]

falsch wrong [rɒŋ] **Nein, das ist falsch.** No, that's wrong.

Familie family ['fæməli] **Familie Blackwell** the Blackwell family

Fan fan [fæn]

fangen catch [kætʃ]

fantastisch fantastic [fæn'tæstɪk]

Farbe colour ['kʌlə]

▶ S.176 Colours

Farm farm [fɑ:m]

fast almost ['ɔ:lməʊst]

Februar February ['februəri]

Federmäppchen pencil case ['pensl keɪs]

fehlen: die fehlenden Wörter the missing words ['mɪsɪŋ]

Fels, Felsen rock [rɒk]

Fenster window ['wɪndəʊ]

Ferien holidays (*pl*) ['hɒlədeɪz]

fernsehen watch TV [,wɒtʃ ti:'vi:]

Fernsehen, Fernsehgerät TV [,ti:'vi:]

fertig 1. mit etwas fertig werden/sein finish sth. ['fɪnɪʃ] **Wir sind fertig.** *(Wir haben es erledigt.)* We're finished. ['fɪnɪʃt] **2.** *(bereit)* ready ['redi] **Wir sind fertig.** *(Wir sind bereit.)* We're ready.

fett fat [fæt]

Figur *(in Roman, Film, Theaterstück usw.)* character ['kærəktə]

Film film [fɪlm]

filmen film [fɪlm]

Finale final ['faɪnl]

finden find [faɪnd] **Freunde finden** make friends **Wie findest du ...?** How do you like ...?

Fisch fish [fɪʃ], *pl* fish

Flasche bottle ['bɒtl]

Fleck spot [spɒt]

Fleisch meat [miːt]

Fluss river ['rɪvə]

folgen follow ['fɒləʊ]

Form (von) form (of) [fɔːm]

fort away [ə'weɪ]

fortfahren (weiterreden) go on [ˌgəʊ_'ɒn]

Foto photo ['fəʊtəʊ] **auf dem Foto** in the photo **Fotos machen** take photos

Fotoapparat camera ['kæmərə]

fotografieren take photos [ˌteɪk 'fəʊtəʊz]

Frage question ['kwestʃn] **eine Frage stellen** ask a question

fragen ask [ɑːsk]

Französisch; französisch French [frentʃ]

Frau **1.** woman ['wʊmən], pl women ['wɪmɪn]

2. Frau Schwarz Mrs Schwarz ['mɪsɪz]

3. (übliche Anrede von Lehrerinnen) **Frau Bell** Miss Bell [mɪs]

frei free [friː]

Freitag Friday ['fraɪdeɪ], ['fraɪdi]

Freizeit free time [ˌfriː 'taɪm]

Freizeitaktivitäten free-time activities [ˌfriːtaɪm_æk'tɪvətiz]

freuen: Freut mich, dich/euch/Sie kennenzulernen. Nice to meet you.

Freund/in friend [frend] **Freunde finden** make friends

freundlich friendly ['frendli]

Freut mich, dich/euch/Sie kennenzulernen. Nice to meet you.

frieren be cold [kəʊld]

froh (glücklich) happy ['hæpi]

Frosch frog [frɒg]

Frucht fruit [fruːt]

früh early ['ɜːli]

Frühling spring [sprɪŋ]

Frühstück breakfast ['brekfəst]

frühstücken have breakfast

fühlen; sich fühlen feel [fiːl]

Füller pen [pen]

fünf five [faɪv]

▶ S.233 English numbers

für for [fɔː], [fə]

Fuß: zu Fuß gehen walk [wɔːk]

Fußball football ['fʊtbɔːl]

Fußboden floor [flɔː]

Futter food [fuːd]

füttern feed [fiːd]

Fütterungszeit feeding time ['fiːdɪŋ taɪm]

G

ganz: das ganze Plymouth, ganz Plymouth all of Plymouth

gar nichts nothing ['nʌθɪŋ]

Garage garage ['gærɑːʒ], ['gærɪdʒ]

Garten garden ['gɑːdn]

Gartenarbeit gardening ['gɑːdnɪŋ]

Gärtnern gardening ['gɑːdnɪŋ]

gebackene Kartoffeln (im Backofen in Fett gebacken) roast potatoes [rəʊst pə'teɪtəʊz]

geben give [gɪv] **Es gibt ...** (Singular) There's ...; (Plural) There are ... **Gibt es (irgendwelche) ...?** Are there any ...? ['eni] **Was gibt es zum Mittagessen?** What's for lunch?

Gebiet area ['eəriə]

Geburtstag birthday ['bɜːθdeɪ] **Ich habe am 5. Mai Geburtstag.** My birthday is on 5th May. **Ich habe im Mai Geburtstag.** My birthday is in May. **Wann hast du Geburtstag?** When's your birthday?

▶ S.182 Birthdays

gefährlich dangerous ['deɪndʒərəs]

gefallen: Wie gefällt dir ...? How do you like ...?

Gefängnis prison ['prɪzn]

Gefühl feeling ['fiːlɪŋ]

gegen against [ə'genst]

Gegend area ['eəriə]

gehen go [gəʊ]; (zu Fuß gehen) walk [wɔːk] **einkaufen gehen** go shopping ['ʃɒpɪŋ] **Los geht's. / Jetzt geht's los.** Here we go. **nach Hause gehen** go home **segeln gehen** go sailing ['seɪlɪŋ] **spazieren gehen** go for a walk [wɔːk] **Wie geht's? / Wie geht es dir/euch/Ihnen?** How are you? **Worum geht es in der Geschichte?** What is the story about? **Es geht um eine Möwe.** It's about a seagull.

gehören: zu etwas gehören (zu etwas passen) go with sth.

Geist ghost [gəʊst]

gelangen (hinkommen) get [get]

gelb yellow ['jeləʊ]

Geld money ['mʌni]

▶ S.194 British money

Gemüse vegetables (pl) ['vedʒtəblz]

genannt werden (heißen) be called [kɔːld]

genug enough [ɪ'nʌf]

geöffnet open ['əʊpən]

Geografie geography [dʒi'ɒgrəfi]

gerade (im Moment) at the moment ['məʊmənt]

Geräusch sound [saʊnd]

gern: Ich tanze/singe/... gern. I like dancing/singing/... **Ich hätte gern ...** I'd like ... [ˌaɪd 'laɪk] (= I would like ...) **Ich würde gern gehen.** I'd like to go. **Was hättest du gern?** What would you like? [wʊd]

gernhaben like [laɪk]

Geschäft (Laden) shop [ʃɒp]

Geschenk present ['preznt]

Geschichte **1.** (vergangene Zeiten) history ['hɪstri] **2.** (Erzählung) story ['stɔːri]

geschieden divorced [dɪ'vɔːst]

Gesicht face [feɪs]

gespannt (aufgeregt) excited [ɪk'saɪtɪd]

Gespenst ghost [gəʊst]

gestern yesterday ['jestədeɪ], ['jestədi]

Getränk drink [drɪŋk]

gewinnen win [wɪn]

Gewinner/in winner ['wɪnə]

gewöhnlich (normalerweise) usually ['juːʒuəli]

Giraffe giraffe [dʒə'rɑːf]

Gitarre guitar [gɪ'tɑː] **Gitarre spielen** play the guitar

glauben (denken) think [θɪŋk]

Glocke bell [bel]

Glück: Viel Glück! Good luck! [lʌk]

glücklich happy ['hæpi]

Gold gold [gəʊld]

Grafschaft (in Großbritannien) county ['kaʊnti]

grau grey [greɪ]

groß big [bɪg] **der/die/das größte ...; die größten ...** the biggest ... ['bɪgɪst]

großartig great [greɪt]

Großeltern grandparents ['grænpeərənts]

Großmutter grandmother ['grænmʌðə]

Großvater grandfather ['grænfɑːðə]

grün green [griːn]

Gruppe group (of) [gruːp]

gruselig scary ['skeəri]

gucken look [lʊk]

▶ S.183 look · see · watch

gut good [gʊd] **gut sein in Kung-Fu / gut Kung-Fu können** be good at kung fu **Danke, gut.** Fine, thanks. **Guten Morgen.** Good morning. [gʊd 'mɔːnɪŋ] **Guten Tag.** Hello. [hə'ləʊ]

Güter goods (pl) [gʊdz]
Gymnastik gymnastics [dʒɪm'næstɪks]

H

Haar, Haare hair [heə]
haben have [hæv], [həv]   **Durst haben** be thirsty ['θɜːsti]   **Hunger haben** be hungry ['hʌŋgri]   **Ich habe im Mai Geburtstag.** My birthday is in May.   **jemand hat Recht** someone is right   **jemand hat Unrecht** someone is wrong   **viel zu tun haben** (beschäftigt sein) be busy ['bɪzi]   **Wann hast du Geburtstag?** When's your birthday?
▶ S.182 Birthdays
Hafen harbour ['hɑːbə]
Hai shark [ʃɑːk]
halb elf (10.30 / 22.30) half past ten ['hɑːf pɑːst]
▶ S.233 English numbers
Halbzeit half [hɑːf], pl halves [hɑːvz]
Hallo. Hello. [hə'ləʊ]
halten hold [həʊld]   **einen Vortrag / eine Rede halten (über)** give a talk (about)
Hand hand [hænd]
handeln: Es handelt von einer Möwe. It's about a seagull.   **Wovon handelt die Geschichte?** What is the story about?
Handy mobile phone [,məʊbaɪl 'fəʊn], (kurz auch:) mobile
hart hard [hɑːd]
Haus house [haʊs]   **nach Hause gehen** go home   **nach Hause kommen** come home   **zu Hause** at home
▶ S.179 home
Hausaufgabe(n) homework ['həʊmwɜːk]   **Hausaufgaben machen** do my / your / ... homework   **Was haben wir als Hausaufgabe auf?** What's for homework?
Heim (Zuhause) home [həʊm]
▶ S.179 home
Heimatstadt hometown [,həʊm'taʊn]
heiß hot [hɒt]
heißen (genannt werden) be called [kɔːld]   **Ich heiße ...** My name is ...   **Wie heißt du?** What's your name?
helfen help [help]
hell bright [braɪt]
herauf up [ʌp]
heraus: aus ... heraus out of ... ['aʊt_əv]
Herbst autumn ['ɔːtəm]

hereinkommen come in [,kʌm_'ɪn]
Herr Schwarz Mr Schwarz ['mɪstə]
herrennen: hinter jm. herrennen run after sb. [,rʌn_'ɑːftə]
herunter down [daʊn]
heute today [tə'deɪ]
hier here [hɪə]   **hier in der Nähe** near here
hierher here [hɪə]
Hilfe help [help]
hinauf up [ʌp]   **auf das Boot hinauf** onto the boat ['ɒntʊ]
hinaus: aus ... hinaus out of ... ['aʊt_əv]
hinbringen take [teɪk]
hinein: in die Küche hinein into the kitchen ['ɪntʊ]
hinfallen fall [fɔːl]
hinkommen (gelangen) get [get]
hinsetzen: sich hinsetzen sit down [,sɪt 'daʊn]
hinter behind [bɪ'haɪnd]   **hinter jm. herrennen** run after sb. [,rʌn_'ɑːftə]
hinüber zu / nach ... over to ... ['əʊvə]
hinunter down [daʊn]
Hobby hobby ['hɒbi]
hoch high [haɪ]
hoffen hope [həʊp]
horchen listen ['lɪsn]
▶ S.193 listen · hear
hören hear [hɪə]
▶ S.193 listen · hear
Hügel hill [hɪl]
Hund dog [dɒg]
Hunger haben be hungry ['hʌŋgri]
hungrig sein be hungry ['hʌŋgri]

I

ich I [aɪ]   **Ich auch.** Me too.
ideal (perfekt) perfect ['pɜːfɪkt]
Idee idea [aɪ'dɪə]
ihm him [hɪm]; (bei Dingen, Tieren) it
ihn him [hɪm]; (bei Dingen, Tieren) it
ihnen them [ðem], [ðəm]
Ihnen (höfliche Anrede) you [juː]
ihr (Plural von „du") you [juː]
ihr: Hilf ihr. Help her. [hɜː]
ihr(e) ... (vor Nomen; besitzanzeigend)
  1. (zu „she") her ... [hɜː, hə]
  2. (zu „it") its ... [ɪts]
  3. (zu „they") their ... [ðeə]
Ihr(e) ... (vor Nomen; besitzanzeigend) (zur höflichen Anrede „you") your ... [jɔː, jə]

im: im Jahr 1580 in 1580   **im Radio** on the radio
Imbiss snack [snæk]
immer always ['ɔːlweɪz]   **immer noch** still [stɪl]
in in [ɪn]; (in Ortsangaben auch oft:) at [æt], [ət]   **in der Beach Road** in Beach Road   **in der Beach Road 8** at 8 Beach Road   **in der Dean Street** in Dean Street   **in der Dean Street 14** at 14 Dean Street   **in der Nacht** at night   **in der Nähe von** near   **in der Schule** at school   **in die Küche (hinein)** into the kitchen   **in England** in England   **in Ordnung** all right   **in Schwierigkeiten sein** be in trouble ['trʌbl]
Information(en) (über) information (about) (no pl) [,ɪnfə'meɪʃn]
Informations- und Kommunikationstechnologie ICT [,aɪ siː 'tiː] (Information and Communication Technology)
Inlineskaten skating ['skeɪtɪŋ]
Inlineskates skates [skeɪts]
Insel island ['aɪlənd]
Instrument instrument ['ɪnstrəmənt]
interessant interesting ['ɪntrəstɪŋ]
interviewen: jn. interviewen interview sb. ['ɪntəvjuː]
irgendwelche: Gibt es irgendwelche ...? Are there any ...? ['eni]
irren: jemand irrt sich (jemand hat Unrecht) someone is wrong [rɒŋ]

J

ja yes [jes]   **Ja, das ist richtig. / Ja, das stimmt.** Yes, that's right.
Jahr year [jɪə]
Jahrgang, Jahrgangsstufe year [jɪə]
Jahrhundert century ['sentʃəri]
Januar January ['dʒænjuəri]
Jeans jeans (pl) [dʒiːnz]
▶ S.189 clothes · jeans
jede(r, s): jeder Tag / jede Farbe / jedes Boot every day / colour / boat ['evri]
jeder (alle) everyone ['evriwʌn], everybody ['evribɒdi]
jemand someone ['sʌmwʌn], somebody ['sʌmbədi]   **Finde jemanden, der ...** Find someone who ...
jene(r, s): jener Ort / jene Fähre / jenes Kleid that place / ferry / dress   **jene Leute** those people
▶ S.198 this, that – these, those
jetzt now [naʊ]

Job job [dʒɒb]
Joghurt yoghurt ['jɒgət]
Judo judo ['dʒuːdəʊ]
Jugendliche(r) kid [kɪd] (infml)
Juli July [dʒuˈlaɪ]
jung young [jʌŋ]
Junge boy [bɔɪ]
Juni June [dʒuːn]

K

Käfig cage [keɪdʒ]
Kalender diary ['daɪəri]
kalt cold [kəʊld]
Kamera camera ['kæmərə]
Kameramann cameraman, pl -men ['kæmrəmən]
kämpfen fight [faɪt]
Kaninchen rabbit ['ræbɪt]
Kantine canteen [kænˈtiːn]
Kapitän/in captain ['kæptɪn]
kaputt gehen break [breɪk] **etwas kaputt machen** break sth.
Karren cart [kɑːt]
Karte (an) card (to) [kɑːd]
Kartoffel potato [pəˈteɪtəʊ], pl potatoes
Käse cheese [tʃiːz]
Kästchen box [bɒks]
Kasten box [bɒks]
Katze cat [kæt]
kaufen buy [baɪ]
kein(e) no [nəʊ] **Es gibt/sind keine …** There aren't any … ['eni] **Ich bin kein Junge.** I'm not a boy. **Ich mag kein Grün.** I don't like green. **er hat keine Zeit** he doesn't have time
Keks biscuit ['bɪskɪt]
kennen know [nəʊ]
kennenlernen meet [miːt] **Freut mich, dich/euch/Sie kennenzulernen.** Nice to meet you.
Kette chain [tʃeɪn]
Kilogramm, Kilo (kg) kilogram ['kɪləgræm], kilo ['kiːləʊ] (kg)
Kilometer (km) kilometre ['kɪləmiːtə], [kɪˈlɒmɪtə] (km)
Kind child [tʃaɪld], pl children ['tʃɪldrən]; (infml auch:) kid [kɪd]
Kino cinema ['sɪnəmə]
Kiste box [bɒks]
Klang sound [saʊnd]
Klasse class [klɑːs]
Klassenkamerad/in classmate ['klɑːsmeɪt]
Klassenzimmer classroom ['klɑːsruːm]

Klavier piano [piˈænəʊ] **Klavier spielen** play the piano
Klebestift glue stick ['gluː stɪk]
Klebstoff glue [gluː]
Kleid dress [dres]
Kleidung, Kleidungsstücke clothes (pl) [kləʊðz]
▶ S.189 clothes · jeans
klein little ['lɪtl]; small [smɔːl]
Klingel bell [bel]
klingen sound [saʊnd]
Klub club [klʌb] **in einen Klub eintreten / sich einem Klub anschließen** join a club [dʒɔɪn]
klug clever ['klevə]
komisch 1. (lustig) funny ['fʌni] 2. (seltsam, merkwürdig) funny; strange [streɪndʒ]
kommen come [kʌm]; (gelangen, hinkommen) get [get] **Ich komme aus Plymouth.** I'm from Plymouth. **Komm, Dad! (Na los, Dad!)** Come on, Dad. **nach Hause kommen** come home
können can [kæn], [kən] **ich kann nicht … / du kannst nicht …** usw. I can't … / you can't … etc. [kɑːnt] **gut Kung-Fu können** be good at kung fu
konnte(n): ich konnte … / du konntest … usw. I could … / you could … etc. [kʊd] **ich konnte nicht … / du konntest nicht …** usw. I couldn't … / you couldn't … etc. [kʊdnt]
Kontrolle (Überprüfung) check [tʃek]
kontrollieren (überprüfen) check [tʃek]
Kopf head [hed]
kopieren copy ['kɒpi]
Korb basket ['bɑːskɪt]
Körper body ['bɒdi]
kosten: Die Kamera kostet … The camera is … **Die DVDs kosten …** The DVDs are … **Was/Wie viel kostet …?** How much is …? **Was/Wie viel kosten …?** How much are …?
▶ S.194 British money
krank sick [sɪk]
Krebs (Tier) crab [kræb]
Kricket cricket ['krɪkɪt]
Küche kitchen ['kɪtʃɪn]
Kuchen cake [keɪk]
Kugelschreiber pen [pen]
Kunst art [ɑːt]
kurz short [ʃɔːt]
Küste coast [kəʊst]

L

lächeln smile [smaɪl]
lachen laugh [lɑːf]
Laden shop [ʃɒp] **Laden an der Ecke („Tante-Emma-Laden")** corner shop ['kɔːnə ʃɒp]
Lampe lamp [læmp]
Landkarte map ['mæp] **auf der Landkarte** on the map
Landwirt/in farmer ['fɑːmə]
lang long [lɒŋ]
langsam slow [sləʊ]
langweilig boring ['bɔːrɪŋ]
lassen: Lass mich dir … zeigen. Let me show you … **Lass(t) uns …** Let's … **Lass(t) uns nach England gehen/fahren.** Let's go to England.
laufen run [rʌn]
laut loud [laʊd]
Leben life [laɪf], pl lives [laɪvz]
leben (wohnen) live [lɪv]
lecker yummy ['jʌmi] (infml)
ledig (alleinstehend) single ['sɪŋgl]
legen (hinlegen, ablegen) put [pʊt]
Lehrer/in teacher ['tiːtʃə]
leicht (einfach) easy ['iːzi]
leid: Es tut mir leid (wegen …) I'm sorry (about …)
leise quiet ['kwaɪət]
lenken steer [stɪə]
lernen learn [lɜːn]
lesen read [riːd]
letzte(r, s) last [lɑːst] **letztes Wochenende / letzten Freitag** last weekend/Friday
leuchtend bright [braɪt]
Leute people ['piːpl]
Licht light [laɪt]
lieben love [lʌv]
Lieblings-: mein Lieblingstier my favourite animal ['feɪvərɪt]
Lied song [sɒŋ]
lila purple ['pɜːpl]
Lineal ruler ['ruːlə]
Liste list [lɪst]
los: Los geht's. / Jetzt geht's los. Here we go. **Was ist los?** What's the matter? ['mætə]
Löwe lion ['laɪən]

M

machen (tun) do [duː]; (herstellen) make [meɪk] **einen Spaziergang machen** go for a walk [wɔːk] **Fotos machen** take photos **Hat es Spaß gemacht?** Was it fun?

Mädchen girl [gɜːl]
Mai May [meɪ]
Mama mum [mʌm]
manchmal sometimes [ˈsʌmtaɪmz]
Mann man [mæn], *pl* men [men]
Mannschaft team [tiːm]
Marine navy [ˈneɪvi]
Markt market [ˈmɑːkɪt]
Marmelade jam [dʒæm]
März March [mɑːtʃ]
Mathematik maths [mæθs]
Maul mouth [maʊθ]
Meer sea [siː] **am Meer** by the sea
Meerschweinchen guinea pig [ˈgɪni pɪg]
mehr more [mɔː]
mein(e) … my … [maɪ]
meistens usually [ˈjuːʒuəli]
Meister/in master [ˈmɑːstə]
Mensa *(Kantine)* canteen [kænˈtiːn]
Menschen people [ˈpiːpl]
Meter metre [ˈmiːtə]
mich me [miː]
Milch milk [mɪlk]
Minute minute [ˈmɪnɪt]
mir me [miː]
mit with [wɪð] **mit dem Bus/Auto fahren** go by bus/car
Mitschüler/in classmate [ˈklɑːsmeɪt]
Mittag: zu Mittag essen have lunch [lʌntʃ]
Mittagessen lunch [lʌntʃ]
mittags at lunchtime [ˈlʌntʃtaɪm]
Mittagszeit lunchtime [ˈlʌntʃtaɪm]
Mitte middle [ˈmɪdl]; *(Zentrum)* centre [ˈsentə]
Mitternacht midnight [ˈmɪdnaɪt]
Mittwoch Wednesday [ˈwenzdeɪ, ˈwenzdi]
Mobiltelefon mobile phone [ˌməʊbaɪl ˈfəʊn], *(kurz auch:)* mobile
möchte: Ich möchte … (haben) I'd like … [ˌaɪd ˈlaɪk] (= I would like …) **Ich möchte gehen.** I'd like to go. **Was möchtest du (haben)?** What would you like? [wʊd] **Was möchtest du essen?** What would you like to eat?
mögen like [laɪk] **Ich mag …** I like … **Ich mag Grün nicht. / Ich mag kein Grün.** I don't like green. [ˈdəʊnt laɪk]
Moment moment [ˈməʊmənt] **im Moment** at the moment **Warte einen Moment. / Moment mal.** Wait a minute.
Monat month [mʌnθ]
▶ S. 182 The months
Mond moon [muːn]

Monster monster [ˈmɒnstə]
Montag Monday [ˈmʌndeɪ, ˈmʌndi]
Morgen *(Vormittag)* morning [ˈmɔːnɪŋ] **am Morgen** in the morning
morgens in the morning [ˈmɔːnɪŋ]
Möwe seagull [ˈsiːgʌl]
MP3-Player, MP3-Spieler MP3 player [ˌempiːˈθriː ˌpleɪə]
müde tired [ˈtaɪəd]
Mund mouth [maʊθ]
Münze coin [kɔɪn]
Museum museum [mjuˈziːəm]
Musik music [ˈmjuːzɪk]
müssen have to [ˈhæv tə] **arbeiten müssen** have to work
Mutter mother [ˈmʌðə]
Mutti mum [mʌm]

N

Na: Na ja, … Well, … [wel] **Na los, Dad!** *(Komm, Dad!)* Come on, Dad. **Na und?** So? [səʊ]
nach 1. *(örtlich)* to [tu], [tə] **nach draußen** outside [ˌaʊtˈsaɪd] **nach drinnen** inside [ˌɪnˈsaɪd] **nach Hause gehen** go home **nach Hause kommen** come home **nach oben** up; *(im Haus)* upstairs [ˌʌpˈsteəz] **nach unten** down; *(im Haus)* downstairs [ˌdaʊnˈsteəz] **2.** *(zeitlich)* after [ˈɑːftə] **nach dem Frühstück** after breakfast **Viertel nach zehn (10.15 / 22.15)** quarter past ten [ˈkwɔːtə pɑːst]
▶ S. 233 English numbers
Nachmittag afternoon [ˌɑːftəˈnuːn] **am Nachmittag** in the afternoon
nachmittags in the afternoon [ˌɑːftəˈnuːn]
Nachrichten news *(no pl)* [njuːz]
Nachspeise dessert [dɪˈzɜːt]
nächste(r, s) next [nekst] **das nächste Bild / die nächste Frage** the next picture/question
Nacht night [naɪt] **in der Nacht** at night
Nachtisch dessert [dɪˈzɜːt]
nachts at night [ət ˈnaɪt]
Nähe: in der Nähe von near [nɪə] **hier in der Nähe** near here
nahe (bei) near [nɪə]
Name name [neɪm] **Mein Name ist Silky.** My name is Silky.
Nase nose [nəʊz]
nass wet [wet]

natürlich *(selbstverständlich)* of course [əv ˈkɔːs]
Naturwissenschaft science [ˈsaɪəns]
Nebensatz sub-clause [ˈsʌbklɔːz]
nehmen take [teɪk]
nein no [nəʊ] **Nein, das ist falsch. / Nein, das stimmt nicht.** No, that's wrong.
nennen *(rufen, bezeichnen)* call [kɔːl]
nett nice [naɪs]
neu new [njuː]
neun nine [naɪn]
▶ S. 233 English numbers
nicht not [nɒt] **Geh nicht.** Don't go. [dəʊnt] **Ich mag Grün nicht.** I don't like green. **Ich weiß (es) nicht.** I don't know. **noch nicht** not … yet [jet]
nie never [ˈnevə]
niemals never [ˈnevə]
niemand no one [ˈnəʊ wʌn], nobody [ˈnəʊbədi]
niesen sneeze [sniːz]
noch: noch einmal again [əˈgen] **noch nicht** not … yet [jet] **immer noch** still [stɪl] **noch ein(e) …** another … [əˈnʌðə]
normalerweise usually [ˈjuːʒuəli]
Notiz note [nəʊt]
November November [nəʊˈvembə]
Null *(in Telefonnummern)* o [əʊ]
Nummer number
nun now [nəʊ] **Nun, …** Well, … [wel]
nur only [ˈəʊnli]; *(einfach nur)* just [dʒʌst]

O

oben *(im Haus)* upstairs [ˌʌpˈsteəz] **nach oben** up; *(im Haus)* upstairs
Obst fruit [fruːt]
Obstsalat fruit salad [ˌfruːt ˈsæləd]
oder or [ɔː]
offen open [ˈəʊpən]
öffnen; sich öffnen open [ˈəʊpən]
oft often [ˈɒfn], [ˈɒftən]
ohne without [wɪˈðaʊt]
Ohr ear [ɪə]
okay OK [ˌəʊˈkeɪ]; all right [ɔːl ˈraɪt]
Oktober October [ɒkˈtəʊbə]
Oma grandma [ˈgrænmɑː]
Onkel uncle [ˈʌŋkl]
Opa grandpa [ˈgrænpɑː]
Orange orange [ˈɒrɪndʒ]
orange(farben) orange [ˈɒrɪndʒ]
Ordnung: in Ordnung *(okay)* all right [ɔːl ˈraɪt]; OK [ˌəʊˈkeɪ]

Ort place [pleɪs]
Ozean ocean ['əʊʃn]

P

paar: ein paar (einige) some [sʌm], [səm]
Papa dad [dæd]
Papier paper ['peɪpə]
Park park [pɑːk]
Partner/in partner ['pɑːtnə]
Party party ['pɑːti]
Pass auf! (Vorsicht!) Watch out! [ˌwɒtʃ_'aʊt]
passen: zu etwas passen (zu etwas gehören) go with sth.
Pause break [breɪk]
Pence pence [pens]
▶ S.194 British money
perfekt perfect ['pɜːfɪkt]
Person person ['pɜːsn]; (in Roman, Film, Theaterstück usw.) character ['kærəktə]
Pfeffer pepper ['pepə]
Pferd horse [hɔːs]
Pfund (britische Währung) pound (£) [paʊnd]
▶ S.194 British money
Piano piano [pɪ'ænəʊ]
Picknick picnic ['pɪknɪk]
pink pink [pɪŋk]
Pizza pizza ['piːtsə]
Plan plan [plæn]
Planet planet ['plænɪt]
Platz place [pleɪs]
Plätzchen (Keks) biscuit ['bɪskɪt]
plötzlich suddenly ['sʌdnli]
Pokal (Trophäe) trophy ['trəʊfi]
Polizist/in police officer [pə'liːs_ˌɒfɪsə]
Porträt (Personenbeschreibung) profile ['prəʊfaɪl]
Poster poster ['pəʊstə]
prallen: gegen etwas prallen hit sth. [hɪt]
Preis (Kaufpreis) price [praɪs]
preiswert (billig) cheap [tʃiːp]
probieren try [traɪ]
Problem problem ['prɒbləm]
Profil (Personenbeschreibung, Porträt) profile ['prəʊfaɪl]
Programm programme ['prəʊgræm]
prüfen (überprüfen) check [tʃek]
Punkt point [pɔɪnt]; (Fleck) spot [spɒt]
putzen clean [kliːn]

Q

Quiz quiz [kwɪz]

R

Rad (Fahrrad) bike [baɪk]   **Rad fahren** ride a bike [ˌraɪd_ə 'baɪk]
Radiergummi rubber ['rʌbə]
Radio radio ['reɪdiəʊ]   **im Radio** on the radio
raten guess [ges]
Ratte rat [ræt]
rauf und runter up and down [ˌʌp_ən 'daʊn]
Recht: jemand hat Recht someone is right
Rede talk [tɔːk]   **eine Rede halten (über)** give a talk (about)
reden (mit) talk (to) [tɔːk]
Referat talk [tɔːk]   **ein Referat halten (über)** give a talk (about)
Regal shelf [ʃelf], pl shelves [ʃelvz]
Regenschirm umbrella [ʌm'brelə]
reich rich [rɪtʃ]
Reihe: Ich bin an der Reihe. (It's) my turn. [tɜːn]
Reihenfolge order ['ɔːdə]
Reim rhyme [raɪm]
Reise trip [trɪp]
reisen travel ['trævl]
Reisende(r) traveller ['trævələ]
Reiten riding ['raɪdɪŋ]
Religion religion [rɪ'lɪdʒən]
rennen run [rʌn]
retten save [seɪv]
richten: etwas auf jn. richten point sth. at sb. [pɔɪnt]
richtig right [raɪt]   **Ja, das ist richtig.** Yes, that's right.
riechen smell [smel]   **an etwas riechen** smell sth.
Riesenrad big wheel [bɪg 'wiːl]
Rinderbraten roast beef [ˌrəʊst 'biːf]
Robbe seal [siːl]
rosa pink [pɪŋk]
rot red [red]
Rucksack rucksack ['rʌksæk]
rufen call [kɔːl]; shout [ʃaʊt]
ruhig (leise) quiet ['kwaɪət]
Rundgang, Rundfahrt (durch) tour (of) ['tʊər_əv]
runter: rauf und runter up and down [ˌʌp_ən 'daʊn]

S

Sache thing [θɪŋ]
sagen say [seɪ]
Sahne cream [kriːm]
Salat (Gericht, Beilage) salad ['sæləd]
Samba samba ['sæmbə]
sammeln collect [kə'lekt]
Samstag Saturday ['sætədeɪ, 'sætədi]
Sand sand [sænd]
Sandwich sandwich ['sænwɪtʃ], ['sænwɪdʒ]
Satz sentence ['sentəns]
sauber machen clean [kliːn]
Schach chess [tʃes]
schauen look [lʊk]
▶ S.183 look · see · watch
▶ S.189 look
Schauspieler/in actor ['æktə]
schicken: jm. etwas schicken send sth. to sb. [send]   **einem Freund/einer Freundin eine SMS schicken** text a friend [tekst]
schieben push [pʊʃ]
schießen: ein Tor schießen score [skɔː]
Schiff ship [ʃɪp]
Schild sign [saɪn]
Schirm umbrella [ʌm'brelə]
schlafen sleep [sliːp]
Schlafparty sleepover ['sliːpəʊvə]
Schlafzimmer bedroom ['bedruːm]
Schlagzeug drums (pl) [drʌmz]   **Schlagzeug spielen** play the drums
Schlange snake [sneɪk]
schlau clever ['klevə]
schlecht bad [bæd]
schließlich at last [ət 'lɑːst]
schlimm bad [bæd]
Schloss castle ['kɑːsl]
Schluss end [end]
Schlüsselwort keyword ['kiːwɜːd]
schmecken taste [teɪst]
Schmetterling butterfly ['bʌtəflaɪ]
Schmuggel; das Schmuggeln smuggling ['smʌglɪŋ]
schmuggeln smuggle ['smʌgl]
Schmuggler/in smuggler ['smʌglə]
schneiden (Film, Video bearbeiten) edit ['edɪt]
schnell fast [fɑːst]
Schokolade chocolate ['tʃɒklət]
schön nice [naɪs]
Schrank cupboard ['kʌbəd]
schreiben write [raɪt]
Schreibtisch desk [desk]
schreien shout [ʃaʊt]
Schritt step [step]
Schuh shoe [ʃuː]

Schule school [skuːl] **in der Schule** at school

Schüler/in student ['stjuːdənt]

Schulfach (school) subject ['sʌbdʒɪkt]
▶ S. 182 School subjects

Schulheft (Übungsheft) exercise book ['eksəsaɪz bʊk]

Schultasche school bag ['skuːl bæg]

schwarz black [blæk]

Schwein pig [pɪg]

schwer (schwierig) hard [hɑːd]

Schwert sword [sɔːd]

Schwester sister ['sɪstə]

schwierig hard [hɑːd]

Schwimmbad, Schwimmbecken (swimming) pool [puːl]

schwimmen swim [swɪm]

Schwimmer/in swimmer ['swɪmə]

Schwimmweste life jacket ['laɪf dʒækɪt]

sechs six [sɪks]
▶ S. 233 English numbers

See 1. (Binnensee) lake [leɪk]
2. (die See, das Meer) sea [siː]

Segelboot sailing boat ['seɪlɪŋ bəʊt]

segeln sail [seɪl] **segeln gehen** go sailing ['seɪlɪŋ]

sehen see [siː]
▶ S. 183 look · see · watch

Sehenswürdigkeiten sights (pl) [saɪts]

sehr very ['veri] **Das hat uns sehr geholfen.** That helped us a lot.

seidig silky ['sɪlki]

sein (Verb) be [biː]

sein(e) ... (vor Nomen; besitzanzeigend)
1. (zu „he") his ... [hɪz]
2. (zu „it") its ... [ɪts]

Seite page [peɪdʒ] **Auf welcher Seite sind wir?** What page are we on?

selbstverständlich of course [əv 'kɔːs]

seltsam strange [streɪndʒ]

senden: jm. etwas senden send sth. to sb. [send]

Sendung (im Radio, Fernsehen) programme ['prəʊgræm]

September September [sep'tembə]

Sessel armchair ['ɑːmtʃeə]

setzen: sich setzen sit [sɪt]

Shorts (kurze Hose) shorts (pl) [ʃɔːts]

sie 1. (Einzahl; weibliche Person) she [ʃiː] **Frag sie.** Ask her. [hɜː]
2. (Einzahl; Ding, Tier) it [ɪt]
3. (Mehrzahl) they [ðeɪ] **Frag sie.** Ask them. [ðem, ðəm]

Sie (höfliche Anrede) you [juː, ju]

sieben seven ['sevn]
▶ S. 233 English numbers

Sieger/in winner ['wɪnə]

singen sing [sɪŋ]

sitzen sit [sɪt]

SMS text [tekst] **einem Freund/ einer Freundin eine SMS schicken** text a friend

Snack snack [snæk]

so 1. (auf diese Weise) like that
2. so cool/nett/leise/... so cool/ nice/quiet/... [səʊ]

Sofa sofa ['səʊfə]

Sommer summer ['sʌmə]

Sonnabend Saturday ['sætədeɪ, 'sætədi]

Sonne sun [sʌn]

Sonntag Sunday ['sʌndeɪ, 'sʌndi]

Spagetti spaghetti [spə'geti]

spannend (aufregend) exciting [ɪk'saɪtɪŋ]

Spaß fun [fʌn] **Spaß haben** have fun [fʌn] **Hat es Spaß gemacht?** Was it fun?

spät late [leɪt] **Du bist spät dran. / Du bist zu spät.** You're late. **Wie spät ist es?** What time is it?

später later ['leɪtə]

spazieren gehen go for a walk [wɔːk]

Spaziergang walk [wɔːk] **einen Spaziergang machen** go for a walk

Spiel game [geɪm]; (Wettkampf, Match) match [mætʃ]

spielen play [pleɪ] **Gitarre spielen** play the guitar **Klavier spielen** play the piano **Schlagzeug spielen** play the drums

Spieler/in player ['pleɪə]

Spielzeug toy [tɔɪ]

Sport; Sportart sport [spɔːt] **Sport treiben** do sport
▶ S. 191 Sports and other activities

Sportunterricht PE [ˌpiː 'iː] (Physical Education)

Sprache language ['læŋgwɪdʒ]

sprechen speak [spiːk]

Sprecher/in speaker ['spiːkə]

springen jump [dʒʌmp]

Sprung jump [dʒʌmp]

Stadt town [taʊn]

Stadtplan map [mæp] **auf dem Stadtplan** on the map

Stammbaum family tree ['fæməli triː]

Star star [stɑː]

Stelle place [pleɪs]; (Job, Arbeitsstelle) job [dʒɒb]

stellen (hinstellen, abstellen) put [pʊt] **eine Frage stellen** ask a question

sterben die [daɪ]

steuern steer [stɪə]

Stift (zum Schreiben) pen [pen]

still quiet ['kwaɪət]

Stimme voice [vɔɪs]

stimmen: Ja, das stimmt. Yes, that's right. [raɪt] **Nein, das stimmt nicht.** No, that's wrong. [rɒŋ]

stoppen stop [stɒp]

stoßen push [pʊʃ] **gegen etwas stoßen** hit sth. [hɪt]

strahlend (leuchtend hell) bright [braɪt]

Strand beach [biːtʃ]

Straße street [striːt]; road [rəʊd]

Student/in student ['stjuːdənt]

Studio studio ['stjuːdiəʊ]

Stuhl chair [tʃeə]

Stunde hour ['aʊə]; (Unterrichts-stunde) lesson ['lesn]

Stundenplan timetable ['taɪmteɪbl]

stürzen fall [fɔːl]

suchen: etwas suchen look for sth. ['lʊk fɔː]

Suppe soup [suːp]

Szene scene [siːn]

T

Tabelle table ['teɪbl]

Tafel board [bɔːd]

Tag day [deɪ]
▶ S. 175 The days of the week

Tagebuch diary ['daɪəri]

Tante aunt [ɑːnt]

Tante-Emma-Laden corner shop ['kɔːnə ʃɒp]

tanzen dance [dɑːns]

Tasche bag [bæg]

Tasse: eine Tasse ... a cup of ... [kʌp]

Team team [tiːm]

Technik, Technologie technology [tek'nɒlədʒi]

Tee tea [tiː]

Teil part [pɑːt]

Telefon telephone ['telɪfəʊn], (kurz auch:) phone [fəʊn]

Teller: ein Teller ... a plate of ... [pleɪt]

Tennis tennis ['tenɪs]

Termin appointment [ə'pɔɪntmənt]

teuer expensive [ɪk'spensɪv]

Theaterstück play [pleɪ]

Tier animal ['ænɪml]

Tipp tip [tɪp]

Tisch table ['teɪbl]

Titel title ['taɪtl]

Toilette toilet ['tɔɪlət]

Top (Oberteil) top [tɒp]
Tor: ein Tor schießen score [skɔ:]
tot dead [ded]
Tourist/in tourist ['tʊərɪst]
tragen (Kleidung) wear [weə]
trainieren practise ['præktɪs]
Training training ['treɪnɪŋ]
Traum dream [dri:m]
traurig sad [sæd]
treffen; sich treffen meet [mi:t]
Treffer: einen Treffer erzielen score [skɔ:]
trinken drink [drɪŋk]
Trommel drum [drʌm]
Trophäe trophy ['trəʊfi]
Tschüs. Bye. [baɪ]
T-Shirt T-shirt ['ti:ʃɜ:t]
tun do [du:] **etwas tun müssen** have to do sth. **etwas tun wollen** want to do sth. [wɒnt] **Tut mir leid.** (I'm) sorry. ['sɒri] **viel zu tun haben** be busy ['bɪzi]
Tür door [dɔ:]
Turm tower ['taʊə]
Turnen gymnastics [dʒɪm'næstɪks]; (Sportunterricht) PE [ˌpi:ˈiː] (Physical Education)
Turnhalle gym [dʒɪm]
Turnschuh trainer ['treɪnə]

U

üben practise ['præktɪs]
über **1.** (räumlich) over ['əʊvə] **2.** (mehr als) over ['əʊvə] **über 400 Jahre** over 400 years **3. über mich/dich/...** about me/you/... [ə'baʊt] **über dich selbst** about yourself [jɔ:'self]
überprüfen check [tʃek]
Überprüfung check [tʃek]
überrascht surprised [sə'praɪzd]
Überschrift title ['taɪtl]
Übung exercise ['eksəsaɪz]
Übungsheft exercise book ['eksəsaɪz bʊk]
Uhr **1.** (Armbanduhr) watch [wɒtʃ]; (Wand-, Stand-, Turmuhr) clock [klɒk] **2. 4 Uhr morgens** 4 am [ˌeɪ 'em] **4 Uhr nachmittags / 16 Uhr** 4 pm [ˌpi: 'em]
Uhrzeit time [taɪm]
um 1 Uhr / 13 Uhr at 1 o'clock [ə'klɒk]
umdrehen (wenden) turn around [ˌtɜ:n ə'raʊnd] **sich umdrehen** turn around

umher: in der Bücherei / auf dem Strand umher around the library/ the beach [ə'raʊnd]
und and [ænd, [ənd] **Und du? / Und was ist mit dir?** What about you? **Und? / Na und?** So? [səʊ]
unheimlich scary ['skeəri]
Uniform uniform ['ju:nɪfɔ:m]
Unrecht: jemand hat Unrecht someone is wrong [rɒŋ]
uns us [ʌs], [əs]
unser(e) ... our ... ['aʊə]
unten (im Haus) downstairs [ˌdaʊn'steəz] **nach unten** down; (im Haus) downstairs
unter under ['ʌndə]
untergehen (Sonne) go down [daʊn]
unterhalten: sich unterhalten (mit) talk (to) [tɔ:k]
Untertitel subtitle ['sʌbtaɪtl]

V

Vater father ['fɑ:ðə]
Vati dad [dæd]
Verabredung appointment [ə'pɔɪntmənt]
Vergangenheit past [pɑ:st]
vergessen forget [fə'get]
verheiratet (mit) married (to) ['mærɪd]
verkaufen sell [sel]
verkehrt wrong [rɒŋ]
verlassen leave [li:v]
verletzt hurt [hɜ:t]
verpassen miss [mɪs]
verrückt mad [mæd]
Vers rhyme [raɪm]
verschieden different ['dɪfrənt]
verstecken; sich verstecken hide [haɪd]
verstehen understand [ˌʌndə'stænd] **Hast du es verstanden?** Did you get it? (infml)
versuchen try [traɪ] **Versuch's mal.** Have a go.
verwenden use [ju:z]
Video video ['vɪdiəʊ]
Videokamera video camera ['vɪdiəʊ kæmrə]
viel a lot (of); lots (of); much [mʌtʃ] **Viel Glück!** Good luck! [lʌk] **viel zu tun haben** be busy ['bɪzi] **Wie viel kosten ...?** How much are ...? **Wie viel kostet ...?** How much is ...?
► S.199 much – many
► S.194 British money

viele a lot (of); lots (of); many ['meni]
► S.199 much – many
vielleicht maybe ['meɪbi]
vier four [fɔ:]
► S.233 English numbers
Viertel: Viertel nach zehn (10.15/ 22.15) quarter past ten ['kwɔ:tə pɑ:st] **Viertel vor elf (10.45/ 22.45)** quarter to eleven ['kwɔ:tə tʊ]
► S.233 English numbers
violett purple ['pɜ:pl]
Vogel bird [bɜ:d]
Volleyball volleyball ['vɒlibɔ:l]
von of [ɒv], [əv]; from [frɒm], [frəm] **von ... bis ...** from ... to ...
vor **1.** (örtlich) in front of [ɪn 'frʌnt ˌəv] **vor der Schule** (vor dem Schulgebäude) in front of the school **2.** (zeitlich) before [bɪ'fɔ:] **vor der Schule** (vor Schulbeginn) before school **vorm Unterricht** before lessons **Viertel vor elf (10.45/ 22.45)** quarter to eleven ['kwɔ:tə tʊ]
► S.233 English numbers
vorbei sein (zu Ende sein) be over ['əʊvə]
vorbereiten: etwas vorbereiten prepare sth. [prɪ'peə]
Vorderseite front [frʌnt]
Vorlieben und Abneigungen likes and dislikes (pl) [ˌlaɪks ˌən 'dɪslaɪks]
Vormittag morning ['mɔ:nɪŋ]
Vorsicht! (Pass auf!) Watch out! [ˌwɒtʃ 'aʊt]
vorsichtig careful ['keəfl]
vorspielen: etwas vorspielen act sth. out [ˌækt 'aʊt]
vorstellen: sich etwas vorstellen imagine sth. [ɪ'mædʒɪn] **Stell dir vor, Dad ...** Guess what, Dad ...
Vorstellung (Idee) idea [aɪ'dɪə]
Vortrag talk [tɔ:k] **einen Vortrag halten (über)** give a talk (about)

W

wählen (aussuchen) choose [tʃu:z]
wahr true [tru:]
Wal whale [weɪl]
wann? when? [wen] **Wann hast du Geburtstag?** When's your birthday.
► S.182 Birthdays
Waren (Güter) goods (pl) [gʊdz]
warm warm [wɔ:m]
warten (auf) wait (for) [weɪt] **Warte einen Moment.** Wait a minute.
warum? why? [waɪ]

was? what? [wɒt] **Was gibt es zum Mittagessen?** What's for lunch? **Was haben wir als Hausaufgabe auf?** What's for homework? **Was hättest du gern? / Was möchtest du?** What would you like? **Was ist denn? / Was ist los?** What's the matter? **Und was ist mit dir?** What about you?

Wasser water ['wɔːtə]

Website website ['websaɪt]

weg away [ə'weɪ]

Weg way [weɪ] **auf dem Weg zu / nach …** on the way to …

wegen: Es tut mir leid wegen … I'm sorry about …

weich soft [sɒft]

weil because [bɪ'kɒz]

weiß white [waɪt]

weit (entfernt) far [fɑː]

weitermachen go on [ˌgəʊ_'ɒn]

weiterreden go on [ˌgəʊ_'ɒn]

welche(r, s) 1. Auf welcher Seite sind wir? What page are we on? **Welche Farbe …?** What colour …? **2.** (aus einer begrenzten Anzahl) which [wɪtʃ] **Welche Klubs …?** (= Welche von diesen Klubs …?) Which clubs …?

wenden (umkehren) turn around [ˌtɜːn_ə'raʊnd]

wenn when [wen]

wer? who? [huː]

werden: wütend/kalt/… werden get angry/cold/… [get]

werfen throw [θrəʊ]

Wettkampf (Match) match [mætʃ]

wichtig important [ɪm'pɔːtnt]

wie 1. (Fragewort) how [haʊ] **Wie alt bist du?** How old are you? **Wie findest du …? / Wie gefällt dir …?** How do you like …? **Wie geht's? / Wie geht es dir/euch?** How are you? **Wie heißt du?** What's your name? **Wie ist sie (so)?** What's she like? **Wie spät ist es?** What time is it? **Wie viel kosten …?** How much are …? **Wie viel kostet …?** How much is …? **2. wie Jungen** like boys [laɪk] **3. der-/die-/dasselbe wie …** the same as …

wieder again [ə'gen]

wiegen weigh [weɪ]

Willkommen in Plymouth. Welcome to Plymouth. ['welkəm]

Winter winter ['wɪntə]

wir we [wiː]

wirklich really ['rɪəli]

wissen know [nəʊ] **…, weißt du. / …, wissen Sie.** …, you know. [nəʊ] **Weißt du was, Dad …** Guess what, Dad …

Witz joke [dʒəʊk]

witzig funny ['fʌni]

wo? where? [weə]

Woche week [wiːk]

Wochenende weekend [ˌwiːk'end] **am Wochenende** at the weekend

Wochentag day of the week

▶ S.175 The days of the week

Woher kommst du? Where are you from?

wohin? where? [weə]

wohnen (leben) live [lɪv]

Wohnung flat [flæt]

Wohnzimmer living room ['lɪvɪŋ ruːm]

wollen: etwas haben wollen want sth. [wɒnt] **etwas tun wollen** want to do sth.

Wort word [wɜːd]

Wortstellung word order ['wɜːd_ˌɔːdə]

Wovon handelt die Geschichte? What is the story about?

Wunsch wish [wɪʃ]

wünschen: sich etwas wünschen make a wish [wɪʃ]

würde: Ich würde gern … I'd like to …

Wurm worm [wɜːm]

wütend angry ['æŋgri]

Y

Yoga yoga ['jəʊgə]

Z

Zahl number ['nʌmbə]

zählen count [kaʊnt] **bis zehn zählen** count to ten

▶ S.233 English numbers

zehn ten [ten]

▶ S.233 English numbers

Zeichen sign [saɪn]

zeichnen draw [drɔː]

Zeichnung drawing ['drɔːɪŋ]

zeigen show [ʃəʊ] **auf etwas zeigen** point to sth. [pɔɪnt] **es zeigt, dass …** it shows that …

Zeile line [laɪn]

Zeit time [taɪm]

Zeitschrift magazine [ˌmægə'ziːn]

Zeitung paper ['peɪpə]

Zentrum centre ['sentə]

zerbrechen break [breɪk]

ziehen pull [pʊl]

Ziffer number ['nʌmbə]

Zoo zoo [zuː]

zu 1. (örtlich) to [tu], [tə] **2. zu spät/kalt/groß/…** too late/cold/big/… [tuː] **3. Es ist Zeit zu gehen.** It's time to go. **Nice to meet you.** Freut mich, dich/euch/Sie kennenzulernen.

zuerst first [fɜːst]

Zuhause home [həʊm]

▶ S.179 home

zuhören listen ['lɪsn] **Hör(t) mir zu.** Listen to me.

▶ S.193 listen · hear

zurück back [bæk]

zurücklassen leave [liːv]

zusammen together [tə'geðə]

zustimmen: jm. zustimmen agree with sb. [ə'griː]

zwei two [tuː]

▶ S.233 English numbers

zweite(r, s) second ['sekənd]

▶ S.233 English numbers

Zwillinge twins (pl) [twɪnz]

zwischen between [bɪ'twiːn]

zwölf twelve [twelv]

▶ S.233 English numbers

infinitive	simple past	
(to) **be**	I/he/she/it **was**; you/we/you/they **were**	sein
(to) **bite** [aɪ]	**bit** [ɪ]	beißen
(to) **break** [eɪ]	**broke**	brechen; zerbrechen
(to) **buy**	**bought**	kaufen
(to) **catch**	**caught**	fangen
(to) **choose** [uː]	**chose** [əʊ]	aussuchen, (aus)wählen; sich aussuchen
(to) **come**	**came**	kommen
(to) **do**	**did**	tun, machen
(to) **draw**	**drew**	zeichnen
(to) **drink**	**drank**	trinken
(to) **eat**	**ate** [et, eɪt]	essen
(to) **fall**	**fell**	fallen, stürzen; hinfallen
(to) **feed**	**fed**	füttern
(to) **feel**	**felt**	fühlen; sich fühlen
(to) **fight**	**fought**	kämpfen
(to) **find**	**found**	finden
(to) **forget**	**forgot**	vergessen
(to) **get**	**got**	bekommen; werden; gelangen, (hin)kommen
(to) **give**	**gave**	geben
(to) **go**	**went**	gehen
(to) **grow**	**grew**	anbauen, anpflanzen
(to) **have**	**had**	haben
(to) **hear** [ɪə]	**heard** [ɜː]	hören
(to) **hide** [aɪ]	**hid** [ɪ]	verstecken; sich verstecken
(to) **hit** sth.	**hit**	gegen etwas prallen, stoßen
(to) **hold**	**held**	halten
(to) **know** [nəʊ]	**knew** [njuː]	wissen; kennen
(to) **leave** [iː]	**left**	verlassen; zurücklassen
(to) **let**	**let**	lassen
(to) **make**	**made**	machen; herstellen
(to) **meet** [iː]	**met** [e]	treffen; sich treffen; kennenlernen
(to) **put**	**put**	(etwas wohin) tun, legen, stellen
(to) **read** [iː]	**read** [e]	lesen
(to) **ride** a bike [aɪ]	**rode** a bike	(Rad) fahren
(to) **run**	**ran**	rennen, laufen
(to) **say** [eɪ]	**said** [e]	sagen
(to) **see**	**saw**	sehen
(to) **sell**	**sold**	verkaufen
(to) **send**	**sent**	schicken, senden
(to) **sing**	**sang**	singen
(to) **sit**	**sat**	sitzen; sich setzen
(to) **sleep**	**slept**	schlafen
(to) **speak** [iː]	**spoke**	sprechen
(to) **swim**	**swam**	schwimmen
(to) **take**	**took**	nehmen, mitnehmen; (weg-, hin)bringen
(to) **tell**	**told**	erzählen, berichten
(to) **think**	**thought**	denken, glauben
(to) **throw**	**threw**	werfen
(to) **understand**	**understood**	verstehen
(to) **wake up**	**woke up**	aufwachen
(to) **wear** [eə]	**wore** [ɔː]	tragen (Kleidung)
(to) **win**	**won** [ʌ]	gewinnen
(to) **write**	**wrote**	schreiben

List of names

Place names
(Ortsnamen)

Aquarium [ə'kweəriəm]
Asia ['eɪʒə] *Asien*
the **Atlantic Ocean** [ət,læntɪk‿'əʊʃn]
  der Atlantik
the **Barbican** ['bɑːbɪkən]
  (Kanonenbastion)
Berlin [bɜː'lɪn]
Blackawton [,blæk'ɔːtn]
Boston ['bɒstən]
Britain ['brɪtn] *Großbritannien*
Buckingham Palace [,bʌkɪŋəm 'pæləs]
the **Caribbean** [,kærɪ'biːən] *die Karibik*
Cawsand ['kɔːsænd]
China ['tʃaɪnə]
Citadel ['sɪtədəl, 'sɪtədel] *Zitadelle*
Coombe Dean [,kuːm 'diːn]
Dartmoor ['dɑːtmɔː]
Devon ['devn]
England ['ɪŋglənd] *England*
Exmouth ['eksməθ]
France [frɑːns] *Frankreich*
Frankfurt ['fræŋkfɜːt]
Germany ['dʒɜːməni] *Deutschland*
the **Great Barrier Reef**
  [,greɪt 'bæriə riːf]
Great Britain [,greɪt 'brɪtn]
  Großbritannien
High Street ['haɪ striːt] *Hauptstraße*
the **Hoe** [həʊ] *(Hügel in Plymouth)*
India ['ɪndiə] *Indien*
Lido ['laɪdəʊ, 'liːdəʊ]
Market Square ['mɑːkɪt skweə]
Mexico ['meksɪkəʊ]
New York [,njuː 'jɔːk]
Northern Ireland [,nɔːðən‿'aɪələnd]
  Nordirland
Plymouth ['plɪməθ]
Plymouth Sound [,plɪməθ 'saʊnd]
Plymstock ['plɪmstɒk]
the **River Plym** [plɪm]
Scotland ['skɒtlənd] *Schottland*
Smeaton's Tower [,smiːtnz 'taʊə]
South Africa [,saʊθ‿'æfrɪkə]
  Südafrika
Stockbridge ['stɒkbrɪdʒ]
Sutton ['sʌtn]
Torquay [,tɔː'kiː]
Totnes ['tɒtnɪs]
the **UK** [,juː 'keɪ] **(= Great Britain
  and Northern Ireland)**
  das Vereinigte Königreich
the **USA** [,juː‿es‿'eɪ] *die Vereinigten
  Staaten von Amerika*
Wales [weɪlz] *Wales*
Wembury ['wembri, 'wembəri]
Woolacombe ['wʊləkəm]

First names
(Vornamen)

Abby ['æbi]
Adam ['ædəm]
Albert ['ælbət]
Amar ['æmə, 'ʌmə]
Bill [bɪl]
Charles [tʃɑːlz]
Dasan ['dæsæn, 'dʌsən]
Dave [deɪv]
Dilip ['dɪlɪp]
George [dʒɔːdʒ]
Grace [greɪs]
Harry ['hæri]
Helen ['helən]
Holly ['hɒli]
Jack [dʒæk]
Jamie ['dʒeɪmi]
Jeff [dʒef]
Jim [dʒɪm]
Joshua ['dʒɒʃuə]
Justin ['dʒʌstɪn]
Karen ['kærən]
Lewis ['luːɪs]
Lily ['lɪli]
Lisa ['liːsə]
Lloyd [lɔɪd]
Lucy ['luːsi]
Luke [luːk]
Lynn [lɪn]
Maggie ['mægi]
Maya ['maɪə]
Megan ['megən]
Melissa [mə'lɪsə]
Molly ['mɒli]
Mukesh ['mʊkeʃ]
Oliver ['ɒlɪvə]
Paul [pɔːl]
Priya ['priːjɑː, 'priːjə]
Robbie ['rɒbi]
Ruby ['ruːbi]
Ryan ['raɪən]
Sam [sæm]
Sanjay ['sændʒeɪ]
Sarah ['seərə]
Simon ['saɪmən]
Sir Francis [sə 'frɑːnsɪs]
Steve [stiːv]
Tim [tɪm]
Tom [tɒm]
Will [wɪl]
Zoe ['zəʊi]

Family names / Surnames
(Familiennamen)

Bell [bel]
Bennett ['benɪt]
Blackwell ['blækwel]
Drake [dreɪk]
Einstein ['aɪnstaɪn]
Hacker ['hækə]
Hart [hɑːt]
Hobbs [hɒbz]
Miller ['mɪlə]
Pascoe ['pæskəʊ]
Sen [sen]
Skinner ['skɪnə]
Taylor ['teɪlə]
Tizzard ['tɪzəd]
Willis ['wɪlɪs]
Wood [wʊd]
Wu [wuː]

Other names
(Andere Namen)

Igor ['iːgɔː]
Inga ['ɪŋə]
Mickey ['mɪki]
Mink [mɪŋk]
Minnie ['mɪni]
Morph [mɔːf]
Omar ['əʊmɑː]
Pip [pɪp]
Pop [pɒp]
Raj [rɑːdʒ]
Sasha ['sæʃə]
Sheba ['ʃiːbə]
Silky ['sɪlki]
Skip [skɪp]
Skype [skaɪp]
Suzie ['suːzi]
Tarzan ['tɑːzæn]
Teddy ['tedi]
Tut [tʌt]

English sounds

[iː]	green, he, sea
[i]	happy, monkey
[ɪ]	big, in, expensive
[e]	red, yes, again, breakfast
[æ]	cat, animal, apple, black
[ɑː]	class, ask, car, park
[ɒ]	song, on, dog, what
[ɔː]	door, or, ball, four, morning
[uː]	blue, ruler, too, two, you
[ʊ]	book, good, pullover
[ʌ]	mum, bus, colour
[ɜː]	girl, early, her, work, T-shirt
[ə]	a partner, again, today

[eɪ]	name, eight, play, great
[aɪ]	time, right, my, I
[ɔɪ]	boy, toilet, noise
[əʊ]	old, no, road, yellow
[aʊ]	town, now, house
[ɪə]	here, year, idea
[eə]	where, pair, share, their
[ʊə]	tour

[b]	boat, table, verb
[p]	pool, paper, shop
[d]	dad, window, good
[t]	ten, letter, at
[g]	good, again, bag
[k]	cat, kitchen, back
[m]	mum, man, remember
[n]	no, one, ten
[ŋ]	song, young, uncle, thanks
[l]	hello, like, old, small
[r]	red, ruler, friend, sorry
[w]	we, where, one
[j]	you, yes, uniform
[f]	family, after, laugh
[v]	river, very, seven, have
[s]	sister, poster, yes
[z]	please, zoo, quiz, his, music
[ʃ]	shop, station, English
[ʒ]	television, usually
[tʃ]	teacher, child, watch
[dʒ]	Germany, job, project, orange
[θ]	thanks, three, bathroom
[ð]	the, this, father, with
[h]	here, who, behind

Am besten kannst du dir die Aussprache der einzelnen Lautzeichen einprägen, wenn du dir zu jedem Zeichen ein einfaches Wort merkst – das [iː] ist der **green**-Laut, das [eɪ] ist der **name**-Laut usw.

English numbers

0 **oh, zero, nil** [əʊ, ˈzɪərəʊ, nɪl]
1 **one** [wʌn]
2 **two** [tuː]
3 **three** [θriː]
4 **four** [fɔː]
5 **five** [faɪv]
6 **six** [sɪks]
7 **seven** [ˈsevn]
8 **eight** [eɪt]
9 **nine** [naɪn]
10 **ten** [ten]

11 **eleven** [ɪˈlevn]
12 **twelve** [twelv]
13 **thir**teen [ˌθɜːˈtiːn]
14 **four**teen [ˌfɔːˈtiːn]
15 **fif**teen [ˌfɪfˈtiːn]
16 **six**teen [ˌsɪksˈtiːn]
17 **seven**teen [ˌsevnˈtiːn]
18 **eigh**teen [ˌeɪˈtiːn]
19 **nine**teen [ˌnaɪnˈtiːn]
20 **twenty** [ˈtwenti]

21 **twenty-one** [ˌtwentiˈwʌn]
22 **twenty-two** [ˌtwentiˈtuː]
23 **twenty-three** [ˌtwentiˈθriː]
...

30 **thir**ty [ˈθɜːti]
40 **for**ty [ˈfɔːti]
50 **fif**ty [ˈfɪfti]
60 **six**ty [ˈsɪksti]
70 **seven**ty [ˈsevnti]
80 **eigh**ty [ˈeɪti]
90 **nine**ty [ˈnaɪnti]
100 **a / one hundred**
[əˈhʌndrəd / ˌwʌnˈhʌndrəd]

101 **one hundred and one**
102 **one hundred and two**
...

1st **first** [fɜːst]
2nd **second** [ˈsekənd]
3rd **third** [θɜːd]
4th **fourth** [fɔːθ]
5th **fifth** [fɪfθ]
6th **sixth** [sɪksθ]
7th **seventh** [ˈsevnθ]
8th **eighth** [eɪtθ]
9th **ninth** [naɪnθ]
10th **tenth** [tenθ]

11th **eleventh** [ɪˈlevnθ]
12th **twelfth** [twelfθ]
13th **thirteenth** [ˌθɜːˈtiːnθ]
14th **fourteenth** [ˌfɔːˈtiːnθ]
15th **fifteenth** [ˌfɪfˈtiːnθ]
16th **sixteenth** [ˌsɪksˈtiːnθ]
17th **seventeenth** [ˌsevnˈtiːnθ]
18th **eighteenth** [ˌeɪˈtiːnθ]
19th **nineteenth** [ˌnaɪnˈtiːnθ]
20th **twentieth** [ˈtwentiəθ]

21st **twenty-first** [ˌtwentiˈfɜːst]
22nd **twenty-second** [ˌtwentiˈsekənd]
23rd **twenty-third** [ˌtwentiˈθɜːd]
...

30th **thirtieth** [ˈθɜːtiəθ]
40th **fortieth** [ˈfɔːtiəθ]
50th **fiftieth** [ˈfɪftiəθ]
60th **sixtieth** [ˈsɪkstiəθ]
70th **seventieth** [ˈsevntiəθ]
80th **eightieth** [ˈeɪtiəθ]
90th **ninetieth** [ˈnaɪntiəθ]
100th **hundredth** [ˈhʌndrədθ]

101st **hundred and first**
102nd **hundred and second**
...

Illustrationen

Roland Beier, Berlin (Umschlaginnenseite Karte icon Ireland castle; S. 143; 148; 151; 153 oben; 157 pencils, bag, ruler; 159 oben re., unten li.; 160 oben re., 2. v. unten li.; 166 Bild 1–4; 167 bags; 168 Mitte, unten; 169 oben; 174; 175 unten, 2. v. unten; 176–180; 184; 185 oben, 2. v. oben; 186; 188 oben; 189; 191 oben; 192–193 oben; 195–196; 197 unten; 200–203; 205 oben, 2. v. oben); **Carlos Borrell**, Berlin (Umschlaginnenseite Karte (M)); **Judy Brown**, Sutton (S. 37); **Cornelsen Schulverlage GmbH**, Berlin (S. 42; 62; 150); **Tobias Dahmen**, Utrecht, Niederlande, www.tobidahmen.de (S. 16; 19; 20–22 oben; 23; 25 unten; 27; 29; 33; 35 unten –36; 40 Morph; 41 Mitte; 43 unten; 45–47; 49; 53 unten; 55; 57; 60–61; 65 oben, unten (M); 66; 70 heads –71; 74–75; 82; 85 Morph–86; 89; 91; 94; 100–101; 104; 109; 114; 117 Mitte, unten; 120–121; 126–127; 133; 153 unten–156; 157 heads, Morph; 158–159 Morph; 160 heads, Morph; 161–166 Morph; 167 Morph; 168 oben; 169 Mitte, unten; 170); **Elke Hanisch**, Köln (S. 8–9; 10 Silky (M); 11 unten, 12–15; 17; 25 Bild 2; 38 (u. 185 unten); 40 Silky; 41 oben; 50; 70 Silky; 80–81; 95; 102–103; 111; 117 oben; 175 oben, 2. v. oben); **Jeongsook Lee**, Heidelberg (Umschlaginnenseite Karte icons; S. 172; 175 Mitte; 183; 188 frogs; 191 unten; 193 unten; 197 oben; 198); **M.B. Schulz**, Düsseldorf (S. 22 Mitte; 24; 34 (M)–35 oben; 40 Lucy, Maya; 43 Bild A–D; 44; 52–53 oben; 72–73; 76–79; 84–85; 87; 93 (u. 96); 98–99; 106–107 (u. 136); 110; 113; 118–119; 123–125; 128; 140–141; 205 Bild 4–6); **Jane Smith**, London (S. 10 Bild 1–10, map (M); 11 map (M))

Bildquellen

Alamy, Abingdon (S. 12 Bild 4: International Photobank; S. 67 Bild 2: Bob Daemmrich, Bild 3: Marv Johnson (RF), Bild 4: Nicholas Burningham; S. 69 unten li. Figuren im Hintergrund (M): The Print Collector, unten re.: Lee Pengelly; S. 92 oben (M): Gregory Davies (RF); S. 120 oben: Jane Hallin, Mitte: Mark Bolton Photography, 2. v. unten: Paul Harrison, unten: David Noton Photography; S. 142 extracurricular activities unten: MBI (RF); S. 146 hockey: Enigma, judo: Andrzej Gorzkowski, hockey stick: keith morris; S. 147 band: Oliver Rossi (RF), models: Corbis Super RF / Steve Prezant (RF)); **Phil Bales**, Plymouth (S. 47 Steve); **John Birdsall**, www.JohnBirdsall.co.uk (S. 21 Uniform dunkelgrün); **Trevor Burrows Photography Ltd**, Plymouth (S. 4 li. Mitte, re. oben, re. unten; S. 5; S. 6 li. oben, re. unten, re. oben; S. 12 Bild 1–3; S. 13 Bild 5, 6; S. 16–20; S. 21 oben, Uniformen rot, dunkelblau, schwarz; S. 23; S. 25–26; S. 28; S. 30; S. 34 Bild 1–3 (M); S. 36 li.; S. 39; S. 41; S. 47 Bill, Maggie, Holly, Lucy; S. 48; S. 54 oben Lehrwerkskinder; S. 56 Justin, Filmstreifen; S. 57 unten li.; S. 58–59; S. 64–65; S. 68; S. 69 oben; S. 80; S. 81 Bild C, Bild D; S. 82 (M); S. 84–85; S. 88; S. 102–103; S. 105; S. 108 Lehrwerkskinder; S. 112–113; S. 115; S. 130; S. 140; S. 154; S. 193; S. 205); **Clipdealer**, München (S. 174 unten: Feverpitch); **Corbis**, Düsseldorf (S. 6 unten li.: Joel W. Rogers); **Cornelsen Schulverlage GmbH**, Berlin (S. 13 Bild 7; S. 31; S. 49; S. 51; S. 63; S. 97; S. 116; S. 141; S. 147 orchestra; S. 150; S. 188

scone); **Gareth Evans**, Berlin (S. 138 li., re.); **Fotolia**, Berlin (S. 146 skating: Kathrin39); **Getty Images**, München (S. 146 canoeing: flickr / 2007 Lothar Knopp / An Lumatic image (RF), climbing gear: Peter Chadwick; S. 147 collecting: Vasiliki Varvaki (RF)); **Stefanie Gira**, Berlin (S. 38; S. 54 Mitte re., Mitte li., unten re., unten li.; S. 66 oben (M), unten; S. 81 unten re.; S. 100); **images.de**, Berlin (S. 69 unten li. Figur im Vordergrund (M): Florilegius); **iStockphoto**, Calgary (S. 4 unten li. (u. 36 re.): matthewleesdixon; S. 6 Mitte li. (u. 90 unten Mitte u. 135 unten Mitte): Maxian; S. 47 twins: RichardUpshur, Melissa: JeffHillman, Jim: alvarez, Sam: jwebb, Helen: SteveLuker; S. 57 cabassa: Rouzes, maracas: tacataca; S. 67 Bild 1: Purdue9394; S. 90 unten li. (u. 135 unten li.): PeskyMonkey, unten re. (u. 135 unten re.): TheDman; S. 91 unten li.: Andyd; S. 142 Latin: AndreaAstes, ethics: marekuliasz; S. 143 Uncle Phil: Maica; S. 145 fried eggs: tamara_kulikova, omelette: Elnur, mashed potatoes: travellinglight, potato salad: WinterStorm, blancmange: DanielTaeger, lemonade: bluehill75, jelly with custard: instamatics, cupcake with chocolate topping: AngiePhotos, muesli: LauriPatterson, rolls: xxmmxx; S. 146 ice skating: YinYang, canoe paddles: 3dvd, climbing rope: Laborer, saddle: amriphoto, skis: walik, snowboard: Silvrshootr; S. 147 choir, clarinet: CEFutcher, acting: sjlocke, photos: empire331; S. 187 2. v. unten: alle12; S. 195 unten: annaia; S. 197 li.: JazzIRT); **National Marine Aquarium**, Plymouth (S. 108 unten re., unten Mitte, unten li.; S. 109; S. 120 2. v. oben); **Okapia**, Frankfurt/Main (S. 4 oben li. (u. 8): imagebroker / Stefan Huwiler); **Picture Alliance**, Frankfurt/Main (S. 92 oben seal (M): Zoonar); **Images courtesy of Plymouth City Council (Arts and Heritage)**. Images taken by Polly Stock Photography www.pollystockphotography.co.uk, Plymouth (S. 70); **Shutterstock**, New York (S. 19 re.: Matthew Benoit; S. 42 li. (u. 190), re.: Robert Spriggs, Mitte: Tatiana Popova; S. 43 unten li.: Morena Valente, unten re.: SmileStudio, oben re.: sagir, oben Mitte: Andreja Donko, oben li.: Oleksiy Mark, unten Mitte: monbibi; S. 47 Lynn: Warren Goldswain, George: rj lerich, Karen: Olga Sapegina, Harry: vgstudio, Bild 1–4: Feliks Kogan, Bild 5: lalan; S. 50 Bild 1: Sergey Peterman, Bild 2: Elena Aliaga, Bild 3: Kirill Smirnov, Bild 4: Marc Dietrich, Bild 5: maxim ibragimov, Bild 6: aarrows, Bild 7: Monticello, Bild 8: Seroff, Bild 9: Nattika, Bild 10: Subbotina Anna, Bild 11: Rob Stark, Bild 12: Africa Studio, Bild 13: sergojpg, Bild 14: Joe Gough, Bild 15: charles taylor; S. 56 Mitte re.: Pavel Lysenko, unten re. (u. 190 oben re.): viki2win; S. 57 oben li.: Yarek Gora, oben Mitte: Shutterstock.com / Pres Panayotov, oben re.: Val Thoermer; S. 62: pakowacz; S. 71 oben Mitte: romvo, unten Mitte: Abramova Kseniya, oben re.: Andresr, oben li.: Morena Valente, unten re.: archidea, unten li.: Rtimages; S. 91 unten Mitte: Elena Elisseeva, unten re.: Karkas, oben re.: kkymek, oben Mitte: vovan, oben li.: Tischenko Irina; S. 92 Mitte: Roland IJdema, unten: Bjorn Stefanson; S. 142 class assembly: Zurijeta, biology: AISPIX by Image Source, Spanish, Italian: alp33, extracurricular activities oben: oliveromg, chemistry: Kiselev Andrey Valerevich, physics: Monkey Business Images, social studies: Dawn Hudson, drama: Elnur, lizard: Angel Simon, tortoise: cynoclub, turtle: DenisNata, cow, goat, one sheep, three sheep, gerbil, budgie, canary: Eric Isselée, parrot: prapass, hamster:

Igor Kovalchuk, mouse: kontur-vid, three mice: Robert Wroblewski; S. 143 oben li.: privilege, Clara: Simon Greig, unten li.: Valentin Mosichev, unten re., unten 2. v. re., unten 3. v. re.: Yuri Arcurs; S. 144 tomatoes: Aleksey Patsyuk, cucumber: Anna Sedneva, broccoli: Dionisvera, lettuce: Bakelyt, carrots: mashe, cauliflower: monticello, peppers: Rusian Anatolevich Kuzmenkov, strawberries: Picsfive, grapes: Protasov A & N, pears: Sandra Caldwell, bananas: Tatiana Popova, cherries, apples, oranges, plums, beans: Valentyn Volkov, grilled steak: Dan Peretz, sausages: de2marco, salami: Peter zijlstra, ham: Michael C. Gray, lamb chops: Robyn Mackenzie, fish fingers, fish filet: Magone, cold cuts: Zvyagintsev Sergey, sweetcorn: Maks Narodenko, roast chicken: Viktor1, peas, mushrooms: Yasonya; S. 145 chocolate: lasha, chocolate cupcake: Aaron Amat, blue cupcake: Ivonne Wierink, chips: Alexandra Lande, hot chocolate: Andrey Shtanko, coffee: Tiplyashin Anatoly, honey: deniss09, butter: Diana Taliun, pasta salad: Igor Dutina, cereals: Kitch Bain, rice: oriori, fried potatoes: lorenzo gambaro, pasta: windu, fruit cake: Margoe Edwards, mineral water: Monticello, boiled eggs: Nattika, scrambled eggs: Nitr, toast: RusGri, orange juice: victoriaKh; S. 146 ice skates: Jami Garrison, inline skates: 2happy, badminton: andromantic, badminton racket: Alexander Dashewsky, hockey helmet: Phoenix79, rowing: corepics, gymnastics: Denys Kurbatov, ice hockey stick: Flashon Studio, riding: Fotokostic, climbing: Frances A. Miller, skiing: gorillaimages, canoe: shutswis, ice hockey: Govorov Pavel, skateboard: HomeArt, snow boarding: Ipatov, windsurfing: Sean Nel, skateboarding: sonya etchison, table tennis: JJ pixs, table tennis bat: Vividz Foto, yoga: Malyugin, volleyball: shutterstock.com / muzsy, ice hockey helmet: Nicholas Piccillo, pads: nito, riding cap: shutswis, riding boots: Timothy Large; S. 147 saxophone: Anton Albert, recorder: Apollofoto, violin: Brian Chase, flute, cello: Fotokostic, trumpet: Katrina Brown, music: Goodluz, drawing: Jeka, internet: LUCARELLI TEMISTOCLE, rapping: Nejron Photo, ballet dancing: Yuri Arcurs; S. 151: GJS; S. 172 re. (u. 177 re.): Dan Gerber, 2. v. re. (u. 177 2. v. re.): jiawangkun, li. (u. 177 li.): Olga Mishyna, 2. v. li. (u. 177 2. v. li.): Jim Barber; S. 173: Monkey Business Images; S. 174 oben: Zurijeta; S. 175: Elnur; S. 179 poster (M): blue67design, girl: Vibrant Image Studio; S. 180 trainers: NY Arkady, shoes: sommthink, map: Volina; S. 181 oben: Gemenacom, Mitte: R-O-M-A, unten: wongstock; S. 182: Alegria; S. 184: Vjom; S. 186 oben (u. 188 tea): Viktor1, unten: Kuricheva Ekaterina; S. 187 oben: NLshop, 2. v. oben: Oleksandr Koval, unten re.: discpicture, unten li.: Olga Lyubkina, unten 2. v. li.: bonchan, unten 2. v. re.: Olinchuk; S. 188 chocolate cake: Elena Larina, strawberry cake: Smit, bread: Brykaylo Yuriy, cornflakes: Oliver Hoffmann, milk: Texturis, cheese: Evgeny Karandaev, sandwich unten: Chris Ieachman, sandwich oben: Daniel Etzold, present: Vasilius; S. 190 oben li.: Olga Lyubkina; S. 191 oben: amasterphotographer, unten: nito; S. 192: SergiyN; S. 195 Mitte: Gordon Ball LRPS; S. 197 oben: Koshevnyk, re.: risteski goce, Mitte: Rob Wilson); **Emma Wood Photography**, Brighton (S. 95)

Titelbild
Trevor Burrows Photography Ltd, Plymouth

Liedquellen
S. 49: *Our house*. Text: Joseph Cathal Smyth, Musik: John Christopher Foreman performed by Madness © EMI Music Publishing LTD und EMI Music Publishing Germany GmbH; S. 103: *Octopus's Garden*. M + T: John Lennon, Paul McCartney, Richard Starkey performed by The Beatles © Startling Music LTD, Discoton Musik Edition GmbH und Universal Music Publishing International MGB LTD

Special thanks to:
The staff and students at **Plymstock School**, Plymouth; **The National Marine Aquarium**, Plymouth/www.national-aquarium.co.uk, **Plymouth City Council**

Zu Beginn und am Ende des Unterrichts

Guten Morgen, Frau …	**Good morning, Mrs/Miss …** *(bis 12 Uhr)*
Guten Tag, Herr …	**Good afternoon, Mr …** *(ab 12 Uhr)*
Entschuldigung, dass ich zu spät komme.	**Sorry I'm late.**
Auf Wiedersehen! / Bis morgen.	**Goodbye. / See you tomorrow.**

Du brauchst Hilfe

Können Sie/Kannst du mir bitte helfen?	**Can you help me, please?**
Auf welcher Seite sind wir, bitte?	**What page are we on, please?**
Was heißt … auf Englisch/Deutsch?	**What's … in English/German?**
Können Sie/Kannst du mir bitte … buchstabieren?	**Can you spell …, please?**
Können Sie es bitte an die Tafel schreiben?	**Can you write it on the board, please?**

Hausaufgaben und Übungen

Tut mir leid, ich habe mein Schulheft nicht dabei.	**Sorry, I don't have my exercise book.**
Kann ich bitte vorlesen?	**Can I read, please?**
Ich verstehe diese Übung nicht.	**I don't understand this exercise.**
Ich kann Nummer 3 nicht lösen.	**I can't do number 3.**
Entschuldigung, ich bin noch nicht fertig.	**Sorry, I haven't finished.**
Ich habe … Ist das auch richtig?	**I have … Is that right too?**
Tut mir leid, das weiß ich nicht.	**Sorry, I don't know.**
Was haben wir (als Hausaufgabe) auf?	**What's for homework?**

Wenn es Probleme gibt

Kann ich es auf Deutsch sagen?	**Can I say it in German?**
Können Sie/Kannst du bitte lauter sprechen?	**Can you speak louder, please?**
Können Sie/Kannst du das bitte noch mal sagen?	**Can you say that again, please?**
Kann ich bitte das Fenster öffnen/zumachen?	**Can I open/close the window, please?**
Kann ich bitte zur Toilette gehen?	**Can I go to the toilet, please?**

Partnerarbeit

Kann ich mit Julian arbeiten?	**Can I work with Julian?**
Kann ich bitte dein Lineal/deinen Filzstift/… haben?	**Can I have your ruler/felt tip/…, please?**
Danke. / Vielen Dank.	**Thank you. / Thanks a lot.**
Du bist dran.	**It's your turn.**